The Politics of Famine in Eur(and Memory

This is the first book to bring together groundbreaking scholarship focusing on the various ways in which famines result from political decision-making, and how the threat, occurrence, relief, or memory of famine is instrumentalized as a political and military tool.

Contributions to this volume reveal the complexities, variations, and motivations behind the instrumentalization of famine by political actors and regimes, and how the politics of perpetrating hunger and the politics of relieving it have often been intertwined. They also address how famine legacies have been subsequently politicized in public debates, educational practices, and popular media; and how these socially and politically constructed memories and myths, in turn, have shaped broader narratives about hunger and humanitarianism both in history and today.

The Politics of Famine in European History and Memory provides a crucial resource for scholars and students from all disciplines interested in the study of famines, as well as those interested in the history of war and troubled pasts more generally.

Ingrid de Zwarte is Assistant Professor of Economic and Environmental History at Wageningen University. Her research focuses on the central role of food and famine in modern warfare. She is the author of *The Hunger Winter: Fighting Famine in the Occupied Netherlands, 1944–45* (Cambridge UP, 2020).

Miguel Ángel del Arco Blanco is Full Professor in the Department of Contemporary History at the University of Granada. His work focuses on the study of fascism, memory, the Spanish Civil War, and post-war Francoism. Currently, he is working on a book about the Spanish famine.

Routledge Studies in Modern European History

111 Educational Internationalism in the Cold War
Plural Visions, Global Experiences
Edited by Damiano Matasci and Raphaëlle Ruppen Coutaz

112 Weapons Law in Western Europe 1550–2020
Gunner Lind

113 Gender, Emotion, and the Origins of Democracy in July Monarchy France
The Liberal Crucible
Jeffrey B. Hobbs

114 The French-German Dynamic in an Age of Conflict, 1925–1963
Enemies, Collaborators, Friends
Elana Passman

115 Britain and Ireland from the Treaty to the Troubles
Independence and Interdependence, c. 1921–1973
Richard Carr

116 "Nazi Fantasy"
Vilém Flusser and History as Site of Experiment
Amos Morris-Reich

117 A Modern History of Andorra
Autonomy in the Pyrenean Borderlands
Martyn Lyons

118 The Belgian Revolt of 1830
Nick Ridley

119 The Politics of Famine in European History and Memory
Edited by Ingrid de Zwarte and Miguel Ángel del Arco Blanco

For more information about this series, please visit: www.routledge.com/Routledge-Studies-in-Modern-European-History/book-series/SE0246

The Politics of Famine in European History and Memory

Edited by Ingrid de Zwarte and Miguel Ángel del Arco Blanco

Routledge
Taylor & Francis Group
LONDON AND NEW YORK

First published 2025
by Routledge
4 Park Square, Milton Park, Abingdon, Oxon OX14 4RN

and by Routledge
605 Third Avenue, New York, NY 10158

Routledge is an imprint of the Taylor & Francis Group, an informa business

The Open Access publication of this volume was supported by generous funding of the Dutch Research Council (NWO) under Grant NWA.1160.18.197 (De Zwarte) and Grant VI.Veni.201H.043 (De Zwarte).

British Library Cataloguing-in-Publication Data
A catalogue record for this book is available from the British Library

Library of Congress Cataloging-in-Publication Data
Names: Zwarte, Ingrid de, 1988– editor | Arco Blanco, Miguel Ángel del editor
Title: The politics of famine in European history and memory /
edited by Ingrid de Zwarte and Miguel Ángel del Arco Blanco.
Description: Abingdon, Oxon ; New York, NY : Routledge, 2025. |
Series: Routledge studies in modern European history ; 119 |
Includes bibliographical references and index.
Identifiers: LCCN 2024062062 (print) | LCCN 2024062063 (ebook) |
Subjects: LCSH: Famines–Europe–History–20th century |
Food supply–Political aspects–Europe–History–20th century
Classification: LCC HC240.9.F3 P65 2025 (print) |
LCC HC240.9.F3 (ebook) | DDC 363.8094–dc23/eng/20250402
LC record available at https://lccn.loc.gov/2024062062
LC ebook record available at https://lccn.loc.gov/2024062063

ISBN: 978-1-032-73757-7 (hbk)
ISBN: 978-1-032-73763-8 (pbk)
ISBN: 978-1-003-46580-5 (ebk)

DOI: 10.4324/9781003465805

Typeset in Times New Roman
by Newgen Publishing UK

Contents

Figures

Tables

Contributors

Georgina Brewis is Professor of Social History at University College London (UCL). Based in IOE, UCL's Faculty of Education and Society, she is a historian of voluntary action, humanitarianism, and higher education with extensive experience in collaborative research projects variously funded by UK research councils, the British Academy, and the Swedish Research Council. Books include *Transformational Moments in Social Welfare: What Role for Voluntary Action* (Policy Press, 2021), *Humanitarianism in the Modern World: The Moral Economy of Famine Relief* (CUP, 2020), and *A Social History of Student Volunteering: Britain and Beyond 1880–1980* (Palgrave, 2014). Georgina has a long-standing interest in the question of archiving and record keeping for voluntary organizations and has directed the British Academy Research Project Archiving the Mixed Economy of Welfare in Britain since 2014. At UCL, Georgina leads Generation UCL: Two Hundred Years of Student Life in London, a research and engagement project marking UCL's bicentenary in 2026.

Igor Cașu is the Director of the National Agency for Archives (since April 2022) and a lecturer at the State University of Moldova, Chişinău, since 1998. In 2016, he was a Fulbright Scholar at Stanford University and Hoover, giving talks on postwar famine at Toronto University, Yale, Harvard, and Stanford. He defended his Ph.D. at Jassy University in Romania in 2000 on Soviet Nationalities Policy in the Moldavian SSR, 1944–89. In 2010, he was Deputy Chair of the Presidential Commission for the Study of the Communist Totalitarian Regime in Moldova. In 2014, he published, in Romanian, a book entitled *The Class Enemy. Political Repressions, Violence and Resistance in Soviet Moldavia, 1924–56*, based on party, KGB, and MVD archives. His recent publications include "The Benefits of Comparison: Famine in Kazakhstan in the Early 1930s in Soviet Context", in *Journal of Genocide Research*, Volume 22, issue 3, 2020, and "Do Starving People Rebel? Hunger Riots as *Bab'y* Bunty in Spring 1946 Soviet Moldavia", in *New Europe College's Yearbook* (Bucharest) 2020, and "Police vs. Party? Institutional Hierarchies and Agency in Soviet Moldavia, 1944–1952", in *Contemporary European History*, vol. 32, no. 1, 2022. He is working on a book on the postwar famine in Soviet Moldavia in the European context, 1946–47.

Marguérite Corporaal is Professor and Chair in Irish Literature in Transnational Contexts at Radboud University in Nijmegen, Netherlands. She was the recipient of an ERC grant for consolidators for a project which investigated early literature of Ireland's Great Famine (2010–15). She is currently the principal investigator and supervisor of the projects Redefining the Region and Heritages of Hunger, both funded by the Dutch Research Council (NWO). She is the author of *Relocated Memories: The Great Irish Famine in Irish and Diaspora Fiction, 1847–1870* (2017). Other recent publications include *The Great Famine and Social Class: Conflicts, Responsibilities, Representations* (co-edited, Peter Lang, 2019),

The Famine Diaspora and Irish American Women's Writing (co-edited, Palgrave, 2024), and *Famines and the Making of Heritage* (co-edited, Routledge, 2024).

Mary Elisabeth Cox is Assistant Professor of International Relations at Central European University in Vienna, Austria. Her first book, *Hunger in War and Peace: Women and Children in Germany, 1914–1924*, was published by Oxford University Press in 2019. Cox is the co-editor of *Hunger Re-Draws the Map: Food, State, and Society in the Era of the First World War* with Dr. Claire Morelon, which is being published by Cambridge University Press and is expected in 2024.

Alex de Waal is Executive Director of the World Peace Foundation and Research Professor at the Fletcher School, Tufts University. He has worked on the Horn of Africa, and on conflict, food security, and related issues since the 1980s as a researcher and practitioner. He served as a senior advisor to the African Union High Level Panel on Sudan and South Sudan. He was listed among *Foreign Policy*'s 100 most influential international intellectuals in 2008 and *Atlantic*'s 29 'brave thinkers' in 2009. De Waal's recent books include: *The Real Politics of the Horn of Africa: Money, War and the Business of Power* (Polity 2015), *Mass Starvation: The History and Future of Famine* (Polity Press, 2018), and *New Pandemics, Old Politics: 200 Years of the War on Disease and Its Alternatives* (Polity Press, 2021). He is co-author (with Willow Berridge, Justin Lynch, and Raga Makawi) of *Sudan's Unfinished Democracy: The Promise and Betrayal of a People's Revolution* (Hurst and Oxford University Press, 2022) and co-editor and contributor to *Accountability for Mass Starvation: Testing the Limits of the Law* (Oxford University Press, 2022).

Ingrid de Zwarte is Assistant Professor of Economic and Environmental History at Wageningen University. Previously, she was a Niels Stensen postdoctoral fellow at the University of Oxford. She completed her PhD in History in 2018 with a thesis entitled *The Hunger Winter: Fighting Famine in the Occupied Netherlands, 1944–45*, which was published by Cambridge University Press in 2020. De Zwarte has written on the Dutch Hunger Winter in journals such as *Population Studies*, *Memory Studies*, *War & Society*, and *International Journal of Heritage Studies* and is co-editor of the volume *Famines and the Making of Heritage* (Routledge, 2024). She is a co-applicant of the NWO-NWA project 'Heritages of Hunger' and also holds an NWO Veni Grant (2021–25) for the project 'Food, Famine and the End of Empire in Indonesia, 1940–50'.

Miguel Ángel del Arco Blanco is Full Professor in the Department of Contemporary History at the University of Granada. His work centres on the study of fascism, the Spanish Civil War, and postwar Francoism. Some of his books published in English are: with Alejandro Quiroga (Eds.), *Right Wing Spain in the Civil War Era: Soldiers of God and Apostles of the Fatherland, 1914–45* (2012), with Peter Anderson (Eds.), *Mass Killings and Violence in Spain, 1936–52. Grappling with the Past* (Routledge, 2014), with Peter Anderson (Eds.), *Franco's Famine. Malnutrition, Disease and Starvation in Post-Civil War Spain* (2021). His latest book is *Crosses of Memory and Oblivion. Monuments to the Fallen of The Spanish Civil War (1936–2022)* (Routledge, 2023). Currently, he is working on a book about the Spanish famine.

Norbert Götz holds the chair of contemporary history at Södertörn University. His current research focuses on humanitarianism, moral economy, global civil society, and international organizations. His interests also include populism and nationalism, political culture, peace and international relations, environmental politics, democracy and the welfare state, and conceptual history. He is the PI of the project "Civil Society without Boundaries: Nordic Humanitarianism Facing the Biafra Crisis" (funded by the Swedish Research Council 2022–25). His latest book is *Humanitarianism in the Modern World: The Moral Economy of Famine Relief* (Cambridge University Press, 2020, OA, co-authored with G. Brewis and S. Werther).

Daniel Maul is Professor of Modern and Contemporary History at the University of Oslo, Norway. He has published widely on issues of global social policy, in particular the history of the International Labour Organization, internationalism, and humanitarian aid with a particular emphasis on American Quakers contribution. His latest monographs include *The International Labour Organization. 100 Years of Global Social Policy* (2019) and *The Politics of Service. American Quakers and the Emergence of International Humanitarian Aid 1917–1945* (De Gruyter, 2024).

Anne van Mourik is a historian at the NIOD Institute for War, Holocaust, and Genocide Studies in Amsterdam. Her research focuses on how societies deal with war and mass violence. She has previously worked on projects examining the role of the Dutch Red Cross during WWII and Dutch colonial violence in Indonesia (1945–1950). Currently, she is pursuing a PhD with her project titled 'Weaponizing the Past: Hunger, War and Textbooks in Germany, 1914–2020', which explores the representation of German hunger during and after WWI and WWII in educational materials. Anne has held fellowships at Freie Universität Berlin and the Georg Eckert Institute for International Textbook Research. She also hosts the podcast series *NIOD Rewind*, where she interviews historians and experts on the history and study of mass violence, war, and genocide.

Cormac Ó Gráda is Professor Emeritus at the School of Economics, University College Dublin. He has published extensively on the economic history of Ireland, on famines in Ireland and globally, and on the Industrial Revolution. His books include *Ireland: A New Economic History* (1994), *Black '47 and Beyond* (1999), *Jewish Ireland in the Age of Joyce: A Socioeconomic History* (2006), *Famine: A Short History* (Princeton, 2009), and *The Hidden Victims: Civilian Casualties of the Two World Wars* (2024).

Yurii Shapoval is Professor and Head (since 1998) of the Centre for Historical Political Studies, Institute of Political and Ethnic Studies, National Academy of Sciences of Ukraine. He was a visiting research scholar at various scholarly institutions, including in Canada, Germany, Poland, the USA, and France. His research interests include the political history and the history of political thought in Ukraine in the 19th to 21st centuries, the politics of memory, the process of decommunization in modern Ukraine, and the Holodomor. He has produced numerous original works based on the hitherto unknown archival sources: *Ukraine from the 1920s to the 1950s: Pages from an Unwritten History* (Naukova dumka, 1993), *Ukraine in the Twentieth Century: The People and Events of a Difficult Time* (Heneza, 2001), and *Touch the History* (Parlaments Edition, 2013).

Filip Slaveski is a senior lecturer in Russian/Soviet and East European History at the Australian National University. He is a historian of the Soviet Empire, focusing primarily on Russia and Ukraine. His work examines mass conflict and its aftermath, particularly the intersections of food crises, mass violence, political control, and their contemporary echoes. Some of his publications include: Slaveski, F. and Shapoval, Y. *Stalin's Liquidation Game: The Unlikely Case of Oleksandr Shums'kyi, His Survival in Soviet Jail, and His Subsequent Arcane Assassination* (Harvard Ukrainian Research Institute, 2025), Slaveski, F. *Remaking Ukraine* *after WWII: The Clash of Central and Local Soviet Power, 1944-1953* (Cambridge University Press, 2021), Slaveski, F. *The Soviet Occupation of Germany: Hunger, Mass Violence and the Struggle for Peace, 1945-1947* (Cambridge University Press, 2013).

Tatjana Tönsmeyer is Professor of Modern European History at Wuppertal University. In her research, she focuses on European history of the 19th and 20th centuries, especially the history of World War II, occupation, and occupied societies. Among her latest publications is "Unter deutscher Besatzung. Europa 1939-1945" (2024), an everyday life history of Europe under World War II Occupation, and the two-volume source edition *Fighting Hunger, Dealing with Shortage. Everyday Life under Occupation in World War II Europe* (ed. by Tatjana Tönsmeyer, Peter Haslinger, Włodzimierz Borodziej, Stefan Martens, Irina Sherbakova) Boston 2021 and online on https://societiesundergermanoccupation.uni-wuppertal.de/.

Steffen Werther is an associate professor at Södertörn University and an analyst at the Swedish Defence Research Agency with a PhD in Modern History from Stockholm University. His research interests cover Waffen-SS ideology, Romani studies, far-right memory politics, veteran studies, and the history of humanitarianism. His publications include *Humanitarianism in the Modern World* (Cambridge University Press, 2020), 'Help Yourself by Helping Others' (*Disasters*, 2021), 'The Scandinavian "Gypsy Friend"' (*Scandinavian Journal of History*, 2022), 'Waffen-SS Veterans and Their Sites of Memory Today' (Oxford University Press, 2017), 'Performing Control in the Swedish Twitter Sphere' (*Frontiers*, 2022), and 'Knowledge Production about Danish Nightmen, Roma and Travelers 1800–1950' (*NORDEUROPAforum*, 2023).

Stephen Wheatcroft is a professorial fellow at the School of Historical and Philosophical Studies at Melbourne University and a Fellow of the Academy of Social Sciences of Australia. He has written on Russian, Soviet, and East European Economic, Social, and Demographic History, especially on food problems, famine, and repression. He received his PhD from the Centre for Russian and East European Studies at Birmingham University under R.W. Davies and M. Lewin and spent two years as a British Council Exchange Student at the Moscow Institute of National Economics in the 1970s working with V.P. Danilov and his school. He moved to Melbourne University in the 1980s. Together with R.W. Davies, he wrote *The Years of Hunger: Soviet Agriculture 1931–33*, the major detailed volume on the Soviet Famine of 1932, he is now working on the Soviet famine of 1946/7 in Moldova, Ukraine, and Russia with Filip Slaveski of ANU.

Introduction

The politics of famine

Ingrid de Zwarte and Miguel Ángel del Arco Blanco

Throughout history, famines have always had political dimensions. Starvation tactics, as old as civilization itself, often took the form of sieges designed to induce famine and starve enemies into submission, profoundly shaping political relations in their aftermath.[1] Beyond starvation strategies, politics also played a role in the sense that all historical famines inherently entailed a failure of those in power to respond adequately to food supply issues and effectively organize relief to prevent a crisis from evolving into a catastrophe.[2] Yet although it is hard to think of a historical famine where politics did not matter at all, politics was arguably a less dominant causal factor in pre-modern times, when state capacity was weak or non-existent, transport and storage were costly, interpersonal trust was crucial, and the surplus above subsistence was small, meaning that not all famines were preventable disasters.

Politics became more pervasive, however, since the late nineteenth century, when globalization processes accelerated, diversifying and adding actors to the global food system and increasing the worldwide access to sufficient and nutritious food. Technological innovations in transport and communication integrated food markets globally and reduced food prices and food price volatility, scientific innovations massively increased crop yields and agricultural production, improvements in health and sanitation strongly reduced the incidence of mortality indirectly related to famine, and the spread of democratic and humanitarian institutions strongly reduced levels of warfare as well as the number of people living in extreme poverty.[3] Already by the mid-twentieth century, we achieved the technical capacity to eradicate famine once and for all.

Yet, paradoxically, the twentieth century also witnessed some of the most lethal famines in history, with the major share of the estimated 90 million famine deaths of the twentieth century occurring in Europe and Asia under totalitarian rule – Hitler's Germany, Stalin's Soviet Union, and Mao's China.[4] Since the 1970s, the major technological advancements above as well as the development of strong institutions and legal frameworks that protect civilians from mass starvation have significantly reduced the geographical spread and lethality of famines. Global humanitarian aid networks became equipped to effectively combat food crises while international law – starting with the 1977 Additional Protocols to the Geneva Conventions and reinforced by the 1998 Rome Statute of the International Criminal Court – explicitly prohibited starvation of civilians as a method of warfare.[5] However, famines are by no means a thing of the past. Given the current escalation of emergency food security levels in Sudan, Gaza, Ethiopia, Mali, and elsewhere, they might even be on the rise again.

The question of why famine, narrowly defined as widespread death from starvation and malnutrition-induced diseases,[6] persists in an era of global over-production and food losses has been the subject of extensive scholarly inquiry. Recent scholarship has focused on demonstrating that modern famines are inherently political, arguing that political processes and

DOI: 10.4324/9781003465805-1

decision-making ultimately determine access to food and failures to respond to food crises. In the ground-breaking volume *The New Famines* (2007), Stephen Devereux and the volume contributors argue that, although famines can be triggered by natural disasters or economic shocks, politics should be central to explanations of famine causation: 'the "new famines" are *political* because they are almost always *preventable*'.[7] In his influential study, *Mass Starvation* (2018a), Alex de Waal further reveals how mass starvation is often the result of political decisions and deliberate strategies, emphasizing the power of hunger as a political and military tool of war and repression. All modern famines, as Devereux and De Waal, among others, conclude, are essentially man-made. They were either caused deliberately or not prevented adequately.[8]

The 'new famine thinking' has brought a paradigm shift in our understanding of famines as being man-made and often preventable disasters. That is not to say that *deliberate* starvation policies were the primary cause of most catastrophic famines since the late nineteenth century. Similar to the misconception that famines result one-dimensionally from natural disasters, population growth, or economic shocks, attributing famines to a single perpetrator overlooks their complexity and the multiple drivers involved. When a famine happens, all sources of food fail or are deliberately disrupted – food production, markets, humanitarian aid, as well as coping strategies to deal with food shocks.[9] In modern times, success or failure in preventing famine therefore inherently involves a wide range of actors and institutions, all connected by an intricate web of power relations across political regimes. One of the present scholarly challenges is thus how to avoid offering new mono-causal explanations for famine causation and to prevent reverting to simplified victim-perpetrator discourses. This calls for shifting the focus from *whether* to *how* and *why* famines are political.

This volume builds on the notion that all modern famines are essentially political events and aims to advance a richer agenda – one which explores the many intricate ways in which they actually are political. It offers the first comparative historical study of what we call 'the politics of famine', which we define as the various ways in which famines result from political decision-making, and how the threat, occurrence, relieve, or memory of famine are instrumentalized as a political and military tool. Contributions to this volume show the complexities, variations, and motivations in which famines were instrumentalized by political actors and regimes, and how the politics of perpetrating hunger and the politics of relieving it were oftentimes mutually imbricated. They also address how famine legacies have been subsequently politicized in public debates, educational practices, and popular media; and how these socially and politically constructed memories and myths, in turn, informed broader narratives about hunger and humanitarianism both in history and today.

The focus of this volume is on Europe, which has a longstanding history of famines.[10] On the one hand, European colonial rule was central to the many famines that occurred in colonial contexts.[11] On the other hand, during the nineteenth and twentieth centuries, the continent itself also suffered from multiple famines, mostly related to periods of warfare, political extremism, totalitarianism, and inter-European occupation and colonization. Previous studies have already highlighted that famines in Ireland (1845–50), Germany (1915–19), Russia (1919–23; 1941–44; 1946–47), Ukraine (1932–33; 1946–47), Spain (1939–42; 1946), Greece (1941–44), the Netherlands (1944–45), and Moldova (1946–47) can all be at least partially attributed to political causes.[12] Focusing on these European famines provides us with an excellent opportunity to explore the manifold, interconnected political dimensions of famine, including the political decision-making and failures of response that impacted their causation, development, and mitigation, as well as their long-term consequences. Given the vastly different context of famines under imperial rule in the Global South – due to different actors, institutions, and racist hierarchies – they fall beyond our scope and warrant a separate study.

This Introduction provides a brief context for the chapters that follow. It begins with an overview of the main theories and concepts in famines studies on which this volume builds – moving from an understanding of famine causation in terms of food availability decline to entitlements failures, to failures in response and accountability, and finally to a new agenda which we propose around the concept of 'the politics of famine'. The next section introduces the ten chapters of this volume. The Introduction concludes with a brief discussion of the four general patterns we discern and introduces a theoretical framework to understand the politics of famine, based on the findings and perspectives presented in the chapters.

Theories of famine

Although most scholars today acknowledge the political factors in famine causation, this was not always the case. Until the 1980s, the prevailing view on famine causation closely followed the ideas presented in Thomas Malthus's famous *An Essay on the Principle of Population* (1798), which argued that population growth is always constrained by natural resources and that famine acts as nature's intervention mechanism to balance population size with the available resources, ensuring that the demand for food does not exceed supply.[13] In the late 1970s, this perspective was fundamentally challenged by Amartya Sen, who argued against the notion that famines are solely caused by a food availability decline (FAD). The publication of Sen's *Poverty and Famines* (1981) marked a paradigm shift in our understanding of famine causation. Sen argued that historical famines were not necessarily caused by FAD but rather resulted from market failures. His 'entitlement approach', built around the case of the Bengal famine of 1943, revealed that certain groups might be unable to obtain enough food for survival even when sufficient food was available in the region. Sen posited that starvation occurs when individuals or households cannot secure enough food through their specific set of entitlements, irrespective of the wider availability of food.[14]

While Sen's entitlements theory and his reconceptualization of famine causation have gained broad scholarly acceptance and remain an indispensable tool for understanding famine vulnerability, it has also been challenged in several fundamental ways. Critics of Sen's theory have pointed toward flaws in his empirical foundation as well as his dismissal of the FAD approach, demonstrating that in many modern famines – including during the Bengal famine – issues with food availability decline, for example, through weather extremes resulting in harvest failures, actually played a crucial role in the famine causation.[15]

Another important challenge to Sen's work is that his economic theory primarily explains *how* specific groups are unable to access adequate food supplies, but it does not fully address *why* food entitlements are organized in certain ways, as this should take into account the power relations that ultimately determine access to food. Significantly, it also downplays the fact that all modern famines are *political*-economic events and that political decision-making can, intentionally or unintentionally, reduce the set of entitlements to food that individuals possess. As Jenny Edkins has pointed out, Sen 'did not consider the possibility that famines could be a product of the social or economic system rather than its failure'.[16]

Recent studies emphasize that FAD, market or entitlement failures, and failures of response were not mutually exclusive in most historical famines. Indeed, in many famines discussed in this volume, natural disasters and harvest failures leading to FAD played some role in the chain of events that eventually resulted in famine, but effective political interventions could have prevented worse from happening. As Cormac Ó Gráda concludes in response to Sen's entitlements approach to the Bengal famine: 'The problem in Bengal in 1943 was not internecine strife, but the failure of the imperial power to make good a harvest shortfall that would have been manageable in peacetime'.[17] In another work, he further explains how, in the face of FAD, effective and compassionate governance can foster competitive markets, enforce sanctions against corruption, and provide well-directed relief.[18] Famines in which FAD and response failures interact may be viewed as what Michael Ellman has coined as 'preventable famines', or FAD2 famines.[19] Applied to the case of the 1946–47 Soviet famine – central to Chapter 4 of this volume (Slaveski et al.) – Ellman convincingly argued that despite FAD caused by harvest failures, famine in the Soviet Union could have been prevented by effective government responses. His theory on FAD2 famines has recently received renewed interest and has been convincingly applied to twentieth-century famines in Europe and the Global South.[20]

As supply and market failures thus inadequately capture the multifaceted nature of famine causation, the field of famine studies has recently shifted its focus toward elucidating the key role of politics in causing or failing to prevent famines, with notions of culpability and accountability at the foreground of ongoing debates.[21] In *The New Famines*, Devereux became an important advocate of moving our understanding of modern famines as being preventable disasters, arguing for an 'analytical focus on failures to prevent famine, rather than on the triggers of food shortage or disrupted access to food'.[22] De Waal strengthened this notion by pointing out that famines are often not just a failure of response but 'a kind of atrocity', and 'that political and legal action is needed to complete the job of eliminating mass starvation', as the two proximate factors in famine causation today remain political and military.[23]

Recent scholarship has thus increasingly conceptualized famines not only as humanitarian disasters but also as atrocities, or even crimes, arguing that mass starvation should be understood as a form of violence inflicted upon civilian populations. Influential in this line of thought has been the concept of 'slow violence', coined by Rob Nixon in his book under the same title, which refers to a kind of 'violence that occurs gradually and out of sight', making it hard to single out a clear perpetrator, contrary to, for example, mass killings or torture.[24] Camilla Orjuela and Swati Parashar rightfully note that applying the concept of slow violence to famines 'expands the understanding of what counts as violence, and challenges the focus on distinct events rather than long-term structures and processes in the conceptualisation of famines'.[25] Significantly, this understanding helps us to move away from viewing famines as a by-product of violence toward recognizing mass starvation can be a form of violence in itself.

In this volume, we aim to deepen and complicate these notions of the political causes of famine in three key ways. The first advancement is that we draw attention to the many different political actors and institutions that may contribute to or fail to prevent famine from happening. Sen famously asserted that democracy plays a crucial role in averting famine, as no substantial famine has ever occurred in a country with functioning democratic institutions such as a free press and free elections, yet history tells us that democracies do not necessarily prevent famine at the global level. This holds particularly when considering the role Western democracies have played in causing or failing to prevent famines in colonial and post-colonial contexts. As Olivier Rubin explains in *Democracy and Famine* (2011): 'In essence, famines are only easy to prevent assuming that it is in the interest of those in power to do so'.[26]

For example, in a recent study, Nicolas Mulder and Boyd van Dijk convincingly explain that mass starvation was rarely seen as a war crime before the late twentieth century because of the central role of blockade strategies in modern warfare. They reveal how the same powerful Western states and the Soviet Union, which used starvation as an instrument of warfare, also took the lead in shaping international law and were thereby incentivized to consistently preserve 'a legal space for starvation'.[27] This underscores the importance of investigating political decision-making at local, national, and international levels, across political regimes, rather than narrowly focusing on the specific regime under which the famine occurred.

A second contribution to the literature this volume makes is highlighting the politics of famine relief. Previous studies have shown the crucial importance of humanitarian aid networks in famine prevention and in alleviating immediate suffering by providing food and other essential resources to those in need. Yet, paradoxically, food relief can also reinforce existing social and economic inequalities. Aid distribution may favor certain groups over others, based on factors such as accessibility or political considerations, thus perpetuating or enhancing pre-existing divisions within societies. Studies have also shown that supposedly 'neutral' and 'impartial' relief efforts oftentimes serve political and geopolitical interests, including those of Western countries, and that it can actually contribute to the escalation of violence as well as weaken the region's capacity to deal with future crises.[28] Chapters in this volume strongly reinforce the notion that humanitarian aid is rarely disinterested or apolitical and that the act of giving food has often been instrumentalized and politicized in modern conflicts.

The third and final advancement this volume aims to make is to integrate the history with the memory of famine, as both are deeply connected. One prime example is the continuous and largely successful plea by Ukrainian president Volodymyr Zelensky to the international community to recognize the Holodomor as a genocide. By invoking the Holodomor as a genocide orchestrated under Stalin's Soviet regime, Zelensky has drawn explicit parallels between Ukraine's famine history and Russia's present-day use of starvation as a method of warfare and genocidal intentions in Ukraine. Chapters in this volume show that Ukraine's reinterpretation of the Holodomor in the context of the ongoing war is not a unique example, but that 'famine pasts are [continuously] used to make sense of the presence' or to serve a specific political agenda.[29] They also focus on how these memories and popular representations shape narratives about hunger and humanitarian aid, and how they establish often simplified victim-perpetrator discourses, which subsequently contribute to later political agendas and humanitarian responses.

Chapter overview

The chapters are thematically arranged according to three dimensions that together encompass the politics of famine: state policies and responses (Part I), the international politics of famine and relief (Part II), and the politicization of famine legacies (Part III). They engage with sixteen European famines that took place between 1845 and 1947, spanning from North to South and from West to East Europe, thereby reflecting the continent's economic, cultural, and political diversity. While we fully recognize the major role European colonial institutions and political actors played in the many famines that took place in the Global South within the same timeframe, these fall beyond the scope of this volume.[30]

The first part of this volume focuses on the role of state policies in the causation and exacerbation of famines as well as political responses – or lack thereof – to prevent food shortages from escalating into famine. In Chapter 1, Miguel Ángel del Arco Blanco unravels the origins of the relatively unknown Spanish famine of 1939–42, demonstrating that this famine, which resulted in an estimated 200,000 deaths, was caused by the autarkic policy adopted by Franco's dictatorship. This autarkic policy, influenced by fascist ideology, eventually resulted in the collapse of both agricultural and industrial production and trade. At the same time, the government's inadequate responses to the famine had profound political, economic, and social consequences. The regime's political supporters grew wealthier and managed to avoid starvation while the lower classes, especially those supportive of the previous Republican political regime (1931–36), were most affected by the hunger conditions. The author concludes that the autarkic policy and control over food distribution provided the dictatorship with an unprecedented tool for exerting social control during the famine.

Perhaps the best-known example of *deliberate* mass starvation policies are those carried out by Nazi Germany during the Second World War (WWII). At the same time, there is still much to learn about how local authorities and societies under pressure navigated these extreme circumstances. In Chapter 2, Tatjana Tönsmeyer examines the centrality of starvation policies of the Third Reich in both Western and Eastern Europe. Deeply convinced that Germany lost the Great War because it lost the battle for food ('*Kampf um die Ernährung*'), early on, Hitler's regime determined that Germany needed to be made 'blockade-safe' by exploiting the occupied territories. In the so-called 'Hunger Plan', German planners decided that several millions of people from the East would need to starve to death in order to succeed in their colonial endeavors as well as to feed the Wehrmacht and German population. Within this context, Tönsmeyer shows how German food policies and genocidal policies intersected, specifically those aimed at Jewish populations and Soviet prisoners of war. In the 'makeshift economies' of the German-occupied territories, she further demonstrates how rationing systems became an instrument of oppression while survival strategies were often criminalized. Local authorities of the occupied areas could often do little to alleviate the food situation, especially not in the East.

Chapter 3 shifts the focus to Eastern Europe. In this chapter, Stephen Wheatcroft and Filip Slaveski offer a comprehensive examination of the political history and demographic impact of famines in the Soviet Union between 1917 and 1947 – a period in which six major famines occurred, making it by far the most famine-stricken region in Europe. Analyzing these famines comparatively, the authors argue that the major causal factors were highly similar. Each of the famines started with food shortages in northern deficit regions. Successive governments subsequently squeezed food producers in southern surplus areas to provide for consumers in the north, thereby demonstrating a governmental disregard for the lives of the peasantry in favor of urban industrial and military populations. However, despite incompetent and detrimental state policies, the authors emphasize that natural factors exacerbated the shortages and argue that the famines were neither intentional nor genocidal. In doing so, they call for a clearer distinction between genocidal famines, instigated by military occupiers, and those Soviet famines that resulted in mass starvation under callous, negligent, and self-serving governments.

The importance of investigating political agency in state policies and responses to famines is highlighted in Chapter 4 by Filip Slaveski, Yurii Shapoval, and Igor Caşu, which focuses on center-periphery relationships in the under-researched 1946–47 Soviet famines. The authors compare the actions and policies of two leading Soviet politicians, Lazar Kaganovich and Aleksei Kosygin, who were sent as Stalin's representatives to respectively Ukraine and Moldova, and shed new light on the decisive roles played by these plenipotentiaries in the state's (mis)management of the famine. Paradoxically, while both Soviet leaders were responsible for the implementation of the central Soviet regime's policies that contributed to the famines in Ukraine and Moldova, they simultaneously proved the most effective advocates for alleviating the widespread suffering.

Beyond political regimes and actors, the causes and development of modern famines cannot be fully understood without considering interventions that transcend national borders.[31] Therefore, Part II shifts the focus to the international politics of famine and relief including the role of blockade warfare during both World Wars and the political dimensions of humanitarianism. In Chapter 5, Ingrid de Zwarte and Miguel Ángel del Arco Blanco present the first comparative study of the controversial role played by the Second World War Allied economic blockade of Europe during famines in Francoist Spain (1939–42), Axis-occupied Greece (1941–44), and the German-occupied Netherlands (1944–45). They argue that the Allied blockade policy had a detrimental effect on the food situation in all three cases, attributing the differences in approach to these famines to a complex interplay of military strategies and political objectives, often with little regard for the affected civilian populations. Like the Axis, the Allies recognized that food and hunger were powerful weapons of warfare, playing a pivotal role in securing the Allied victory and shaping the post-war world in their favor.

The other two chapters of Part II engage with transnational humanitarianism, which is often perceived as 'neutral' or depoliticized but, in reality, rarely lacks underlying political motives. Chapter 6, authored by Norbert Götz, Georgina Brewis, and Steffen Werther, offers a fresh perspective on humanitarian appeals, the allocation of relief, and aid accounts through the concept of the 'moral economy'. It proposes a new periodization of humanitarianism, taking a 'supply-side perspective' to famine relief that focuses on the mechanisms of relief efforts. They examine three highly different cases that are representative of distinct phases of humanitarian action in modern history: the Great Irish Famine of the 1840s ('ad hoc humanitarianism'), the famine in Soviet Russia in 1921–22 ('organized humanitarianism'), and the Ethiopian famine of the mid-1980s ('expressive humanitarianism') – the only non-European famine discussed in this book. The authors conclude that the development of humanitarian reasoning was driven more by cultural changes in a changing political landscape than by the emergencies it was intended to address.

Daniel Maul's Chapter 7 presents another interesting case study of transnational humanitarian responses to famine, investigating the American and British Quaker aid to Germany in the aftermath of the First World War. His chapter shows that the Quaker relief efforts to defeated Germany involved an intricate network of relationships between victors and vanquished, donors and recipients, public and private actors, and religious and professional interests, which Maul examines in relation to the broader political, economic, and cultural contexts of aid-giving. As such, Quaker aid to Germany illuminates the tensions inherent in humanitarian action in general, and hunger relief in particular. Together, the contributions to Part II demonstrate the significant influence wielded by those who control the distribution of aid, and how these power dynamics shape not only the immediate relief efforts but also the post-famine political landscape.

The final part of the volume testifies to the fact that memory and myth-making constitute crucial aspects of the politics of famine. Chapters in Part III elucidate how the recollection of European famines, much like the memories of any traumatic event, was reflected in current political and social agendas, shaping people's understanding of the present and their expectations for the future.[32] Cormac Ó Gráda's contribution in Chapter 8 offers a critical reflection on the sesquicentennial commemorations of the Great Irish Famine in the mid-1990s. He analyses the political, official, and popular discourses that asserted a shared collective memory of the catastrophe among the Irish people, 150 years after the event. He challenges this claim of 'communal suffering' with historical insights that reveal that the impact of the Irish Famine was highly unequal and divisive, thus arguing that 'collective memory', as expressed in the 1990s commemorations, was largely an artifact or myth.

Formal education and popular culture also contribute to myth-making and the politicization of famine legacies. In Chapter 9, Mary Elisabeth Cox and Anne van Mourik offer an insightful analysis of the evolving narratives on the Allied naval blockade (1914–19) and widespread hunger conditions in Germany from the end of First World War through the Weimar era – a topic that has hitherto been overlooked by scholarship. Analyzing textbooks and films, the authors show how dominant narratives and myths about the blockade emerged well before National Socialists ascended to power. Foregrounding the complex memory politics in Germany during the early interwar years, they show how textbooks and films functioned as powerful socio-political tools for conveying hunger narratives and contributed to the anti-Allied discourses that would play a pivotal role in the mounting international tensions of the later interwar years.

Part III concludes with Chapter 10 by Marguérite Corporaal, who shows how European famine legacies have been used to give meaning to recent societal issues and how they have been instrumentalized in contemporary political debates. Covering a wide range of examples connected to various nineteenth- and twentieth-century famines, her chapter discusses how present political agendas have led to a reinterpretation of European famine histories. In addition, the chapter analyzes strategies employed in recent famine heritage projects aimed at engaging contemporary generations and incorporating broader global communities with Europe's famine past in a politically unstable present. Corporaal concludes that these strategies include the use of so-called 'multidirectional memory', the recovery of lost and subaltern histories, and dramatization of history to generate affect. The final part of this book thus underscores the importance of recognizing how Europe's famine pasts continue to influence contemporary discourses and political dynamics.

The volume concludes with an Afterword by famine expert Alex de Waal, who offers insightful reflections on the contributions of this volume and the politics of famine in the past, present, and future. Drawing on insights from the chapters and bringing in contemporary controversies, he addresses three key questions: can we make sense of famine denialism? How can we understand variations in the politics of mass starvation? And how have humanitarian scripts shaped the representation of past famines and the permission of current ones? He sadly concludes that while the era of tolerating 'faminogenic' practices seemed to have ended with the triumph of liberal norms in the early 2000s, the wars in Ukraine, Gaza, Sudan, Ethiopia, and elsewhere appear to signal a return to such practices, threatening to elevate 'starvation diplomacy' over humanitarian norms once again.

Understanding the politics of famine

Together, the authors of this volume shed light on the complexities of the political dimensions to the European famines of the nineteenth and twentieth centuries. As such, the chapters engage with what we may call the current 'political turn' in famine studies, which, in this volume, is rooted in four general dimensions we discern within the politics of famine: first, the role of political decision-making that, intentionally or unintentionally, directly contributes to causing famine; second, political failures to prevent famine from happening; third, the politics of humanitarian aid; and fourth, the politicization of famine memory, which in turn influences how famines are addressed in the present and in the future.

Drawing on the insights and findings from the chapters, Figure 0.1 presents a framework for how we may understand these four political dimensions to interact in the causation, development, and long-term consequences of famine. Political decision-making that directly contributes to famine causation includes genocidal intentions, using hunger as a tool for repression or social control, the conduct of war and military strategies (e.g., sieges, scorched earth tactics, blockades), and economic planning. These political strategies and policies can either directly cause famine or induce FAD and market failures that result into famine. Political failures of response help explain why famine is not averted when FAD, market failures and/or political decision-making are creating serious issues with the food supply or access to food. These political failures of response result from a wide range of reasons, including political intent, mismanagement, inability to implement famine preventions measures (especially in times of war), political neglect, or denial.

As this volume shows, humanitarian aid responses also play a central role both in the failure to prevent famine and in their development. The political dimensions of humanitarian aid are often driven by local, domestic, and geopolitical interests – frequently influenced by political

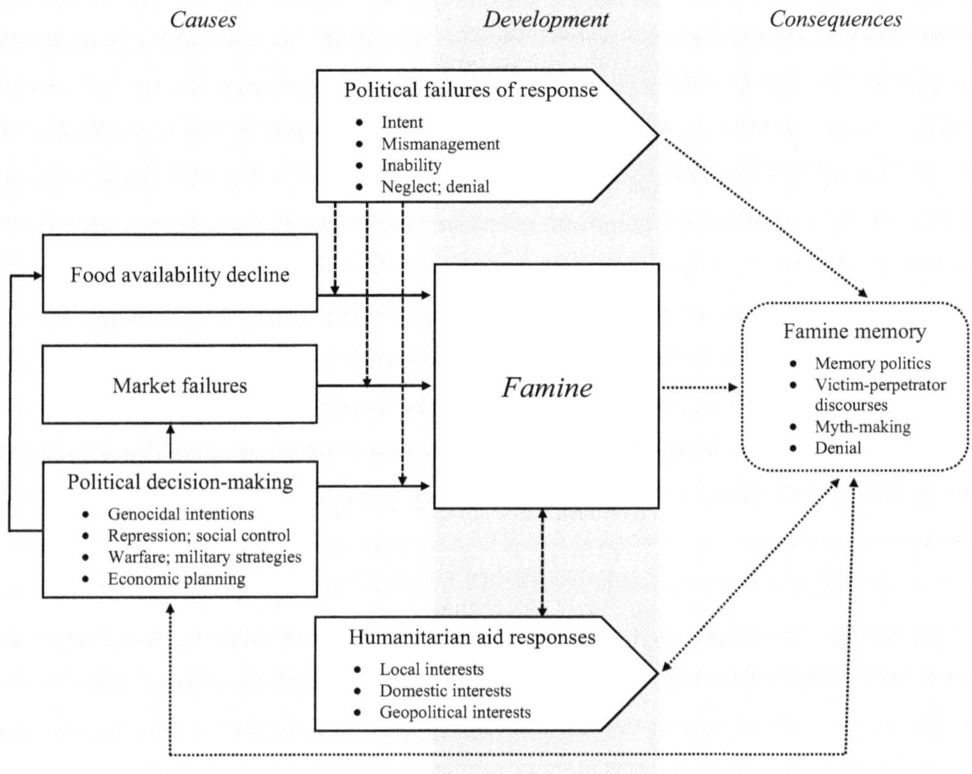

Figure 0.1 Framework for understanding the politics of famine.

motivations across these levels. Finally, this volume seeks to integrate famine memory in our understanding of the politics of famine. We view famine memory as intrinsically fluid and socially, culturally, and politically constructed. It is deeply shaped by individual and collective memories of the event, as well as by political and humanitarian responses during the crisis. The political dimensions include memory politics, the creation of simplified victim-perpetrator discourses, myth-making, and denial – all of which significantly influence political ideologies and subsequent responses to famine.

Examining the role of political decision-making in Europe's modern history of famine, chapters to this volume complicate the picture on perpetratorship and argue for a clearer distinction between political-military intent and political negligence or mismanagement. Chapter 2 (Tönsmeyer) discusses a clear example of deliberate starvation tactics, examining how and why these evolved in Nazi Germany. As Tönsmeyer shows, Nazi food policies initially aimed at wholesale requisitioning of food to feed the German Wehrmacht and civilian population. However, in the course of the war, particularly following the invasion of the Soviet Union, these policies progressively evolved into starvation policies, including the so-called 'Hunger Plan', which aimed to starve and decimate the population of Eastern Europe and repopulate the Soviet territories with ethnic German settlers. Significantly, she explains how 'the acceleration and radicalization of German anti-Semitic measures happened precisely within this context of extreme supply problems', leading to the deaths of millions of Soviet prisoners of war and civilians through deliberate starvation.[33] The forced starvation of Jews, Roma, Sinti, and other so-called 'useless eaters' (*nutzlose Esser*) in concentration camps and euthanasia facilities across the Nazi Empire further demonstrates how central starvation was to the genocidal policies of Nazi Germany.[34]

There is considerable debate whether the Ukrainian famine of 1932–33, known as the 'Holodomor', should also be viewed as a genocidal famine. Several recent studies indicate that the famine was entirely man-made, engineered by the Soviet leadership under Stalin to target ethnic Ukrainians, evidenced by policy directions and disproportionate excess mortality among this part of the population.[35] In this volume, Wheatcroft and Slaveski (Chapter 3) 'argue against the growing consensus that claims Soviet famines were genocidal', finding 'little evidence that the state intentionally used famine as a means to kill Ukrainians as a specific ethnic group'. They also challenge current claims that deny that there were serious food crises from which the famines originated, showing that harvest losses and ongoing food supply problems under influence of misguided economic planning objectives played a crucial role in triggering periods of extreme hunger in the Soviet Union. Political decisions based on gross miscalculations and misjudgments exacerbated the situation and effectively caused the famines, especially because government policies favored urban and military populations over peasant lives, diverting famine to food-producing regions.

Some other famines might be better described as 'foreseen' rather than intentional. In this context, 'foreseen' also seems more appropriate than 'preventable', as the latter implies political structures and actors that could actively work to stop a famine through effective intervention methods, which are often absent in authoritarian regimes. Chapter 1 (Del Arco Blanco) on autarky-driven Francoist Spain and Chapter 4 (Slaveski et al.) on the 1946–47 Soviet famines in Ukraine and Moldova both testify to the central role of political mismanagement and negligence in the failure to prevent famine in the absence of intent to inflict mass starvation.

The volume's case studies further demonstrate that democratic regimes can also contribute to famine, especially when relief efforts were purposely withheld or delayed for political and military reasons. Examples include the Second World War famines in Axis-occupied Greece in 1941–44 and the German-occupied Netherlands in 1944–45.[36] Common misconceptions about the causes of these famines persist until today, unilaterally blaming the German occupier for creating famine conditions through extortive policies or, in the case of the Netherlands, by allegedly blocking food supplies from reaching the starving population.[37] As Chapter 5 (De Zwarte and Del Arco Blanco) shows, the detrimental role of the Allied economic blockade and refusal to allow food aid – prioritizing military considerations over humanitarian concerns – in exacerbating famine have received far less attention. Their differential approaches to famine and relief in wartime Europe were driven by various political motivations: enforcing neutrality in Spain, securing post-war alliances in Greece, and defeating the enemy in the Netherlands. The oversight in literature on the detrimental role of the blockade is perhaps understandable, given the construction of post-war victim-perpetrator narratives, where the Allies were seen as the main victors and saviors.[38] At the same time, these examples highlight the central role of geopolitical interests in the causes, development, and outcomes of a famine.

As many chapters in this volume demonstrate, both hunger and food can be powerful tools for repression or negotiation, making 'the politics of food' an integral part of the politics of famine. In Francoist Spain, autarky and access to food provided the dictatorship with an unparalleled tool for social control, as it 'allowed the dictatorship to reward its social supporters and control and punish the lower social classes', especially those with Republican affiliations. The power exerted through control over food is also well demonstrated by the German occupation of societies across Europe, which included the criminalization of survival strategies, as discussed in Chapter 2 (Tönsmeyer). Within these systems of control, members of occupied societies were hierarchized and ascribed survival chances, with Jews placed at the bottom of these racist and utilitarian hierarchies, which again stresses the intersection between starvation and genocidal policies.

Food can also be a powerful tool for political and diplomatic purposes during times of famine, with humanitarian organizations assuming a central role in mediating political agendas. As Daniel Maul shows in Chapter 7, in the immediate years after First World War, American and British Quaker organizations provided large-scale relief in the former 'enemy states' Germany and Austria, supported by official state agencies like Herbert Hoover's American Relief Administration. Maul explains how Hoover's involvement was based on humanitarian as well as political considerations: 'What Hoover feared most was that starvation might ultimately contribute to a revolutionary overthrow of the country's new democratic order [...] From his point of view, American aid was the prime weapon to fight this danger'. In the case of Greece during Second World War, the perceived 'neutrality' of the Swedish Red Cross was used by the Allies to set up a relieve scheme that worked in their advantage, allowing them to obtain vital intelligence during the war while simultaneously seeking to establish a stronghold in strategically important post-war Greece.

News media have historically played an important role in the representations of famine, with the power to either politicize or depoliticize them, thereby influencing political and humanitarian interventions. Mounting public pressure following new reports on starvation in Greece led the British Foreign Office to fear that the suffering might create 'permanent anti-British feeling in those countries which may well dictate the post-war policies'. This concern subsequently contributed to their decision to breach their blockade policy in 1942 and allow a Red Cross relief scheme. Television, as a new medium after the war, further advanced the mediatization of famine, often invoking recurrent famine tropes – such as the famished mother and child – aimed at evoking sympathy and prompting calls for aid.[39] The media-driven humanitarianism of the late twentieth century, which culminated during the Ethiopian famine of 1982–84, is what Götz et al. (Chapter 6) define as 'expressive humanitarianism': 'a media-driven understanding of disasters and relief efforts and an emphasis on celebrity, spectacle, and mass participation in relief'. While expressive humanitarianism fostered 'specific moral economies in which donors and relief agencies endowed their allocations with altruistic meaning', it also revealed the 'depoliticizing power' that media can exert through their representations of famines – a highly problematic dynamic, given the deeply political nature of famine and the many local, domestic, and geopolitical interests involved.

This brings us to our final observation about the power of social and political representations of famine in memory and myth-making. Chapter 10 (Corporaal) demonstrates how famine legacies are continuously invoked to make sense of the present and politicized to serve meaning in present-day debates. As Corporaal explains, political events 'condition in what ways famines are remembered and what dimensions of these famine pasts are recollected or forgotten'. Indeed, famine denialism also plays a role in the politics of famine, as evidenced by the denialist policies in the Soviet Union following the devastating famines of the 1930s and 1940s, but also in Spain, where the famine was subsequently silenced by the Francoist regime. Starting from 1978, democratic governments neglected to establish active memory policies concerning the country's traumatic past, mostly because it still proved inconvenient to current political agendas, resulting in the famine being largely disregarded. It is only with recent academic research and the introduction of active memory policies that the country has started to acknowledge and narrate its famine history.[40]

At the same time, this volume also reveals how memory politics and myth-creating can serve as powerful tools in processes of nation-building and self-identification, helping to construct an internal victim group while 'othering' of those deemed responsible for the catastrophic suffering. Analyzing the sesquicentennial commemorations of the Great Irish Famine in the mid-1990s, Ó Gráda (Chapter 8) challenges the moment when Irish people across the world began to share a communal memory of that catastrophe, questioning how the memory of 'such an uneven and divisive disaster' be ever truly be collective. In post-First World War and Weimar Germany, wartime hunger narratives were similarly used 'to foster a sense of unity' and to legitimize post-war governmental policies. The authors in Chapter 9 convincingly argue that by portraying the Allied blockade as 'an inhumane action by a terrible enemy', these victim-perpetrator discourses eventually became ingrained in popular and political memory, influencing Nazi policies and starvation politics of the 1940s – a case in point for including memory and myth-making in our understanding of the politics of famine.

On the other side of the spectrum are famine myths that evolve for propaganda purposes. A good example in this volume is the myth surrounding the miraculous salvation of the Netherlands from starvation by the Allies through the legendary food drops at the end of the Dutch 'Hunger Winter'. This myth effectively obscured the role the Allies' rigid blockade policy played in the same famine. The simplified victim-perpetrator discourses that accompany famine myth-making thus go beyond mere rhetoric strategies aligned with contemporary political agendas; they play a decisive role in shaping post-famine political allegiances.

Taken together, the chapters broaden our understanding of what constitutes 'the politics of famine'. They move beyond a narrow focus on intent and simplified perpetrator roles to reveal the complexities and variations in how famine can be used as a political or military tool. This spectrum ranges from the overt use of starvation as a method of warfare and repression to more covert forms of exploiting (or threatening) hunger and using the promise of food for propaganda or sociopolitical control, even when such motives are denied. This expanded view also broadens our understanding of who is culpable, accountable, or complicit in preventing famine. With global hunger on the rise again after decades of decline, affecting more than 37 million people at emergency levels of hunger or worse,[41] understanding the politics of famine is an urgent task beyond academic circles. It calls on the international community to critically examine their own complex roles in addressing the future of famine.

Acknowledgments

The authors wish to thank Anne-Lise Bobeldijk, Marguérite Corporaal, Alex de Waal, Ewout Frankema, and Cormac Ó Gráda for their insightful feedback on earlier versions of this Introduction.

Notes

1 See various chapters in Guido Alfani and Cormac Ó Gráda, eds., *Famine in European History* (Cambridge: Cambridge University Press, 2017).

2 See various chapters in Jessica Dijkman and Bas van Leeuwen, eds., *An Economic History of Famine Resilience* (London: Routledge, 2020).

3 Niek Koning, *Food Security, Agricultural Policies and Economic Growth: Long-term Dynamics in the Past, Present, and Future* (London: Routledge, 2017); Amartya Sen, 'Liberty and Poverty: Political Rights and Economics', *The New Republic*, 210, no. 10 (1994): 31–7; Gordon Conway, *The Doubly Green Revolution: Food for All in the Twenty-First Century* (Ithaca: Cornell University Press, 1998);

Daniel A. Sumner, 'Recent Commodity Price Movements in Historical Perspective', *American Journal of Agricultural Economics*, 91 (2009): 1250–6.

4 Tatjana Tönsmeyer, Peter Haslinger, and Agnes Laba, eds. *Coping with Hunger and Shortage under German Occupation in World War II* (Cham: Springer International Publishing, 2018); Adam Tooze, *The Wages of Destruction: The Making and Breaking of the Nazi Economy* (New York: Penguin, 2008): 513–51; Robert W. Davies and Stephen Wheatcroft, *The Years of Hunger: Soviet Agriculture, 1931–1933* (New York: Palgrave, 2004); Anne Applebaum, *Red Famine: Stalin's War on Ukraine* (London: Allen Lane, 2017); Frank Dikötter, *Mao's Great Famine* (London: Bloomsbury, 2014).

5 Alex De Waal, *Mass Starvation: The History and Future of Famine* (Cambridge: Polity Press, 2018a).

6 This definition is based on Ó Gráda, who defines famines as 'a shortage of food or purchasing power directly leading to excess mortality from starvation or hunger-induced diseases'. Cormac Ó Gráda, *Famine. A Short History* (Princeton: Princeton University Press, 2009): 3–6. For clear definitions of 'famine', see also: Stephen Devereux, *Famine in the Twentieth Century*. Working Paper 105 (Brighton: Institute of Development Studies, 2000); Paul Howe and Stephen Devereux, 'Famine Intensity and Magnitude Scales: A Proposal for an Instrumental Definition of Famine', *Disasters* 28, no. 4 (2004): 353–72.

7 Devereux, 'Introduction: From "Old Famines" to "New Famines"', in Devereux, ed, *The New Famines: Why Famines Exist in an Era of Globalization* (London: Routledge, 2006), 11.

8 De Waal, *Mass Starvation*; Devereux, 'From "Old Famines" to "New Famines"', 4–5.

9 Devereux, 'From "Old Famines" to "New Famines"',, 11; Jessica Dijkman and Bas van Leeuwen, 'Resilience to Famine ca. 600 BC to Present: An Introduction', in Dijkman and Van Leeuwen, eds, *An Economic History of Famine Resilience* (Routledge: London, 2020): 8–10.

10 For a longer-term perspective on famines in Europe, see: Guido Alfani and Cormac Ó Gráda, eds. *Famine in European History* (Cambridge: Cambridge University Press, 2017).

11 Mike Davis, *Late Victorian Holocausts* (New York: Verso, 2017); Janam Mukherjee, *Hungry Bengal: War, Famine and the End of Empire* (London: Hurst & Company, 2023); Yan Slobodkin, *The Starving Empire: A History of Famine in France's Colonies* (Ithaca: Cornell University Press, 2023); Gregg Huff, 'Causes and Consequences of the Great Vietnam Famine, 1944–1945', *Economic History Review*, 72, no. 1 (2019): 286–316; Pierre van der Eng, 'Missing Millions: Java's 1944–45 Famine in Indonesia's Historiography', *Modern Asian Studies*, 58, no. 2 (2024): 563–583.

12 E.g., Cormac Ó Gráda, *Black '47 and Beyond: The Great Irish Famine in History, Economy, and Memory* (Princeton: Princeton University Press, 1999); Peter Gray, *Famine, Land and Politics: British Government and Irish Society, 1843-50* (Dublin: Irish Academic Press, 1999); Mary Cox, *Hunger in War and Peace: Women and Children in Germany, 1914–1924* (Oxford: Oxford University Press, 2019); Stephen Wheatcroft, 'Eastern Europe (Russia and the USSR)', in Guido Alfani and Cormac Ó Gráda, eds, *Famine in European History* (Cambridge: Cambridge University Press, 2017); Stephen Wheatcroft and Robert W. Davies, *Years of Hunger: Soviet Agriculture, 1931–1933* (New York: Palgrave Macmillan, 2009); Nicholas Ganson, *The Soviet Famine of 1946-47 in Global & Historical Perspective* (New York: Palgrave, 2009); Declan Curran, Luciuk Lubomyr, and Andrew G. Newby, *Famines in European Economic History: The Last Great European Famines Reconsidered* (Abingdon: Routledge, 2015); Applebaum, *Red Famine*. Miguel Ángel del Arco Blanco and Peter Anderson, *Franco's Famine: Malnutrition, Disease and Starvation in Post-Civil War Spain* (New York: Bloomsbury Academic, 2021); Violetta Hionidou, *Famine and Death in Occupied Greece, 1941–1944* (New York: Cambridge University Press, 2006); Ingrid de Zwarte, *The Hunger Winter: Fighting Famine in the Occupied Netherlands, 1944–1945* (Cambridge: Cambridge University Press, 2020).

13 Robert Thomas Malthus, *An Essay on the Principle of Population*. Joyce E. Chaplin, ed. (New York: W. W. Norton, 2018 [1798]).

14 Amartya Sen, *Poverty and Famines: An Essay on Entitlement and Deprivation* (Oxford: Oxford University Press, 1981).

15 Devereux, 'Famine in the Twentieth Century', 9, 20; Idem, 'Sen's Entitlement Approach: Critiques and Counter-Critiques', *Oxford Development Studies* 29 (2001): 245–63; Meghnad Desai, 'The Economics

of Famine', in G. A. Harrison, ed, *Famine* (Oxford: Oxford University Press, 1988): 112–14. Ó Gráda, 'Sufficiency and Sufficiency and Sufficiency: Revisiting the Greta Bengal Famine of 1943–44' in *Eating people Is Wrong and Other Essays on Famine, Its Past and Its Future* (New Jersey: Princeton University Press, 2015): 38–91.

16 Jenny Edkins, 'The Criminalization of Mass Starvations: From Natural Disaster to Crime against Humanity', in *The New Famines*, 53.

17 Ó Gráda, *Eating People Is Wrong*, 90–91.

18 Idem *Famine*, 13; Idem, 'Famines Past, Famine's Future', *Development and Change* 42, no. 1 (2011): 49–69. See also: Idem, *Black '47 and Beyond: The Great Irish Famine in History, Economy, and Memory* (Princeton: Princeton University Press, 1999): 4–10; Andrew Newby, *Finland's Great Famine, 1856-68* (Cham: Springer, 2024).

19 Michael Ellman, 'The 1947 Soviet Famine and the Entitlement Approach to Famines', *Cambridge Journal of Economics* 24, no. 5 (2000): 603–30.

20 See, for example: Gregg Huff, 'The Great Second World War Vietnam and Java Famines', *Modern Asian Studies* 54, no. 2 (2020): 618–53; Ó Gráda, *Famine*, 241.

21 Ó Gráda, *Famine*; Devereux, *The New Famines*; Jenny Edkins, *Whose Hunger? Concepts of Famine, Practices of Aid* (Minneapolis: Minnesota University Press, 2000); Alex De Waal, 'The End of famine? Prospects for the Elimination of Mass Starvation by Political Sction', *Political Geography*, 62 (2018b): 184–95; David Marcus, 'Famine Crimes in International Law', *American Journal of International Law*, 97, 2 (2003): 245–81; Bridget Conley, Alex de Waal, Catriona Murdoch, and Wayne Jordash QC, *Accountability for Mass Starvation: Testing the Limits of the Law* (Oxford: Oxford University Press, 2022).

22 Devereux, 'From 'Old Famines' to 'New Famines', 7.

23 De Waal, *Mass Starvation*, 11; passim.

24 Rob Nixon, *Slow Violence and the Environmentalism of the Poor* (Cambridge, MA: Harvard University Press, 2013).

25 Camilla Orjuela and Swati Parashar, 'Memory and Justice after Famines: An Introduction', *Third World Quarterly* 45, no. 2 (2024): 249.

26 Olivier Rubin, *Democracy and Famine* (Abingdon: Routledge, 2011), 1.

27 Nicholas Mulder, and Boyd van Dijk, 'Why Did Starvation Not Become the Paradigmatic War Crime in International Law?', in Ingo Venzke, and Kevin Jon Heller, eds, *Contingency in International Law: On the Possibility of Different Legal Histories* (Oxford: Oxford University Press, 2021): 368.

28 Mike Zmolek, 'Aid Agencies, NGO's and Institutionalisation of Famine', *Economic and Political Weekly* 25 (1990): 37–48; Joanna Macrae and Anthony B. Zwi, 'Food as an Instrument of War in Contemporary African Famines: A Review of Evidence', *Disasters* 16 (1992): 299–321; David Keen, *The Benefits of Famine: A Political Economy of Famine and Relief in Southwestern Sudan 1983–1989* (Princeton: Princeton University Press, 1994); Alex de Waal, *Famine Crimes: Politics & the Disaster Relief Industry in Africa* (London: Villiers Publications, 1997); Haris Gazdar, 'Pre-modern, Modern and Postmodern Famine in Iraq, 1990–203', in *The New Famines*, 127–142; José C. Martínez and Brent Eng, 'The Unintended Consequences of Emergency Food Aid: Neutrality, Sovereignty and Politics in the Syrian Civil War, 2012-15', *International Affairs* 92 (2016): 153–73.

29 Marguérite Corporaal and Ingrid De Zwarte, 'Introduction: Famines and the Making of Heritage', in Corporaal and De Zwarte, eds, *Famines and the Making of Heritage* (London: Routledge, 2024), 1.

30 E.g., Mukherjee, *Hungry Bengal*; Slobodkin, *The Starving Empire*; Van der Eng, 'Missing Millions'; Huff, 'The Great Second World War Vietnam and Java Famines'.

31 De Waal, *Famine Crimes*; Norbert Götz, Georgina Brewis, and Steffen Werther, *Humanitarianism in the Modern World: The Moral Economy of Famine Relief* (Cambridge: Cambridge University Press, 2020); Bertrand M. Patenaude and Joan Nabseth Stevenson, *Bread + Medicine American Famine Relief in Soviet Russia, 1921–1923* (Chicago: Hoover Institution Press, 2023); Daniel Maul, *The Politics of Service. American Quakers and the Emergence of International Humanitarian Aid 1917–1945* (Berlin: De Gruyter, 2024); Paul C. Vincent, *The Politics of Hunger: The Allied Blockade of Germany,*

1915–1919 (Athens: Ohio University Press, 1985); Clotilde Druelle-Korn, *Feeding Occupied France during World War I: Herbert Hoover and the Blockade* (Cham: Palgrave, 2019).

32 Alex De Waal, 'Memory and the Social Meanings of Famine', *Third World Quarterly*, 45, no. 2 (2023): 439–43; Corporaal and De Zwarte, eds., *Famines and the Making of Heritage*.

33 Gesine Gerhard, 'Food and Genocide: Nazi Agrarian Politics in the Occupied Territories of the Soviet Union', *Contemporary European History* 18, no. 1 (2009): 45–65; Tooze, *The Wages of Destruction*.

34 Susanne Knittel, *The Historical Uncanny: Disability, Ethnicity, and the Politics of Holocaust Memory* (New York: Fordham University Press, 2015): 38–39.

35 E.g., Andrea Graziosi, 'Why and in What Sense Was the Holodomor a Genocide?', in Lubomyr Luciuk and Lisa Grekul, eds, *Holodomor: Reflections on the Great Famine of 1932–1933 in Soviet Ukraine* (Kingston: The Kashtan Press, 2008); Andrei Markevich et al., 'Causes of the Ukrainian Famine Mortality', *Review of Economic Studies* (2024): online pre-publication. DOI: https://doi.org/10.1093/restud/rdae091

36 Hionidou, *Famine and Death in Occupied Greece*; De Zwarte, *The Hunger Winter*.

37 Violetta Hionidou, 'We Went through a Lot That … Cannot Be Discussed, Cannot Be Written: Remembering the Greek Famine of the Early 1940s', in *Famines and the Making of Heritage*; De Zwarte, *The Hunger Winter*, 7, 44. For misconceptions about the causes of the Hunger winter: Lizzie Collingham, *Taste of War: World War II and the Battle for Food* (New York: Penguin, 2012): 176; Ian Buruma, *1945: Biografie van een Jaar* (Amsterdam: Atlas Contact, 2013): 65.

38 Dan Stone, *Goodbye to All That?: The Story of Europe Since 1945* (Oxford: Oxford University Press, 2014): 60–62.

39 Margaret Kelleher, *The Feminization of Famine: Expressions of the Inexpressible?* (Durham: Duke University Press, 1997); De Zwarte and Lindsay Janssen, 'Recalling the Hunger Winter: Evoking Famine Memory beyond the National', *Memory Studies* 17, no. 2 (2024): 221.

40 Miguel Ángel del Arco Blanco and Deborah Madden, 'Spain's Hunger Years: A Lack of Musealisation of a Traumatic Past', in Corporaal and De Zwarte, eds, *Famines and the Making of Heritage*; Gloria Román Ruiz, 'Representations of the Spanish Hunger Years (1939–1952) in Recent Secondary School History Textbooks', *Paedagogica Historica*, 59, no. 6 (2022): 1345–66.

41 WFP, 'Global Hunger Crisis', via: www.wfp.org/global-hunger-crisis. Last accessed: 9 September 2024.

References

Alfani, Guido and Cormac Ó Gráda, eds. *Famine in European History*. Cambridge: Cambridge University Press, 2017.

Applebaum, Anne. *Red Famine: Stalin's War on Ukraine*. London: Allen Lane, 2017.

Buruma, Ian. *1945: Biografie van een Jaar*. Amsterdam: Atlas Contact, 2013.

Collingham, Lizzie. *Taste of War: World War II and the Battle for Food*. New York: Penguin, 2012.

Conley, Bridget, Alex de Waal, Catriona Murdoch, and Wayne Jordash QC. *Accountability for Mass Starvation: Testing the Limits of the Law*. Oxford: Oxford University Press, 2022.

Conway, Gordon. *The Doubly Green Revolution: Food for All in the Twenty-First Century*. Ithaca: Cornell University Press, 1998.

Corporaal, Marguérite and Ingrid De Zwarte, eds. *Famines and the Making of Heritage*. London: Routledge, 2024.

Cox, Mary. *Hunger in War and Peace: Women and Children in Germany, 1914-1924*. Oxford: Oxford University Press, 2019.

Curran, Declan, Luciuk Lubomyr, and Andrew G. Newby. *Famines in European Economic History: The Last Great European Famines Reconsidered*. Abingdon: Routledge, 2015.

Davies, Robert W. and Stephen Wheatcroft. *The Years of Hunger: Soviet Agriculture, 1931–1933*. New York: Palgrave, 2004.

Davis, Mike. *Late Victorian Holocausts*. New York: Verso, 2017.

De Waal, Alex. *Famine Crimes: Politics & The Disaster Relief Industry in Africa*. Villiers Publications: London, 1997.

De Waal, Alex. *Mass Starvation: The History and Future of Famine*. Cambridge: Polity Press, 2018a.
De Waal, Alex. 'The End of Famine? Prospects for the Elimination of Mass Starvation by Political Action'. *Political Geography*, 62 (2018b): 184–95.
De Waal, Alex. 'Memory and the Social Meanings of Famine'. *Third World Quarterly*, 45, no. 2 (2023): 439–43.
De Zwarte, Ingrid. *The Hunger Winter: Fighting Famine in the Occupied Netherlands, 1944–1945*. Cambridge: Cambridge University Press, 2020.
De Zwarte, Ingrid and Lindsay Janssen, 'Recalling the Hunger Winter: Evoking Famine Memory beyond the National'. *Memory Studies*, 17, no. 2 (2024): 213–27.
Del Arco Blanco, Miguel Ángel, and Peter Anderson. *Franco's Famine: Malnutrition, Disease and Starvation in Post-Civil War Spain*. New York: Bloomsbury Academic, 2021.
Del Arco Blanco, Miguel Ángel, and Deborah Madden. 'Spain's Hunger Years: A Lack of Musealisation of a Traumatic Past', in Corporaal and De Zwarte, eds, *Famines and the Making of Heritage*. London: Routledge, 2024.
Desai, Meghnad. 'The Economics of Famine', in G. A. Harrison, ed, *Famine*. Oxford: Oxford University Press, 1988: 112–14.
Devereux, Stephen. *Famine in the Twentieth Century*. Working Paper 105, Brighton: Institute of Development Studies, 2000.
Devereux, Stephen. 'Sen's Entitlement Approach: Critiques and Counter-Critiques', *Oxford Development Studies* 29 (2001): 245–63.
Devereux, Stephen. ed. *The New Famines: Why Famines Exist in an Era of Globalization*. London: Routledge, 2007.
Dijkman, Jessica and Bas van Leeuwen. 'Resilience to Famine ca. 600 BC to Present: An Introduction', in Jessica Dijkman and Bas van Leeuwen, eds, *An Economic History of Famine Resilience*. London: Routledge, 2020: 1–13.
Dikötter, Frank. *Mao's Great Famine*. London: Bloomsbury, 2014.
Druelle-Korn, Clotilde. *Feeding Occupied France during World War I: Herbert Hoover and the Blockade*. Cham: Palgrave, 2019.
Edkins, Jenny. *Whose Hunger? Concepts of Famine, Practices of Aid*. Minneapolis: Minnesota University Press, 2000.
Edkins, Jenny. 'The Criminalization of Mass Starvations: From Natural Disaster to Crime against Humanity', in Stephen Devereux, ed, *The New Famines: Why Famines Exist in an Era of Globalization*. London: Routledge, 2006: 50–65.
Ellman, Michael. 'The 1947 Soviet Famine and the Entitlement Approach to Famines', *Cambridge Journal of Economics* 24, no. 5 (2000): 603–30.
Eng, Pierre van der. 'Missing Millions: Java's 1944–45 Famine in Indonesia's Historiography', *Modern Asian Studies* 58, no. 2 (2024): 563–83. DOI: https://doi.org/10.1017/S0026749X24000027.
Ganson, Nicholas. *The Soviet Famine of 1946-47 in Global & Historical Perspective*. New York: Palgrave, 2009.
Gazdar, Haris. 'Pre-Modern, Modern and Postmodern Famine in Iraq, 1990-203', in Stephen Devereux, ed, *The New Famines: Why Famines Exist in an Era of Globalization*. London: Routledge, 2006: 127–42.
Gerhard, Gesine. 'Food and Genocide: Nazi Agrarian Politics in the Occupied Territories of the Soviet Union', *Contemporary European History* 18, no. 1 (2009): 45–65.
Götz, Norbert, Georgina Brewis, and Steffen Werther. *Humanitarianism in the Modern World: The Moral Economy of Famine Relief*. Cambridge: Cambridge University Press, 2020.
Gray, Peter. *Famine, Land and Politics: British Government and Irish Society, 1843-50*. Dublin: Irish Academic Press, 1999.
Graziosi, Andrea. 'Why and in What Sense Was the Holodomor a Genocide?', in Lubomyr Luciuk and Lisa Grekul, eds, *Holodomor: Reflections on the Great Famine of 1932–1933 in Soviet Ukraine*. Kingston: The Kashtan Press, 2008.
Hionidou, Violetta. *Famine and Death in Occupied Greece, 1941–44*. Cambridge: Cambridge University Press, 2006.

Hionidou, Violetta. 'We Went Through a Lot That … Cannot Be Discussed, Cannot Be Written: Remembering the Greek Famine of the Early 1940s', in Marguérite Corporaal and Ingrid De Zwarte, eds, *Famines and the Making of Heritage*. London: Routledge, 2024.
Howe, Paul and Stephen Devereux. 'Famine Intensity and Magnitude Scales: A Proposal for an Instrumental Definition of Famine', *Disasters*, 28, no. 4 (2004): 353–72.
Huff, Gregg. 'Causes and Consequences of the Great Vietnam Famine, 1944–1945', *Economic History Review*, 72, no. 1 (2019): 286–316.
Huff, Gregg. 'The Great Second World War Vietnam and Java Famines', *Modern Asian Studies*, 54, no. 2 (2020): 618–53.
Keen, David. *The Benefits of Famine: A Political Economy of Famine and Relief in Southwestern Sudan 1983–1989*. Princeton: Princeton University Press, 1994.
Kelleher, Margaret. *The Feminization of Famine: Expressions of the Inexpressible?* Durham: Duke University Press, 1997.
Kiernan, Ben. 'The Demography of Genocide in Southeast Asia: The Death Tolls in Cambodia, 1975–79, and East Timor, 1975–80', *Critical Asian Studies*, 35, no. 4 (2003): 585–97.
Knittel, Susanne. *The Historical Uncanny: Disability, Ethnicity, and the Politics of Holocaust Memory*. New York: Fordham University Press, 2015.
Koning, Niek. *Food Security, Agricultural Policies and Economic Growth: Long-term Dynamics in the Past, Present, and Future*. London: Routledge, 2017.
Macrae, Joanna and Anthony B. Zwi. 'Food as an Instrument of War in Contemporary African Famines: A Review of Evidence', *Disasters* 16 (1992): 299–321.
Malthus, Robert Thomas. *An Essay on the Principle of Population*. Edited by Joyce E. Chaplin. New York: W. W. Norton, 2018 [1798].
Marcus, David. 'Famine Crimes in International Law', *American Journal of International Law*, 97, no. 2 (2003): 245–81.
Markevich, Andrei, Natalya Naumenko, and Nancy Qian, 'The Causes of the Ukrainian Famine Mortality', *The Review of Economic Studies* (2024): DOI: https://doi.org/10.1093/restud/rdae091.
Martínez, José C. and Brent Eng, 'The Unintended Consequences of Emergency Food Aid: Neutrality, Sovereignty and Politics in the Syrian Civil War, 2012-15', *International Affairs* 92 (2016): 153–73.
Maul, Daniel. *The Politics of Service. American Quakers and the Emergence of International Humanitarian Aid 1917–1945*. Berlin: De Gruyter, 2024.
Mukherjee, Janam. *Hungry Bengal: War, Famine and the End of Empire*. London: Hurst & Company, 2023.
Mulder, Nicholas and Boyd van Dijk. 'Why Did Starvation Not Become the Paradigmatic War Crime in International Law?', in Ingo Venzke and Kevin Jon Heller, eds, *Contingency in International Law: On the Possibility of Different Legal Histories*. Oxford: Oxford University Press, 2021.
Newby, Andrew. *Finland's Great Famine, 1856-68*. Cham: Springer International Publishing, 2024.
Nixon, Rob. *Slow Violence and the Environmentalism of the Poor*. Cambridge: Harvard University Press, 2013.
Ó Gráda, Cormac. *Black '47 and Beyond: The Great Irish Famine in History, Economy, and Memory*. Princeton: Princeton University Press, 1999.
Ó Gráda, Cormac. *Famine. A Short History*. Princeton: Princeton University Press, 2009.
Ó Gráda, Cormac. 'Famines Past, Famine's Future', *Development and Change*, 42, no. 1 (2011): 49–69.
Ó Gráda, Cormac. *Eating People Is Wrong and Other Essays on Famine, Its Past and Its Future*. New Jersey: Princeton University Press, 2015.
Orjuela, Camilla and Swati Parashar. 'Memory and Justice after Famines: An Introduction', *Third World Quarterly* 45, no. 2 (2024): 247–58.
Patenaude, Bertrand M. and Joan Nabseth Stevenson. *Bread + Medicine American Famine Relief in Soviet Russia, 1921–1923*. Chicago: Hoover Institution Press, 2023.
Román Ruiz, Gloria. 'Representations of the Spanish Hunger Years (1939–1952) in Recent Secondary School History Textbooks', *Paedagogica Historica*, 59, no. 6 (2022): 1345–66.
Rubin, Olivier. *Democracy and Famine*. Abingdon: Routledge, 2011.

Sen, Amartya. *Poverty and Famines: An Essay on Entitlement and Deprivation.* Oxford: Oxford University Press, 1981.

Sen, Amartya. 'Liberty and Poverty: Political Rights and Economics', *The New Republic*, 210, no. 10 (1994): 31–7.

Slobodkin, Yan. *The Starving Empire: A History of Famine in France's Colonies.* Ithaca: Cornell University Press, 2023.

Stone, Dan. *Goodbye to All That?: The Story of Europe Since 1945.* Oxford: Oxford University Press, 2014.

Sumner, Daniel A. 'Recent Commodity Price Movements in Historical Perspective', *American Journal of Agricultural Economics*, 91 (2009): 1250–6.

Tönsmeyer, Tatjana, Peter Haslinger, and Agnes Laba, eds. *Coping with Hunger and Shortage under German Occupation in World War II.* Cham: Springer International Publishing, 2018.

Tooze, Adam. *The Wages of Destruction: The Making and Breaking of the Nazi Economy.* New York: Penguin, 2008.

Van der Eng, Pierre. 'Missing Millions: Java's 1944–45 Famine in Indonesia's Historiography'. *Modern Asian Studies*, 58, 2 (2024): 1–21.

Vincent, Paul C. *The Politics of Hunger: The Allied Blockade of Germany, 1915–1919.* Athens: Ohio University Press, 1985.

Wheatcroft, Stephen. 'Eastern Europe (Russia and the USSR)', in Guido Alfani and Cormac Ó Gráda, eds, *Famine in European History.* Cambridge: Cambridge University Press, 2017.

Wheatcroft, Stephen and Davies, Robert W. *Years of Hunger: Soviet Agriculture, 1931–1933.* New York: Palgrave Macmillan, 2009.

Zmolek, Mike. 'Aid Agencies, NGO's and Institutionalisation of Famine', *Economic and Political Weekly* 25 (1990): 37–48.

Part I

State policies and responses

1 The autarkic policy

The origin of the Spanish famine, 1939–42, 1946

Miguel Ángel del Arco Blanco

Between 1939 and 1952, Spain endured a protracted post-war crisis period during Franco's regime, commonly referred to as 'the years of hunger' (*los años del hambre*), characterised by shortages and hardship that still resonate in the memories of many Spaniards today. Within this challenging era, a full-blown famine occurred between 1939 and 1942 and again in 1946. Between 1939 and 1942 alone, famine claimed at least 200,000 lives. It disproportionately affected the lower classes, particularly day labourers and workers with Republican affiliations, who were directly targeted or faced greater challenges in accessing food in the wake of Francoism's 'victory.' Their wives and families also suffered, with many women becoming widowed mothers because of the execution, imprisonment, or exile of their husbands.

The famine experienced a second intense episode in 1946, the demographic impact of which has yet to be fully assessed. It was particularly severe in the southern regions (Murcia, southern Castile-La Mancha, Andalusia, and Extremadura). During these years, deaths from starvation, an increase in infectious diseases, increased living costs, forced emigration, child abandonment, heightened criminal activity, hunger riots, and other secondary effects such as neurological and anthropometric disorders were observed, although these have been scarcely studied until recently.[1]

During the Spanish hunger years, Francoism did everything in its power to conceal the famine and evade its responsibility. However, it could not erase the stark reality of hunger in Spain, where many men and women were collapsing in the streets, a fact acknowledged by both the regime's own documents and British diplomats.[2] In response to the hunger conditions, Francoist politicians and propaganda devised three explanatory myths and circulated them, which remain ingrained in the collective memory of Spaniards. First, the famine was attributed to the destruction wrought by the Civil War (1936–39). However, numerous historians have demonstrated that the war's consequences were not particularly devastating for the Spanish economy and, on their own, could not account for either the famine or more than a decade of economic collapse.[3]

The second Francoist myth attributed the famine to natural causes: specifically, a 'persistent drought' (*pertinaz sequía*) that supposedly led to a decline in agricultural yields and subsequent food shortages. However, this claim is debunked by historians and meteorologists, who point out that the 1940s were not notably drier than the 1930s or 1950s. While there was a severe drought in the agricultural year of 1944–45, typical for the Mediterranean climate, it did not affect all regions of Spain and therefore cannot fully explain the widespread hardship endured by the Spanish people. Recent studies further refute the notion of a 'stubborn drought,' as there was no significant variation in rainfall in the subsequent years.[4]

Third and finally, Franco's regime attempted to justify the famine by citing the international situation: initially, the Second World War (1939–45), and later, the supposed isolation imposed by the Allies (1945–53). However, these claims have long been contested. During the war, the

DOI: 10.4324/9781003465805-3

'New State' willingly aligned itself with fascist powers, exporting raw materials and foodstuffs, which prompted the Allies to impose an economic blockade. After 1945, during the Cold War, Spain resumed trade relations with Western and even Eastern European countries.[5]

Of course, war, international relations, and climate cannot be disregarded when explaining the famine. However, the primary cause did not stem from these factors. As this chapter aims to demonstrate, the severe collapse of the Spanish economy and the ensuing famine originated from human decisions: specifically, the adoption of an autarkic policy by the 'New State' at the conclusion of the Civil War on 1 April 1939. As early as January 1940, Marshal Philippe Petáin, the French ambassador in Madrid who would later become the head of Vichy France, recognised this reality. After outlining Spain's food difficulties, Petáin attributed the situation to Francoist authorities: 'it has not been understood in high places that after the horrible Civil War, the policy adopted by the government has prevented the country's rapid recovery.'[6]

To illustrate the political origins of the famine and the political utility of autarky, the chapter is structured as follows: the first section outlines the autarkic policy and demonstrates that it was voluntarily embraced by Franco's dictatorship. The second section analyses the disastrous repercussions of this policy on the economy. Finally, I conclude by reflecting on the dictatorship's exploitation of autarky for social control through hunger.

Autarkic policy and its voluntary adoption by Franco's regime

Autarky was an ultranationalist economic policy devised during the Civil War, strongly inspired by fascism, which promoted the Spanish nation's expansionist ambitions. The central idea was to establish an economy that was independent (autarkic) of the outside world, viewing foreign capital and trade as threats to the nation. To achieve this goal, the Spanish state assumed a dominant role in the economy, prioritising supreme national interests to 'enlarge the nation.'[7] After the end of the Civil War, the country renounced imports and tried to achieve self-sufficiency by producing everything domestically, while also seeking to generate exports to maintain a positive balance of payments. Extreme interventionist measures were implemented, stifling the Spanish economy and obstructing any potential for economic recovery or development.[8]

However, autarky transcended mere economic policy; it also represented a genuine cultural project aligned with the ethos of the 'New State' in 1939–52 that emerged from a Civil War framed as a 'Crusade' against 'anti-Spain' forces. For the leaders and ideologues of Francoism, autarky was deemed essential for the nation's revival. Following the Civil War and the perceived national decline under liberalism and the Second Republic (1936–39), Spain needed to isolate itself to rejuvenate, excise the perceived malign influences from the national community, and, drawing on spiritual virtues, envision a 'New Spain' with lofty imperial aspirations.[9]

These ultranationalist objectives were mirrored in the economic realm: to secure the revival of the 'New Spain,' the state forcibly intervened in the economy. The aim was to strive towards economic self-sufficiency, asserting that Spain would produce all its necessities within its borders, disregarding both opportunity costs and environmental constraints. It was believed that by doing so, Spain could not only meet the demands of the domestic market but also achieve a positive balance of payments through exports (first with food products and raw materials and after the alleged industrialisation with the export of manufactured goods). With the surplus generated from this unconventional strategy, the country's reconstruction would be funded, and more significantly, the economy would be industrialised to facilitate the establishment of a new empire.[10]

The entire autarkic vision rested on a series of myths that shed light on the ultranationalist and unrealistic ideology of Francoism and its dictator. It was purported that Spain possessed unparalleled natural resources that would enable it to attain its objectives. For Franco, a nation's wealth was not measured by its gold reserves but by the resources within its territory, and in his idealised and romanticised vision of Spain, it was abundant in them. In an interview from August 1938, he asserted:

> Spain is a privileged country capable of achieving self-sufficiency. We have everything we must sustain ourselves, and our production is abundant enough to ensure our subsistence. We have no need to rely on imports, and therefore, our standard of living remains unchanged from before the war.[11]

It was thus deemed to be sufficient to rely on the country's natural resources, exploit them forcefully, and promote their exports to ensure the resurgence of 'New Spain.' This belief, rooted more in national faith than in the reality of the country's resources, was supported by a group of technicians and economists who advocated for the adoption of autarky. One of their major concerns was fuel, upon which Spain was entirely dependent. Consequently, after the Civil War in 1939, conferences were held and papers were published claiming, almost as a spiritual dogma, that Spanish geography was 'very rich in minerals: lignites, slate,' which remained untapped and would serve as the 'raw material' for the 'initiation of the new artificial oil industry.'[12] The issue came to the attention of '*Generalissimo*' Franco, who, convinced of this miracle, provided financial and political support to an Austrian chemist to develop a miraculous synthetic petrol. When the scam became evident, there was no further mention of the miracle that had been announced months earlier by some regime newspapers.[13]

While Francoist myths denied decades later that the autarkic policy was voluntarily adopted, there is ample evidence to show that autarky was voluntarily adopted by Franco's dictatorship.[14] First, we have documents and testimonies, some written by Franco himself. The dictator was a fervent supporter of the adoption of this economic policy, perfectly consistent with his ultra-nationalism. Thus, in his personal notes written years later, he justified the adoption of autarky in the following way:

> The optimal aspiration was a balanced budget. The poor state of many sectors of the country did not matter. The resources the nation possessed were neither used to promote its economic development nor to achieve a favourable balance of payments by importing production equipment, nor having achieved this, to support the currency by stabilising it.[15]

Franco was not the only one who believed in the impossible dream of autarky. Juan Antonio Stanzes, a military naval engineer and childhood friend of the '*Caudillo*,' also shared this conviction. Serving as Minister of Industry and Trade between 1938 and 1939, Suanzes was a devout Catholic and ultranationalist who viewed the Civil War as an opportunity to regenerate Spain. He was deeply committed to achieving economic independence and harboured constant suspicions of foreign capital and interests. In the final stages of the war, he implemented measures to control production and supply and to drive Spanish industrialisation. He continued these efforts from the *Instituto Nacional de Industria* (National Institute of Industry), a macro-holding of national companies directly inspired by the *Istituto per la Riconstruzione Industriale* (Institute for Industrial Reconstruction) of Italian fascism, of which he was a staunch advocate. Through publications, conferences, and leveraging his personal relationship with Franco, Suanzes consistently advocated for autarkic measures. When criticised by some technicians and economists for the economy's deterioration, he accused them of being unpatriotic. Even during the famine in 1942, he maintained this optimism, declaring himself an 'optimist by nature' and asserting that Spain would find 'the way' to overcome 'the brutal difficulties inherent in the circumstances.'[16]

This optimism permeated a range of literature published at the time, explicitly endorsing autarky as the path to the economic, political, and cultural regeneration of the country. These ideas were regularly articulated in economic reports submitted to the government. Particularly noteworthy is one from August 1939, issued at the end of the Civil War and just before the outbreak of Second World War. It precisely delineated the characteristics of the economic system being implemented:

> Economic policy must be oriented in such a way as to secure for the state the indispensable direction of production, making it a useful instrument in the service of national interest. It is a fundamental tenet of the totalitarian state that production is a means (...) to enable and maintain the homeland's independence (...) In economic policy, this will facilitate urban, industrial, agricultural, and mining reconstruction; the revitalisation of all our resources; and the stabilisation of our external balance of payments in Spain's best interests until we achieve autarky.[17]

The autarkic programme was not limited to these documents or reports; it was put into practise. Francoism began adopting autarky in the final days of the war in January–February 1939, coinciding with international recognition by the Allies. In the months between the end of the war (1 April 1939) and the outbreak of Second World War (1 September 1939), autarkic institutions were established, and its most important policies were developed, attracting both attention and criticism from abroad.[18] Simultaneously, during 1939 the 'New State' reaffirmed its alignment with the Axis powers, a stance further emphasised with the onset of the conflict, evidenced by significant economic collaboration with them. It was during this period, before the outbreak of global conflict, that the first effects of the irrational economic policy were felt, and that the Spanish famine began.

Reality and the results of autarky

During the Civil War in 1936–39, Spain was divided into two opposing sides: on the one hand, the 'loyalist' or Republican side, supporters of the democratic regime established in 1931. On the other side, the insurgent or rebel side ('nationalists'), which after the failed military coup of July 1936 began to build the authoritarian 'New State' headed by Francisco Franco. The food situation and living conditions were not dire on the rebel side, and they managed to establish a productive system that, with the assistance of Germany, Italy, and Portugal, was quite efficient and enabled the Generalissimo's troops to win the war in April 1939. The situation was significantly more challenging on the Republican side, where from 1937 onwards, food conditions deteriorated in an increasingly densely populated territory. With the Fall of Madrid and the other Republican-controlled regions in February–April 1939, food became a weapon of war for the 'National Army.' Simultaneously with the announcement of an imperial Spain, after 1 April of that year, bread was distributed to the population in central locations in the capital, such as the Puerta del Sol. However, the post-war reality was markedly different.[19]

From the final stages of the Civil War, and especially in the early months of 1939, the Francoist authorities began to implement the autarkic policy.[20] During this period, a series of laws were enacted that formed the foundation of this fascist-inspired economic system. For instance, on 10 March 1939, the *Comisaría General de Abastecimientos y Transportes* (General Commissariat for Supplies and Transport) was established, which was tasked with overseeing 'all aspects related to national supplies and the transportation of materials intended for it.' It reported to the Ministry of Industry and Trade, the ministerial portfolio that encompassed all autarkic policy-making. Rationing, which was introduced on 14 May 1939 and lasted until 1952, ultimately depended on this institution. The goal of rationing was not only to ensure food for the population but also to limit the consumption of certain foodstuffs to reduce imports and obtain products for industrialisation or to achieve a favourable balance of payments. Autarkic interventionism would prove counterproductive for the economy, but it also fostered unprecedented corruption: in the case of hunger in Spain, participation in the regime's institutions meant either suffering hunger or finding a path to wealth.[21]

Autarky was a determining factor in the evolution of agriculture in these years. Through its numerous institutions (National Wheat Service, Provincial Agricultural Boards, Local Agricultural Boards), the dictatorship regulated the mandatory areas for planting each crop to ensure production. Farmers were thus forced to deliver a certain quota at officially fixed prices to the state, which would compensate them at official prices. However, both production and yields per hectare declined because of various factors associated with the autarkic policy: the establishment of low remunerative prices, which discouraged farmers from producing surpluses, the absence of organic fertilisers (due to the decline in livestock due to war and hunger) and inorganic fertilisers (due to import restrictions), the near absence of pesticides and plant protection products (because of disruption of international trade and the shortage of foreign currency for their import), and the challenges in supplying fuel and agricultural machinery.[22]

In addition, there was another determining factor that contributed to the famine conditions: the spectacular increase in black-market trade in agricultural products. Farmers (small, medium, large-sized) diverted part of their production to illegal markets, where prices increased exponentially. For many producers, both landowners and tenant farmers, this dynamic saved them from famine or even helped enrich them. However, for the lower rural and urban classes without access to agricultural production (day labourers or workers), the consequences were dire, as they could not afford these commodities on the black market due to the exorbitant prices.[23]

The agricultural results were devastating during the post-war, which explains the extreme food situation of a large part of the population. Because of autarkic intervention and its policy of setting prices that were too low, the area officially cultivated with cereals decreased significantly during the post-war period. It was not until the mid-1950s that the hectares cultivated in 1935 were reached. The example of wheat is instructive: while 4,554 hectares were cultivated in Spain in 1935, only 3,496 were cultivated in 1939. The decrease in cultivated area and the lack of fertilisers and pesticides also explain the significant drop in production: if in 1935, 4,300 million tonnes of wheat were produced, after the war it was on average 3,000 million tonnes for the entire 1940s. However, there were some particularly extreme years, which coincided with the famine: in the 1940 harvest, only 2,395 million tonnes of wheat were produced (44.3 per cent less than in 1935) and in 1945, 2,262 million tonnes (47.4 per cent less than in 1935). These official statistics reveal the decline in production, but they do not reveal the extent of the hardship, as a large proportion of the harvest was diverted into the black market at exorbitant prices, making bread unaffordable for more modest households.[24] Thus, the Spanish famine was caused both by the decline in food availability due to decreased agricultural production and by difficulties in accessing it caused by inflation, the black market, or the distribution of food by the dictatorship. In both aspects, the autarkic policy was decisive.

The autarky also had a devastating effect on the industry. The 'New State' created a series of state-owned industries under the National Institute of Industry, which aimed to enforce and redirect the industrialisation of the country for military and expansionist purposes. The consequences were disastrous. In addition to limiting economic development by competing with the private capital that Franco's regime was wary of (especially foreign capital), economists describe a decline in the secondary sector, describing those years as the 'night of Spanish industrialisation.' Many companies were paralysed by a lack of raw materials, fuels, or capital goods that had previously been purchased abroad. Similar to agricultural production, the pre-war industrial production index (1935) did not recover until 1950. The autarky was a decisive brake on recovery after the war: while the Gross Domestic Industrial Product of belligerent countries recovered shortly after the end of Second World War (Germany and France in three, and Italy in five), it did not recover in Spain until 1954, no less than 15 years after the end of the Civil War.[25]

Autarkic interventionism also reached foreign trade, which was considered key to obtaining the funds needed to force the country to industrialise or buy foodstuffs. For imports and exports, a range of institutions, regulations, and inexplicable preferences (such as import licences) was established that further complicated the normal supply of national needs. Although the shortage of foreign currency and the need for national reconstruction seemed to justify the intervention and the omnipresent role given to the Ministry of Industry and Trade, the truth is that this system favoured enrichment, corruption, and the loyalty of certain personalities and companies sympathetic to the regime, aggravating supply problems.[26] The autarkic dream was far from being fulfilled: after the war, in 1939, both exports and imports plummeted compared to 1935. By 1940, the country's exports were 41.8 per cent lower in peseta terms than in 1935. Imports were also significantly reduced: in 1940, Spain imported 39.74 per cent fewer goods than in 1935. These figures provide an idea of the extent of hunger among the population.[27]

All of the above shows that the autarkic policy profoundly impacted the development of the economy, which produced low figures throughout the 1940s: it was not until 1951 and 1952 that the Gross Domestic Product (GDP) and GDP per capita indices of 1935, respectively, recovered. The economist Higinio París Eguilaz, a key figure in the economic measures adopted during the Civil War by the rebels and Franco's adviser on economic affairs, wrote critical reports throughout the 1940s warning of the dismal state of the economy. His reports became increasingly harsh. A 1950 report reached the council of ministers and was crystal clear: autarky had been adopted voluntarily, had devastating effects, and should be abandoned:

> *The State had embarked on interventionism without taking into account any economic principle* and carried out by inept and, in many cases, immoral and corrupt personnel [...] A system of special taxes had been established, without considering the factors of price formation (...), thus causing the formation of a black market, favoured in many cases by the official supply agencies, due to the corruption of some of their officials (...). All this led to a per capita income lower than that in 1936 (...). The government's argument, spread in official speeches and press editorials, that *the present decline in the standard of living is due to our civil war and the world war is false and must be rejected* [italics mine].

The report concluded with a devastating warning: 'If the present economic-social system is not modified, *the Spanish people will face dark hours and tragic days*; the longer it is prolonged, the more difficult it will be to avoid these prospects.'[28] From 1951 onwards, the autarky was relaxed. The economy and the living conditions of the population gradually improved.[29]

Politics and the Francoist famine

Politics also conditioned the development and consequences of the Spanish famine, explaining which social groups were most affected. As we shall see, the management of famine through autarkic mechanisms was a key instrument of social control that favoured the establishment and perpetuation of Franco's regime, as well as the extension of the autarkic policy throughout the 1940s.

The Franco regime cannot be understood without considering the Spanish Civil War, which brought it to power. It was on the battlefield that those who rallied around General Francisco Franco destroyed the elected government of the Spanish Second Republic (1931–36). For Francoists, the war represented a crucial moment in the history of Spain, in which a group of 'true Spaniards' had taken up arms against a Republic controlled by 'foreign' Bolshevik, atheist, and criminal enemies. Thus, they painted the conflict as a 'Crusade' against foreign demons and the values of atheism, Freemasonry, and Marxism. This is why they proclaimed that they had taken up arms in defence of the real Spain and its spiritual values. Indeed, for them, the war constituted no less than the definitive fight between 'God' and the 'Godless.'[30]

From this perspective, they believed that victory in the war would bring an end to the decadence of the Second Republic and usher in a reborn and 'New Spain.' However, victory on the battlefield did not suddenly herald the arrival of this promised future. For millions of supporters of the defeated Popular Front government, there still remains to be dealt with. This is an important reason why, after 1939, Francoists kept alive their 'war culture' and why they continued to try to fight their 'Crusade.' Through the sacralisation of political discourse and the fostering of myths, symbols, heroes, martyrs, commemorations, and values, they fought to keep alive the 'spirit of 1936.' By doing so, they preached victory, not reconciliation, and punishment rather than forgiveness. At the very centre of these post-war beliefs stood the autarkic notion that Spain needed to 'close in upon herself' to save herself from the 'danger to her very being and substance,' represented by 'the sickness of Europe' and 'the secularisation of life, laicism, naturalism, positivism, humanism, rationalism, liberalism.'[31]

This atmosphere of victory and revenge conditioned social and economic relations during the Spanish famine. While it lasted (1939–42), the dictatorship and its supporters controlled the production, supply, and distribution of food through autarkic interventionism. Franco's regime garnered support from social groups that had also backed the Nazis in Germany and the Fascists in Italy, especially the middle classes, and, of course, members of the upper classes who had joined the fight against the Second Republic. However, perhaps the most crucial base of support came from the young men who had joined Franco's side during the Civil War. Upon returning to their towns and villages at the war's end, they swiftly began to assume control of the local institutions of the 'New State.'[32] These groups implemented and benefited from the policy of autarky at the grassroots level. As fervent supporters of the regime's culture of war, they saw autarky as a potent weapon to vanquish their enemies. By giving them this leeway, the regime also secured their support for their control of national and local life and allowed them to escape from famine or even to enrich themselves.

Those belonging to the wealthier social strata could evade famine; they possessed financial resources, naturally, but often also had beneficial political connexions and secure access to black market foodstuffs. As reported by a representative of the British embassy in Madrid in April 1931, those overseeing food supplies were 'exploiting the black market.' Being associated with the regime and participating in its institutions provided people with a pathway to access food and even to enrichment: French diplomacy pointed to the *Falange* (the single party) as the primary culprit for corruption and food shortages. The army, ever-loyal to Franco, was also implicated in numerous instances of corruption, as it enjoyed complete tolerance and impunity in the distribution and sale of food during the famine.[33]

Moreover, many rural smallholders and tenant farmers found a means to escape the worst effects of hunger: although it often required circumventing official policies, in a rationed economy, they had the advantage of relying on their own agricultural production. A significant portion of the harvest was clandestinely stored and used for subsistence. Not surprisingly, these groups clandestinely sold their produce on the black market, particularly if they had political connexions. It was precisely among these social strata—the agrarian middle and lower middle classes—that Francoism found its broadest social support.[34]

The lower classes, some of whom had aligned with the political project of the Second Republic, were the hardest hit by famine: rural and urban wage labourers, women, the elderly, or children from families disrupted by the war or the dictatorship's retaliatory policies such as firing squads, imprisonment in prisons, concentration camps, loss of employment, or exile. They were the ones who suffered deaths from starvation or infectious diseases, as they did not have the means to purchase or barter on black markets.[35] With wages frozen at pre-war levels and unions dismantled, lower classes faced a staggering rise in the cost of living (between 1935 and 1940 inflation rose by 145.2 per cent). Many people could not find employment, often as a punishment for their political views. In those years, many landowners in Andalusia refused to hire day labourers, shouting at them: 'Aren't you hungry? Now eat the Republic' (as a punishment for their support to the Republican regime). Many Republicans were imprisoned or conscripted into labour battalions, and those who were free struggled to find employment because of their political backgrounds. Without access to agricultural production or food distribution channels, they could not survive on the meagre rations provided by the regime alone. Therefore, these individuals had no choice but to resort to daily acts of resistance to obtain sustenance, such as theft, consumption of by-products, or selling items on the black market.[36]

Autarky provided the Francoist authorities with a potent tool to oppress their political adversaries during the famine. Those who had been defeated in the war did not enjoy the same leniency as the regime's supporters when it came to breaking the law, engaging in black-market activities, or obtaining food from the rationing system to alleviate famine. For example, approximately 90 per cent of those convicted of '*estraperlo*' (illegal trading) in Almería and Málaga provinces belonged to the poorer social groups: rural labourers, workers, the unemployed, and impoverished housewives. Thus, while grassroots supporters of the regime thrived, those from the defeated side faced fines, imprisonment, and forced labour camps. Local Francoists also leveraged their control over local resources to exert strict social control over individuals from the defeated side. Those who risked the wrath of local authorities were putting their crucially needed supplies in jeopardy.[37]

Francoist authorities did not deliberately seek to starve the defeated to death or to compromise their health. However, the scarcity resulting from their policies, coupled with the ethos of a war culture that legitimised the prosperity of the victors at the expense of the defeated identified with lower classes, led to dire consequences. The grim fate of those on the losing side now lay in the hands of their triumphant neighbours, who both justified and intensified their plight.[38] It is noteworthy that autarky served as an effective means of marginalising the defeated from political life. Of course, famine and hunger had already marginalised much of the population, as vast segments were malnourished and fatigued. In 1940, in Madrid, for instance, it was common to witness men, women, and children collapsing in the streets due to food shortages. Not to mention the numerous deaths from starvation that were recorded in the south of Spain at that time.[39]

Consequently, the defeated lacked both the will and the means to publicly oppose the Francoist State. In Álava (Basque Country), despite dire economic conditions, Francoist authorities did not encounter any protests. In fact, they remarked that 'if these wretches had something to eat, the number of protests would skyrocket, but for now, empty stomachs keep people quiet.' During the Spanish famine, survival always took precedence.[40]

While hunger and scarcity spread throughout the country, the authorities of the 'New State' used food as an instrument of control to condition the political attitudes of the population. The ration cards of the autarkic policy grouped the population into different categories according to gender and social needs. As was the case in other parts of Europe at the time, the food supplied by Franco's rationing system was insufficient for survival, either because of its scarcity or its poor quality. Nevertheless, the population had no choice but to rely on it: the country was filled with queues of men and women who, from the early hours of the morning, waited for long hours in an orderly manner to purchase the limited quantities available at official prices.[41]

During these difficult years, Francoism implemented its social policies through its institutions, demanding loyalty to the regime in return. Perhaps the best-known was Auxilio Social, created during the war and inspired by the Nazi '*Winter Relief*' (*Winterhilfe*). This institution, under the control of the Falange, was completely overwhelmed by the scale of the famine. However, the poorest and most desperate families, often with a Republican background, had no choice but to turn to soup kitchens or even surrender their children to be fed and re-educated by the regime's victors. Control over food is an unparalleled tool for social discipline.[42]

Conclusions

The autarkic policy was inherent to the nature of the Francoist regime: inspired by fascism, it aligned perfectly with its anti-democratic, ultranationalist, and imperial ideology. It was not imposed by external or internal circumstances but was voluntarily adopted by Franco and the elites of the dictatorship as a means of securing Spain's independence and promoting its expansion.

The consequences of autarky were devastating throughout the 1940s. So much so that, in 1939–42 and 1946, it was the determining factor in the emergence of the Spanish famine. Undoubtedly, the Spanish Civil War and the nutritional conditions of the Spanish population (particularly those on the Republican side, where certain urban social groups received woefully inadequate rations, especially during the war's final phases) must be considered. However, it was a human decision—the adoption of an unattainable and irrational autarkic policy—that triggered the disaster. This disaster was not only economic but also stemmed from the imperial and pro-Axis tendencies of the Franco regime during the early years of the Second World War, which led to an economic blockade by the Allies (see Chapter 5 of this book). The international factor was not the decisive element in the second episode of the famine. In 1946, in addition to the autarkic policy, we must consider the impact of the drought in the southern part of the country in the preceding year.

Autarky was consistent with Franco's victory over the Republicans in the war. Despite its dismal economic results, autarkic interventionism provided the dictatorship with an effective tool to reward its social supporters and to control and punish the more modest social classes who, in many cases, had supported the Second Republic. At the same time, it allowed its supporters to escape starvation and even to enrich themselves.

Notes

1 Miguel Ángel del Arco Blanco, 'Famine in Spain during Franco's Dictatorship (1939–1952)', *Journal of Contemporary History*, 56, no. 1 (2021), 3–27. Miguel Ángel Del Arco Blanco and Peter Anderson, eds, *Franco's Famine. Malnutrition, Disease, and Starvation in post-Civil War Spain* (London: Bloomsbury, 2021). Isabel Del Cura González and Rafael Huertas García-Alejo, *Alimentación y enfermedad en tiempos de hambre: España, 1937–1947* (Madrid: CSIC, 2007). Antonio D. Cámara, José M. Martínez

Carrión, Javier Puche, Josep-Maria Ramon-Muñoz, 'Height and Inequality in Spain: A Long-term Perspective', *Journal of Iberian and Latin American Economic History*, 37, no. 2 (2019), 205–238.

2 Miguel Ángel Del Arco Blanco, 'Morir de hambre. Autarquía, escasez y enfermedad en la España del primer franquismo', *Pasado y Memoria*, 5 (2006), 241–258.

3 Carlos Barciela, 'La economía y la guerra', *Pasado y Memoria*, 8 (2009), 13–34. Pablo Martín Aceña y Elena Martínez Ruiz, eds., *La economía de la Guerra Civil* (Madrid: Marcial Pons, 2006).

4 Cayetano Tames, *El régimen de humedad de la España Peninsular en relación con la agricultura durante el periodo 1940–1953* (Madrid: Instituto Nacional de Investigaciones Agronómicas, 1954), 11. Fernando Sánchez Rodrigo and Mariano Barriendos, 'Reconstruction of Seasonal and Annual Rainfall Variability in the Iberian Peninsula (16th–20th Centuries) from Documentary Data', *Global and Planetary Change*, 63, no. 2–3 (2008), 256.

5 Juan Carlos Pereira Castañares, 'De centinela de Occidente a la conspiración masónica-comunista. La política exterior del franquismo', in Ángel Viñas, ed., *En el combate por la historia: la República, la Guerra Civil, el Franquismo* (Barcelona: Pasado y Presente, 2020), 659–677. Matilde Eiroa, *Las relaciones de Franco con Europa Centro-Oriental (1939–1955)* (Barcelona: Ariel, 2001).

6 Centre des Archives Diplomatiques de Nantes (CADN), Madrid, AMBASSADE, 396PO/C/1/131, 4 January 1940.

7 This nationalist verbiage can be seen in some of the legislation of the time: Decree 9 March, *Fuero del Trabajo* (Boletín Oficial del Estado -BOE-, 10 March 1938).

8 Ángel Viñas, *Guerra, dinero, dictadura. Ayuda fascista y autarquía en la España de Franco* (Barcelona: Crítica, 1984). Antonio Gómez Mendoza, *De mitos y milagros. El Instituto Nacional de Autarquía (1941–1963)* (Barcelona: Fundación Duques de Soria y Edicions de la Universitat de Barcelona, 2000).

9 Michael Richards, *A Time of Silence. Civil War and the Culture of Repression in Franco's Spain, 1936–1945* (Cambridge: Cambridge University Press, 1998).

10 Carlos Barciela, María Inmaculada López Ortiz, Joaquín Melgarejo Moreno and José A. Miranda, *La España de Franco (1939–1975). Economía* (Madrid: Síntesis, 2001).

11 Franco's statements to Henri Massis, *Candide,* 18 August 1939. See: www.generalisimofranco.com/Discursos/prensa/00028.htm, last accessed 16 May 2024.

12 Luis Bermejo, 'El problema de los carburantes en España', in *Aspectos y problemas de la nueva organización de España: ciclo de conferencias* (Barcelona: La Neotipa, 1939), 239.

13 Paul Preston, *Franco, Caudillo de España* (Barcelona: Debate, 2019), 522–523. Ignacio Martínez de Pisón, *Filek: el estafador que engañó a Franco* (Barcelona: Seix Barral, 2018).

14 The myths can be found in Franco's own words: Francisco Franco Salgado-Araujo, *Mis conversaciones privadas con Franco* (Barcelona: Planeta, 2005), 343. They can also be found in the works of certain Francoist historians published even after the death of the dictator: Ricardo de la Cierva, *Historias de la corrupción* (Barcelona: Planeta, 1992), 286–287.

15 Francisco Franco, *'Apuntes' personales del Generalísimo sobre la República y la Guerra Civil,* ed. Luis Suárez Fernández (Madrid: Fundación Nacional Francisco Franco, 1987), 44. Carlos Velasco Murviedro, 'Las pintorescas ideas económicas de Franco', *Historia* 16, 83 (1985), 19–28.

16 Miguel Ángel Del Arco Blanco, 'Juan Antonio Suanzes: Industry, Fascism and Catholicism', in Alejandro Quiroga and Miguel Ángel del Arco Blanco, eds., *Right-wing Spain in the Civil War Era. Soldiers of God and Apostles of the Fatherland, 1914–1945* (London: Continuum, 2012), 148–176. Elena San Román, *Ejército e industria: el nacimiento del INI* (Barcelona: Crítica, 1999). Real Academia de la Historia (RAH), Archivo Juan Antonio Suanzes, G, box 37, registro 2678, 'Nuevas notas de política económica'; registro 2677, 6-6-1939 y 10-8-1939; box 38, registro 2726, Discurso sobre la autarquía pronunciado en la Escuela Superior del Ejército, 11-6-1942; box 10, register 1008, 1-7-1945, Notas para una conferencia sobre la autarquía; and also box 118, register 8390, 14-8-1942 y 1-9-1942.

17 Autarchic literature: Rafael Gay de Montellá. *Autarquía. Nuevas orientaciones de la Economía* (Barcelona: Bosch, 1940). Antonio de Miguel, *Autarquía* (Madrid: Diana, 1941). The report cited: *Documentos inéditos para la historia del Generalísimo Franco. Vol. I.* Madrid, Fundación

Nacional Francisco Franco, 1992, Informe económico del Ministerio de Industria y Comercio, 9 August 1939, 572–573.

18 Allan G. B. Fisher, *Economic self-Sufficiency* (Oxford: Clarendon Press, 1939).

19 Michael Seidman, *The Victorious Counterrevolution: The Nationalist Effort in the Spanish Civil War* (Madison: University of Wisconsin Press, 2011). Ainhoa Campos Posada, 'Madrid o "La capital espectro": la utilización del hambre como arma de guerra y posguerra por el franquismo'. Miguel Ángel del Arco Blanco, ed. *Los años del hambre. Historia y memoria de la posguerra franquista* (Madrid: Marcial Pons, 2020b), 77–96. Alba Nueda Lozano, *El hambre como arma. Escasez republicana en la guerra civil española* (Granada: Comares, 2024).

20 There was some precedent during the war, although it was limited to the control of agricultural production and not foreign trade or supply. For example: Decree-Law 'De Ordenación Triguera' of 23 August 1937 (BOE 25/8/1937).

21 Law 10 March 1939 creating the Comisaría General de Abastecimiento y Transportes (BOE 12/3/1939). Orden de 14 de mayo de 1939 (BOE 17/5/1939). Carlos Barciela López, 'Franquismo y corrupción económica', *Historia Social* 30 (1998), 83–96.

22 Carlos Barciela López, 'Los costes del franquismo en el sector agrario: la ruptura del proceso de transformaciones', in Ramón Garrabou, Carlos Barciela López and José Ignacio Jiménez Blanco, eds., *Historia agraria de la España Contemporánea. 3. El fin de la agricultura tradicional (1900–1960)* (Barcelona 1986), 383–455. María Inmaculada López Ortiz, 'Los efectos de la autarquía en la agricultura murciana'. *Revista de Historia Económica*, XIV, 3 (1996), 591–618. Including production traded on the black market, Christiansen argues that the decline in wheat yields was due to a lack of fertiliser and a shortage of working cattle, rather than state intervention. Thomas Christiansen, *The Reason Why. The Post-Civil War Agrarian Crisis in Spain* (Zaragoza, 2012).

23 Carlos Barciela López, 'La España del estraperlo'. José Luis Garcia Delgado', *El primer franquismo. España durante la Segunda Guerra Mundial* (Madrid: Siglo XXI, 1989). José Manuel Naredo, 'La incidencia del «estraperlo» en la economía de las grandes fincas del Sur', *Agricultura y Sociedad*, 19, 1981, pp. 81–129. Miguel Ángel del Arco Blanco, *Hambre de siglos. Mundo rural y apoyos sociales del franquismo en Andalucía Oriental (1936–1951)* (Comares: Granada, 2007), 343–346.

24 Xavier Tafunell Sambola, Carlos Barciela López, Josep Fontana and Albert Carreras. *Estadísticas históricas de España: siglos XIX-XX* (Bilbao: Fundación BBVA, 2005), 302–303, 307.

25 Albert Carreras, 'La producción industrial española, 1842–1981: construcción de un índice anual', *Revista de Historia Económica*, 2, 1 (1984), 127–157. Enric Morellá, 'El producto industrial de posguerra: una revisión (índices sectoriales, 1940–1958)', *Revista de Historia Industrial*, 10, 1, 1992, 125–143. Tafunell, Barciela, Fontana and Carreras. *Estadísticas históricas*, 398 (we follow the index elaborated by Carreras). Jordi Catalán, *La economía española y la segunda guerra mundial* (Barcelona: Ariel, 1995). Jordi Catalán, 'Economía e industria: la ruptura de posguerra en perspectiva comparada', *Revista de Historia Industrial*, 4, 1993, 120.

26 Ángel Viñas, Julio Viñuela, Fernando Eguidazu, Carlos Fernández Pulgar and Senen Florensa, *Política comercial exterior en España (1931–1975). Tomo I* (Madrid: Banco Exterior de España, 1979), 294–295, 252–267.

27 Antonio Tena, 'Sector exterior', in Tafunell Sambola, Xavier, Carlos Barciela, Josep Fontana and Albert Carreras, eds, *Estadísticas históricas de España: siglos XIX-XX*. 2a. edición revisada y ampliada (Bilbao: Fundación BBVA, 2005), 605.

28 Fundación Nacional Francisco Franco, Documento 25989, *Informe de Higinio Paris: la situación económica actual de España, 1950.*

29 Jordi Maluquer de Motes, *La economía española en perspectiva histórica. Siglos XVIII-XXI* (Barcelona: Pasado y Presente, 2014).

30 Hugo García, 'Relatos para una guerra. Terror, testimonio y literatura en la España nacional', *Ayer* 76 (2009) 143–176. Javier Rodrigo, *Cruzada, paz, memoria. La guerra civil en sus relatos* (Granada: Comares, 2013).

31 Michael Richards, *A Time of Silence*, 23; Michael Richards, 'From War Culture to Civil Society. Francoism, Social Change and Memories of the Spanish Civil War', *History and Memory* autumn (2002), 14, 1–2, 93–120.

32 Julián Sanz Hoya, *España en camisa azul. Falange, cultura política y poderes locales* (Granada: Comares, 2023), 27–36.
33 The National Archives (TNA), Public Record Office (PRO), Foreign Office (FO) 371/26890, 28-4-1941. CADN, Madrid, AMBASSADE, 396PO/C/1/131, 19-12-1939. Miguel Ángel Del Arco Blanco, 'La corrupción en el franquismo. El fenómeno del "Gran Estraperlo"', *Hispania Nova* 16 (2018), 637–638.
34 Miguel Ángel del Arco Blanco, *Hambre de siglos*, 167–177, 343–346.
35 Miguel Ángel del Arco Blanco, 'Famine in Spain', 14–20.
36 Teresa Ortega López, 'Las miserias del fascismo rural. Las relaciones laborales en la agricultura española, 1936–1948', *Historia Agraria*, 43 (2007), 544–548. Jordi Maluquer de Motes, *La inflación en España. Un índice de precios al consumo, 1830–2012* (Madrid, 2013), 76. Francisco Cobo Romero and Teresa María Ortega López, *Franquismo y posguerra en Andalucía Oriental: represión, castigo a los vencidos y apoyos sociales al régimen franquista, 1936–1950* (Granada: Universidad de Granada, 2005). Gloria Román Ruiz, 'Pícaros de Posguerra'. Turning to crime to survive famine and malnutrition in early Francoism (1939–52), in Miguel Ángel del Arco Blanco and Paul Anderson, eds., *Franco's Famine. Malnutrition, Disease and Starvation in post-Civil War Spain* (London: Bloomsbury, 2021) 114–136.
37 Archivo Histórico Provincial de Almería, Guardia Civil, 734, 735, Files of the Fiscalía Provincial de Tasas of Almería. Year 1945; and Archivo Histórico Provincial de Málaga, Guardia Civil, 12580, Files of the Fiscalía Provincial de Tasas of Málaga. Year 1944. Daniel Lanero Táboas, *Historia dun ermo asociativo. Labregos, sindicatos verticais e políticas agrarias en Galicia baixo o Franquismo* (A Coruña: Tresctres, 2011).
38 Paul Preston, *The Politics of Revenge: Fascism and the Military in Twentieth-century Spain* (London: Routledge, 2003).
39 TNA, FO 371/24509, Prof. Starkey Memorandum, November 1940. Archivo General de la Administración (AGA), Presidencia del Gobierno (PG), Delegación Nacional de Provincias (DNP), box 20495, 1 March 1940.
40 AGA, PG, DNP, box 20691, 1946–1947. Some examples: TNA, PRO, FO 371/26890, *Visit Report*, 28 December 1940 to 8 January 1941. Samuel Hoare, *Ambassador in Special Mission* (London: Collins, 1946), 30. *I Documenti Diplomatici Italiani*. Decima serie: 1943–1948, Vol. VI. (Roma: Libreria Dello Stato, 1992), 507, and Vol. IV, 599.
41 Miguel Ángel del Arco Blanco, 'Hunger and the Consolidation of the Francoist Regime (1939–1951)', *European History Quarterly* 40, 3 (2010), 458–483.
42 Ángela Cenarro Lagunas, *La sonrisa de Falange: Auxilio Social en la guerra civil y en la posguerra* (Barcelona: Crítica, 2005). Ángela Cenarro Lagunas, *Los niños del auxilio social* (Madrid: Espasa, 2009). Gloria Román Ruiz, 'Mothers and Children without Bread. Hunger in the Auxilio Social Cocinas de Hermandad and Comedores Infantiles during post-war Francoism (1939–1940)', *Culture & History Digital Journal*, 13, 2 (2024).

References

Barciela López, Carlos, 'Los costes del franquismo en el sector agrario: la ruptura del proceso de transformaciones', in Ramón Garrabou, Carlos Barciela and José Ignacio Jiménez Blanco, eds, *Historia agraria de la España Contemporánea. 3. El fin de la agricultura tradicional (1900–1960)*, 383–455. Barcelona: Crítica, 1986.

Barciela López, Carlos, 'La España del estraperlo', in José Luis García Delgado, ed., *El primer franquismo. España durante la Segunda Guerra Mundial*, 105–123. Madrid: Siglo XXI, 1989.

Barciela López, Carlos, 'Franquismo y corrupción económica', *Historia Social*, 30 (1998), 83–96.

Barciela López, Carlos, 'La economía y la guerra', *Pasado y Memoria*, 8 (2009), 13–34.

Barciela López, Carlos; López Ortiz, María Inmaculada; Melgarejo, Moreno; Joaquín, y Miranda Encarnación; J. Antonio, *La España de Franco (1939–1975). Economía*. Madrid: Síntesis, 2001.

Bermejo, Luis, 'El problema de los carburantes en España', in *Aspectos y problemas de la nueva organización de España*, 221–252. Barcelona: La Neotipia, 1939.

Cámara, Antonio D.; Martínez Carrión, José M.; Puche, Javier; Ramón-Muñoz, Josep-María, 'Height and Inequality in Spain: A Long-term Perspective', *Journal of Iberian and Latin American Economic History*, 37, 2 (2019), 205–238.

Campos Posada, Ainhoa, 'Madrid o "La capital espectro": la utilización del hambre como arma de guerra y posguerra por el franquismo', in Miguel Ángel Del Arco Blanco, ed., *Los años del hambre. Historia y memoria de la posguerra franquista*, 77–96. Madrid: Marcial Pons, 2020.

Carreras, Albert, 'La producción industrial española, 1842–1981: construcción de un índice anual', *Revista de Historia Económica*, 2, 1 (1984), 127–157.

Catalán, Jordi, 'Economía e industria: la ruptura de posguerra en perspectiva comparada', *Revista de Historia Industrial*, 4 (1993), 111–144.

Catalán, Jordi, *La economía española y la segunda guerra mundial*. Barcelona: Ariel, 1995.

Cenarro Lagunas, Ángela, *La sonrisa de Falange: Auxilio Social en la guerra civil y en la posguerra*. Barcelona: Crítica, 2005.

Cenarro Lagunas, Ángela, *Los niños del auxilio social*. Madrid: Espasa, 2009.

Christiansen, Thomas, *The Reason Why. The Post Civil-War Agrarian Crisis in Spain*. Zaragoza: Prensas Universitarias de Zaragoza, 2012.

De la Cierva, Ricardo, *Historias de la corrupción*. Barcelona: Planeta, 1992.

De Miguel, Antonio, *Autarquía*. Madrid: Diana, 1941.

Del Arco Blanco, Miguel Ángel, 'Morir de hambre. Autarquía, escasez y enfermedad en la España del primer franquismo', *Pasado y Memoria*, 5 (2006), 241–258.

Del Arco Blanco, Miguel Ángel, *Hambre de siglos. Mundo rural y apoyos sociales del franquismo en Andalucía Oriental (1936–1951)*. Granada: Comares, 2007.

Del Arco Blanco, Miguel Ángel. 'Hunger and the Consolidation of the Francoist Regime (1939–1951)', *European History Quarterly*, 40, 3 (2010), 458–483.

Del Arco Blanco, Miguel Ángel, 'Juan Antonio Suanzes: industry, fascism and catholicism', in Alejandro Quiroga and Miguel Ángel del Arco Blanco, eds., *Right-wing Spain in the Civil War Era. Soldiers of God and Apostles of the Fatherland*, 1914–1945, 148–176. London: Continuum, 2012.

Del Arco Blanco, Miguel Ángel, 'La corrupción en el franquismo. El fenómeno del "Gran Estraperlo"', *Hispania Nova*, 16 (2018), 637–638.

Del Arco Blanco, Miguel Ángel, ed., *Los años del hambre. Historia y memoria de la posguerra franquista*. Madrid: Marcial Pons, 2020.

Del Arco Blanco, Miguel Ángel, 'Famine in Spain during Franco's dictatorship (1939–1952)', *Journal of Contemporary History*, 56, 1 (2021), 2–27.

Del Arco Blanco, Miguel Ángel and Anderson, Paul, eds., *Franco's Famine. Malnutrition, Disease and Starvation in post-Civil War Spain*. London: Bloomsbury, 2021.

Del Cura González, Isabel and Huertas García-Alejo, Rafael, *Alimentación y enfermedad en tiempos de hambre: España, 1937–1947*. Madrid: CSIC, 2007.

Di Febo, Giuliana, *Ritos de guerra y de victoria en la España franquista*. Bilbao: DDB, 2002.

Eiroa, Matilde, *Las relaciones de Franco con Europa Centro-Oriental (1939–1955)*. Barcelona: Ariel, 2001.

Fisher, Allan George Barnard, *Economic Self-Sufficiency*. Oxford: Clarendon Press, 1939.

Franco, Francisco, *Apuntes personales del Generalísimo sobre la República y la Guerra Civil*. Ordenados y transcritos por L. Suárez Fernández. Madrid: Fundación Nacional Francisco Franco, 1987.

Franco Salgado-Araujo, Francisco, *Mis conversaciones privadas con Franco*. Barcelona: Planeta, 2005.

García Delgado, José Luis, ed., *El primer franquismo. España durante la Segunda Guerra Mundial*. Madrid: Siglo XXI, 1989.

Gay de Montellá, Rafael, *Autarquía. Nuevas orientaciones de la Economía*. Barcelona: Bosch, 1940.

Gómez Mendoza, Antonio, *De mitos y milagros. El Instituto Nacional de Autarquía (1941–1963)*. Barcelona: Fundación Duques de Soria y Edicions de la Universitat de Barcelona, 2000.

Lanero Táboas, Daniel, *Historia dun ermo asociativo. Labregos, sindicatos verticais e políticas agrarias en Galicia baixo o Franquismo*. A Coruña: Tresctres, 2011.

López Ortiz, María Inmaculada, 'Los efectos de la autarquía en la agricultura murciana'. *Revista de Historia Económica*, XIV, 3 (1996), 591–618.

Maluquer de Motes, Jordi, *La inflación en España. Un índice de precios al consumo, 1830–2012.* Madrid: Banco de España, 2013.

Maluquer de Motes, Jordi, *La economía española en perspectiva histórica. Siglos XVIII-XXI.* Barcelona: Pasado y Presente, 2014.

Martín Aceña, Pablo y Martínez Ruiz, Elena, eds., *La economía de la Guerra Civil.* Madrid: Marcial Pons, 2006.

Martínez de Pisón, Ignacio, *Filek: el estafador que engañó a Franco.* Barcelona: Seix Barral, 2018.

Morellá, Enric, 'El producto industrial de posguerra: una revisión (índices sectoriales, 1940–1958)', *Revista de Historia Industrial*, 10, 1 (1992), 125–143.

Naredo, José Manuel, 'La incidencia del «estraperlo» en la economía de las grandes fincas del Sur', *Agricultura y Sociedad*, 19 (1981), 81–129.

Nueda Lozano, Alba, *El hambre como arma. Escasez republicana en la guerra civil española.* Granada: Comares, 2024.

Ortega López, Teresa, 'Las miserias del fascismo rural. Las relaciones laborales en la agricultura española, 1936–1948', *Historia Agraria*, 43 (2007), 531–553.

Paul Preston, *The Politics of Revenge: Fascism and the Military in Twentieth-century Spain.* London: Routledge, 2003.

Pereira Castañares, Juan Carlos, 'De "centinela de Occidente" a la conspiración masónica-comunista. La política exterior del franquismo', in Ángel Viñas, ed., *En el combate por la historia: la República, la Guerra Civil, el Franquismo*, 659–677. Barcelona: Pasado y Presente, 2020.

Preston, Paul, *Franco, Caudillo de España.* Barcelona: Debate, 2019.

Richards, Michael, *A Time of Silence. Civil War and the Culture of Repression in Franco's Spain, 1936–1945.* Cambridge: Cambridge University Press, 1998.

Richards, Michael, 'From War Culture to Civil Society. Francoism, Social Change and Memories of the Spanish Civil War', *History and Memory*, 14 (2002), 93–120.

Román Ruiz, Gloria, 'Pícaros De Posguerra. Turning to crime to survive famine and malnutrition in early Francoism (1939–52)', in Miguel Ángel del Arco Blanco and Paul Anderson, eds., *Franco's Famine. Malnutrition, Disease and Starvation in post-Civil War Spain,* 114–136. London: Bloomsbury, 2021.

Román Ruiz, Gloria, 'Mothers and Children without Bread. Hunger in the Auxilio Social Cocinas de Hermandad and Comedores Infantiles during post-War Francoism (1939–1940)', *Culture & History Digital Journal*, 13, 2 (2024).

San Román, Elena, *Ejército e industria: el nacimiento del INI.* Barcelona: Crítica, 1999.

Sánchez Rodrigo, Fernando and Barriendos, Mariano, 'Reconstruction of Seasonal and Annual Rainfall Variability in the Iberian Peninsula (16th–20th Centuries) from Documentary Data', *Global and Planetary Change*, 63, 2–3 (2008), 243–257.

Seidman, Michael, *The Victorious Counterrevolution: The Nationalist Effort in the Spanish Civil War.* Madison: University of Wisconsin Press, 2011.

Tafunell Sambola, Xavier; Barciela López, Carlos; Fontana, Josep; and Carreras, Albert, eds., *Estadísticas históricas de España: siglos XIX-XX.* Bilbao: Fundación BBVA, 2005.

Tames, C., *El régimen de humedad de la España Peninsular en relación con la agricultura durante el periodo 1940–1953.* Madrid: Instituto Nacional de Investigaciones Agronómicas, 1954.

Tena, Antonio, 'Sector Exterior', in Xavier Tafunell, Carlos Barciela, Josep Fontana and Albert Carreras, eds., *Estadísticas históricas de España: siglos XIX-XX.* Bilbao: Fundación BBVA, 2005.

Velasco Murviedro, Carlos, 'Las pintorescas ideas económicas de Franco', *Historia* 16, 83 (1985), 19–28.

Viñas, Ángel, *Guerra, dinero, dictadura. Ayuda fascista y autarquía en la España de Franco.* Barcelona: Crítica, 1984.

Viñas, Ángel; Viñuela, Julio; Eguidazu, Fernando; Fernández Pulgar, Carlos; and Florensa, Senen, *Política comercial exterior en España (1931–1975). Tomo I.* Madrid: Banco Exterior de España, 1979.

2 War, occupation and the politics of causing and fighting hunger in World War II

Tatjana Tönsmeyer

The Russian full-scale war of aggression against Ukraine, which started in early 2022, revived a knowledge which Europe had been happy to forget: wars disrupt the sowing and harvesting of food crops. They damage agriculture by intoxicating the soil and by leaving behind motor oils, explosives or other remnants of the fighting. But wars also cause breakdowns of economies by destroying production, disrupting distribution chains and damaging infrastructures. The combined consequences of all this were felt globally when due to the fighting in Ukraine grain prices exploded in the global South.

Though the degree in a highly interdependent world may be new, the phenomena as such are not. European societies experienced similar conditions during World War II. The consequences thereof for people living in occupied countries were in those times aggravated by ruthlessly implemented German exploitation policies. Research within this realm has for many years focused on policies of exploitation. This history has by and far been written as economic macro-history with an interest in assessing the contributions of various countries regarding the German war effort. Much attention has, for example, been paid to the highly industrialized countries in Western Europe like France, without which Germany could not have continued the war for six years.[1] Other studies have taken a perpetrator-centred approach, paying close attention to those who enacted starvation policies.[2] As a result, we know how different German institutions organized exploitation and that hunger policies were deeply rooted in anti-Semitism and racism, resulting in mass starvation in the occupied territories of the Soviet Union, especially in the cities.[3] A third strand of research has focussed on the exploitation of forced labour, paying special attention to the management of forced labour by German authorities, on living and working conditions in the Third Reich (much less in occupied territories), and especially on Jewish slave labour.[4]

Only recently has the question "Being hungry, whar do peole do?" – usually adopted to look to subsistence economies of pre and early modern times[5] – been applied to the everyday life of societies under German occupation. In doing so, the focus has shifted from aggregated data of macroeconomics and a focus on the heads of the Berlin Nazi administrations to local communities and their members, who tried to deal with scarcity and struggled to survive in times when starvation hit whole societies.[6] While shortage took different forms and concerned different commodities, scarcity made itself felt rather quickly in occupied Europe. It hit occupied Soviet cities, where the situation became one of utmost destitution and desperation already in late summer and autumn of 1941. But mortality rates rose very quickly in Axis-occupied Greece as well. Further in the north, it was the so-called Dutch Hunger Winter that cost about 20.000 people's lives in 1944–45. Wherever hunger raged, the effect was felt directly, but hunger played its part indirectly as well, because malnutrition and dire living conditions such as a lack of heating material, catastrophic sanitary conditions and insufficient medical care increased

DOI: 10.4324/9781003465805-4

people's exposure to tuberculosis, influenza and other illnesses.[7] Compared to this, most countries in Western Europe were better off. Nevertheless, the gnawing sensation of hunger and the general scarcity were on many people's minds.

This chapter therefore examines national socialist exploitation policies before it turns to the economies of shortage in occupied societies. Special attention will be paid to rationing systems as an instrument used all over occupied Europe to fight shortages. Make-shift economies and the criminalization of survival strategies by the German occupying personnel will be another important issue. In addressing the interaction between "the occupiers" and "the occupied" (both groups were far from homogenous) in supply situations, this chapter further aims to contribute to the growing body of literature on how occupation moulded the social order all over occupied Europe.

Exploitation policies

Leading national socialists regarded it as a lesson learnt from World War I that the lost "battle for food" ("*Kampf um die Ernährung*") led to the breakdown of the German home front and, as a consequence, to defeat. Believing that Germany was overpopulated and endangered of being cut off from imports by blockades, acquiring "*Lebensraum*" in terms of space as well as food was deemed essential. Medical experts backed such assumptions. As early as 1921, they warned that childhood malnutrition due to World War I's blockade led to "an intensive racial worsening of the growing generation".[8] Therefore, Hitler himself advised Wehrmacht officers in February of 1939 that "the food question [is] … the most vital problem … that demands being solved by expansion".[9]

The man in charge of dealing with this was Herbert Backe. He was appointed State Secretary (*Staatssekretär*) to Minister of Agriculture Richard Walther Darré, when Darré took office as Minister of Agriculture. Later on, he became head of the food commission in the Four-Year-Plan administration.[10] Backe was among the top officials who – only a few days after Hitler met the military leadership on 4 November 1940 – were informed by Hermann Göring, leading the Four-Year-Plan administration, about the decision to invade the Soviet Union. It became his task to set up plans which would enable the German Wehrmacht to lead this war as a "*Blitzkrieg*". This was considered possible only if supplies were not brought in from Germany, to spare the population of hardships. Instead, troops would be fed from Soviet soil, and "surpluses" would be requisitioned for the home front. These policies were tightly interconnected with the envisaged "elimination of all [Soviet] political leaders", especially the "Bolshevik-Jewish intelligentsia":[11] The breakdown of the Soviet state was considered a prerequisite for ruthlessly requisitioning foodstuffs. Military and civil personnel, even before the German assault on the Soviet Union started, were well aware that this meant that "many millions" – some sources speak explicitly of "30 million" – were going to be starved to death.[12]

Plans were set up to divide the Soviet Union into so-called deficit zones – like the forest regions of Belarus or northern and central Russia – and zones in Ukraine, southern Russia and the Caucasus, which were believed to produce surpluses.[13] But as early as July 1941, it proved to be impossible to rob the local population of its supply and secure the hinterland of the Wehrmacht at the same time. As a consequence, more selective hunger policies were implemented which differentiated between smaller sub-regions and various groups of local populations. The non-Jewish population in the former Baltic countries, in Western Ukraine and the Caucasus, as well as those working for the German war effort, were to be fed to some degree. It is worth noting that the acceleration and radicalization of German anti-Semitic measures happened precisely within this context of extreme supply problems: German decision-makers selected the Jewish population as "useless eaters" and tried to reduce supply problems by murdering them. The same was true regarding Soviet prisoners of war who were already under German control. Though numbers are difficult to obtain, educated guesses speak of four million victims of the German starvation policies on Soviet territory.[14]

Chances of survival were, as a consequence, massively influenced by the availability of resources not taken by the occupiers. In this regard, it is important to note that from the onset of the fighting, withdrawing Soviet troops, particularly NKWD (People's Commissariat of Internal Affairs) forces, were ordered to destroy anything that might be useful to the occupier. This scorched-earth policy hit the civilian population severely by diminishing its resources from very early on.[15] The fighting added to the destruction; many of the Soviet cities were bombed out and resources were destroyed. Exploitation therefore often impacted impoverished populations such as, for example, in Ukraine, where many had still vivid memories of another famine – the Holodomor of 1932–33.

Furthermore, while German officers initially handed out receipts for compensation for grain requisitioning, peasants soon realized that redeeming these notes was nearly impossible. The policy was stopped fairly quickly anyway; advancing troops took to expropriations without compensation or very small ones paid in roubles. The longer the fighting lasted, the more looting became a common problem. Taking the area of the Centre Army Group operating in the Soviet Union as an example, towns and villages were overrun several times. As a result, the land was stripped of food over a range of 800 to 1000 kilometres and turned into a so-called *Kahlfraßzone* [Nazi term for zones deliberately deprived of food supplies for the population]. Plundering by individual German soldiers further aggravated the situation.[16] Last but not least, the longer the war lasted and the more the partisan movement grew, the more local peasants had to feed resistance fighters as well (and to fear German reprisals for doing so).[17]

Compared to this, the situation was less horrible in other parts of occupied Europe, but in Greece, the circumstances were very dire as well. In Piraeus and Athens, mortality rates were five to seven times higher in the winter of 1941–42 than the previous year. Medical reports pointed out that hunger was the direct cause of at least one-third of these deaths.[18] Distribution of foodstuffs was part of the problem causing the catastrophic situation. The breakdown of state structures exacerbated the situation, and hunger on the islands was largely due to trading and fishing restrictions imposed by the occupiers in the Mediterranean.[19]

In France, where about half of the population experienced hunger as well, the wealthy banker Charles Rist noted in his diary: "People talk of nothing else but provisions and supply".[20] This was not just a feeling, the shortage was real. Already in October 1941, the prefect of Paris warned that diseases might be transmitted by eating stewed cats.[21] Schoolchildren in rural Aude listed in June 1941 that they had already eaten a hedgehog, grass snakes, a fox, frogs, a squirrel, a cat, a falcon and a badger.[22] As severe as this was, deaths from hunger occurred rather rarely in Western European countries (or not at all, like in Denmark). This was due to the fact that here exploitation but not starvation policies were implemented. Furthermore, exploitation itself took different forms from Eastern Europe. Though, as a result of German demands, national economies were transformed into a war-oriented system of autarky,[23] in contrast to Eastern and South Eastern Europe, German occupation in Western and Northern Europe as well as in the Protectorate of Bohemia and Moravia did not take the production factors, but mostly the output.[24] In France, this policy only partly succeeded, and the country therefore also lost much of its labour and foodstuff.[25]

Massive intervention in the industry was nevertheless rather rare, with exceptions like the sequestration of individual plants of the iron and steel industry in Lorraine (France), aluminium and electricity generation in Norway or the chemical industry in the Netherlands testing the overall rule.[26] On the factory level, a set of regulations made sure that German demands were met.[27] Price policy regarding foodstuff was meant to stimulate the delivery of agrarian products.[28] The resulting scarcity that hit local populations was aggravated by the fact that Wehrmacht soldiers went on shopping tours to such great scales that, for example, the *Wehrmachtsintendant* for Belgium warned his superiors that this might lead to "the selling-out" of the country.[29]

Rationing systems and the attribution of survival chances

Introducing rations was actually the answer to war-induced shortages in occupied Europe at the administrative level. Based on nutritional research in the early twentieth century,[30] they were thought to regulate the distribution of food, usually based on different age categories like children, young persons, grown-ups and old people and extra categories like "heavy labour" or "pregnant and breast-feeding women". Rural populations were usually thought to be able to sustain themselves, without taking into consideration if the individual actually worked in agriculture or had a garden or not.[31]

What might seem well-ordered in bureaucratic terms nevertheless confronted cardholders with many problems on a daily basis. Cards and coupons were only valid during a specific time or in certain shops, regardless of whether the goods were available or not. Even from an administrative standpoint, the handling was complicated because the same ration strips sometimes allowed for the purchase of different goods in different quotas. For example, in the Protectorate of Bohemia and Moravia, the same strips usually allowing to buy 125 grams of butter and 250 grams of synthetic honey allowed cardholders in mid-December 1942 to purchase 250 grams of raisins or prunes and 150 grams of almonds or nuts, as part of a Christmas donation in twelve big cities and industrial towns. Two weeks later, the same strips were valid for purchasing an additional 100 grams of sultanas or almonds elsewhere in the Protectorate.[32] Because of the regulations themselves, inefficiencies and fraud of all kinds were commonplace.

Rations were not only difficult to regulate, but they were also usually very low and did not provide enough food to live on.[33] This was especially true for Eastern Europe. In the Polish district of Radom, a region with heavy industry as well as agriculture, inhabitants in early November 1939 were entitled to 200 grams of bread per day, 200 grams of sugar and salt each per month and flour not exceeding 400 grams per month. The rural population had to supply itself via the market, which was next to impossible because trading flour and foodstuff was virtually prohibited. Exemptions were only made regarding fruit and vegetables.[34] In the Soviet Union, the population was worse off. Even those working for the German war effort were only entitled to food of the lowest quality and quantity. While some military commanders set up rations to stabilize relations between the occupying forces and the local population in the hinterland, meat rations were only handed out in tiny portions in the winter and were gained from waste. Further, these regulations were only guidelines for the German bureaucracy, and were not to be publicly communicated.[35]

All over occupied Europe, two groups were accorded special rations: ethnic Germans were entitled to above-average rations, whereas rations for Jews, especially in Eastern Europe, were usually so low that nobody could survive on them. In the Radom district in Poland, Jews only received rations for children up to ten years, and in Ukraine rations for Jewish persons were not to exceed those for (non-Jewish) children up to fourteen years. Jews were anyway only to be supplied in case food was available. In Belarus, where the non-Jewish local population was only supplied with those foodstuffs that were left over from Wehrmacht requisitions, German agencies decided to economize on rations for Jews. If they were supplied at all, their rations were set by the 403rd *Sicherungsdivision* (and other military units as well) at 125 grams of

bread, 14 grams of flour and 11 grams of groats daily, which was about half what non-Jewish local people received.[36]

Further examples could be easily added. They all show the racist segregation of societies, implemented by German occupation authorities who by and large determined the supply situation. Trying to find supplies where shortage prevailed was essential for members of the occupied societies all over Europe. Systems of rationing in this regard were meant to regulate access to food. On the one hand, they were based on categorizing populations according to the racist and utilitarian conceptions of the occupiers, represented in higher rations for ethnic Germans and those who did so-called "heavy" or "very heavy labour". On the other hand, those who were perceived as so-called "useless eaters" like the Jewish population found themselves at the bottom of Nazi categorizations and were not meant to survive. Soviet prisoners of war in German concentration camps or patients in hospitals, especially if mentally ill, as well as large groups of the overall Soviet population, were in many cases doomed to starvation as well.[37]

Aside from those groups, rationing actually meant that not just "minority groups", however numerous, but whole societies in Eastern and Western Europe were categorized and thereby hierarchized according to German perceptions. This categorization had direct consequences for the everyday life of all these peoples: rations determined survival chances, and they were attributed not just to some, but to all members of occupied societies. Since exploitation on behalf of the German war efforts was the general German intention with shortage resulting from it, the attribution of survival chances by rations was a widely shared experience in occupied Europe.

Make-shift economies across occupied Europe

Scarcity and especially serious forms of malnutrition, if prevailing for weeks, have a very strong impact on people's everyday lives. In a hunger crisis, the preoccupation with food, even before the situation becomes fatal, may become so intense that it has the power to overturn the starving person's normal morality and sense of self. In the later phases of marasmus, the human body tries to sustain itself from protein taken from its own muscles and cells, thereby severely damaging the heart and causing a breakdown of the immune system. Already before this phase, the progressing malfunctioning of the immune system has made people prone to dysentery, typhus and other illnesses. Keneally therefore argues that whereas about 10 per cent of the deaths caused by famine result from the final phase of starvation, most people die from infectious diseases their bodies have no defence against any longer,[38] especially when medication, heating material in winter and sanitary articles, especially soap, are also in short supply.[39]

Shortage and especially hunger are phenomena that very quickly came to influence people's lives on a day-to-day basis tremendously. As the German occupation during World War II concerned up to 230 million people,[40] the numbers affected were very high. Furthermore, compared to peacetime, occupied societies were characterized by important shifts in gender and age composition: adult men were to a large degree absent – be it at the front, in captivity, dead or away for labour-related reasons, especially forced labour. Those struggling to cope with occupation were, to a much higher percentage than in peacetime societies, women, children and the elderly people.[41] Especially babies and small children were endangered by the prevailing scarcity, and so were the elderly and sick people. Marcel Junod of the Red Cross observed in starving Athens that especially women tended to go without food to spare it for their children.[42]

Organizing food was generally a woman's task. Usually, their first step was trying to find shops that sold products they were entitled to according to the rations. However, due to German requisitions, lower productivity of agriculture, price control and disruptions in distribution, many shops were ill-supplied and goods could not be bought without queuing for hours. Jacques

Biélinky, describing the French capital in September 1940, noted in his diary: "The queues are getting longer and longer and are overgrowing Paris".[43] In front of a dairy shop where 60 small parcels of butter were distributed, he counted 350 people waiting in line.[44] Another entry, still from September 1940, says: "Queues without end where potatoes are being sold. To buy two and a half kilos one has to wait in line for more than three hours. Totally exhausted women are sitting at the kerb".[45]

Since rations and what was being sold in shops were not sufficient to survive on them alone, people had to look for other supply strategies. Hundreds of thousands of people all over Europe had to turn to make-shift economies. The term was first used with regard to the rural poor in England and describes an economy that was based on their survival strategies. During World War II occupation, these strategies included growing vegetables and fruits wherever possible to sustain their families and themselves and using all kinds of preservation techniques. Further on, "*Ersatz*" ("substitute" in terms of materials and products) was the word of the day. Especially bread was partly baked from surrogates, such as corn flour, which was legal in France but not liked, or from rye, which people complained about in the Protectorate, or from local traditional surrogates like chestnut on Crete.[46]

Hoarding, bartering, and sometimes smuggling were other possibilities for how people tried to cope with scarcity. Of great everyday importance were black markets. The overall picture is that everyone went there, and almost everyone condemned it. Accusations of black marketeering mirrored social dynamics. Generally speaking, people in the cities blamed peasants, workers blamed the rich, and the old bourgeoisie blamed parvenu shopkeepers.[47] Wherever authorities had a hand in black market operations, they were despised by the common people – a situation from which political radicalism could grow as it happened in Greece.[48] But more widespread, in fact, was blaming "the Jews", though they were surely the weakest protagonists on the scene.[49]

If nothing else was left for bartering, some women took to prostitution. Oral history reports from Smolensk tell us that women, aware of the pressing situation, often thought of contacts between local women and German soldiers with a mild moral condemnation but accepted it because "generally, you worked wherever you could".[50] The reaction of local men was different. Recollections from the Smolensk countryside talk about an old custom being revived when a girl was caught with a German: "The boys tied her skirt over her head, and she had to run home with the bottom part of her body bare".[51]

Criminalizing survival strategies

Local populations experienced the German occupation in many ways, among them exploitation, but as well in criminalizing their make-shift economies, for example, by restricting mobility. As a result, travelling to the countryside to gather agricultural products became difficult or outright dangerous. In the occupied territories of the Soviet Union, German authorities and their auxiliaries suspected people not registered locally (so-called "*Ortsfremde*") to be members of the partisan movements.[52]

Another way of criminalizing make-shift economies was to limit all kinds of trade to markets determined by the occupiers and severely punish any trading outside of these.[53] Along with marketplaces, the goods that were allowed for trading were limited as well. In Nizhyn, in Ukraine, the local *Wehrmacht* commander on 1 May 1942 announced a prohibition on selling "meat (pork, beef, mutton, goat, poultry etc.), fats, potatoes, pearl barley, millet, flour, grain, milk, butter, cream, quark (i.e. milk curds), eggs".[54] There was nothing much left to be sold and bought, and Nizhyn was not an exception. In Ukraine, these restrictions hit the peasant population, which compared to Soviet times was locally better fed due to the possibility of working in family gardens, but lived in constant fear because of German reprisals.[55]

In their intention to restrict all kinds of transactions, German occupation authorities even defined what was considered junk, and therefore unfit for bartering. Punishment in case of infringement was severe, since the German authorities saw these transactions as smuggling or, as they put it, "*Schleichhandel*", which was an anti-Semitic code word indicating that they suspected Jews to be involved. Regulations like these gave German soldiers an even stronger position in market encounters than they already had: soldiers were present in shops and on markets everywhere in occupied Europe. Compared to local people, they could afford more. Due to financial manipulations in currency exchange rates, their pay made shopping tours possible, especially when supplemented with additional funds from home. Furthermore, German authorities intended to give soldiers, especially those coming from the Eastern front, a good time in France, and therefore offered to convert unspent Russian roubles into francs on favourable terms.[56] The same was true for Belgium, where the Wehrmacht logistics department acknowledged that enabling German soldiers to shop "led to a high degree to the sell-out of the country".[57] The purchasing power of German soldiers was not limited to their pay. In those parts of occupied Europe, where trade was transacted rather by ways of bartering, cigarettes, tobacco and alcohol were more important than cash. Soldiers, due to the Wehrmacht allowances, had access to these substitute currencies. If not or just in a way that proved not sufficient for their needs and wants, they simply bartered goods they had confiscated.[58]

As these examples show, soldiers were part of the make-shift economies in occupied countries in many ways: they were customers on restricted markets, with higher purchasing power than the average local population, and with access to goods for barter, because of their army allowances or their power to confiscate. Given this situation, their involvement in local markets caused prices to rise, to the disadvantage of local customers. Local seller... in a dangerous situation, since a soldier, if not satisfied with a proposed transaction, could always accuse a local person of transgressing orders. Last but not least, soldiers were active in black market operations, be it on a small scale or in larger operations, such as when entire wagonloads found their way to the black market, which could hardly have been done without their involvement, including higher-ranking officers.[59]

Occupation, shortage and social order

Occupation caused shortage. Shortage in itself had consequences as far as the social order of occupied societies was concerned, since it put these societies under severe social pressure. Hunger and severe scarcity are often perceived as equalizing forces within a society. In fact, rations could blur social distinctions since they were usually higher for a person doing heavy labour than for white-collar professionals. At the same time, members of well-to-do households could afford it more easily to buy on the black market whereas (lower) middle-class families often found themselves in between. Therefore, a supply system based on rations had paradoxical consequences since its mechanisms of blurring and emphasizing social distinctions within a society worked at the same time.

This can be shown by an example taken from the Netherlands. Here, many working-class men were entitled to higher rations than white-collar people because of heavy labour but could use them only partially or not at all since they often lacked the money to buy these "luxury" goods, such as meat or fat. Therefore, working-class families often sold their ration coupons on the black market to people who were better off and spent the money gained to buy potatoes here. This way they supplemented the potatoes bought in shops within the rationing systems with potatoes bought from the black market, because the shops would not sell them any beyond the rationing system. The longer the situation lasted, the more annoyed those affected became: working-class families were not actually starving, but often had to accept eating meals without meat and fat and consisting largely of dry potatoes and bread baked with a high percentage of substitutes like pulses. Middle-class households were annoyed because they were not entitled to rations which allowed them to keep their standard of living and had to use up (some of) their property to be able to shop on black markets. Less affected were well-off families, who could afford it more easily to buy on the black market. Usually, they bought everyday products in the shops and had high-caloric goods like fatty fish or cheese delivered to them by a trusted black marketer.[60]

These mechanisms of social pressure were not just privately experienced. In fact, disturbances in traditional social settings were visible in public. Long queues in front of shops, which appeared all over Europe, became a new social space of scarcity and of attributing privilege in societies of shortage. Since only those in front of a queue had a good chance of buying the sought-after goods, there were fierce debates on who should be privileged by having a right to these places. In France, older men, accompanying their wifes when shopping, showed their medals from World War I pointing to their merits for the fatherland, and thereby demanded their right to a place at the head of the queue together with their wives. Aside from generational issues, more often it was established social hierarchies that were reversed in wartime queues. In Marseille, Italian women, normally from the lower stratum of the working class, were said to have pushed to the front of queues saying, "Priority to the victors". In Brittany, women who cooked for the Germans were given special rights to go to the head of queues. Since these women too were usually poor, housewives from respectable families resented making way for them. After the war, these women were quite frequently accused of "sleeping with the *boches*" (German soldiers) – and had their heads shaven after liberation for "collaboration".[61]

As scarcity put whole societies under pressure, people looked for someone to blame. Especially, farmers were often confronted with incompatible demands since the occupiers made them deliver high quotas of their produce and punished offenses severely, particularly in occupied Eastern Europe. At the same time, members of resistance movements accused them of collaborating with the enemy, and enraged city-dwellers accused them of earning a fortune on their misery by asking too high prices. In fact, in rural Belarus and Ukraine for the first time ever consumer goods like sewing machines arrived in the villages by way of bartering. Where scarcity turned into a hunger crisis, the social dynamics could fuel armed resistance, such as in Greece, where it let people to believe that they might be better off within the resistance movement. In the partisan regions of the Soviet Union, peasants in many places tried to defend their produce from either being taken by the occupiers or by partisan units. As a consequence, the situation locally resembled a civil war with everyone fighting everyone.[62]

Not only in civil war-like settings but also elsewhere, enduring shortages and especially severe hunger crises had – and continue to have – massive consequences on how those affected perceive(d) the social world they live in. For some, the solidarity within families and close circles of friends became extremely important. Diaries, for example, show that the little food that was available was shared with those people one had close personal ties with.[63] When starving became commonplace, like in ghettos or in the hunger regions of the Soviet Union and Greece, time and again, parents, especially mothers, starved themselves to death giving the food they could find to their children.[64]

Since research on the social dynamics resulting from shortage and hunger during World War II is still in its early stages, there is yet much to learn on how decisions were taken, shifting norms were debated, fought or accepted and generally speaking how scarcity was dealt with practically, on a day-to-day basis, but socially, politically or morally as well. Though the results so far show growing social tensions within societies and ego documents emphasize the importance of family structures and circles of close friends, the social world of those concerned probably was not as restricted as it might seem at first hand.[65] Even for Soviet cities where shortage and hunger were common features under occupation, there is more than episodic evidence that women and children living near POW camps tried to help those imprisoned. Their situation was disastrous. From those imprisoned, about 1.8 million POWs died in the winter of 1941/42 alone, mostly from hunger and disease. To help, women and children threw bread over the fences, handed in parcels at the gates or hid food along paths used by labour columns. Doing this was dangerous, since German guards used to shoot at women as well as children, with fatal consequences.[66]

With examples like this, the question is: why did these people do what they did? Why did they risk their lives for men they did not know by sharing their rations in times of shortage? One explanation is that they seemed to have shared it in the belief that if women and children all over the occupied territories of the Soviet Union acted the same way they did, their husbands, fathers, sons or brothers might have a chance to survive as well.[67] How many men indeed survived because of this is impossible to tell. But these episodes of helping let us catch a glimpse of the abovementioned decisions taken: women and children integrated men they did not know personally into their "universe of obligations". Helen Fein coined this term to describe the circle of individuals and groups towards whom obligations are owed, to whom rules apply and whose injuries call for amends.[68]

Shortage and hunger crises put occupied societies under pressure with the effect that social cohesion was affected. These effects had many facets: growing class antagonisms, turning to a family-structured world, but as well adapting social rules to living under occupation. This might include a reframing of who belonged to one's universe of obligations in the light of the occupiers' norms, regulations and institutions. Regarding the Jewish populations such a reframing indeed often happened. As mentioned earlier, Jews had a very weak position when bartering or on the black market. Prices and exchange rates in these situations tell their own stories of social proximity or distance. Peasants usually asked much higher prices from people they did not know than from those known to them.[69]

The same is true for barter between Jews and non-Jews. Barter was one of the few possibilities left for Jews in ghettos exchanging whatever possession they might still have for food. Some Jews in occupied Poland who went into hiding with non-Jews came to understand that they were "bartering" for their lives: if no possessions were left, they were in danger that those they stayed with turned them over to the Polish gendarmerie or killed them, mostly with the help of fellow villagers.[70] On black markets, Jews were in very weak positions as well – paying the highest prices and risking denunciation. With non-Jews, domestic and German authorities, especially in Western Europe sometimes turned a blind eye knowing that without the black market people could not survive.[71] Jews couldn't hope for such leniency; they were punished in any case.

Conclusion

Black markets and barter were just two examples of spaces within the economies of scarcity that had their own rules and morality that people had to learn to survive. They, as well as queues in front of shops or ration cards, represented contexts where the social order of occupied societies materialized. This social order was not totally different from pre-war times insofar as internal cleavages according to class, religion, education, ethnicity, gender and so on prevailed.

But occupation as shown in regard to exploitation and the resulting shortage categorized and hierarchized *all* members of occupied societies and ascribed survival chances to them according to the racist and utilitarian conceptions of the occupiers. Jews found themselves at the bottom of these racist and utilitarian hierarchies of the occupiers' perception, which was essential for attributing survival chances that affected them severely even before mass murder began. Thereby, occupation put the societies concerned under severe pressure. This, in turn, set free social dynamics that directly and indirectly influenced people's everyday lives, setting it aside from pre- and post-war times – as a consequence of Nazi politics of occupation within which mass murder, hunger policies, starvation and exploitation played key roles.

Notes

1 Christoph Buchheim, Marcel Boldorf, eds., *Europäische Volkswirtschaften unter deutscher Hegemonie 1938–1945*. München: Oldenbourg, 2012; Adam Tooze, *The Wages of Destruction. The Making and Breaking of the Nazi Economy*. London/New York: Allen Lane, 2006. Alan S. Milward, *The New Order and the French Economy*. Oxford: Oxford University Press, 1970.

2 Christian Gerlach, *Krieg, Ernährung, Völkermord. Forschungen zur deutschen Vernichtungspolitik im Zweiten Weltkrieg*. Hamburg: Hamburg Edition, 1998; Christian Gerlach, *Kalkulierte Morde. Die deutsche Wirtschafts- und Vernichtungspolitik in Weißrussland 1941 bis 1944*. Hamburg: Hamburg Edition, 1999; Gesine Gerhard: 'Food and Genocide. Nazi Agrarian Politics in the Occupied Territories of the Soviet Union', in *Contemporary European History*, 18, 1 (2009), 45–65; Dieter Pohl, *Die Herrschaft der Wehrmacht. Deutsche Militärbesatzung und einheimische Bevölkerung in der Sowjetunion 1941–1944*, pp. 183–200. Oldenbourg, 2011; Wigbert Benz, *Hans-Joachim Riecke. Vom Hungerplaner vor, zum 'Welternährer' nach 1945*. Berlin: Wissenschaftlicher Verlag Berlin, 2014; Christoph Dieckmann and Babette Quinkert, eds., *Kriegsführung und Hunger 1939–1945. Zum Verhältnis von militärischen, wirtschaftlichen und politischen Interessen*. Göttingen: Wallstein, 2015.

3 Nicholas Terry: '"Do not burden one's own army and its hinterland with unneeded mouths!" The Fate of the Soviet Civilian Population Behind the "Panther Line" in Eastern Belorussia, October 1943–June 1944', in Christoph Dieckmann and Quinkert Babette, eds., *Kriegsführung, Kriegsführung und Hunger 1939–1945. Zum Verhältnis von militärischen, wirtschaftlichen undpolitischen Interessen*, pp. 185–209. Göttingen: Wallstein, 2015; Karel Berkhoff, '"Wir sollen verhungern, damit Platz für die Deutschen geschaffen wird". Hungersnöte in den ukrainischen Städten im Zweiten Weltkrieg', in Babette Quinkert and Jörg Morré, eds., *Vernichtungskrieg, Reaktionen, Erinnerung. Die deutsche Besatzungsherrschaft in der Sowjetunion 1941–1944*, pp. 54–75. Paderborn: Brill Schoningh, 2014; Tanja Penter, *Kohle für Stalin und Hitler, Arbeiten und Leben im Donbass 1929 bi 1953*. Essen: Klartext, 2010; Norbert Kanz, 'Das Beispiel Charkow: Eine Stadtbevölkerung als Opfer der deutschen Hungerstrategie 1941/42', in Christian Hartmann, Johannes Hürter, Ulrike Jureit, eds., *Verbrechen der Wehrmacht. Bilanz einer Debatte*, 136–144. München: C.H. Beck, 2005.

4 Marc Buggeln and Michael Wildt, eds., *Arbeit im Nationalsozialismus*. München: De Gruyter Oldenbourg, 2014; Dieter Pohl and Tanja Sebta, eds., *Zwangsarbeit in Hitlers Europa. Besatzung, Arbeit, Folgen*. Berlin: Metropol 2013; Jürgen Hensel and Stephan Lehnstaedt eds., *Arbeit in den nationalsozialistischen Ghettos*. Osnabrück: Fibre Verlag, 2013; Karsten Linne and Florian Dierl, eds., *Arbeitskräfte als Kriegsbeute. Der Fall Ost- und Südosteuropa 1939–1945*. Berlin: Metropol, 2011.

5 E.P. Thompson, 'The Moral Economy of the English Crowd in the Eighteenth Century', in Dorothy Thompson, ed., *The Essential E.P. Thompson*, pp. 316–377. New York, 2001.

6 Tatjana Tönsmeyer, Peter Haslinger, Włodzimierz Borodziej, Stefan Martens and Irina Sherbakova, eds., *Fighting Hunger, Dealing with Shortage. Everyday Life under Occupation in World War II Europe. A Source Edition*. 2 vols. Leiden/Boston: Brill, 2021. See as well the online-portal 'Societies under German occupation', https://societiesundergermanoccupation.uni-wuppertal.de/

7 Mark Mazower, *Inside Hitler's Greece. The Experience of Occupation, 1941–1944*. New Haven: Yale University Press, 2001. Generally, Violetta Hionidou, *Famine and Death in Occupied*

Greece. 1941–1944. New York: Cambridge University Press, 2006; Ingrid de Zwarte, *The Hunger Winter. Fighting Famine in the Occupied Netherlands, 1944–1945*. Cambridge: Cambridge University Press, 2020.

8 Citied in Alice Weinreb, *Modern Hungers. Food and Power in Twentieth-Century German,* p. 51. New York: Oxford University Press, 2017. Jonas Scherner, 'Germany, Blockade and Strategic Raw Materials in the Era of the Two World Wars', *The International History Review*, published online 04-03-2024; https://doi.org/10.1080/07075332.2024.2323497.

9 Citied in Rolf-Dieter Müller, 'Die Mobilisierung der deutschen Wirtschaft für Hitlers Kriegsführung', in Bernhard R. Kroener, Rolf-Dieter Müller and Hans Umbreit, eds., *Organisation und Mobilisierung des deutschen Machtbereichs. Erster Halbband: Kriegsverwaltung, Wirtschaft und personelle Ressourcen 1939-1941*, pp. 349–689, 397. Stuttgart, 1988.

10 Gerhard, 'Food and Genocide. Nazi Agrarian Politics in the Occupied Territories of the Soviet Union', in *Contemporary European History* 18, 1 (2009): 46, 50.

11 Christoph Dieckmann, 'Das Scheitern des Hungerplans und die Praxis der selektiven Hungerpolitik im deutschen Krieg gegen die Sowjetunion', in Christoph Dieckmann and Babette Quinkert, eds., *Kriegführung und Hunger*, pp. 88–122, 93ff. Göttingen: Wallstein, 2015.

12 Citied in Christian Streit, *Keine Kameraden, Die Wehrmacht und die sowjetischen Kriegsgefangenen 1941–1945*. Stuttgart: Deutsche Verlags-Anstalt, 1978, p. 63 and in Dieckmann, 'Das Scheitern des Hungerplans und die Praxis der selektiven Hungerpolitik im deutschen Krieg gegen die Sowjetunion', p. 97.

13 Gerhard, 'Food and Genocide. Nazi Agrarian Politics in the Occupied Territories of the Soviet Union', *Contemporary European History* 18, 1 (2009): 56f.

14 Ibid and Dieckmann, Scheitern, p. 111, 118f. Focusing on Belarus, see Gerlach, Morde, pp. 265–318, on Soviet cities Alex J. Kay: *Empire of Destruction. A History of Nazi Mass Killing*. New Haven: Yale University Press, 2021, pp. 116–145.

15 Karel Berkhoff, *Harvest of Despair. Life and Death in Ukraine under Nazi Rule*. Cambridge/Mass: Harvard University Press, 2004, pp. 17–24.

16 Sergei Kudryashov, 'Living Conditions in the Occupied Territories of the USSR, 1941–1944', in Christoph Buchheim and Marcel Boldorf (Hg.), *Europäische Volkswirtschaften unter deutscher Hegemonie 1938–1945*. München: Oldenbourg, 2012, pp. 53–65, 55f. On requisitions on a local level see e.g. Laurie A. Cohen, *Smolensk under the Nazis. Everyday Life in Occupied Russia*. University of Rochester Press 2013, p. 97; Michaela Christ, *Die Dynamik des Tötens. Die Ermordung der Juden in Berditschew*, Frankfurt am Main: Fischer Taschenbuch Verlag, 2011, p. 75; Mazower, *Inside Hitler's Greece. The experience of Occupation, 1941–1944*. New Haven: Yale University Press, 2001, p. 23.

17 Tatjana Tönsmeyer, 'Farming Farming under Occupation. Rural Actors and the Social Dynamics of Occupation during World War II', in Liesbeth van de Grift, Dietmar Müller and Corinna R. Unger, eds., *Living with the Land. Rural and Agricultural Actors in Twentieth-Century Europe*, 133–154, a handbook. Berlin: De Gruyter, 2022, pp. 133–154.

18 Mazower, *Inside Hitler's Greece. The Experience of Occupation, 1941–1944*. New Haven: Yale University Press, 2001, p. 40.

19 Mazower, *Inside Hitler's Greece*, p. 27f.; Violetta Hionidou, 'Why Do People Die in Famines? Evidence from Three Island Populations', *Continuity and Change* 56, 1 (2002), 65–80.

20 Charles Rist, *Une saison gâtée: Journal de la guerre et de l'occupation, 1939–1945*, ed. Jean Noel Jeanneney, Paris 1983, p. 413 (entry for 3 July 1944).

21 Richard Vinen, *The Unfree French. Life under the Occupation*. London: Allen Lane, 2006, p. 216.

22 Ibd., p. 228.

23 Marcel Boldorf, 'Neue Wege zur Erforschung der Wirtschaftsgeschichte Europas unter nationalsozialistischer Hegemonie', in Christoph Buchheim and Marcel Boldorf, eds., *Europäische Volkswirtschaften unter deutscher Hegemonie 1938–1945*. München: Oldenbourg, 2012, pp. 1–23, 6.

24 Hein Kleman and Sergei Kudryashov, *Occupied Economies. An Economic History of Nazi-Occupied Europe, 1939–1945*. London: Berg, 2012, p. 174.

25 Kleman and Kudryashov, *Occupied Economies*, pp. 368 and 437.

26 Adam Tooze, *The Wages of Destruction. The Making and Breaking of the Nazi Economy*. London/ New York: Allen Lane, 2006, p. 389f.

27 Boldorf, Wege, p. 8.

28 Boldorf, Wege, p. 13f.

29 Götz Aly, *Hitlers Volksstaat. Raub, Rassenkrieg und nationaler Sozialismus*. Frankfurt am Main 2005, p. 114.

30 Nick Cullather, *The Hungry World. America's Cold War Battle against Poverty in Asia*, Cambridge/ Mass, 2010, pp. 28–33.

31 Tatjana Tönsmeyer, 'Hungerökonomien. Vom Umgang mit der Mangelversorgung im besetzten Europa des Zweiten Weltkrieg', *Historische Zeitschrift* 310 (2015), 662–704, 669–673.

32 Versorgungsanzeiger. Wochenblatt für die Versorgungs- und Ernährungspraxis/Zásobovací zpravodaj. Týdeník pro zásobovácí a vyživovací praxi, 12.12.1942, p. 9.

33 With Denmark being the exemption to this rule.

34 Robert Seidel, *Deutsche Besatzungspolitik in Polen. Der Distrikt Radom 1939–1945*. Paderborn: Ferdinand Schöningh, 2006, p. 122f.

35 Jörn Hasenclever, *Wehrmacht und Besatzungspolitik in der Sowjetunion. Die Befehlshaber der rückwärtigen Heeresgebiete 1941–1943* Paderborn: Schöningh, 2010, p. 287, 291, 302. Pohl, *Die Herrschaft der Wehrmacht. Deutsche Militärbesatzung und einheimische Bevölkerung in der Sowjetunion* 1941–1944, p. 184f. Jürgen Kilian, *Wehrmacht und Besatzungsherrschaft im Russischen Nordwesten 1941–1944. Praxis und Alltag im Militärverwaltungsgebiet der Heeresgruppe Nord*. Paderborn: Ferdinand Schöningh, 2012, p. 274, 284, 292, 299. Gerlach, Motde, p. 277. Wirtschaftsinspektion Mitte, Chefgruppe Landwirtschaft [Office of Economic Administration, Central Area, Agricultural Command Group] to the Gebietskommissar [District Commissar] for Minsk, 4 September 1941. National Archive Belarus: Fonds 393, 3/14.

36 On ethnic Germans e.g Seidel, *Deutsche Besatzungspolitik in Polen. Der Distrikt Radom 1939–1945. Paderborn: Ferdinand Schöningh*, p. 124; Gerhard Wolf, *Ideologie und Herrschaftsrationalität. Nationalsozialistische Germanisierungspolitik in Polen*. Hamburg: Hamburger Edition, 2012, p. 223f., On Jews in the Radom district Seidel, *Deutsche Besatzungspolitik in Polen. Der Distrikt Radom 1939–1945. Paderborn: Ferdinand Schöningh*, p. 124, on Jews in Ukraine Wendy Lower: *Nazi Empire-Building and the Holocaust in Ukraine*. Chapel Hill: University of North Carolina Press, 2005, p. 139, on nutrition policies regarding Jewish populations in Belarus Gerlach, *Kalkulierte Morde. Die deutsche Wirtschafts- und Vernichtungspolitik in Weißrussland 1941 bis 1944*, p. 668ff.

37 Dieter Pohl, *Verfolgung und Massenmord in der NS-Zeit 1933–1945*. Darmstadt 2003, p.40f.

38 Thomas Keneally, *Three Famines. Starvation and Politics*, New York: Publics Affairs, 2011, p. 12ff.

39 On the closing of pharmacies, sequestration of medicine, and the overall lack regarding health care, see e.g. Gerlach, *Kalkulierte Morde. Die deutsche Wirtschafts- und Vernichtungspolitik in Weißrussland 1941 bis 1944*. Hamburg: Hamburg Edition, 1999, p. 290f.

40 Dieter Pohl 'Herrscher and Unterworfene. "Die deutsche Besatzung und die Gesellschaften Europas"', in Dietmar Süß and Winfried Süß, eds., *Das 'Dritte Reich'. Eine Einführung*. München: Patheon, 2008, 267–285, 276.

41 On the concept of occupied societies, see Tatjana Tönsmeyer, 'Besatzungsgesellschaften. Begriffliche und konzeptionelle Überlegungen zur Erfahrungsgeschichte des Alltags unter deutscher Besatzung im Zweiten Weltkrieg', Version: 1.0, in: *Docupedia-Zeitgeschichte*, 18.12.2015a. http://docupedia.de/zg/toensmeyer_besatzungsgesellschaften_v1_de_2015. Accessed 14 June 2024.

42 Mazower, *Inside Hitler's Greece. The experience of Occupation, 1941–1944*, p. 36.

43 Entry for 13 September 1940. Die Verfolgung und Ermordung der europäischen Juden durch das nationalsozialistische Deutschland 1933–1945 (VEJ). Ed. by the Bundesarchiv, the Institut für Zeitgeschichte and the Lehrstuhl für Neuere und Neueste Geschichte an der Albert-Ludwigs-Universität Freiburg, München 2012, vol. 5, doc. 243, p. 613.

44 Entry for 16 September 1940. Die Verfolgung und Ermordung der europäischen Juden durch das nationalsozialistische Deutschland 1933–1945 (VEJ), vol. 5.

45 Entry for 22 September 1940. Die Verfolgung und Ermordung der europäischen Juden durch das nationalsozialistische Deutschland 1933–1945 (VEJ), vol. 5.

46 On France Vinen, French, p. 219. On the Protectorate: Report about the complaints to the Office of Reich's Protector, 11 June 1942. National Archive Prague, Státní tajemník u řišského protektora v Čechách a na Moravě 109-4/1335, box 81. On Greece Fleischer, Hagen, Schwert and Olive. 'Besatzungsalltag in der "Festung Kreta", 1941–1945. Eine Dokumentation', in Willi Benning, ed., *'Lern im Leben die Kunst ... '. Festschrift für Klaus Betzen*, 81–178. Athen: University of Athen, 1995, p. 102.

47 Vinen, *French*, p. 224.

48 Mazower, *Inside Hitler's Greece. The Experience of Occupation, 1941–1944*, p. 52–56.

49 Mark Mazower, *Salonica. The City of Ghosts. Christians, Muslims, and Jews, 1430–1950*. New York: Vintage, 2006, p. 395; Christoph Dieckmann, *Deutsche Besatzungspolitik in Litauen 1941–1944*, Göttingen: Wallstein, 2011, p. 1064f.

50 Cohen, *Smolensk*, p. 224.

51 Cohen, *Smolensk*, p. 225.

52 Berkhoff, *Harvest of Despair. Life and Death in Ukraine under Nazi Rule*. Cambridge/Mass: Harvard University Press, 2004, p. 177; Gerlach, *Kalkulierte Morde. Die deutsche Wirtschafts- und Vernichtungspolitik in Weißrussland 1941 bis 1944*, p. 218ff.

53 On Poland Tomasz Szarota, *Warschau unter dem Hakenkreuz. Leben und Alltag im besetzten Warschau, 1.10.1939 bis 31.7.1944*. Paderborn: Ferdinand Schöningh, 1985, p. 128f. On Belarus: Decree issued by the Kreiskommissar Grodno, 14 October 1941. Gosudarstvennyj Archiv Grodnenskoj oblasti (GAGrO), F. 1, Op. 1, d. 15, p. 2.

54 State Archive of the region of Tschernihiw, department Nizhyn, R–4394, op. 1, d. 3, l. 227.

55 Berkhoff, *Harvest of Despair. Life and Death in Ukraine under Nazi Rule*. Cambridge/Mass: Harvard University Press, 2004, p. 130–140.

56 Aly, *Hitlers Volksstaat. Raub, Rassenkrieg und nationaler Sozialismus*. Frankfurt am Main 2005, p. 102 and pp. 114–139.

57 Aly, *Hitlers Volksstaat*, p. 114.

58 Tomasz Szarota, *Warschau unter dem Hakenkreuz. Leben und Alltag im besetzten Warschau, 1.10.1939 bis 31.7.1944*, p. 124; Stephan Lehnstaedt, *Okkupation im Osten. Besatzeralltag in Warschau und Minsk 1939–1944*. München: Oldenbourg, 2010, pp. 165–176.

59 See e.g. regarding Belgium Gérard Libois, José Gotovitch, *L'an 40. La Belgique occupée*, Bruxelles: CRISP, 1971, p. 338f.

60 Ralf Futselaar, 'Incomes, Class, and Coupons. Black Markets for Food in the Netherlands during the Second World War', *Food & History* 8, 1 (2010): pp. 171–198, 181–183, 187, 189. On rural populations, see Tatjana Tönsmeyer, 'Farming Farming under Occupation. Rural Actors and the Social Dynamics of Occupation during World War II', pp. 133–154.

61 Vinen, *The Unfree French. Life under the Occupation*. London: Allen Lane, 2006, p. 217f. and Fabrice Virgili, *Shorn Women: Gender and Punishment in Liberation France*. Oxford: Berg, 2002.

62 Gerlach, *Kalkulierte Morde. Die deutsche Wirtschafts- und Vernichtungspolitik in Weißrussland 1941 bis 1944*, p. 248f; Dieckmann, *Deutsche Besatzungspolitik in Litauen 1941–1944*, p. 1093; Alexander Brakel, 'Das allergefährlichste ist die Wut der Bauern'. Die Versorgung der Partisanen und ihr Verhältnis zur Zivilbevölkerung, *VfZ*, 55 (2007): pp. 393–424. Browning, Christopher, *Remembering Survival. Inside a Nazi Slave-Labor Camp*. New York: W. W. Norton & Company, 2010, pp. 393–424. Daniel Romanovsky, 'The Soviet Person as a Bystander of the Holocaust. The Case of Eastern Belorussia', in David Bankier, ed., *Nazi Europa and the Final Solution*, Jerusalem, 2003, pp. 276–306, 293f. On Greece Mazower, *Inside Hitler's Greece. The Experience of Occupation, 1941–1944*, pp. 24–28, 108–132. On Belgium, see generally Futselaar, 'Incomes, Class, and Coupons. Black Markets for Food in the Netherlands during the Second World War', *Food & History* 8, 1 (2010), p. 184f. Here the reluctance of farmers to deliver their produce was very widespread, and punishment here is a lot less severe than in the occupied territories of the Soviet Union. See e.g. a report for the West of Flanders: Centre d'études et de documentation guerre et société contemporaine (CEGESOMA): AA 78/6 (Controledienst Kortrijk).

63 For examples, see Tönsmeyer, 'Hungerökonomien. Vom Umgang mit der Mangelversorgung im besetzten Europa des Zweiten Weltkrieg', *Historische Zeitschrift* 310 (2015), pp. 662–704, p. 679.
64 Mazower, *Inside Hitler's Greece. The Experience of Occupation, 1941–1944*, p. 36.
65 Tatjana Tönsmeyer, *Unter deutscher Besatzung, Europa 1939–1945*, München: C.H. Beck, 2024.
66 On the mortality of POWs Pohl, Verfolgung und Massenmord, p. 40f; for examples of helping Berkhoff, *Harvest of Despair. Life and Death in Ukraine under Nazi Rule*, pp. 95–104 and p. 109f and Lower, *Nazi Empire-Building and the Holocaust in Ukraine*, p. 64f.
67 Berkhoff, *Harvest of Despair. Life and Death in Ukraine under Nazi Rulev*, pp. 95–104.
68 Fein, Helen, 'Genocide and State Murders in the Twentieth Century'. Lecture at the United States Holocaust Memorial Museum, 24 October 1995.
69 Futselaar, Incomes, p. 181. Vinen, *The Unfree French. Life under the Occupation*, p. 225. On especially high prices that Jews had to pay Christopher Browning *Remembering Survival. Inside a Nazi Slave-Labor Camp*. New York: W. W. Norton & Company, 2010, p. 57. Christ, *Die Dynamik des Tötens. Die Ermordung der Juden von Berditschew, Ukraine 1941–1944*. Frankfurt: Main, 2011, p. 153f.
70 Jan Tomasz Gross/Irena Grudzińska Gross: *Golden Harvest. Events at the Periphery of the Holocaust*, New York: Oxford University Press, 2012, pp. 50–57. Jan Grabowski, *Hunt for the Jews. Betrayal and Murder in German-Occupied Poland*, Bloomington: Indiana University Press, 2013, pp. 63–86. Natalia Aleksiun, 'Gender and the Daily Lives of Jews in Hiding in Eastern Galicia', *Nashim: A Journal of Jewish Women's Studies and Gender Issues* 27 (2014): 38–61, p. 38 und p. 46.
71 Vinen, *The Unfree French. Life under the Occupation*, p. 225. Szarota, *Warschau unter dem Hakenkreuz. Leben und Alltag im besetzten Warschau, 1.10.1939 bis 31.7.1944*, p. 129.

References

Aleksiun, Natalia, 'Gender and the Daily Lives of Jews in Hiding in Eastern Galicia, in *Nashim*', *A Journal of Jewish Women's Studies and Gender Issues* 27 (2014): 38–61.

Aly, Götz, *Hitlers Volksstaat. Raub, Rassenkrieg und nationaler Sozialismus.* Frankfurt am Main: S. Fischer Verlag, 2005.

Benz, Wigbert, *Hans-Joachim Riecke. Vom Hungerplaner vor, zum 'Welternährer' nach 1945.* Berlin: Wissenschaftlicher Verlag Berlin, 2014.

Berkhoff, Karel, *Harvest of Despair. Life and Death in Ukraine under Nazi Rule*. Cambridge/Mass: Harvard University Press, 2004.

Berkhoff, Karel, ' "Wir sollen verhungern, damit Platz für die Deutschen geschaffen wird". Hungersnöte in den ukrainischen Städten im Zweiten Weltkrieg', in Babette Quinkert and Jörg Morré, eds., *Vernichtungskrieg, Reaktionen, Erinnerung. Die deutsche Besatzungsherrschaft in der Sowjetunion 1941–1944*, 54–75. Paderborn: Brill Schoningh, 2014.

Boldorf, Marcel, 'Neue Wege zur Erforschung der Wirtschaftsgeschichte Europas unter nationalsozialistischer Hegemonie', in Christoph Buchheim and Marcel Boldorf, eds., *Europäische Volkswirtschaften unter deutscher Hegemonie 1938–1945*, 1–23. München: Olenbourg, 2012.

Brakel, Alexander, '"Das allergefährlichste ist die Wut der Bauern". Die Versorgung der Partisanen und ihr Verhältnis zur Zivilbevölkerung', *VfZ*, 55 (2007): 393–424.

Browning, Christopher, *Remembering Survival. Inside a Nazi Slave-Labor Camp*. New York: W. W. Norton & Company, 2010.

Buchheim, Christoph and Boldorf, Marcel, eds., *Europäische Volkswirtschaften unter deutscher Hegemonie 1938–1945*. München: Olenbourg, 2012.

Buggeln, Marc and Wildt, Michael, eds., *Arbeit im Nationalsozialismus*. München: De Gruyter Oldenbourg, 2014.

Christ, Michaela, *Die Dynamik des Tötens. Die Ermordung der Juden von Berditschew, Ukraine 1941–1944*. Frankfurt: Main, 2011.

Cohen, Laurie A., *Smolensk under the Nazis. Everyday Life in Occupied Russia*. Rochester NY: University of Rochester Press, 2013.

Cullather, Nick, *The Hungry World. America's Cold War Battle against Poverty in Asia*. Cambridge/ Mass: Harvard University Press, 2010.

de Zwarte, Ingrid, *The Hunger Winter. Fighting Famine in the Occupied Netherlands, 1944–1945*. Cambridge: Cambridge University Press, 2020.

Dreyfus, Jean-Marc. 2013. *Die Verfolgung Und Ermordung Der Europälschen Juden Durch Das Nationalsozialistische Deutschland 1933–1945. Band 5, West-Und Nordeuropa 1940–Juni 1942*. Edited by Katja Happe, Michael Mayer, and Maja Peers. Berlin: Oldenbourg Wissenschaftsverlag.

Dieckmann, Christoph, *Deutsche Besatzungspolitik in Litauen 1941–1944*. Göttingen: Wallstein, 2011.

Dieckmann, Christoph, 'Das Scheitern des Hungerplans und die Praxis der selektiven Hungerpolitik im deutschen Krieg gegen die Sowjetunion', in Christoph Dieckmann and Babette Quinkert, eds., *Kriegführung und Hunger*, 88–122. Göttingen: Wallstein, 2015.

Dieckmann, Christoph and Quinkert, Babette, eds., *Kriegsführung und Hunger 1939–1945. Zum Verhältnis von militärischen, wirtschaftlichen und politischen Interessen*. Göttingen: Wallstein, 2015.

Fein, Helen, 'Genocide and State Murders in the Twentieth Century'. Lecture at the United States Holocaust Memorial Museum, 24 October 1995.

Fleischer, Hagen, Schwert and Olive, 'Besatzungsalltag in der "Festung Kreta", 1941–1945. Eine Dokumentation', in Willi Benning, ed., *Lern im Leben die Kunst ... Festschrift für Klaus Betzen*, 81–178. Athens: University of Athens, 1995.

Futselaar, Ralf, 'Incomes, Class, and Coupons. Black Markets for Food in the Netherlands during the Second World War', in *Food & History* 8, 1 (2010): 171–198.

Gerhard, Gesine, 'Food and Genocide. Nazi Agrarian Politics in the Occupied Territories of the Soviet Union', in *Contemporary European History* 18, 1 (2009): 45–65.

Gerlach, Christian, *Krieg, Ernährung, Völkermord. Forschungen zur deutschen Vernichtungspolitik im Zweiten Weltkrieg*. Hamburg: Hamburg Edition, 1998.

Gerlach, Christian, *Kalkulierte Morde. Die deutsche Wirtschafts- und Vernichtungspolitik in Weißrussland 1941 bis 1944*. Hamburg: Hamburg Edition, 1999.

Grabowski, Jan, *Hunt for the Jews. Betrayal and Murder in German-Occupied Poland*. Bloomington: Indiana University Press, 2013.

Gross, Jan Tomasz and Gross, Irena Grudzińska, *Golden Harvest. Events at the Periphery of the Holocaust*. New York: Oxford University Press, 2012.

Hasenclever, Jörn, *Wehrmacht und Besatzungspolitik in der Sowjetunion. Die Befehlshaber der rückwärtigen Heeresgebiete 1941–1943*. Paderborn: Schöningh, 2010.

Hensel, Jürgen and Lehnstaedt, Stephan, eds., *Arbeit in den nationalsozialistischen Ghettos*. Osnabrück: Fibre Verlag, 2013.

Hionidou, Violetta, 'Why Do People Die in Famines? Evidence from Three Island Populations', *Continuity and Change* 56, 1 (2002): 65–80.

Hionidou, Violetta, *Famine and Death in Occupied Greece. 1941–1944*. New York: Cambridge University Press, 2006.

Kanz, Norbert, 'Das Beispiel Charkow: Eine Stadtbevölkerung als Opfer der deutschen Hungerstrategie 1941/42', in Christian Hartmann, Johannes Hürter, and Ulrike Jureit, eds., *Verbrechen der Wehrmacht. Bilanz einer Debatte*, 136–144. München: C.H. Beck, 2005.

Kay, Alex J., *Empire of Destruction. A History of Nazi Mass Killing*. New Haven: Yale University Press, 2021.

Keneally, Thomas, *Three Famines. Starvation and Politics*. New York: Publics Affairs, 2011.

Kilian, Jürgen, *Wehrmacht und Besatzungsherrschaft im Russischen Nordwesten 1941–1944. Praxis und Alltag im Militärverwaltungsgebiet der Heeresgruppe Nord*. Paderborn: Ferdinand Schöningh, 2012.

Kleman, Hein and Kudryashov, Sergei, *Occupied Economies. An Economic History of Nazi-Occupied Europe, 1939–1945*. London: Berg, 2012.

Kudryashov, Sergei, 'Living Conditions in the Occupied Territories of the USSR, 1941–1944', in Christoph Buchheim and Marcel Boldorf, eds., *Europäische Volkswirtschaften unter deutscher Hegemonie 1938–1945*, 53–65. München: Oldenbourg, 2012.

Lehnstaedt, Stephan: *Okkupation im Osten. Besatzeralltag in Warschau und Minsk 1939–1944*. München: Oldenbourg, 2010.
Libois, Gérard and Gotovitch, José, *L'an 40. La Belgique occupée*. Bruxelles: CRISP, 1971.
Linne, Karsten and Dierl, Florian, eds., *Arbeitskräfte als Kriegsbeute. Der Fall Ost- und Südosteuropa 1939–1945*. Berlin: Metropol, 2011.
Lower, Wendy, *Nazi Empire-Building and the Holocaust in Ukraine*. Chapel Hill: University of North Carolina Press, 2005.
Mazower, Mark, *Inside Hitler's Greece. The Experience of Occupation, 1941–1944*. New Haven: Yale University Press, 2001.
Mazower, Mark, *Salonica. The City of Ghosts. Christians, Muslims, and Jews, 1430–1950*. New York: Vintage, 2006.
Milward, Alan S., *The New Order and the French Economy*. Oxford: Oxford University Press, 1970.
Müller, Rolf-Dieter, 'Die Mobilisierung der deutschen Wirtschaft für Hitlers Kriegsführung', in Bernhard R. Kroener, Rolf-Dieter Müller and Hans Umbreit, eds., *Das Deutsche Reich und der Zweite Weltkrieg, 10 vol. vol. 5, part 2: Organisation und Mobilisierung des deutschen Machtbereichs. Erster Halbband: Kriegsverwaltung, Wirtschaft und personelle Ressourcen 1939–1941*, 349–689. Stuttgart: DVA/Deutsche Verlags-Anstalt, 1988.
Penter, Tanja, *Kohle für Stalin und Hitler, Arbeiten und Leben im Donbass 1929 bi 1953*. Essen: Klartext, 2010.
Pohl, Dieter, *Verfolgung und Massenmord in der NS-Zeit 1933–1945*. Darmstadt: Wissenschaftliche Buchgesellschaft, 2003.
Pohl, Dieter, 'Herrscher and Unterworfene. "Die deutsche Besatzung und die Gesellschaften Europas"', in Dietmar Süß and Winfried Süß, eds., *Das 'Dritte Reich'. Eine Einführung,* 267–285. München: Patheon, 2008.
Pohl, Dieter, *Die Herrschaft der Wehrmacht. Deutsche Militärbesatzung und einheimische Bevölkerung in der Sowjetunion 1941–1944*, 183–200. Main: Oldenbourg, 2011.
Pohl, Dieter and Sebta, Tanja (eds.), *Zwangsarbeit in Hitlers Europa.* Besatzung, Arbeit, Folgen: Berlin:Metropol, 2013.
Romanovsky, Daniel, 'The Soviet Person as a Bystander of the Holocaust. The Case of Eastern Belorussia', in David Bankier, ed., *Nazi Europa and the Final Solution,* 276–306. Jerusalem, 2003.
Scherner, Jonas, 'Germany, Blockade and Strategic Raw Materials in the Era of the Two World Wars', in *The International History Review*, published online 04-03-2024; https://doi.org/10.1080/07075332.2024.2323497.
Seidel, Robert, *Deutsche Besatzungspolitik in Polen. Der Distrikt Radom 1939–1945*. Paderborn: Ferdinand Schöningh, 2006.
Streit, Christian, *Keine Kameraden, Die Wehrmacht und die sowjetischen Kriegsgefangenen 1941–1945*. Stuttgart: Deutsche Verlags-Anstalt, 1978.
Szarota, Tomasz, *Warschau unter dem Hakenkreuz. Leben und Alltag im besetzten Warschau, 1.10.1939 bis 31.7.1944*. Paderborn: Ferdinand Schöningh, 1985.
Terry, Nicholas, '"Do Not Burden One's Own Army and Its Hinterland with Unneeded Mouths!" The Fate of the Soviet Civilian Population Behind the "Panther Line"', in Christoph Dieckmann and Quinkert Babette, eds., *Kriegsführung und Hunger 1939–1945. Zum Verhältnis von militärischen, wirtschaftlichen und politischen*, Interessen, 185–209. Göttingen: Wallstein, 2015.
Thompson, E.P., 'The Moral Economy of the English Crowd in the Eighteenth Century', in Dorothy Thompson, ed., *The Essential E.P. Thompson,* 316–377. New York: The New Press, 2001.
Tönsmeyer, Tatjana, 'Besatzungsgesellschaften. Begriffliche und konzeptionelle Überlegungen zur Erfahrungsgeschichte des Alltags unter deutscher Besatzung im Zweiten Weltkrieg', Version: 1.0, in: Docupedia-Zeitgeschichte, 18.12. 2015a. http://docupedia.de/zg/toensmeyer_besatzungsgesellschaften_v1_de_2015. Accessed 14 June 2024.
Tönsmeyer, Tatjana, 'Hungerökonomien. Vom Umgang mit der Mangelversorgung im besetzten Europa des Zweiten Weltkrieg', *Historische Zeitschrift,* 310 (2015b): 662–704.

Tönsmeyer, Tatjana, Haslinger, Peter, Borodziej, Włodzimierz, Martens, Stefan and Sherbakova, Irina, eds., *Fighting Hunger, Dealing with Shortage. Everyday Life under Occupation in World War II Europe. A Source Edition*. 2 vols. Leiden/ Boston: Brill, 2021.

Tönsmeyer, Tatjana, 'Farming Farming under Occupation. Rural Actors and the Social Dynamics of Occupation during World War II', in Liesbeth van de Grift, Dietmar Müller und Corinna R. Unger, eds., *Living with the Land. Rural and Agricultural Actors in Twentieth-Century Europe*, 133–154, a handbook. Berlin: De Gruyter, 2022.

Tönsmeyer, Tatjana, *Unter deutscher Besatzung, Europa 1939–1945*. München: C.H. Beck, 2024.

Tooze, Adam, *The Wages of Destruction. The Making and Breaking of the Nazi Economy*. London/ New York: Allen Lane, 2006.

Vinen, Richard, *The Unfree French. Life under the Occupation*. London: Allen Lane, 2006.

Virgili, Fabrice, *Shorn Women: Gender and Punishment in Liberation France*. Oxford: Berg, 2002.

Weinreb, Alice, *Modern Hungers. Food and Power in Twentieth-Century German*. New York: Oxford University Press, 2017.

Wolf, Gerhard, *Ideologie und Herrschaftsrationalität. Nationalsozialistische Germanisierungspolitik in Polen*. Hamburg: Hamburger Edition, 2012.

3 Food crises, extreme hunger and famine in Russia and the USSR[1]

Stephen Wheatcroft and Filip Slaveski

The Russian Empire and Soviet Union in the first half of the twentieth century experienced far more famines than any other European country. Food crises causing extreme hunger, famine and mass starvation were undoubtedly very important political factors in Soviet history, but they have been inadequately understood. This chapter attempts an new assessment of the three periods of food crisis and extreme hunger in Russia and the Soviet Union: 1917–22, 1927–33 and 1941–47, which contained as many as six famines.[2] Although natural and political factors played a role in all of these extreme events, this chapter will argue that the causes of these famines were complex, varied by region and developed incrementally, arising from ongoing food supply problems. They involved the government in taking extra-ordinary measures to protect the food supply of different regions and groups at different times, but like many societies they tended to favour the more influential, wealthy and articulate population in the towns, and especially the capital over the peasantry.

Famine is a term used in many (but not all) languages to distinguish between different degrees of hunger. It is used to indicate an extra-ordinarily high degree of hunger, which was life-threatening and which was believed to require extra-ordinary relief measures from the State. The problem of when to declare a famine is particularly complicated for historical societies operating under different and harsher demographic regimes, and especially for those whose languages do not have a word for famine, and whose histories do not have the long tradition of appeals to the State for extra-ordinary famine assistance. This applies to Russian and Ukrainian history of famine, because, until very recently, neither Russian nor Ukrainian languages had separate words for famine. Their words *'golod'* and *'holod'* referred to both hunger and famine, with no distinction. Historically their societies also lacked the traditional emphasis placed on such a distinction, with the state only beginning to take on a sense of responsibility for feeding people in a famine from the late nineteenth century.[3] Before using the term famine, we will need to unpack some of its meanings and provide a definition that we will try to use consistently throughout this chapter.

Development economists Paul Howe and Stephen Devereux (H&D) have proposed an instrumental definition of famine that takes into consideration both 'magnitude' in terms of the size of population experiencing excess mortalities caused by hunger and 'intensity' in terms of death rates as a proportion of the population.[4] Their stages in the scale of famine magnitude (see Table 3.1) begin with 'minor famines', where mortality is less than 1,000 people per year; 'moderate famines', with mortality between 1,000 and 10,000; 'major famines', with mortality between 10,000 and 100,000; 'great famines', with mortality between 100,000 and 1 million; and 'catastrophic famines', with mortality exceeding 1 million. It seems reasonable for historians to accept these scales. Their five stages of the intensity of famine measured mortality rates per 10,000 population per day and were associated with different rates of wasting

DOI: 10.4324/9781003465805-5

and/or prevalence of oedema. To make our historical work comparable, we can easily adopt these scales of magnitude, noting that they automatically increase as we deal with larger and larger territorial units. Producing historically comparable famine intensity indicators is more complex. We generally do not have rates of wasting and have only scattered reports on the incidence of oedema. Yet we do have other indicators of food crisis (e.g., food consumption survey and price data) that we can use. We are also more used to dealing with mortality rates per thousand population per year, and when dealing with shorter periods we generally break the period up into months and adjust the monthly data to their annual equivalents, meaning the annual rate that would apply if the shorter-term rate were to hold throughout the year.[5]

For our historical studies, we also need some information not included by H&D. We need to know the duration of the crises in months. Annual mortality figures for famines lasting less than a year will clearly be less accurate than the annualized results of monthly mortality data that only covers the crisis months. This is particularly important for famines that are related to harvest conditions, with a harvest year spanning from July to June in the following calendar year. We also need to know the normal levels of mortality at the time. The H&D intensity scales relate to modern societies, where normal levels of mortality are around eight deaths per thousand population (in 2021, 6.8 per thousand in Ethiopia and 11.6 per thousand in Somalia). This is less than a third of what they were in Russia on the eve of World War I (WW1) and less than a half on the eve of World War 2 (WW2). This will not greatly influence the higher stages of the famine spectrum where we can accept the H&D mortality levels, but for lower levels it is more appropriate for us to scale down the HD ratios above their normal level to fit in with these famine levels. The rates have been worked out on a per thousand per year basis for different normal mortality levels in Table 3.1.

Finally, a few words about the expression 'extra-ordinary measures', which is a term very familiar in Soviet history because of its relationship to the Extra-ordinary Commission (ChK) – a powerful political agency with a dreadful history. The ChK was empowered to carry

Table 3.1 Comparison of classifications of intensity of hunger related to annualized mortality rates for modern and historical periods according to different durations of food crisis

	Mortalities per thousand per year			*Multiples of normal death rates*		
	H&D Modern	*Soviet Union 1940*	*Russia 1913*	*H&D Modern*	*Soviet Union 1940*	*Russia 1913*
Normal	10	20	30	1	1	1
1-Insecure	10–18	20–28	30–35	1.8	1.4	1.2
2-Food Crisis	18–37	28–40	35–40	3.7	2	1.3
3-Famine	37–180	40–180	40–180	18	9	6
4-Severe Famine	180–550	180–550	180–550	55	28	18
5-Extreme Famine	550+	550+	550+	55+	28+	18+

Sources: 'Modern', calculated from Howe and Devereux (2004); '1900–50', our estimates are based on the normal mortality figures for Russia in 1913 and the USSR in 1940, available in *Narodnoye Khozyaistvo SSSR v 1956g. (Statisticheskii sbornik)* Moscow 1956 p. 243 where the crude death rate in Russia in 1913 is given as 30.2 deaths per thousand and for the USSR in 1940 as 18.3 per thousand. We round these figures to give the normal rates for Russia in 1913 at 30 and in the USSR in 1939 at 20. The mortality rates for levels 3 to 5 are set the same as for the H&D scales. This results in multiple levels above normal for the USSR in 1940 at 9 and for Russia in 1913 at 6. Our levels 1 and 2 are fitted into the gap between the norm level and level 3 in proportion to the gaps between the H&D multiples and were then rounded.[6]

out extra-judicial repression against those accused of counter-revolutionary acts, sabotage and speculation in times when the state felt threatened by enemies and famine. The history of Soviet famines is more deeply connected to the history of extra-ordinary measures than is often realized.

This chapter is divided into five sections. The first four sections chronologically consider the history and the demography of the food crises of pre-1917, 1917–22, 1927–33, 1941–47. The final section critically looks at the explanations that have been and are currently used to explain the famines with special reference to recent debates on the 1932–33 famine.

Extreme hunger and famine in Russia before October 1917

Russia did not have a tradition of the central government providing relief for peasants in times of extreme hunger as occurred in Western Europe,[7] and this may explain why a separate word for famine never developed in these times.[8] Under serfdom, care for the peasants in times of hunger was the responsibility of the landowners and not the central government. The Tsar and his government were primarily concerned with the task of organizing grain supplies for the court, the army and the capital. Moscow was located in a food-deficit region, requiring large grain shipments up the Volga.

When Peter the Great moved the capital from Moscow to St. Petersburg in 1703, which was 800 kilometres further to the North in a region even more deficient in grain supplies and more difficult to provision, the government needed to provide the food supply. Initially, Peter levied a tax in kind on all landowners who were required to provide the necessary grain and transport it to St Petersburg.[9] This levy concept proved to be very inefficient and was quickly replaced by a monetary tax that was used to buy grain from private contractors, who arranged to buy the grain and transport it in bulk from places where it was cheaper to produce and transport. This resulted in the development of commercial landowner farms in favourable locations along the rivers in the producer regions. Later in the eighteenth century, Catherine the Great improved the northern food supply by building canals and by expanding agricultural production into the great fertile new black earth regions in the South of the country. This eventually led to an explosion in grain production and export, when railways linked these new supply areas to the ports and the Northern cities.

On the eve of WWI, the northern consumer region (NCR), which included the Moscow and St Petersburg Industrial regions, was annually requiring six million tons of grain and the military another million tons. This grain was provided by the three surplus producer regions: the central producer regions (CPR) of the Volga and Black-Earth Region; the southern producer region (SPR) of Ukraine and North Caucasus; and the eastern producer region (EPR) of Urals, Kazakhstan and Siberia.[10] In addition, the SPR also regularly exported large amounts of grain – about ten million tons a year – which was the main source of foreign capital used to purchase capital equipment needed to industrialize the country.

Although there had been some earlier attempts to develop a granary system capable of providing some relief in difficult years, it was only after the Emancipation of the serfs in 1861 that the state began taking on responsibility for caring for peasants that had earlier been assigned to serf owners. The earlier systems were reformed with the central government working with newly established local government agencies (*Zemstva*). As this coincided with the large expansion of grain production and marketings in the new lands in the south of Russia, it enabled large amounts of relief to be provided to the distressed peasants in the harvest failures in the CPR in 1892 and 1905. These were the first periods of local grain shortage and extreme hunger that received extra-ordinary relief,[11] which greatly reduced the elevated mortality that would have otherwise occurred. Ironically, there was little appreciation of the achievements of the Tsarist government's relief work at the time, although some historians have later noted its importance.[12]

WWI and the wartime blockades placed on food imports caused an enormous strain on food supply systems in all grain-importing countries. But the crisis was totally unexpected in Russia, where the government expected the cessation of exports would result in a glut of about ten million tons of grain per year and a reduction in its price. The increase in demand for grain by the army from one million tons to three million tons in the first year of the war, and then rising to six million tons in 1916, was expected to offset only a fraction of the unexported grain. In the patriotic fervour of war, the government and the army were suspicious of the Jewish and foreign firms of private grain traders who normally handled the grain trade and military provisioning. They took the extra-ordinary decision of trying to bypass the private traders and deal directly with the producers to buy the additional three million tons of grain at what they thought would be a low but appropriate price. In doing this, they co-opted into their service the agricultural and statistical specialists in the local zemstvo, which had the effect of disarming in advance a potentially dangerous political group that had been active in the 1905 Revolution.

The government, on the orders of the Tsar and against all economic advice, also took the extra-ordinarily unwise decision of introducing abstinence for the duration of the war.[13] The government therefore lost an extremely important revenue item, at a time when government expenditure was greatly increasing. The only way that increased military expenditure could be paid for was by printing more money, and this introduced an inflationary pressure causing all prices to rise, including grain prices.

When grain prices began to rise and the new state procurement agencies found it difficult to buy grain at the official low price, the army was given the right to impose a form of martial law on the grain supply regions and to forbid the inter-regional transport of private grain, until state collections had been completed.[14] The result of this action was to greatly disrupt the normal inter-regional grain transfers to the civilian population in the NCR. When in the autumn of 1916 the food crisis for the civilian population in the NCR increased as a result of private traders being unable to get sufficient priority on the overworked transport system to transport their grain, the Minister of Agriculture took the next extra-ordinary step of declaring a monopoly on inter-regional grain transfers and taking over the entire supply of the civilian population of the NCR as well as the army. There was an immediate increase in state grain procurements from the 1916 harvest, which was much larger than the state procurements from the 1914 and 1915 harvests. However, it was insufficient to cover all the additional requirements of the civilian population. Petrograd was placed on rations causing food riots to break out that led to the February Revolution and the collapse of the Tsarist Empire.

The Russian historian Neferov has been one of the few historians to note the significance of the prevalence of widespread hunger in the events leading up to the Russian Revolution of 1917.[15] After the February Revolution, the Provisional government was hampered by its continued involvement in the war and its delays in resolving the agrarian problem. Meanwhile, nationalism was leading to the splintering of the former Russian Empire. The loss of Finland, Poland and the Baltic Provinces, which were all grain deficit regions, would only ease the grain supply problem. However, the loss of Ukraine, with the authority of the Central Rada first recognized by the Provisional Government in July 1917, would seriously reduce available supplies of grain.

The early Soviet famines of war and revolution, 1917–22

The Bolshevik Soviet Government took power in 1917 amid these extra-ordinary urban food problems, which had been caused by policies pursued by the Tsarist government. Lenin, the leader of the Bolsheviks, had initially, and with good reason, refused to support the peasant seizure of land from the large estates, which would inevitably lead to the breakup of the commercial farms that largely fed the complex but essential inter-regional grain transfers. But in the end, realizing it was inevitable and that opposing it would be massively unpopular, he changed his policy and opportunistically supported a move that would greatly complicate future Northern supplies. At the same time, he declared the end of the war and accepted the spontaneous disbanding of an army that they could not feed. Finally, early in 1918, the capital was moved back to Moscow, making it easier to feed its large population. When the Bolsheviks pulled out of the Great War with Germany and Austria, the British and French moved to prevent the armaments that they had supplied to Russia from falling into German hands by occupying parts of Russia and extending the blockade to Russia.

The food supply to the army and the large NCR, already severely strained, would deteriorate as civil war and intervention disturbed inter-regional supplies of grain. Instead of the six million tons of grain required from the three producer regions, the civil war disrupted supplies from SPR, EPR and, for a while, from parts of CPR. The situation was particularly serious for Petrograd/Leningrad, the capital and the largest city, which was in the north of the NCR and particularly distant from potential food supply regions.

Levels of famine were registered in Petrograd above the famine threshold of 40 per thousand for three whole years: in 1918 at 45 deaths per thousand population per year, in 1919 at 72 deaths per thousand per year and in 1920 still above famine level but down to 49 deaths per thousand per year. The monthly data show above 40 per thousand levels in 14 months from July 1918 to August 1919, with a peak in April 1919 at 95 deaths per thousand population. There was then a slight reduction below famine levels for two months after the harvest of 1919 (34/1,000 in September 1919 and 38/1,000 in October 1919) before resuming a spell of seven more months above 40 from November 1919 to May 1920, peaking in February 1920 at 91 per thousand. Moscow during this period only registered famine mortality for one calendar year 1919, at 45 deaths per thousand per year. In monthly terms, Moscow mortality exceeded 40 deaths per thousand for the similar two periods, with a larger break at the time of harvest. This was for nine months from October 1918 to June 1919, with a peak at 68 in March 1919 and with a break below 40 for the four months of July to October 1919. Then, from November 1919 until March 1920, there was a continuation of mortality above 40 levels.[16]

Petrograd, with a population initially over 2 million people, was the worst affected city in the NCR. The entire urban population in the NCR comprised 5.1 million people, according to the 1920 census. An estimated excess mortality of 20 per thousand for three years would therefore amount to about 300,000 excess deaths in the NCR, which qualifies as a great famine. An elevated mortality of 10 per thousand in the local rural population (20 million people according to the 1920 census) would amount to a further 2 million excess deaths, which qualifies as a catastrophic famine. However, mortality at this time was also greatly affected by pandemic illnesses, especially cholera and typhus, which complicates the picture.[17]

There was little that could be done to stabilize the situation whilst the Bolsheviks faced Civil and Interventionist wars, supported by a blockade and massive assistance of arms and munitions from Britain and France. When the blockade came to an end on 16 March 1921, Lenin immediately took steps to partially restore the market by replacing the requisitioning policy with a tax in kind and allowing peasants to engage in limited local trade with their remaining grain (the New Economic Policy: NEP). Significantly, international trade and inter-regional trade between surplus producer regions and consumer regions would remain in the hands of the state. Had the weather for the 1921 Soviet harvest been fine the famines may have ended and Soviet history would have been very different.

The serious drought during the late spring and early summer of 1921, coming at a time when the countryside was bereft of its reserves following earlier requisitions, produced another more serious famine in the Central Producer Regions. It came at a time when the northern cities were coming out of famine and were already beginning to recover their populations and when the government had partly restored the grain collection mechanism and was in the process of changing its procurement policy. The role of the Anglo-Soviet Trade Agreement (1921), the lifting of the blockade, and the receipt of American food aid were crucial factors in providing relief to a situation that would have been much worse without them.[18]

Saratov was, at the time, the largest town in the Volga in the worst affected area during the southern famine. Its mortality levels had been high in earlier years because of the spread of epidemic illnesses, but following the drought in 1921 mortality rose to severe famine levels, with 67 deaths per thousand of the population in 1921, and to extreme famine levels, with 83 deaths per thousand in 1922.[19] The area covered by the 1921–22 famine had a population of about 31 million in the CPR and another 12 million in SPR and with excess mortality rates for this whole area above 10 per thousand the magnitude of excess deaths probably reached 5 million. It far exceeded the scale of the great Northern famine, and both should be classified as catastrophic famines, with an overall duration of four years.

Extreme food shortages from 1927 and famine in 1932–33

The food problems of 1927–33 differed from problems in the earlier famine period because they occurred in peacetime. At the same time, they followed a similar pattern of northern urban food problems followed by a southern rural famine after harvest failures, which were partly weather-induced. The main causes of the food crisis that began in the autumn of 1927 and culminated in the famine of 1932–33 were the Soviet government's attempts to collect too much grain at low prices, to ignore the changed conjuncture on the market caused by poor weather and lower grain yields, and to continue using exaggerated planning figures and ignore objective assessments of the real level of grain production. Aspects of the conjunctural problem have been well documented.[20] Here we will concentrate on the fundamental planning problems that tragically became the modus operandi of the way the Stalinist system handled the grain problem.

Exaggerations in planning potential were partly the results of the extra-ordinary scientific enthusiasm that had already begun to bear fruit in Western Europe, with fertilizers and improved agricultural methods raising yields significantly and expecting them to increase even more in the future. The Soviet's first five-year plan under Stalin projected an increase in Soviet grain yields by 35 per cent (more than an extra 30 million tons), which would have solved the grain problem.[21] This increase was to be achieved by using simple and inexpensive ways of improving agrotechnology. Given the low level of Soviet grain yields of the time, and the achievements of increasing yields in Western Europe, it was not unrealistic to assume that some dramatic improvements could be made. But the scale of expectations, and the presumption that they could be made with little or no expense, was completely unrealistic.

Nevertheless, despite the objections of statisticians and agricultural specialists, unrealistic plans were forced through the government by the Workers-Peasant Inspectorate and a group of politically favoured fanatics who quickly moved into key economic positions and determined the dangerous and rash style of running the economy.[22] Additionally, there was a real problem of over-estimation of the grain yield, as corrections were applied to compensate for alleged underestimation of visual assessments of yields. Government officials, supported by enthusiastic inspectorate officials, went too far and forced the statisticians to overcompensate. This over-estimation of planning possibilities and distortion of the agricultural potential reality were, at the time, denounced by the statistical leader N. Osinskii as 'plan-constructivism'.[23] This combination of excessive planning targets and exaggerated claims of agricultural production became an important aspect of the Stalin planning system that contributed greatly to the tragedy of the famine of 1932–33 and also to the subsequent famine of 1946–47.

In terms of dimension, the 1932–33 famine was at its most intense for a shorter duration than the 1918–22 famine. The threatening food problem in the NCR, in 1927–33, never developed into a famine. Annual mortality levels in Moscow were secretly reported to have risen by over 26 per cent from 13 per thousand per year in 1928 to 16 per thousand in 1931. This did cause the government great concern but, despite the large percentage growth, it did not qualify as a food crisis level in our classification. However, this was at a time when all demographic statistics were secret and when there were great pressures to conceal embarrassing statistics, so the real level may have been higher. In the following years, as mortality rates rose in SPR, the rate in Moscow city is reported to have fallen to 15 per thousand in 1932 and 1933. Furthermore, 1933 is a period when we think that demographic statistics became more reliable than earlier.[24]

While the demographic statistics became slightly more reliable after 1932, they still remained secret. These more reliable secret statistics showed annual mortality in Ukraine rising overall from 16 per thousand per year in 1931 to 21 in 1932 and to well over famine levels at 61 per thousand in 1933; the rural levels went even higher at 70 per thousand. The situation differed by oblast, with low below-famine levels in the industrial Donetsk and with the highest levels not in the main grain-producing oblasts of the south (Odesa and Dnepropetrovsk) but in Kyiv and Kharkiv oblasts, where the two largest cities were located. Mortality in Kyiv oblast rose from 16 in 1931 to 26 (crisis level) in 1932 and 97 in 1933 – more than double the base famine level of 40. However, the annual rate for Kyiv city was much lower, and by some reports just below 40. Monthly rates (in annual equivalents) in Kyiv oblast rose above famine levels of 40 per thousand per year for seven months from January to July 1933, and above 180, at severe famine levels, for three months: 209 per thousand in May 1933, 316 in June 1933 and 206 in July 1933. The highest monthly figure for Kyiv city was 'only' 67 per thousand in March 1933. In the Lower Volga Krai, annual mortality in 1933 was also well above famine levels at 59 per thousand per year, and here the rate for Saratov city (the largest town in the Lower Volga) was only slightly lower than the rural rate at 56 per thousand. In the final section, we provide an explanation for the high mortality rates in Kyiv oblast and relatively lower rates in Kyiv city.

Since we are dealing with high famine mortality rates for most of Ukraine with a population of about 30 million, we end up estimating the famine to be of catastrophic magnitude of 3–4 million deaths for Ukraine and 5–6 million for all of the USSR. Unlike in previous famines, this famine was far less associated with infectious diseases and more so with direct starvation.

Extreme food shortages from 1941 to 1947 and famines in 1942–43 and 1946–47

The 1946–47 postwar famine was linked to the wartime food problems in a similar way as the urban and rural famines of 1918–22 and 1927–33. There were initial severe supply problems in NCR, and especially in besieged Leningrad, as Germany pursued a genocidal policy of occupying and disrupting the normal transfers of supplies from the main grain surplus-producing regions in the South and Centre. This was followed by a rural crisis in parts of the formerly surplus areas when very poor weather produced a harvest failure in 1946 and a famine in the first half of 1947.[25]

In the first three desperate years of the war, from 1941 to 1944, the German and Romanian occupation of Ukraine and Moldova had forced the bulk of the burden for feeding the Red Army and the unoccupied parts of the NCR onto the unoccupied parts of the CPR and the EPR. However, in 1944, after its liberation the SPR was immediately required to resume its role as a major grain supplier to the NCR allowing the CPR and EPR to recover. The Soviet government's decision to export 2.1 million tons of grain in 1944 and 1945 was a grave mistake. This excessive extraction of grain from Moldovan SSR and Ukrainian SSR in 1944–45 and 1945–46, at a time of weakness, placed them at great risk, especially when combined with attempts in 1946 to reduce the scale of private plots, which had been so advantageous in earlier periods of crisis. When drought struck in the Southwest, these areas faced famine.[26]

Mortality rates in the German and Romanian occupied parts of the USSR, where genocidal policies were carried out, would undoubtedly have been very high, but data are not available. Data are available for the besieged civilian population of Leningrad, where annual mortality for 1942 rose to 260 deaths of civilian population per thousand population per year, which places it high in the severe famine category of intensity (above 180) and more than twice as high as any levels recorded anywhere in the Soviet Union in the previous famine periods. The monthly data show severe famine levels for nine months from December 1941 to July 1942, with the highest rate of 1,126 in February 1942 – double the extreme famine threshold of 550. The extreme famine level was exceeded in four months, from January to April 1942, with levels above 500 in December 1941 and in May 1942. The annual mortality rate for Moscow, the main town in NCR that was not besieged, rose from 20 per thousand in 1941 to 36 per thousand in 1942, which was high on the food crisis level, but below our famine limit of 40 per thousand.

Most unoccupied parts of the USSR had similar levels of hunger-related mortality that only periodically rose to famine levels in places of refugee concentration and in locations recently under enemy occupation. Kyiv city registered 50 deaths per thousand population per year in 1944 and Kishinev registered 46 in 1945, although this was partly due to typhus and other epidemic illnesses. The only other towns to register famine mortality levels in annual data well after liberation were Kishinev (Moldovan SSR) and Izmail (Ukrainian SSR) during the 1947 famine.

During the 1946–47 crisis, famine levels of mortality were only recorded in the Moldovan SSR at 81 deaths per thousand per year and in some of the new parts of Western Ukraine, specifically in Izmail oblast with rates of 69. The monthly data show ten months above 40 in Moldovan SSR from December 1946 to August 1947, with two peaks in February 1947 at 160 and then after a small fall again in June 1947 at 157. Izmail oblast had nine months above 40, with an even higher single peak of 178 in March 1947. In both locations, the main cities Kishinev and Izmail had mortality rates lower than for the larger area as a whole – for Moldovan SSR and Kishinev with a significant difference (81 for Moldovan SSR and 49 for Kishinev), but for Izmail a much smaller difference (69 for the oblast and 65 for the city). Across all of the USSR, there were about 700,000 more deaths registered in the famine year of 1947 compared to the non-famine year of 1948, when population numbers were relatively stable and in the absence of epidemics, a disparity we are currently investigating. Of these, 270,000 deaths were in Ukrainian SSR and 130,000 in Moldovan SSR.

Explanations for extreme hunger and famines in Russia and the USSR

Political factors have undoubtedly played a major role in the reasoning given to explain extreme hunger and famine. This is because there is a political advantage to be gained by blaming disasters and catastrophes on your enemies. Those who want an explanation in order to blame someone should be treated with great caution.

The history of the blame game in relation to the famines is clear: the Bolsheviks blamed the Tsarist government, White guards, kulaks, Ukrainians, and other 'bourgeois' nationalists for the early famines, whilst the anti-Bolsheviks blamed the Bolsheviks for all famines. The German and Romanian invaders looked for an excuse to increase the feelings of blame against the

Bolsheviks and incite anti-Bolshevik and Nationalist forces, during WWII. Future nationalists, years after these events, blamed the anti-nationalist policies of the Bolsheviks for the 1932–33 and 1946–47 famines. We do not rule out the fact faulty Tsarist government policies, resistance to the Bolsheviks, and Bolshevik repressive policies against peasants and especially against Ukrainians all played a role – they certainly did, at different times in different places and to different extents. The questions are to assess the relative importance of these different factors, how they interacted over time in different places, and, even more importantly, to ask whether the outcome of famine would have occurred without them.

Following the opening of the Soviet archives and the appearance of much secret demographic, economic and political material from the late 1980s we were able to get a much more complete and better understanding of why these famines occurred. Most attention, so far, has been paid to explaining the 1932–33 famine. Twenty years ago, Davies and Wheatcroft used the newly available archival material to produce a major explanation of the combination of factors that operated over a sequence of harvest crises to culminate in the famine of 1932–33.[27] They described the conjuncture of factors contributing to the mounting crises and the errors in policy that were caused by ignorance, conceit, ruthlessness, and reluctance to admit mistakes. In their conclusions, they stated that, after their thorough research of all the available archival evidence, they disagreed with the conclusions of Robert Conquest, who was cited to have claimed that the famine was caused on purpose.[28] After reading a pre-publication, Conquest agreed with Davies and Wheatcroft that the available data did not indicate that the famine was caused intentionally and requested them to clarify his position that he did not think that the famine was caused by Stalin intentionally but 'that with resulting famine imminent, he [Stalin] could have prevented it, but put "Soviet interest" other than feeding the starving first – thus consciously abetting it'.[29]

At this point and for the next decade, it looked as though academic opinion was agreeing on the complex causes of the 1932–33 famine. In 2017, in the introduction to their authoritative survey of the history of European famines, Cormac Ó Gráda and Guido Alfani referred to the recent 'voluminous literature' presenting the 'famines ravaging Ukraine in 1931–33 and Moldova in 1946–47 as deliberately engineered for political reasons by the Soviet authorities' with the writings on the Irish famine, and commented: 'In the case of Ireland, this view was once influential in nationalist rhetoric, but the verdict of modern scholarship is much more nuanced'.[30] At the time, Ó Gráda and Alfani stated that:

> in the case of Ukraine, most recent literature has tempered this interpretation, suggesting instead that, although Stalin and the Soviet government did indeed take decisions that exacerbated the consequences of poor harvests caused by adverse weather [...], the crises were not intentional but, rather the consequences of poor judgement.[31]

We would add, not just poor judgement, but the consequences of the modus operandi by which the system was being run. In other words, the political causes of the famines can be attributed to the systematic process of exaggerating possibilities, denying inconvenient reality, risking the lives of the vulnerable and covering up their deadly mistakes.

However, in recent years, the situation has changed and, as we will see below, there have been increasing claims that the famine was caused on purpose (often citing Conquest as a source for this claim) and that there was no real shortage of grain.[32] It is now widely claimed that the famine was a genocide. For a while, it was even claimed the Holodomor (the new name for the Ukrainian famine) was the largest genocide the world had ever seen, with over 7 million Ukrainian fatalities.[33] Fortunately, Ukrainian historians and demographers have been able to moderate the excessive claim of over 7 million fatalities and we should be grateful to them for that.

The claim that the famine was a genocide had been adopted by Ukrainian Emigres in Canada as soon as the concept of genocide was invented and accepted by the United Nations in 1948. Pressure mounted within the Ukrainian community both for the adoption of a special word, *holodomor*, to describe the 1932–33 hunger instead of *holod*, and not just to call it a famine, but to call it a genocide. James Mace promoted this idea in America as the executive director of the U.S. Commission on the Ukraine famine (1986–90) and in the USIA publication *Problems of Communism* where it was firmly rebuffed.[34] The idea did not catch on at the time with the American academic community. Mace was replaced as the author of a major commissioned volume for the Harvard Ukrainian Research Institute by the slightly more moderate Robert Conquest and eventually left the USA for Ukraine in 1993, where there was more support for his ideas.[35]

The idea of the *Holodomor* as a genocide of over 7 million deaths was promoted by Ukrainian President Viktor Yushchenko after the Orange Revolution in 2004 and became more popular later, after the Maidan Uprising of 2014. The genocide idea was promoted by Ukrainian nationalist politicians as an event of key importance in Ukrainian national identity. They have consequently attempted to separate the understanding of the Holodomor from the history of food problems, even going as far as to deny that there was a food problem. Other Ukrainian historians have attempted a more sophisticated compromise suggesting that there was a union-wide food problem, but that at a key moment in the autumn of 1932 the all-union food problem took on a more sinister significance in Ukraine as a genocidal famine.[36]

Our studies have shown that the autumn of 1932 was the point at which the all-union food crisis became a famine, which in regions like Kyiv Oblast became a severe famine for six months. This was the time when the food crisis was intensifying all over the USSR, and mortality rates rose to over 40 per cent for several months in several regions. There was certainly a bias against Ukraine at this time, and Soviet politicians were quick to blame anyone who drew attention to the famine occurring in Ukraine at that time as Ukrainian Nationalists, but this does not mean that the famine was being caused on purpose.

As these arguments were mounting in the year before the Maidan Uprising, Wheatcroft and his collaborators argued in two rival conferences of Ukrainian historians in Kyiv in the autumn of 2013 that explanations of the famine needed to take into account the location and timing of mortality excesses and presented detailed rayon (district-level) maps and graphs of monthly mortality to demonstrate this.[37] It is a sign of the internal Ukrainian political conflict of the time that there were only two historians who attended both of these conferences.

The maps produced by the Wheatcroft team showed that, contrary to many claims, famine levels of mortality did not dramatically fall from rayon to rayon when crossing the Ukrainian border to Russia and that it was not highest in the main regions of central grain procurement, where the 'blacklisted'[38] villages and farms were located.[39] Instead, the highest levels of mortality were in Kyiv Oblast in its southern rayons, with very sharp downward changes at its borders with Vinnytsia and Odesa Oblasts, which were both more important for central grain procurements. Wheatcroft suggested that an explanation for the higher mortality in these regions might well be the fact that Kyiv Oblast contained Kyiv city – the largest urban concentration in Ukraine – and that its allocation of central grain supplies had been cut as a result of the grain procurement plan not being fulfilled.[40] In these circumstances, the Kyiv Oblast party committee would have needed to organize de-centralized collections of grain to feed Kyiv city to avoid it having mortality levels higher than in the rural areas of Kyiv Oblast. Naturally, the Kyiv committee could only operate within their own oblast. This is an explanation that fits the facts.

Serhii Plokhy, the prominent American Ukrainian historian and director of the Ukrainian Research Institute at Harvard University (HURI), Oleh Wolowyna, and other leading Ukrainian demographers who were all at the Academy of Sciences Conference in Kyiv have responded to this argument in a series of articles on regional and monthly famine losses.[41] Plokhy and the demographers agree that our figure of up to 6 million deaths overall with about a half in Ukraine. They also agree that the rise in mortality in Ukraine was less serious in the major grain collecting regions than in Kyiv oblast and that the reason for this needs to be explained. However, Plokhy claims that there were more blacklistings in Kyiv Oblast than in other Ukrainian oblasts.[42] Plokhy has now turned the previous argument about the famine being focused on the main grain collection regions on its head and argues that the relatively lower mortality there could have been a result of more state aid being directed to grain collection areas.

Our critics fail to note that the mortality rate for Kyiv city (in 1933 at 38–40 deaths per thousand per year, rising to a monthly peak of 67 in annual equivalents) is relatively low, and, by our definition, qualifies as a food crisis level mortality and not as famine level mortality. By contrast, the rural mortality rate in Kyiv Oblast was 99 deaths per thousand per year, rising to a monthly peak of 316 in annual equivalents in June 1933. This was significantly more than the city rate and qualifies as a severe famine level – even higher than the highest level recorded in the 1918–21 famine period. The exceptional nature of Kyiv city mortality being so low in comparison with rural areas can be seen by comparing it with the situation in the Lower Volga, where rural mortality rates at 59 per thousand in 1933 were only about 6 per cent higher than the rates in its largest city Saratov, which registered a famine rate of 56 per thousand that same year. The conclusion that blacklisting was not such a major cause of the extra-ordinary famine mortality thus still stands.

In any case, to invalidate the argument that it was de-centralized collections of grain used in urban locations within the oblast that were the direct cause of high mortality and not the centralized collections that were to be shipped out to Moscow, it would be necessary to distinguish between blacklistings ordered by the central grain collection agencies and those ordered by local officials. The data that Plokhy cites on the HURI Historical Atlas gives no such breakdown. Plokhy has also claimed that our hypothesis has not been substantiated by evidence on the special policies adopted by Kyiv officials and that it does not take into account the fact that not all areas of Kyiv Oblast suffered equally, nor that many rayons of Kharkiv Oblast suffered at similar levels.[43] In response, it is important to point out that there was no need for a special policy on de-centralized collections because they, and using milling levies, were part of the system by which local urban areas were expected to feed themselves. In 1933, the amount of grain received from the milling levy would have been very small[44] and, consequently, local leaders would have needed to place greater emphasis on the de-centralized collections.

The fact that there was also high mortality in parts of Kharkiv oblast does not weaken this argument. Although Kharkiv had more industry that was managed by the All-Union Ministries and therefore received better supplies than Kyiv, it still faced a greater shortage of grain supply from central collections compared to the more favoured Industrial and Mining region of Donetsk Oblast whose industrial workers and miners received full central supplies. Additionally, Kharkiv had a greater need for urban supplies than oblasts with smaller cities, making decentralized collections more important there as well. Of course, this does not deny the fact that too much grain had previously been withdrawn from these oblasts by the central collectors, which was key to causing the famine. However, if the grain was being taken from the Ukrainian countryside to feed the starving Ukrainian cities, then it does complicate the genocidal argument.

More recently, econometricians Andrei Markevich, Natasha Naumenko and Nancy Qian (MNQ) have published a widely distributed NBER Working Paper[45] that, despite the complex and impressive-looking detailed workings that it contains, fails to make any real progress in improving our understanding in three areas that it addresses: (1) It presents an incorrect description of the controversy over the causation of Ukrainian famine mortality; (2) it makes misleading claims about the availability of grain in the famine period in Ukraine and the USSR as a whole, together with the astonishing claim that weather was not an important factor in the famine; and (3) it makes unjustifiable claims about the intentionality of a government policy of anti-Ukrainian bias, which it suggests is responsible for 92 per cent of famine deaths in Ukraine. The paper may well have identified a widespread level of correlation between declared Ukrainian ethnicity in 1926 and elevated mortality in 1933, which might be a sign of anti-Ukrainian bias in the way the political system worked, but this tells us nothing about intentionality.

The paper begins by noting the existence of controversy over excess Ukrainian mortality, which they see in stark terms as being between those like Conquest, who 'believe that the famine was a "terror" intentionally waged by the Soviet government against Ukraine', and those like Davies and Wheatcroft, 'who argue that the high famine mortality in Ukraine was an unintended consequence of policies with no inherent anti- Ukrainian bias'.[46] This claim needs to be corrected on both sides. The positions of Conquest and Davies/Wheatcroft are far closer than MNQ claim. As we have mentioned above, Conquest made it perfectly clear in 2003 that he did not think that Stalin had purposely inflicted famine on the Ukrainians. Wheatcroft and Davies, in their conclusion in 2004, had stated that they did 'not at all absolve Stalin from responsibility for the famine. His policies towards the peasants were ruthless and brutal'. And that the famine had been caused by a complex of factors that included 'wrongheaded policies', 'the modus operandi of the Soviet system as it was established under Stalin'. Russian history, the experience of the civil war, the international situation, the intransigent circumstances of geography and weather and, above all, the decision to industrialize the country at breakneck speed were all partly responsible for causing the famine.[47]

MNQ are presenting an incorrect account of a conflict, which doesn't exist in the way they claim. Wheatcroft agrees with most of Conquest's reformulation of his views, apart from the claim that 'he [Stalin] could have prevented it'. The problems are to question at what stage could he have prevented it? And at what cost? There is no doubt that when it came to the crunch of who would be most favourably treated in a desperate situation, Stalin and the political leadership would ensure that the Northern cities were fed first, before Ukraine. The main difference in views on the famine is not about whether there was bias or not, but about whether the famine was intentionally caused or not. Having examined the evidence Conquest announced that he was on the same side as Davies and Wheatcroft. Many of those who claim there was an intention to cause a famine (including MNQ) are very eager to recruit Conquest into their camp and deny his defection.

Following the introduction, the MNQ paper presents a simple food accounting balance that attempts to show that there was no grain shortage in 1932–33. Unlike earlier versions of their paper that had used highly unreliable official harvest figures their balances in the 2023 and 2024 versions now use corrected figures which show a per capita level of grain production of 0.79 kg per person per day in 1932 in Ukraine and 1 kg per person per day in USSR less UkSSR. They compare these figures with the normed grain consumption figure for heavy labourers (0.78 kg per person per day) and claim that this shows that there should have been no grain shortage. The problem with this argument is that it fails to recognize that about 10 per cent of grain would always be required for seed and that about 30 per cent would regularly be required for livestock feed. It is therefore simply wrong to argue that there was no grain problem in these years. Table 3.2 compares the MNQ figures on grain availability with those calculated with seed and livestock feed allocations deducted.

Table 3.2 Grain availability in Ukraine SSR and in USSR less UkSSR, 1930 and 1932

Ukraine	*Population*	*Production*	*Seed*	*Livestock feed*	*Net*	*Tons per cap per year*	*Kgms per cap per day*	*Heavy labour norm*
UkSSR								
1930	30.8	23.2	2.3	7	13.9	0.45	1.24	0.78
1932								
(a) 1930 level seed and feed	31.3	8.1	2.3	7	−1.2	−0.04	−0.10	0.78
(b) 1930 est	31.3	8.1	1	3	4.1	0.13	0.36	0.78
(c) MNQ	31.3	8.1	0	0	8.1	0.26	0.71	0.78
USSR-UkSSR								
1930	126.7	60.1	6	38	16.1	0.13	0.35	0.78
1932								
(a) 1930 level seed and feed	131.5	48	6	38	4	0.03	0.08	0.78
(b) 1930 est	131.5	48	4	20	24	0.18	0.50	0.78
(c) MNQ	131.5	48	0	0	48	0.37	1.00	0.78

The more realistic versions of the grain balance show that in 1930 per capita grain production in UkSSR less the amount needed for seed and livestock feed left 1.24 kilogram per person per day for food, which was well above the amount needed for heavy labour norm. So no signs in 1930 of grain shortage. But in 1932, with the low level of grain production, if the 1930 levels of seed and livestock feed had been deducted nothing would have been left for human consumption. If the amounts of grain used as seed were reduced to more realistic levels, the amount of grain left for human consumption would only have been half of the heavy labour norm. This presents signs of grain shortage. MNQ makes the impossible assumption that no grain was used as seed or livestock feed, and that is the basis of their argument for claiming that there was no grain shortage in Ukraine.

Similarly for USSR less UkSSR, the per capita grain production in 1930 less seed and livestock feed resulted in only half of the heavy labour norm level. If the 1930 level seed and feed allocations were deducted from the 1932 level of grain production, then per capita levels of production net of these seed and feed levels would leave about a tenth of the heavy labour norm. If more realistic reduced levels of seed and feed were applied, per capita levels left for human consumption would be about 36 per cent below the heavy labour norm. Again, it takes the MNQ presumption of no sowings and no livestock to exceed the heavy labour norm by 28 per cent, but this is an impossible scenario.

Regarding their proof that there is a correlation between high mortality and high proportion of Ukrainians in the population at the rayon and oblast levels inside and outside Ukraine, we repeat the statement made four years ago at the Wisconsin Workshop that they may well be correct, but such a bias is more likely to be a result of the way the system and local officials worked than a conscious state policy. There is no doubt that there was a conscious state policy of political repression against Ukrainians during the famine in 1933 – the rolling back of Ukrainization which led to the arrest of thousands with many executed by the state in the Terror of 1937 – as there was in other republics.[48] We need to understand the complex interplay between this repression mostly in urban areas, broader repression against Ukrainian peasants protesting collectivization in the countryside and hunger, instead of postulating a conscious state policy to starve Ukrainians

Finally, concerning the weather, Naumenko's modelling indicates a high correlation between her weather variables and yield variations, as did Wheatcroft's earlier study 40 years ago.[49] If grain production was critically low in these years, as indicated in the corrected Table 3.2 then poor weather caused high losses of grain production in 1932 (too much dampness at harvest time), and a very low level of grain production in 1931(drought and excessive heat during flowering and filling out stages of plant phenology) would result in an overall reduction in local reserves, which would certainly impact the famine. But the deaths would not necessarily be in the areas of harvest shortfall. If the MNQ models were looking for a simple relationship between separate variables of mortality and grain yield and were not capturing the complex reality of the system, then the failure of their model to show these relationships seems more likely to be demonstrating a failure in their model rather than that weather causing harvest failures and losses were not contributing to the food problem and famine. Overall, their models may have shown that there was some local anti-Ukrainian bias in the way the Soviet system worked, but they have not shown that it was intentionally placed there by policy, and their suggestion that there was no shortage of grain and that weather was unimportant is demonstrably false.

Conclusion

Recently, and especially since Russia's terrible full-scale invasion of Ukraine in 2022, there has been a great surge of writings supporting the official Ukrainian government's claim that the famine was a genocide intended to destroy any idea of Ukrainian nationhood. Our survey finds the Soviet famines emerged from a complex interplay of numerous factors, within a long-established and growing food problem scenario in which state policies and especially its 'modus operandi' were major causes. Soviet leaders' attitudes and, at times, specific policies toward Ukraine can help to explain the severity of famine there, but we find little evidence that the state intentionally used famine as a means to kill Ukrainians as a specific ethnic group as per the Ukrainian government's claims. We also disagree with a range of other qualifications put forward by some scholars, which aim to satisfy different definitions of genocide. We note the extreme and catastrophic levels of hunger-related mortality with their peaks in the city of Leningrad in 1919 and 1942 and in the rural areas of Ukraine and especially Kyiv Oblast in 1933, with parts of Moldova and Ukraine reaching extreme famine levels in their peaks in 1947. We have attempted to clarify the situation by objectifying the classification of famine and other spectra of hunger and by relating the 1932–33 famine to other periods of food problem and hunger in this troubled period.

Notes

1 'Research for this chapter was assisted work funded by the Australian Research Council (ARC) for Discovery Project, "The Last Soviet Famine, 1946/47: Drought and food crises in war's aftermath" (DP210100278).'

2 There was also a serious famine in Kazakhstan in 1929–33 associated with the forced settlement of the nomads, which has been discussed elsewhere. See Robert Kindler, *Stalin's Nomads: Power and Famine in Kazakhstan,* University of Pittsburgh Press, 2018; and Sarah Cameron, *The Hungry Steppe: Famine, Violence, and the Making of Soviet Kazakhstan*, Cornel University Press, 2018; and S.G. Wheatcroft, 'The Complexity of the Kazakh Famine: Food Problems and Faulty Perceptions', *Journal of Genocide Research* (2021): 23.

3 For further discussion of this, see A.S. Ermolov, *Nashi Neurozhai i prodovol'stvennii vopros*, St. Petersburg, 1909; A. Lindenmeyer, *Poverty Is Not Vice: Charity, Society and the State in Imperial Russia*, Princeton University Press, 1996.
4 Paul Howe and Stephen Devereux, 'Famine Intensity and Magnitude Scales: A Proposal for an Instrumental Definition of Famine', *Disasters* (2004): 28: 4: 353–72.
5 Wheatcroft first began annualizing monthly mortality data in his comparisons of the urban famines of 1918–20 in his SIPs discussion papers in the 1970s and 1980s. See S.G. Wheatcroft, 'Population Dynamic and Factors Affecting It in the Soviet Union in the 1920s and 1930s', Birmingham University, Centre for Russian and East European Studies Discussion Papers, SIPS nos 1–2 (Birmingham, 1976); and S.G. Wheatcroft, 'Famine and Factors Affecting Mortality in the USSR: The Demographic Crises of 1914–1922 and 1930–33', SIPS nos 21–22 (Birmingham, 1982).
6 These stages are similar to the scales subsequently adopted by the UN-accredited IPC. See IPC Global Partners. 2021 Integrated Food Security Phase Classification Technical Manual Version 3.1. Evidence and Standards for Better Food Security and Nutrition Decisions. Rome FAO, p. 36.
7 A.S. Ermolov, *Nashi Neurozhai i prodovol'stvennii vopros*, St. Petersburg, 1909; A. Lindenmeyer, *Poverty Is Not Vice: Charity, Society and the State in Imperial Russia*, Princeton University Press, 1996.
8 See S.G. Wheatcroft, 'Famines', in W.H. McNeill, ed., *Berkshire Encyclopaedia of World History*, 2005, pp. 728–33; and S.G. Wheatcroft, 'Famine, Food Problems and Imperialism', in John M. MacKenzie (ed.), *The Encyclopedia of Empire*, John Wiley and Sons, 2016.
9 See Robert Jones, *Bread upon the Waters. The St. Petersburg Grain Trade and the Russian Economy, 1703–1811*, University of Pittsburg Press, 2013.
10 For a description of these regions and their pre-revolutionary development, see S.G. Wheatcroft, 'The Crises and the Condition of the Peasantry in Late Imperial Russia', in E. Kingston-Mann and T. Mixter (eds), *Peasant Economy, Culture and Politics of European Russia, 1800–1921*, Princeton University Press, 1991, pp. 128.
11 Earlier harvest failures of 1868, 1873, 1881 were even more severe in parts of NCR, especially in Finland and the Baltic provinces but were not recognized as famines at the time.
12 See R.G. Robbins, *Famine in Russia, 1891–1892: The Imperial Government Responds to a Crisis*, Columbia University Press, 1975; and S.G. Wheatcroft, 'The 1891-92 Famine in Russia: Towards a More Detailed Analysis of Its Scale and Demographic Significance', in L. Edmondson and P. Waldron (eds.), *Economy and Society in Russia and the Soviet Union, 1860–1930*, Macmillan, 1992, pp. 44–64.
13 See D. Christian, 'Prohibition in Russia, 1914–1925', *Australian Slavonic and East European Studies* (1995): 9: 2: 89–118.
14 See N.D. Kondratiev, *Rynok khlebov I ego regulirovanie vo vremya voiny I revolyutsii*, 1922 (reprinted 1991); and L.T. Lih, *Bread and Authority in Russia*, University of California Press, 1990, 1914–1921.
15 S. Neferov, 'Prodovol'stvennii krizis v Petrograde nakanune Fevlral'skoi revolyutsii', *Quaestio Rossica* (2017): 5: 3: 635–55.
16 The sources of data for the 1917–23 food crises were first listed in Wheatcroft 1976, 1982, and 1997 with graphs in Wheatcroft, 2017, p. 224.
17 See S.G. Wheatcroft, 1976, 1982 and 1983.
18 See H.H. Fisher, *The Famine in Soviet Russia, 1919–1923: The Operations of the American Relief Administration*, Stanford University Press, 1927.
19 See S.G.Wheatcroft, 'Famine and Epidemic Crises in Russia, 1918–1922: The Case of Saratov', *Annales de Demographie Historique* (1983): 329–353; S.G.Wheatcroft, 'Soviet Statistics of Nutrition and Mortality during times of Famine, 1917–1922 and 1931–33', *Cahiers du Monde russe* (1997): 38: 4: 1–34. Note we only have relatively reliable statistical data for mortality in the major towns in these years, and mortality in these towns may be inflated to some extent by them including deaths of refugees from other areas. In later years, steps were taken to exclude refugee mortality in the cities. See S.G. Wheatcroft, 'Pokazateli demograficheskogo krizisa v period goloda v SSSR' (Indicators of Demographic Crisis in the Soviet Famine), in *Golod v SSSR, 1929-33*, vol. 3, book 2, Moscow, 2013 [*Famine in USSR, 1929-33*].

20 See M. Lewin, *Russian Peasants and Soviet Power*, George Allen & Unwin, 1968; Alec Nove, *An Economic History of the USSR, 1917–1991*, Penguin, 1992; E.H. Carr and Davies, *The Foundations of a Planned Economy,* Macmillan, 1926–1929.

21 The planned increase in grain production from 73 million tons in 1927 to 106 million tons in 1932 would allow an additional 7.7 million tons of grain to be exported, an additional 2 million tons for urban, industrial and military use, and it would still leave an additional 18 million tons for the rural sector, which would be 27 per cent better off; *Pyatiletnii plan razvitiya Nar. Khoz. SSSR*, vol. 2, part 1, Moscow, 1929, p. 333.

22 The roles of Yu.Yakovlev, V. Kuibyshev, S. Ordzhonikidze and later N. Voznesenskii were most critical. See Davies and Wheatcroft, 1975, pp. 790–802; Wheatcroft, 2019, pp. 1013–35.

23 The claim was that as plans had to be fulfilled, the statisticians were under pressure to report fulfillment, even when it did not occur. For a history of harvest evaluations, see Wheatcroft, *Soviet Statistics under Stalinism*.

24 The reason for this has been explained many times, most recently in Wheatcroft 2019.

25 S.G. Wheatcroft, 'The Soviet Famine of 1946/47, the Weather and Human Agency in Historical Perspective', *Europe Asia Studies* (2012): 64: 6: 987–1005.

26 See F. Slaveski and S.G.Wheatcroft, *The Last Soviet Famine, 1946/47* (in progress).

27 Davies and Wheatcroft, *The Years of Hunger: Soviet Agriculture, 1931–1933*, Palgrave-Macmillan, 2004.

28 R. Conquest, *Hearing before the Committee on Foreignn Relations United States Senate, Ninety-Eighth Congress, Second Session, on S. 2456: A Bill to Establish a Commission to Study the 1932-33 Famine Caused by the Soviet Government in Ukraine*, Washington, DC, 1984: 45, 61; and R. Conquest, *The Harvest of Sorrow: Soviet Collectivization and the Terror Famin*e, London, 1986: 196.

29 Letter from Robert Conquest to Davies and Wheatcroft, September 2003, reproduced in Davies and Wheatcroft, *The Years of Hunger: Soviet Agriculture, 1931–1933*, Palgrave-Macmillan, 2004, p. 441 footnote 145.

30 Alfani and O'Grada, 'Famines in Europe: An Overview', in *Famine in European History*, Cambridge, 2017, p. 23.

31 Alfani and O'Grada, 2017, *Famines in Europe*, p. 23. They cite Davies and Wheatcroft, 2004; and O'Grada, 2009, to support this.

32 Anne Appelbaum, *Red Famine: Stalin's War on Ukraine*, Allen Lane, 2017; and Markevich, A., Naumenko, N., Qian, N., 'The Causes of Ukrainian Famine Mortality, 1932-33', Working Paper 29089, NBER, Washington DC, USA, 2023 are the main examples. The latter will be discussed below.

33 See Victor Yushchenko, 'Holodomor', *The Wall Street Journal*, 27/11/2007, available on net -https://web.archive.org/web/201206099185004/http://www.president.gov.ua/en/news/8296.html?Print Version

34 James E. Mace, 'Famine and Nationalism in Soviet Ukraine', *Problems of Communism*, 1984, vol. 33: 37–50, and the exchange between Wheatcroft and Mace, 'Ukrainian Famine', *Problems of Communism*, 1985, vol. 34: 132–138.

35 Wheatcroft had been planning to write a joint article with Kulcytskii and Maksudov arguing against the large 7 million figure for famine deaths being advocated by Robert Conquest but withdrew when Kulcytskii insisted on calling the famine a genocide.

36 See Kulcytskii, *The Famine of 1932–1933 in Ukraine: An Anatomy of the Holodomor*, Canadian Institute of Ukrainian Studies Press, Edmonton, 2018; Andrea Graziosi, 'The Soviet 19312–1933 Famines and the Ukrainian Holodomor: Is a New Interpretation Possible, and What Would Its Consequences Be?', *Harvard Ukrainian Studies*, 2004: 27: 1–4, 97–115; and Naimark, N.M., *Stalin's Genocides (Human Rights and Crimes against Humanity)*, Princeton University Press, 2010.

37 The first conference covered three Ukrainian famines of 1921–23, 1932–33 and 1946–47, was organized by five Academic Institutions and was dominated by demographers and historians who subscribed to the genocide thesis. The second conference purely on the 1933 famine in Ukraine was organized by the Ukrainian Institute of National Memory and was dominated by historians who opposed the genocide argument. It is a sign of the political conflict of the time that there were only two historians who

attended and had their work published in the proceedings of both conferences and they were the leading Russian historian Viktor Kondrashin and the Australian historian Stephen Wheatcroft. The first volume produced under an editorial team of M. Antonovich, G. Boryak, O. Gladun and S.Kul'cytskii was entitled Holod v Ukraini u pershii polovini XX stollittya: prichini ta naslidki (1921–1923, 1932–1933, 1946–1947). Materiali Mizhnarodnoi Naukovoi Konferentsii, Kiiv 20–21 listopada 2013, Kiiv 2013 and was a simple paperback. The second volume edited by V. Soldatenko was entitled Golod, 1933. Ukraintsi, Zbirnik naukovykh prats, Kiiv 2013 and was lavishly produced.

38 'Blacklisted' meant being listed for special treatment for failing to fulfil central grain collections, with special searches and no rights to receive any traded items. This could happen to different entities: villages, collective farms or cooperatives.

39 S.G. Wheatcroft, A. Garnaut, I. Leikin, 'Mapping crude death rates in Ukraine in 1933 and explaining the rain patterns', pp. 219–225, with maps produced in colour; and S.Wheatcroft and A. Garnaut, 'Potery naseleniya v otdelnykh raionakh SSSR (1929–1934) statistiki, karty I sravnitel'nii Analiz (osoboe polozhenie Ukrainy)', pp. 376–391, with maps and graphs in colour on 7 end pages.

40 For cuts in grain supply plans, see Davies and Wheatcroft, *The Years of Hunger*, pp. 185–7 and 406–7. Workers and employees on central rations were transferred to lowest category 3 list, as early as February 1931 TsDAVO, F.1, op. 6, d. 204, ll. 76–8, and more cuts were to follow.

41 In 2016: Oleh Wolowyna, Serhii Plokhy, Nataliia Levchuk, Omelian Rudnytskyi, Alla Kovbasiuk, Pavlo Shevchuk, Regional variations of 1932–34 famine losses in Ukraine, Canadian Studies in Population, 43, no.3–4 (2026): 175–202. In Nataliia Levchuk, Oleh Wolowyna, Omelian Rudnytskyi, Alla Kovbasiuk, Regional 1932–1933 'Famine Losses: A Comparative Analysis of Ukraine and Russia', *Nationality Papers* (2020): 48: 3, 492–512; and also in Oleh Wolowyna, 'A Demographic Framework for the 1932–1934 Famine in the Soviet Union', *Journal of Genocide Research*, (2020): 23: 4: 501–26. Also separately Serhii Plokhy, 'Mapping the Great Famine', in *Harvard Ukrainian Studies*, (2015–2016): 43: 1–4: 385–430 and reproduced as Chapter 8 under the same title in S. Plokhy, *The Frontline: Essays on Ukraine's Past and Presen*t, Harvard, 2024, and on-line as part of the HURI Historical Atlas: The Great Famine Project: https://gis.huri.harvard.edu/mapping-the-great-famine

42 He gave no details or source for that claim and the distribution of blacklisted entities (farms and villages) on his maps does not support it. Presumably, they are based on the work of Dr. Heorhiy Papaskin of the Institute of Ukrainian History and the maps that he prepared for the HURI Great Famine Project that are on the web. See Map 11: Government Policy, Blacklisted Localities, https://gis.huri.harvard.edu/media-gallerey/detail/1382384/1085780. This map shows about 200 blacklisted entities in just 7 of the 78 rayon of Kyiv Oblast. Of the nine rayons with the highest recorded levels of mortality in the oblast, only two (Volodarskii and Rzhyshevskii) are listed as having any blacklisted entities.

43 See Plokhy, *The Frontline*, p. 127.

44 The milling levy *(merchuk)* was a levy that was placed on private milling of grain part of which was to be made available for local use. For figures showing the overall fall in milling levy collected in the famine year, see Davies and Wheatcroft, p. 469.

45 A. Markevich, N. Naumenko, N. Qian, The Causes of Ukrainian Famine Mortality, 1932–33, Working Paper 29089, NBER, 2021–2023. A final 2024 version has just been accepted for publication by *Review of Economic* Studies.

46 MNQ, 2024, p. 1

47 Davies and Wheatcroft, 2004, p. 441 Furthermore, in the commentary that Wheatcroft prepared for the discussion of this paper at the Wisconsin Workshop on June 18, 2020, he wrote that he thought 'that it was probably likely that there was a tendency for there to be local ethnic bias [against Ukrainians] in terms of local allocation of scarce resources in a famine'. But that 'The extent to which there was a central and conscious ethnic bias strikes me as less certain'. Full comments available on request.

48 Filip Slaveski and Yurii Shapoval, *Stalin's Liquidation Game: The Unlikely Case of Oleksandr Shums'kyi, His Survival in Soviet Prison, and His Subsequent Arcane Assassination* (HURI/Harvard university Press, 2025) in press.

49 S.G. Wheatcroft, 'The Significance of Climate and Weather Change on Soviet Agriculture', Birmingham University, CREES Discussion Papers, SIPS:11, Birmingham, 1977.

References

Alfani, G. and Ó Gráda, C., eds. *Famine in European History*, Cambridge, 2017.Antonovich, M., Boryak, G., Gladun, O. and Kul'cytskii, S., eds., *Holod v Ukraini u pershii polovini XX stollittya: prichini ta naslidki (1921–1923, 1932–1933, 1946–1947). Materiali Mizhnarodnoi Naukovoi Konferentsii*, Kyiv2013.

Applebaum, Anne, *Red Famine: Stalin's War on Ukraine*, Allen Lane, 2017.

Cameron, Sarah, *The Hungry Steppe: Famine, Violence, and the Making of Soviet Kazakhstan,* Cornell University Press, 2017.

Carr, E.H. and Davies, R.W., *The Foundations of a Planned Economy, 1926–1929*, Macmillan, 1969.

Christian, David, 'Prohibition in Russia, 1914–1925', *Australian Slavonic and East European studies,* vol. 9, no. 2 (1995): 89–118.

Conquest, Robert, *The Harvest of Sorrow: Soviet Collectivization and the Terror Famine*, Hutchinson, 1986.

Davies, R.W. and Wheatcroft, S.G., 'Further Thoughts on the First Soviet Five Year Plan', *Slavic Review*, vol. 34, no. 4 (1975, December), 790–802.

Davies, R.W. and Wheatcroft, S.G., *The Years of Hunger: Soviet Agriculture, 1931–1933*, Palgrave-Macmillan, 2004.

Ermolov, A.S., *Nashi Neurozhai i prodovol'stvennii vopros*, St. Petersburg, 1909.

Fisher, H.H., *The Famine in Soviet Russia, 1919–1923: The Operations of the American Relief Administration*, Stanford University Press, 1927.

Gosplan, *Pyatiletnii plan razvitiya Nar. Khoz. SSSR*, vol. 2, part 1, Moscow, 1929.

Graziosi, Andreas, 'The Soviet 19312–1933 Famines and the Ukrainian Holodomor: Is a New Interpretation Possible, and What Would Its Consequences Be?', *Harvard Ukrainian Studies*, vol. 27, nos 1–4 (2004), 97–115.

Groman, V.G. ed., *Problem Urozhai.* Kyiv, 1927.

Howe, Paul and Devereux, Stephen, 'Famine Intensity and Magnitude Scales: A Proposal for an Instrumental Definition of Famine', *Disasters*, vol. 28, no. 4 (2004): 353–72.

Jones, Robert, *Bread upon the Waters. The St. Petersburg Grain Trade and the Russian Economy, 1703-1811*, University of Pittsburg Press, 2013.

Kindler, Robert, *Stalin's Nomads: Power and Famine in Kazakhstan*, University of Pittsburgh Press, 2018.

Kondratiev, N.D., *Rynok khlebov i ego regulirovanie vo vremya voiny i revolyutsii,* Moscow, 1922 (reprinted 1991).

Kulcytskii, *The Famine of 1932–1933 in Ukraine: An Anatomy of the Holodomor*, Canadian Institute of Ukrainian Studies Press, 2018.

Levchuk, Nataliia, Wolowyna, O., Rudnytskyi, O., and Kovbasiuk, A., 'Regional 1932–1933 Famine Losses: A Comparative Analysis of Ukraine and Russia', *Nationality Papers*, vol. 48, no. 3 (2020). 492–512.

Lewin, Moshe, *Russian Peasants and Soviet Power*, George Allen & Unwin, 1968.

Lih, L.T., *Bread and Authority in Russia, 1914–1921*, University of California Press, 1990.

Lindenmeyer, A., *Poverty Is not Vice: Charity, Society and the State in Imperial Russia,* Princeton University Press, 1996.

Mace, James, E., 'Famine and Nationalism in Soviet Ukraine', *Problems of Communism*, vol. 33, May–June (1984): 37–50.

Markevich, A., Naumenko, N., and Qian, N., 'The Causes of Ukrainian Famine Mortality, 1932–33', Working Paper 29089, NBER, Washington DC, USA, 2023.

Naimark, N.M., *Stalin's Genocides (Human Rights and Crimes against Humanity),* Princeton University Press, 2010.

Neferov, S., 'Prodovol'stvennii krizis v Petrograde nakanune Fevlral'skoi revolyutsii,' *Quaestio Rossica*, vol. 5, no. 3 (2017): 635–55.

Nove, Alec, *An Economic History of the USSR, 1917–1991*, Penguin, 1992.

Plokhy, S., 'Mapping the Great Famine', *Harvard Ukrainian Studies*, vol. 43, no. 1–4 (2015): 385–430.

Robbins, R.G., *Famine in Russia, 1891–1892: The Imperial Government Responds to a Crisis*, Columbia University Press, 1975.

Slaveski, Filip, and Shapoval, Yuri, *Stalin's Liquidation Game: The Unlikely Case of Oleksandr Shums'kyi, His Survival in Soviet Prison, and His Subsequent Arcane Assassination,* HURI/Harvard University Press, 2025.

Soldatenko, V., ed., *Golod 1933: Ukraintsi, Zbirnik naukovykh prats*, Kyiv2013.

Wheatcroft, S.G., 'Population Dynamic and Factors Affecting It in the Soviet Union in the 1920s & 1930s', Birmingham University, CREES Discussion Papers, SIPS: 1-2, Birmingham, 1976.

Wheatcroft, S.G., 'The Significance of Climate and Weather Change on Soviet Agriculture', Birmingham University, CREES Discussion Papers, SIPS: 11, Birmingham, 1977.

Wheatcroft, S.G., 'Famine and Factors Affecting Mortality in the USSR: The Demographic Crises of 1914–1922 & 1930–33', SIPS: 21–22, Birmingham, 1982.

Wheatcroft, S.G., 'Famine and Epidemic Crises in Russia, 1918–1922: The Case of Saratov', *Annales de Demographie Historique*, (1983), 329–352.

Wheatcroft, S.G., 'The Crises and the Condition of the Peasantry in Late Imperial Russia', in E. Kingston-Mann and T. Mixter (eds.), *Peasant Economy, Culture and Politics of European Russia, 1800–1921*, Princeton University Press, 1991.

Wheatcroft, S.G., 'The 1891–92 Famine in Russia: Towards a More Detailed Analysis of Its Scale and Demographic Significance', in L. Edmondson and P. Waldron (eds.), *Economy and Society in Russia and the Soviet Union, 1860–1930*, Macmillan, 1992.

Wheatcroft, S.G., 'Soviet Statistics of Nutrition and Mortality during Times of Famine, 1917–1922 and 1931-33', *Cahiers du Monde russe*, vol. 38, no. 4 (1997), 525–557.

Wheatcroft, S.G., 'Suchasne uyavleniya pro priroda ta riven' smertnosti. Shd chas goloda 1931–1933 rokiv v Ukrainii' (Current Knowledge of the Level and Nature of Mortality in the Ukrainian Famine of 1931–3), in V.Vasil'ev and Yu. Shapovala (eds.), *Komandiri velikogo golodu: Poizdki V.Molotova I L.Kaganovicha v Ukrainu ta na Pivnichnii Kavkaz, 1932-1933 rr.*, 2001: 179–94.

Wheatcroft, S.G., 'Famines', in W.H. McNeill (ed.), *Berkshire Encyclopaedia of World History*, 2005: 728–33. Berkshire Publishing Group.

Wheatcroft, S.G., 'Pokazateli demograficheskogo krizisa v period goloda v SSSR'. [Indicators of Demographic Crisis in the Soviet Famine], in *Golod v SSSR, 1929-33* [*Famine in USSR*, 1929–33] (2013): vol. 3, part 2, pp. 719–771. International Fund Democracy.

Wheatcroft, S.G., 'Famine, Food Problems and Imperialism', in John M. MacKenzie (ed.), *The Encyclopedia of Empire,* John Wiley and Sons, 2016.

Wheatcroft, S.G., 'Famines in Russia and the USSR', in Alfoni and O' Grada (eds.), *Famines in Europe*, Cambridge University Press, 2017.

Wheatcroft, S.G., 'Soviet Statistics under Stalinism: Reliability and Distortions in Grain and Population Statistics', *Europe Asia Studies*, vol. 71, no. 6 (2019), 1013–1035.

Wheatcroft, S. G., 'The Complexity of the Kazakh Famine: Food Problems and Faulty Perceptions', *Journal of Genocide Research*, vol. 23, no. 4 (2021), 593–597.

Wheatcroft, S.G. and Garnaut, A., Potery naseleniya v otdelnykh raionakh SSSR (1929–1934) statistiki, karty I sravnitel'nii Analiz (osoboe polozhenie Ukrainy), in Soldatenko, V. (ed.), *Golod 1933. Ukraintsi, Zbirnik naukovykh prats*, 2013: 376–39. SGW respond.

Wheatcroft, S.G., Garnaut, A., and Leikin, I., 'Mapping Crude Death Rate in Ukraine in 1933 and Explaining the Rain Patterns', in Antonovich, M., et al. (eds.), *Holod v Ukraini u pershii polovini XX stollittya: prichini ta naslidki (1921–1923, 1932–1933, 1946–1947). Materiali*, 2013. Kyiv 219–25.Wheatcroft, S.G. and O' Grado, Cormac, 'The European Famines of World Wars 1 and 2: Causes and Consequences', in Alfoni & O' Grada (eds.), *Famines in Europe*, Cambridge University Press, 2017.

Wolowyna, O., 'A Demographic Framework for the 1932–1934 Famine in the Soviet Union', *Journal of Genocide Research*, vol. 23, no. 4 (2020): 501–26.

Wolowyna, O., Plokhy, S., Levchuk, N., Rudnytskyi, O., Kovbasiuk, A., and Shevchuk, 'Regional Variations of 1932-34 Famine Losses in Ukraine', *Canadian Studies in Population*, vol. 43, no. 3–4 (2016): 175–202.

Yushchenko, V., 'Holodomor', *The Wall Street Journal*, vol. 26, no. November (2007).

4 Centre-periphery relations in the Soviet post-war famine of 1946–47[1]

Filip Slaveski, Yurii Shapoval and Igor Caşu

For much of Soviet History, the relationship between Soviet central authorities and their representatives on the local level was often strained. Central authorities had the power to appoint or remove people from their positions yet, even in a dictatorship, had less control over how local authorities exercised their power. This problem not only plagued Soviet authorities but also their Tsarist predecessors. It emerged primarily from the tension between attempting to control a vast geographical territory comprising millions of people while seeking to centralise that control in the capital and usually in one individual. One remedy to this dilemma available to the Tsar or Soviet leader was the plenipotentiary (*upolnomochennyi*)—trusted subordinates whom leaders could arm with extraordinary powers and send out into the peripheries of the empire to investigate local leaders, bring them to heel and/or manage the numerous crises that habitually emerged there: military conflict, insurrection, food crises and more. Centre-local or centre-periphery relations and the historical role played by plenipotentiaries within them have thus long been a closely studied topic in Soviet and post-Soviet studies.[2]

This chapter, for the first time, presents a comparative analysis of the role played by two leading Soviet politicians, Lazar Kaganovich and Aleksei Kosygin, sent by Stalin as plenipotentiaries to Ukraine and Moldova respectively in 1947, then in the grip of famine. This famine raged primarily in these Soviet republics during 1946–47 and was felt across the Soviet Union, killing approximately one million people.[3] The analysis offered here sheds new light on the role played by these plenipotentiaries in the state's management of this famine; the last in Soviet History but little studied.[4] The key insight is that although this famine shows similarities and differences with previous famines in Soviet history in its causes, anatomy and consequences, the roles played by plenipotentiaries in 1946–47 were especially decisive. Kosygin and Kaganovich were both implementers of central policies that were helping to make famine but, at the same time, the most effective advocates to alleviate the suffering caused by it, at least for some members of the affected population. This dual role, and their significant power to exercise it, encourages new assessments of centre-periphery relations between Moscow, Kyiv and Chisinau under Stalin.

Background to the famine

The Soviet Union was the only warring power to experience famine in the immediate aftermath of the Second World War (WWII). Many of the millions of Soviet wartime dead and those killed in famine afterward died in the south-western region of the Soviet Union, especially Ukraine.[5] This region, the breadbasket of the Soviet Union, formed the epicentre of military operations and occupations that left it underpopulated, its infrastructure in ruins and its agricultural sector barely operational. These consequences of the war continued to play out years afterward,

DOI: 10.4324/9781003465805-6

limiting the pace and scope of post-war recovery. The Soviet leadership failed to anticipate both the severity and enduring nature of these consequences on the recovery of the agricultural sector when it resumed control over this region from 1944 onwards. Given its success in avoiding mass famine in wartime, the leadership was optimistic that recovering control of this region, especially Ukraine and Moldova, would secure food supplies for the remainder of the war and the immediate post-war period.

This optimism was founded on the past, not the present. Before the war, the grain harvest of this region, mostly Ukraine, had contributed greatly to feeding the major cities and towns in the north of the Soviet Union and providing grain exports. When this region was occupied by Axis powers in 1941–44, alternate grain surplus regions in the centre and the east of the Soviet Union had to try to make up as much of the loss as much as they could. This led to them being heavily taxed in these years and drained of their grain reserves. In 1944 and 1945, when the southwestern region was fully back under Soviet control, it was taxed heavily while taxes on central and eastern regions were relaxed, and food reserves were replenished there. In 1945 alone, all of the six million tons of inter-regionally transported grain destined for the North came from the southwest, especially Ukraine.

The leadership's optimism waned in the face of the slow recovery of the agricultural sector in the southwest region. Even the massive amount of 6 million tonnes of grain it procured from here was less than the state anticipated and needed. Indeed, this was about half of what the state managed to procure from Ukraine in 1940 (11.1 million tonnes). The state continued to procure more and more grain from the smaller amount produced, trying to sustain its food exports and feed the military as well as a rapidly growing domestic population swelled by demobilisations from the military and the incorporation of new or reconquered territories into the Soviet Union in the final stages and immediate aftermath of the war.

But this massive procurement reduced the food available to the population in the region producing it while the state also reduced the amount of grain it redistributed back to these areas to fund the urban rationing system. Compared to 1940, when the state reallocated 8 million tonnes of grain back to Ukraine for its domestic food consumption, in 1945 it allocated only 2.1 million.[6] This disparity and the state's failure to reinvest sufficiently in the devastated agricultural sector here put the majority of the population working in it and the urban recipients dependent on rations at great risk of starvation in the event of post-war shock. The shock came in the summer of 1946 when a massive drought took hold in the southwestern region. The grain harvest, which usually fed the nation, failed, pushing the Soviet Union into the massive famine that it had avoided during WWII and since the last mass famine of 1932–33.

Famine threatened to de-stabilise the Soviet regime at the height of its domestic and international prestige as one of the 'Big Three' victors in WWII. The collective farm system, the backbone of the Soviet economy and the major structure of state control in the countryside came under increased stress. It had bonded the majority of the peasant population [*kolkhozniki*] to a collective farm [*kolkhoz*] on which they laboured to produce food for the state since the early 1930s. *Kolkhozniki* were generally reluctant to work on the farms when they received only a share of the grain or income from produce that remained after the state procured it. They survived on the farms by supplementing this paltry share by farming the small plot of private land permitted to them, where they could grow their own food.

To combat impending famine, the state attempted to both increase grain production and reduce the level of rural food consumption. It transferred land from *kolkhozniki's* private plots to the *kolkhozy*, hoping that *kolkhozniki* would spend more time working on the latter rather than the former. Increased grain procurement from the failed harvest and reducing the capacity of *kolkhozniki* to produce their own food made it nigh impossible for many *kolkhozniki* to remain on the *kolkhozy*, as the law required of them, and survive. Millions of them thus fled for the cities, but also for 'better' regions such as in western Ukraine that were mostly not collectivised, less affected by drought and where more food was thought to be available.

Joining collective farmers were other rural dwellers not directly engaged in agriculture: teachers, low-level officials, and others, whom the state removed from the bread ration system and also confiscated or reduced the size of their private plots, transferring the land to the *kolkhozy* from September 1946. This policy affected about 27.5 million rural dwellers across the Soviet Union and 2.5 million in Ukraine.[7] The largely uncontrolled exodus of *kolkhozniki* and rural dwellers took place in the midst of a massive anti-Soviet insurgency waged in western Ukraine by nationalist forces, who threatened to draw hungry and disaffected Ukrainians into their ranks. At the same time, millions of men were being demobilised from the army, which, the leaders feared, could turn out of control as they returned home to a hungry and angry countryside.

Central authorities placed local ones in an impossible situation from the summer of 1946, pushing them to procure more and more grain from starving people as famine worsened, even when it was clear that more grain than had already been procured simply did not exist. The centre did not listen to reporting from its own officials stressing this problem, instead replacing them for failing to procure more grain, in some cases arresting them. Most officials who followed orders from above to keep their jobs undermined their capacity to control their localities as mortality increased and social order broke down. Some officials sought to balance conflicting central and local priorities, and a few broke ranks to protect their localities, with limited success. Stalin sent Kaganovich to Ukraine and Kosygin to Moldova with different remits, but at the top of their list was dealing with those local officials whom Stalin chided for failing to find non-existent grain and falling for 'lies' of starving peasants claiming that they had no more grain to give up.[8]

Kaganovich's mission to Ukraine

On 4 March 1947, Ukrainian newspapers reported on the proceedings of the previous day's Plenum of the Central Committee of the Communist Party of Ukraine CP(b)U held in Kyiv. The most pressing news from the Plenum was that, suddenly, it now considered inappropriate that Nikita Khrushchev should continue to combine the posts of Chairman of the Council of Ministers (the government) and First Secretary of the Central Committee of the CP(b)U (party).[9] This combination of party/state leadership posts had never been a problem before, indeed, Stalin himself had occupied them on the all-Union level. The Plenum approved the replacement of Khrushchev as party head with one of Stalin's closest associates, Lazar Kaganovich, from Moscow, leaving Khrushchev as head of government. The Plenum also adopted a resolution on urgent measures to prepare for the spring sowing of 1947 in the countryside, which gave some indication to readers as to the reasons behind Kaganovich's appointment.[10]

Kaganovich last occupied the post of Ukrainian party head from 1925 to 1928 and last dealt with agricultural questions in Ukraine in the previous famine, the Holodomor, in 1932–33. Now with famine raging again, Kaganovich was coming back to and would stay in Ukraine as party head until 26 December 1947. Khrushchev and Kaganovich were old comrades, who had been friendly with each other since the Russian Revolution in 1917, all the way through the war with Germany. However, the current situation strained their relationship greatly. In his memoirs, Kaganovich wrote: 'Khrushchev, in my impression, accepted the decision of the Central Committee to relieve him of his duties as First Secretary of the Central Committee of the Communist Party of Ukraine with resentment'.[11] This was an understatement. Khrushchev was not only insulted by his demotion but also fearful of its future consequences. He understood fully that Stalin no longer trusted him. One of Khrushchev's biographers assessed his replacement as the 'chief communist' of Ukraine by Kaganovich this way: 'Of course, for him it was a serious slap in the face, but Khrushchev did not show any displeasure, knowing full well that everything depended on Stalin'.[12] Khrushchev thus tread very carefully in his dealings with Kaganovich, understanding also that Kaganovich could be an incredibly dangerous political opponent, who could turn any economic problem into a political one to be resolved in his favour.

The key economic problem at the time was grain. The failed grain harvest of the previous year had contributed to the famine that raged in Ukraine. By some calculations, the 1946 summer grain harvest in Ukraine amounted only to 8.9 million tonnes (barn), of which 3.3 million tonnes were procured by the state. This amount was drastically below the state's procurement target of 5.9 million tonnes, which it had already allocated to feeding the rest of the country, the military and for export.[13] Due to the failed harvest, by September 1946 the state also had to delay its abolition of wartime food rationing it had promised the population in 1946, as well as price and monetary reforms, supposed to improve post-war living standards. Soviet leaders now aimed to implement these reforms with a successful summer harvest in 1947, which they anticipated would bring Ukraine and the southwest region out of famine.

Khrushchev understood all of these problems well. He was a faithful Stalinist, who had proven himself as an effective and trustworthy party leader. He was working hard to improve procurements of grain as Moscow demanded, much to the detriment of starving farmers who produced the grain. Why, then, did Stalin send Kaganovich to Ukraine to displace Khrushchev? In short, it is clear Stalin no longer trusted Khrushchev to solve the grain problem and was sending his trusted plenipotentiary to do so. What is unclear and requires explanation are the reasons why this was the case.

We begin our explanation with an analysis of the Plenum of the Central Committee of the All-Union Communist Party of Bolsheviks (ACP[b]) in February 1947 in Moscow. The Plenum itself was supposed to consider the issue of preparing a new party program, but Stalin added a fourth item to the agenda, 'Issues of the rise of agriculture'. The report, 'On measures to boost agriculture in the post-war period', was entrusted to the Deputy Chairman of the Council of Ministers of the USSR, Andrei Andreev. Andreev reported that as soon as it became clear that the Voronezh, Kursk, Oryol, Tambov (Russian Oblasts), as well as parts of Ukraine and Moldova suffered from drought, Stalin raised the question of food and fodder assistance to collective farms from state reserves, assistance with tractors and everything else necessary. But plenum documents indicate otherwise. Stalin first paid attention to drought-stricken oblasts in Ukraine, not Russia, stressing that the grain procurement campaign was failing in Ukraine.[14]

Stalin's focus on Ukraine was reflected in the special resolution adopted after the Plenum, 'On strengthening party and Soviet work in Ukraine'. But what needed to be 'strengthened' in the spring of 1947? After all, though not an agricultural specialist, Khrushchev had always paid serious attention to agriculture throughout his entire stay in Ukraine, from 1938 to the end of 1949. Khrushchev understood that any Ukrainian leader needed to tend foremost to the two major issues in the country: grain and nationalism. Ukrainian leaders were generally removed for failing to export enough Ukrainian grain to the centre and/or to suppress sufficiently anti-Soviet Ukrainian nationalism. Or, at least, they would be accused of failing on one or both of these issues by their enemies. Khrushchev prioritised discussions of agricultural development at the highest party levels during his post-war control of Ukraine, placing these discussions at the top of the agenda of party plenums sixteen times from 1945 to 1949, at which he often spoke. On his initiative, the Central Committee resumed the practice of holding republican meetings of leaders in various branches of agricultural production in 1946. While the famine was occurring, he held numerous broader meetings on agriculture with lower-level state and party representatives, in which about 11,000 people took part. Khruschev simply could not be charged with not seeking to strengthen agriculture.

But the agricultural sector needed more than Krushchev's attention to be strengthened. During the war, tens of thousands of farms and villages were ruined, tractors and hundreds of thousands of heads of livestock stolen from the country, as well as basic farm implements.[15] Rebuilding the agricultural sector from this point of devastation was incredibly difficult, particularly because the consequences of war continued to unravel long after it ended in 1945, indeed, into the famine and the following years. At the same time, Moscow continued to extract far more resources from the sector than it invested into it. 'Reconstruction' then was hampered by both devastation and government policy. It could only be considered impressive on paper. As a result, Khrushchev could boast at the end of 1945 that almost all of the sector had been rebuilt, that is 27,500 collective farms, 784 state farms and 1,277 Machine Tractor Stations in Ukraine. But their condition was extremely weak, with massive labour, draught power and equipment shortages continuing. Mostly women did the bulk of hard agricultural labour by hand to try to make up for this deficit.

Exacerbating the enduring consequences of wartime devastation and limiting recovery were economically unjustified plans for massive procurements of Ukrainian grain coming from Moscow. Such plans were instituted ever since the Soviets reconquered Ukraine in 1944. In 1944 and 1945, the state had confiscated almost everything from many collective farms including fodder and seed funds. Therefore, many farms had nothing left to pay the collective farmers' workdays, that is the days registered by the collective farm leadership for which collective farmers were paid, mostly in grain and rarely in cash. In 1945, an average of 400 grams of bread was planned for distribution each labour day per collective farmer, although almost none received this amount.[16]

This was evident to the Ukrainian leadership from reports in March 1946 it received from the People's Commissariat of State Security (NKGB) of Ukraine, which included excerpts from letters from families of military personnel in the southwest region. One of these letters from Odesa Oblast dated February 1946 reads: 'Misha, we work on a collective farm, and we have to sit hungry without bread, without flour, without cereals. If you go to ask for help on the collective farm, they say: "You need to work", but when you do the work, they turn your nose up at you and don't give you anything. This is not life, but torture'.[17] Another letter, from Kherson oblast, notes: 'Kolya, we have 656 workdays, but nothing was given for them. I've already been to the district, they told me: "Let the collective farm help", but on the collective farm they refer to the district ... It's impossible for us to live like this any longer. Your father was killed, you have been in the army since 1944, your mother is sick, but we are not receiving any help ...'[18] Police warned the leadership that it had already intercepted 5,550 letters concerning starvation in Odesa oblast in January and February 1946 alone, that is before the drought hit in the summer. Many more letters would have passed through the police censorship net.

Khrushchev often brought failures of the collective farm system to the attention of Stalin and other central leaders when seeking assistance for the food crises which raged across Ukraine even before the drought and famine hit in the summer of 1946. In February, the Union government gave collective farms in the southern regions a food loan of 16,325 tonnes of grain as aid with military families at the top of the hierarchy for receiving it.[19] But this amount was nowhere near enough to improve the situation on collective farms. Farmers remained malnourished even before the onset of drought and then famine from the middle of 1946. When the harvest failed, given the previous years' extraction of grain, now there was simply not enough grain available to the state to sustain its feeding of urban dwellers and the military and still provide further 'aid' to the countryside, which it expected to feed itself.

The state eventually paused foreign grain exports in the spring of 1947 in recognition of this shortage, but the damage of years of massive grain procurements in the southwest and the failed harvest could not be recuperated now. Further, farmers only had limited capacity to feed themselves from their own food sources, which the state had curtailed by its reduction and even confiscation of private plots of land from September 1946. Problems with livestock farming and draught power remained, which only further burdened collective farmers with additional ploughing work by hand which sapped their energies and health. This worsening food situation was further aggravated by unfavourable weather conditions at the time. The winter of 1945–46 in most areas had little snow, with frequent thaws, and April, May and June 1946 were the driest in the previous 50 years in the region, producing massive drought at harvest time. It did rain in July 1946, but the air temperature remained very high at 31–36 degrees Celsius, and in August even 36–39 degrees.[20] Soil moisture levels became dangerously low. The weather clearly contributed greatly to the destruction of crops on many farms.

The mail excerpts and broader reports on that sharp deterioration in the conditions of the already struggling agricultural sector in Ukraine (as in other regions of the Soviet Union) from the end of 1945 and then food troubles from the spring of 1946 carried special weight with the Ukrainian and all-Union leadership for two reasons. First, leaders feared instability in military ranks (mostly military-aged men were still mobilised) caused by food crises affecting their families at home. Second, the reports were prepared by the security services.[21] Unlike information about food difficulties communicated to them by other government agencies such as the Ministry of Health, when communicated by the police, there was little concern over their veracity.

It was clear to the Soviet leadership even before the failed harvest in the summer of 1946, that it needed to revise its agricultural policy to avoid a worsening of the food crisis and further social unrest. This revision included refraining from further expansion of sown areas without a corresponding increase in material and technical resources that would enable successful sowing, as well as reducing the volume of mandatory state procurements of food and increasing the prices that the state paid to farms for this food (they were symbolic). These measures would reduce the unrealistic expectations placed on farmers to produce unrealisable quantities of food for the state. More positive reforms were also necessary: to increase the material interest of collective farmers in their work, increase investments in agriculture, reduce administrative interference in the affairs of collective farms and move from extensive to intensive development of agriculture. But the leadership in Moscow took no such action, and leaders in Kyiv followed suit. They had to plan to expand the sowing acreage to ‘increase productivity’, as Moscow demanded, though without the commensurate increase in resources, even seed, which it demanded.

These unfavourable conditions in agriculture impacted both the harvest on collective farmland on which farmers worked to produce food for the state and on their private plots in Ukraine and across the southwestern region. To make matters worse for farmers, the taxes on food produced on these plots also increased (farmers always had to provide a portion of this food to the state as tax). Other taxes also increased, and farmers were required to take out state loans (*zaimy*), which was effectively a tax.

As the grain harvest failed in the midst of drought in the summer of 1946 and the material conditions of the peasantry further deteriorated, there were few avenues of survival. As collective farmers they did not have internal passports required for travel, they were bound to their farms that they could not leave without permission. Many farmers were authorised to leave for seasonal labour stints in the cities, often in winter, but were always required for the sowing and harvesting. Now, in the midst of the summer harvest, millions left in search of food and work illegally and risked arrest and punishment. In June 1946 alone, about 160,000 people were caught by the police at L'viv central railway station in western Ukraine, mostly collective farmers from east and south Ukraine without documentation.[22] There were many more who slipped past the police.

As in the spring sowing, despite the advice of agricultural experts and in the midst of these most unpropitious agricultural conditions, the Ukrainian leadership made them worse in the 1946 summer harvest. Following the instructions of Moscow, it began another 'battle for the harvest', that is to procure as much grain from the failed harvest as possible from Ukraine into state coffers. In July 1946, the Council of Ministers (Sovmin) of Ukraine and the Central Committee of the CP(b)U approved the plan that came from Moscow—to procure 340 million poods of grain [5.5 million tonnes] and the July Party Plenum demanded the unconditional fulfilment of this target.[23] Moreover, on July 22, 1946, Moscow increased the grain procurement plan for Ukraine to 362 million 750 thousand poods [5.9 million tonnes].[24] Moscow's 'logic' to deal with failed harvest was not to leave grain in drought-stricken areas where starving people needed it most, but to take more grain from these areas to control its distribution. This control was, fundamentally, the entire point of the collective farm system. While Khrushchev had sought to reduce the plan earlier and there was some wrangling over plan targets between Kyiv and Moscow, now, none of the Ukrainian leadership spoke out against this increased plan. Clearly, the consequences of the drought were intensified by Moscow and helped to create famine. Central leaders disregarded the specific conditions and capacities of the Ukrainian agricultural sector, demanding from their Ukrainian subordinates that mandatory grain procurement plans be fulfilled at any cost.

Collective farms were placed under incredible pressure to realise these impossible procurement targets and were punished for failing to do so. In this atmosphere, collective farm chairs, those responsible for meeting the targets on the farm, began to hide some of the grain from harvesting, risking being condemned as 'pests and saboteurs', mostly for seeking to feed their farmers. Corruption was also rife.[25] But it was quite difficult to hide the grain since the progress of grain procurements was monitored by authorised representatives of the USSR Ministry of Procurement. There were 1,550 of them in only 53 rayons of Kyiv Oblast alone, and tens of thousands more across Ukraine.[26] Khrushchev grew more and more dissatisfied with the behaviour of collective farm chairs as well as local leaders, some of whom he felt tolerated their chairs' deceit in hiding grain or 'failures' in procuring it. Khrushchev issued a resolution via Sovmin on 4 October 1946, to crack down on 'pests' and 'saboteurs' within the collective farm system.

From the beginning of 1946 until October of that year, the Ukrainian government and the Central Committee of the CP(b)U adopted more than ten resolutions concerning grain procurements, adding measures to meet targets and to punish those who did not. Khrushchev's language in private Politburo meetings betrayed his increasing frustration with what he perceived to be the lack of will and competence among his own party and government representatives in the regions to enforce procurement targets.[27] But these measures did not save Khrushchev from pressure from Moscow. Indeed, Stalin expressed his own frustrations towards Khrushchev for these same failings, using the same insults against Khrushchev that he used against his underlings. For example, on October 5, 1946, a telegram was sent to Kyiv addressed to Khrushchev from the Council of Ministers of the USSR (then headed by Stalin) warning that the Ukrainian leadership 'still continues to stand aloof from the matter of grain procurement', is not waging the 'necessary struggle for the complete and timely implementation of state procurement plans' and that 'in a number of cases there is a direct concealment of grain from the state'.[28]

Khrushchev responded to these political charges by agreeing with Stalin's analysis but still trying to stress the objective reasons for the failure to meet procurement targets (drought) and offering alternatives. In October, Khrushchev wrote a letter to Stalin about the progress of grain procurements in Ukraine, reporting that the grain procurement plan was 61 per cent fulfilled, that 'many facts have been revealed of threshed grain settling on collective farms, withholding from the state by individual collective farms of threshed grain in waste, and theft of bread from collective farms'.[29] He also wrote to Minister for Trade Anastas Mikoyan, asking that, considering that many collective farms could not fulfil the plan for food crops, could the state accept other grain crops for grain procurements, that is, to deliver them instead of wheat and rye?[30] Mikoyan rejected this request. Collective farms and collective farmers were prohibited from selling bread in markets on 31 July 1946, until the mandatory procurement targets were met.

In Moscow, Stalin and much of the central leadership perceived Khrushchev's letters as an attempt to justify the failure to fulfil the grain procurement plan and more as evidence of the insufficient dedication and competence of the Ukrainian leadership to the growing problem. Moscow's tone towards Khrushchev sharpened further on November 4, 1946, when the Minister of Procurement of the USSR Boris Dvinsky sent Khrushchev the following order:

> Despite repeated instructions to strengthen the procurement of food crops, you are not paying enough attention to this most important process. As of October 20, your republic has delivered 120,783 thousand poods of rye and wheat; 111,097 thousand poods remain for delivery. I order that the district police departments be instructed to check the delivery of food crops on the personal accounts of collective farms and state farms and to all collective farms and state farms that are yet to meet their procurement targets and demand the complete delivery in the shortest possible time. Bring to justice those responsible for the deliberate delay in delivery of food crops.[31]

On November 26, 1946, Khrushchev (like some leaders of other regions of the USSR) received a telegram from Stalin accusing him of curtailing grain procurements. It also contained a demand to put an end to the 'un-Bolshevik attitude' towards the implementation of the grain procurement plan and to punish those who hid grain.[32] In November–December 1946, the Politburo of the Central Committee of the CP(b)U weekly considered the issue of the progress of grain procurements without bringing any tangible improvements.

Being directly accused by Stalin not only of the shortcomings but now of the same crimes as Khrushchev accused his own subordinates signalled to Khrushchev that he was in danger of losing his position as head of Ukraine or even worse. In his memoirs, Khrushchev recalled a chilling telegram he received from Stalin on December 17, 1946:

> Stalin sent me a rude, insulting telegram, which said that I was a dubious person, that I was writing notes in which I proved that Ukraine could not fulfil state procurements and was asking for a huge number of ration cards to feed people. This telegram had a devastating effect on me. I understood the tragedy that hung not only over my person personally, but also over the Ukrainian people [...].[33]

When Khrushchev, according to his memoirs, began to give Stalin detailed information about the severity of starvation, he further drew Stalin's ire: 'Softness! They are deceiving you, they are deliberately reporting this in order to elicit pity from you and force you to use up your reserves...'. Khrushchev further explained that Stalin believed that he 'was succumbing to local Ukrainian influence, that they were putting such pressure on me and that I had become almost a nationalist, untrustworthy'.[34] Khrushchev was thus failing the key test of any Ukrainian leader: failing to procure enough grain and failing to battle nationalism (or falling to it).

Khrushchev was 'failing' this test fundamentally because there was simply much less grain to procure than the state imagined in its plans. Khrushchev travelled a lot around at this time and was well-informed by the security services about the desperation in the countryside. Khrushchev's real crime was not only failing to procure enough grain but to outline to Stalin the objective difficulties responsible for the failed harvest—the ongoing effects of war and severe drought (government policy of course the other unspoken difficulty). Stalin was not used to this style of communication. Khrushchev's reports on the severity of famine at his requests for help not only irritated Stalin but also provided evidence to him that Khrushchev had exhausted his capacity to improve the situation and meet the targets. Stalin decided not to leave the problem of organising the spring sowing, the success of which he hoped would ensure a good 1947 harvest and break the famine, to this 'failure' of a leader. This is the primary reason Stalin decided to send Lazar Kaganovich to Ukraine.

Kaganovich was one of Stalin's closest and trusted associates. Stalin considered him an 'expert' on Ukraine. Kaganovich was born there and was head of the Ukrainian communist party in the 1920s. He was one of the chief drivers of the collectivisation of Ukrainian agriculture in the 1930s and, like Stalin, among those chiefly responsible for the Holodomor. But Kaganovich's actions in 1947 should not be a priori demonised because of this, nor Khrushchev's actions be idealised in this analysis. The differences in leadership style between both of these faithful Stalinists were not great. We should be especially critical of Khrushchev's memoirs, which paint a much more compassionate picture of his character in dealing with famine than records of his conversations with Stalin and his colleagues, as well as his actions at the time. Khrushchev also grew up in Ukraine, but neither he nor Kaganovich considered themselves 'Ukrainian' in the narrow sense of 'ethnic identity' in the Soviet system nor in a broader sense of belonging to a Ukrainian heritage distinct and independent from Russia's. Neither would have risen through the Stalinist ranks had they exhibited this attitude or failed to exhibit the same loyalty towards Stalin and willingness to engage in repression and violence towards their colleagues and the population in general.

However, Kaganovich was far more advanced in these violent respects than Khrushchev. He immediately demonstrated this by intensifying repression against lower party and state officials in establishing broader control over key portfolios across party and state institutions. Kaganovich replaced not only Khrushchev as head of the party in this respect, but also many of his functions in his remaining post as head of the government. They did work together at different points, but as already intimated, this was difficult to do given Kaganovich's personality. To make matters worse, the stress of this period surely contributed to Khrushchev falling ill, removing him from day-to-day operations. Kaganovich became thus the most decisive leader in managing the famine and battling the anti-Soviet nationalist insurgency in western Ukraine at this time, as well as managing the information flow from Ukraine to Moscow. He had a much better sense than Khrushchev of how to speak to Stalin properly, to report only the information that Stalin needed to know, and how to request assistance for Ukraine without drawing the ire of the Boss (*vozhd*).

Kaganovich immediately got to work after his arrival in Kyiv. Already on March 10, 1947, the Politburo of the Central Committee of the CP(b)U, under Kaganovich's control as head of the party, passed a resolution on the agricultural work plan for 1947. Four days later, it reviewed the resolution of the plenum of the Central Committee of the ACP (b) of March 3, 1947, 'On urgent measures to prepare for spring sowing in the Ukrainian SSR'[35] and established urgent security measures in the countryside. Partly as a response to Stalin's own concern about the sabotage and theft of grain, he communicated to Khrushchev the previous year, Kaganovich passed two Politburo resolutions on 14 and 18 March to protect seed materials sent to Ukraine for the spring sowing.[36] To stop the outflow of farmers from the countryside in search of food to cities and other regional areas, which threatened labour shortages for the sowing period and broader social unrest, Kaganovich issued instructions to lower levels of power: the regional committees, district party committees, executive committees of regional and district councils in March as well, to help return these farmers to their places of origin 'for the period of work on processing crops and harvesting'.[37] The heads of enterprises, institutions and organisations were also prohibited from hiring collective farmers who did not have the appropriate documents from the collective farms.[38]

These measures provided greater scope to prosecute farmers and especially local officials. Stalin expected this. When sending Kaganovich to Ukraine, he knew well that the distinctive feature of his plenipotentiary was that in order to achieve his goal, he was never afraid to act as harshly as possible and never afraid to break the law. Moreover, Kaganovich was inherently suspicious even of his closest comrades and even more so of lower-level officials. Just like after his arrival to Ukraine in 1933, he directed the removal and arrest of thousands of collective farm chairs, heads of district party committees and district executive committees. Kaganovich did not bring repression to the sector, but he clearly intensified the scale of repression and its direction towards local officials. Already in 1946 in Chernihiv Oblast, for instance, 728 collective farm chairs were replaced (often more than once) and every 16th collective farm chair in Ukraine was imprisoned. In 1946 and in the first quarter of 1947, before Kaganovich's arrival to Ukraine, 1,312 collective farm chairs were sentenced, of which 513 were sentenced to three years in prison, 219 to 5 years, 112 to 10 years and 2 were shot.[39] Upon Kaganovich's arrival, during the first eight months of 1947, almost 38 per cent of the secretaries of district party committees, 64 per cent of the chairmen of executive committees, and two-thirds of the directors of Machine Tractor Stations were replaced.[40] This broader purge affected thousands of people and wrought more serious sentences for those arrested than previously.[41]

To organise grain procurements from the summer harvest and speed them up, the Kyiv leadership sent representatives from numerous state and party bodies to those regions that were slowest in fulfilling the grain procurement plans. These representatives were picked because they had experienced during the Holodomor in confiscating 'surplus' grain from peasants in order to fulfil the plans. Many of them were 'sharp-edged' people (*ostrye liudi*), as Khrushchev called them, Lenin's term for his favourite people to send to the countryside in the 1920s to take food from the peasantry without mercy. Khrushchev had started to send such people to the countryside even earlier, in October 1946, but it was only now under Kaganovich they were recruited and sent en masse.

Some historians have argued that Kaganovich worked 'without the same energy' during his return to Ukraine in 1947 compared to 1933, that is, without exercising the same amount of influence.[42] The facts cited above confirm that this is not so. Kaganovich's energy not only boiled down to punishing people for failing to procure enough grain but also explained this failure by their supposed sympathies for Ukrainian nationalism and, in extreme cases, their support for the anti-Soviet nationalist insurgency being waged in western Ukraine. On June 10, 1947, the Politburo of the Central Committee of the CP(b)U adopted Kaganovich's resolution 'On improving the ideological and political education of personnel and on the fight against manifestations of bourgeois-nationalist ideology'. At one of the meetings with the first secretaries of the regional party committees, Kaganovich stated that every case of failure to fulfil planned targets in industry and agriculture would be considered a manifestation of Ukrainian bourgeois nationalism.[43] Gradually, the campaign against Ukrainian artists, writers, and scientists accused of 'sympathy' towards nationalism became increasingly powerful. Devastating articles about them appeared in the press.[44]

Kaganovich began preparations for the next Plenum of the Central Committee CP(b)U with the agenda 'The fight against nationalism as the main danger in the Communist Party of Ukraine'.[45] Some evidence gives reason to believe that Kaganovich attached great importance to this agenda. A former Ukrainian communist party leader confided to Yurii Shapoval that Kaganovich had prepared a list of prominent people for arrest. Kaganovich went with this list to Moscow to see Stalin, but Stalin stopped Kaganovich from launching this broader purge seemingly deeming that further repression was unnecessary. After all, Kaganovich had done his job. As discussed below, the 1947 grain harvest was successful, procurement targets were mostly met, and Ukraine began to emerge from the famine. On December 26, 1947, Kaganovich was relieved of the post of First Secretary of the CP(b)U.[46] Khrushchev resumed this post and the Council of Ministers of the Ukrainian SSR was headed by Demiyan Korotchenko.

Khrushchev could be returned to party head after his demotion, partly because Stalin had regained a degree of trust in him. Kaganovich can take some credit for this. As early as May 1947, he worked with Khrushchev to request from Stalin 'corrections' to the September 1946 law on 'economising bread' that removed 2.5 million Ukrainians, mostly rural workers and dependents, from the bread ration list. Some were removed incorrectly, Kaganovich wrote. As a result, 636,000 of them were starving and in dire need of food aid, as well as their dependent children. Moreover, hundreds of thousands of those hospitalised for starvation also needed immediate aid. Kaganovich effectively confirmed the severity of the famine and the need for the aid that Khrushchev had been requesting from the previous year. He also intimated to Stalin that these people were 'ours', that is, low-level officials and teachers more sympathetic to the state than Ukrainian farmers. Stalin gave some of the aid that Kaganovich and Khrushchev requested, though, as always, too little and too late to make much of a difference. But by doing so, Stalin signalled that he no longer perceived this kind of request, at least when made with his plenipotentiaries, as a sign of the weakness of the Ukrainian leadership as he had clearly done so throughout 1946. As we shall see later, Stalin had already begun to lean towards providing specific food aid to relieve the famine in 1946 in the worst affected border regions between Ukraine and Moldova, which increased in 1947 based partly on the reporting of his other plenipotentiary, Aleksei Kosygin, to which we now turn.

Kosygin's mission to Moldova

Famine raged even more severely to the west of Ukraine in 1946 and 1947 in Moldova, which was then known as the Moldavian Soviet Socialist Republic (MSSR). Some comparisons between Kaganovich and Kosygin's mission in Ukraine and MSSR respectively provide a good indication of centre-periphery relations between Moscow and different republics at this time and the unique features of famine therein. Like Ukraine, the MSSR was devastated by war. During WWII, Romania and Germany had extracted thousands of tonnes of grain and removed thousands of draught animals, tractors and a range of farm implement as well as people as labour, all of which hindered post-war recovery.

While the Soviet reconquest in 1944 initiated much-needed 'reconstruction' in the war-torn MSSR, 'reconstruction' also limited recovery in many ways. The Soviets continued to extract as much grain as possible, mostly from rebuilt collective farms on the left bank of the Dniester River and individual farmers on the right, as collectivisation commenced on the right bank only very slowly after the war. The MSSR also faced droughty weather from the summer of 1945, which heavily impacted harvest yields and increased food shortages. These conditions applied in the border regions of Ukraine, Izmail and Chernvitsi Oblasts, i.e. south of Bessarabia and northern Bukovina, Romania's territories before 1940. To make matters worse, the MSSR was the epicentre of a massive typhus outbreak in 1945, which killed thousands.[47] As in Ukraine, the agricultural sector was already on the brink of catastrophe. The scene was already set for possible famine, which hit with the most serious drought in the summer of 1946 and the Soviet regime's response to it.

Despite the similarities between them, the MSSR did not occupy a major space in the strategic imagination of Soviet leaders as did Ukraine. It was one of the small Soviet republics which, although food-rich, provided only a very small portion of the economy. There was no insurgency waged against Soviet power which was not a site of Cold War tensions. Moscow understood the close cultural and ethnic relations between many Moldovans and their former occupiers in the Romanians and was thus wary of potential 'nationalist diversions' in the MSSR, but not to the same extent as in Ukraine or the Baltics.[48] The main problem was that the structures of Soviet political control were much less developed in the MSSR, and its political leadership was less well-known to Moscow. The leadership's main economic role was to facilitate a massive extraction of grain from the MSSR and keep nationalism at bay, thereby sustaining the MSSR as a safe extraction-based periphery.

Kosygin's remit as a plenipotentiary to MSSR was much narrower than Kaganovich's in Ukraine and also much shorter. He spent only ten days in the MSSR compared to almost a year for Kaganovich. Kosygin did not go to the MSSR to reshape its political structure. He did try to improve how it functioned, mostly in preparation for the spring 1947 sowing. His was more a fact-finding mission, to find out if the local leadership's reports about famine and massive mortality rates, the worst in the entire Soviet Union, were accurate and to decide whether or not to advise Stalin to send further food aid for which the political leadership had already requested from Moscow.

Kosygin immediately reported to Stalin one day after arriving in Moldova on 25 February 1947, the famine was severe, mortality was massive and the local leadership was to blame for both developments. Yes, the drought had precipitated the famine, Kosygin explained, but it was the failure of the leadership of the MSSR to deal with the signs of famine promptly and to take action to reduce the incidence of mortality that led to the current catastrophe. Only by framing famine in this way, as an isolated problem only within the MSSR, could Kosygin confirm to Stalin that it was occurring. Those dying from famine, however, were referred to as suffering from 'dystrophy', a Soviet medical term, which could be used as a euphemism to marginalise or exclude altogether political factors as a cause of famine deaths.[49]

Kosygin continued his artifice when immediately requesting further food aid, noting that the aid that Moscow had already delivered was enough to have combatted the famine, which, in fact, it was not. The aid was too small and delivered too late making a significant difference. But Kosygin was not only referring to specific 'aid' set by Moscow in response to requests from the MSSR leadership to deal with the famine. He was referring also to Moscow's massive reduction in procurement targets in MSSR in light of the 1946 harvest, which was far greater than in Ukraine. Any analysis of import-export grain balances in the MSSR shows that Moscow redistributed more grain back into the MSSR than it had procured in 1946. That this shift in policy failed to stem the famine frustrated Stalin immensely, explaining his anger towards more and more requests for aid. While Kosygin certainly embellished the role of local leadership in causing the famine, it is clear that the leadership misdirected the food it received. It consistently used the food to prop up rationing systems in urban areas at the expense of supporting rural populations where more people were starving, even when that food had been designated by Moscow for farmers.[50]

Misdirection aside, it was the Moscow leadership's massive extraction of grain from the MSSR in 1944 and 1945 and commensurate failure to rebuild the agricultural sector, exacerbated by drought, that caused the famine. The famine could not be arrested by Stalin's policy shift in 1946. Even the large amount of aid that Kosygin requested from Stalin in March 1947, the major peak of the famine, could only stem mass mortality temporarily. This aid included: doubling the number of people to be fed by the MSSR government from 100,000 to 200,000, doubling the number of hospital places for those severally ill from dystrophy from 20,000 to 40,000, increasing orphanage places from 10,000 to 22,000 and for the all-Union government to release 30 million roubles for the MSSR to cover the expenses in combatting dystrophy.[51]

Kosygin received most of the requested aid from Stalin from March 1947 and it clearly helped reduce dystrophy rates, at least temporarily.[52] The official number of dystrophy cases recorded in the MSSR was 240,537 people at the end of March 1947 (more than 10 per cent of the population). This number fell to 123,763 three months later, by mid-May 1947. But this relief package was only designed to run for three months and ended in June, crucially, before the 1947 harvest came in.[53] Dystrophy rates rebounded as food aid dried up. The local party leader, 1st secretary of the Communist Party of Moldavia (C(b)PM), Nicolae Coval, asked Stalin to extend Kosygin's aid package to September when the harvested food would become fully available. Stalin gave permission for only piecemeal aid, less than half of what Coval had requested. His messages were as clear to the Moldovans as they were to the Ukrainians.[54] 'Food aid' would only come with a successful harvest. Only this would break the famine. Fortunately, the good grain harvest in 1947 did just this, though localised food crises in the MSSR continued into 1948.

Coval needed to be careful in making this request for food before the harvest to arrest the spike in mortality. Local leaders were removed from their positions for making the same requests for food aid as Stalin's plenipotentiaries. Coval's predecessor, Nikita Salogor, much like Khrushchev in June 1946, raised the alarm to Moscow of impending famine due to drought and asked for a reduction in the grain procurement plan for MSSR. Stalin acceded to some of Salogor's requests, but as punishment for making them, Stalin dismissed him from his post as 1st secretary of the Central Committee of the C(b)PM two weeks later.[55] Coval clearly understood the lesson of his predecessor—never to ask for a reduction in procurement but to fulfil it as much as possible at any cost. Coval did so and sought aid only as an extension of Kosygin's plan, rather than on his own accord.

This approach was entirely in keeping with the 'management' style, where Coval sought to balance minimising the severity of famine in his communications with Moscow yet still seeking aid. A good example of this occurred in December 1946, when Coval established a government commission to combat dystrophy but did not participate in its activities from the start and thus sent a signal to the county and district party leaders that the issue was not overriding. The commission thus did nothing. Kosygin chided Coval in front of other party leaders for this failure, as well as 'hiding' the severity of the famine,[56] when other government representatives, especially in the Ministry of Health, communicated its severity to Moscow more accurately. This was part of Kosygin's broader attempt, like Kaganovich's, to blame the local leaders for their own famines, rather than state policies.

That Coval's negligence, unlike Salogor's activism, was not a sackable office, tells us a great deal about the Stalinist system in the peripheries. As far as we can see, Kosygin never suggested to Stalin that Coval be removed. Even after the famine was over and its scale evident, he was not removed from his post until 1950 for other reasons. The primary reason for Coval's retention is that he fits well into the new mould of local officials who became prominent in the post-war period. As long as they were loyal and ran their localities stably, it mattered less how corrupt they were. Stalin seems to have come to terms with this arrangement, a resolution to the old problem plaguing Russian and Soviet History, after launching massive and ultimately futile anti-corruption campaigns aimed at bringing local officials to heel in the immediate post-war years.

Easing up the party ideal after the war of the disciplined ascetic 'Bolshevik cadre' and accepting this 'arrangement', helped to cement Soviet rule across the Union, especially in Central Asia and the Caucuses, even decades after Stalin's death.[57] The conditions in which the population lived in these areas mattered far less to the centre.

Conclusion

Similar to Moldova, the fate of the starving population in Ukraine in 1946–47 also assumed a low priority for the central leadership but for different reasons. Ukrainian peasants could not be disentangled from the suspicions of the leadership over their nationalist and thus anti-Soviet tendencies. This suspicion clearly worsened the severity of the famine, in part because central leaders could punish local officials seeking food aid to alleviate the suffering of Ukrainians as bourgeois nationalists. Centre-periphery relations changed significantly in different parts of the Soviet Union after the war, but in Ukraine, they stayed the same as in the 1930s. Whereas Stalin could treat famine in MSSR as an exceptional case, and even privately, admit that it was occurring and offer massive relief, he could not do so in Ukraine. That the famine was most severe in MSSR helped in this decision. The famine probably killed 125,000 people in MSSR, about 5 per cent of the population.[58] But also this 'special treatment' was only possible towards a small republic, which was not a major food producer and mattered little to his broader strategic thinking.

Though the famine was also severe in Ukraine, Stalin treated it much the same as in the previous famine. The number of excess deaths in the worst affected areas of Ukraine tripled in 1947 compared to 1948 when population numbers were relatively stable. These are only the registered deaths, close to 300,000 across Ukraine in 1947 alone, not to mention those we could count in late 1946 and more who died as food refugees across the country who were not registered by the authorities which would mean hundreds of thousands more.[59] People also starved in Russia. Despite the famine's severity, to deal with it in Ukraine, Stalin made few exceptions, sending one of the architects of the previous famine, the Holodomor, and a key proponent in the massive purge of the Ukrainian elite in 1933. This was Kaganovich's old stomping ground.

On the other hand, Kaganovich had to stomp more lightly than in 1933. Some things had changed in the post-war period. It is inconceivable that Kaganovich would have asked Stalin for as much famine relief for hundreds of thousands of Ukrainians in 1933 as he did in 1947. He did so now because many of these people, mostly low-level officials and teachers who were arbitrarily taken off the food rationing system, served as a post-war skeleton of Soviet influence in the countryside rife with insurgency. Relief was, as always, mostly strategic.

Also, the mostly broader shift across the Union towards less severe repression against individuals through the courts rather than entire groups by police as in the 1930s meant those repressed mostly kept their lives and suffered less severe prison sentences than in the 1930s. Stalin rejected Kaganovich's attempt to increase the scale of the massive purges against the post-war Ukrainian elite to 1930s levels. These continuities and differences across the pre- and post-war period and the agency of Soviet leaders in 1946 and 1947 were key determinants of the famine, but it was the unchanging logic of the Stalinist system that helped to make it.

Notes

1 The chapter is produced from research funded by the Australian Research Council (ARC) for Discovery Project, "The Last Soviet Famine, 1946–47: Drought and food crises in war's aftermath" (DP210100278).

2 Especially since the opening of the Soviet archives, centre-periphery studies have formed part of "revisionist" historians' works against the "totalitarian model" of Soviet history. A general introduction can be found in Donald J. Raleigh, ed. *Provincial Landscapes: Local Dimensions of Soviet Power, 1917–1953* (Pittsburgh: University of Pittsburgh Press, 2001). A host of "localised" studies in the immediate postwar period include: Karl D. Qualls, *From Ruins to Reconstruction: Urban Identity in Soviet Sevastopol after World War II* (Ithaca: Cornell University Press, 2009) and Filip Slaveski, *Remaking Ukraine after World War II: The Clash of Local and Central Soviet Power* (Cambridge: Cambridge University Press, 2021). On the conduct of Stalin's plenipotentiaries in the previous famine of 1923/33 in Ukraine, see V. Vasilev and Iu. Shapoval eds. *Komandiry velikogo goloda: Poezdki V. Molotova i L. Kaganovicha v Ukrainu i na Severnyi Kavkaz, 1931–1933 gg.* (Kyiv: Heneza, 2001).

3 On the number of famine deaths, see Yurii Shapoval, "Holod 1946–1947 rokiv v Rosiyi ta v Ukraïni: potreba porivnyal'noho analizu" in *Ukrayina XX st.: kul'tura, ideolohiya, polityka*: *Zb. St.* (Kyiv, 2008), 343 and M. Ellman, "The 1947 Soviet Famine and the Entitlement Approach to Famines", *Cambridge Journal of Economics,* vol. 24, no. 5 (2000): 611–617.

4 Only a handful of monographs have been published in the famine in addition to a small number of essay and document collections, mostly in Ukraine and Moldova, compared to over 20,000 for the Holodomor. Some include: V. F. Zima, *Golod v SSSR 1946–1947 godov: proiskozhdenie i posledstviya* (Moscow, 1996); N. Ganson, *The Soviet Famine of 1946–47 in Global & Historical Perspective* (New York, Palgrave, 2009); V. M. Kyrychenko and S. M. Tymchenko, *Holodne povoienne lykholittia* (Zaporizhzhia, 1996) and O. Veselova, V. Marochko, O. Movchan, *Holodomory v Ukraïne, 1921–1923, 1932–1933, 1946–1947: Zlochyny Proty Narodu.* (Kyiv, 2000).

5 There is debate over the total number of Soviet casualties in WWII. For a Russian estimate, see G. F. Krivosheev, ed. *Rossiia i SSSR v voinakh XX veka. Poteri vooruzhennykh sil: Istoriko-statisticheskoe issledovanie* (Moscow: Olma-Press, 2001).

6 For all above import/export data, see Russian State Archive of the Economy (RGAE), f. 1884, op. 61, dd. 37, 43, 53, 78, 122.

7 Slaveski, *Remaking Ukraine after WWII*, 14.

8 Memuary N. S. Hrushheva, *Voprosy Istorii*, 11 (1991): 38.

9 *Povidomlennya pro plenum TsK KP(b)U, Radians'ka Ukraïna 1947, 4 bereznia.*

10 Central State Archive of Public Organisations of Ukraine (TsDAHOU) f. 1, op. 1. spr. 736, ark. 4–10.

11 L. M. Kaganovych, *Pamiatnye zapiski rabochego, kommunista-bol'shevika, profsoiuznogo, partiinogo i sovetsko-gosudarstvennogo rabotnika* (Moscow, 1996), 488.

12 V. N. Shevelev, *N. S. Khrushchev* (Rostov-on-Don, 1999), 68.

13 For grain production/procurements, see Stephen G. Wheatcroft, "The Soviet Famine of 1946–1947, the Weather and Human Agency in Historical Perspective" *Europe-Asia Studies*, vol. 64, no. 6 (2012).

14 *Komunistychna partiia Radians'koho Soiuzu v rezoliutsiiakh i rishenniakh z'ïzdiv, konferentsiĭ i plenumiv TsK* t. 6 (Kyïv, 1980), 216–217.

15 V. K. Baran and V. M. Danylenko, *Ukraïna v umovah systemnoi kryzy (1946–1980)* (Kyiv: Al'ternatyvy, 1999), 37.

16 I. M. Makoviĭchuk and Iu. H. Pyliavets', "Holod na Ukraïni u 1946–1947 rr.", *Ukraïns'kyĭ istorychnyĭ zhurnal* no. 8 (1990): 15.

17 Archive Department of the Security Service of Ukraine (HDA SBU), f. 16, op. 1, spr. 0566, ark. 272.

18 HDA SBU f. 16, op. 1, spr. 0566, ark. 272.

19 Makoviĭchuk and Pyliavets', "Holod na Ukraïni u 1946–1947 rr.".

20 Makoviĭchuk and Pyliavets', "Holod na Ukraïni u 1946–1947 rr.", 18.

21 TsDAHOU f. 582 op. 16 spr. 3152, ark. 10.

22 *Holod v Ukraïni, 1946–1947. Dokumenty i materialy* (Kyiv, New York: 1996), 53.

23 Makoviĭchuk and Pyliavets', "Holod na Ukraïni u 1946–1947 rr.", 18.

24 Central State Archive of Supreme Bodies of Power and Government of Ukraine (TsDAVOU) f. 2 op. 7 spr. 3144, ark. 63.

25 TsDAVOU f. 2, op. 7, d. 5036.

26 Imakoviĭchuk and Pyliavets', "Holod na Ukraïni u 1946–1947 rr.", 22.

27 TsDAHO f. 1 op. 6 spr. 995.
28 *Holod v Ukraïni, 1946–1947,* 86.
29 TsDAHOU f. 2, op. 7, spr. 3659, ark. 39–40.
30 TsDAHOU f. 2, op. 7, spr. 3731, ark. 19.
31 *Holod v Ukraïni, 1946–1947,* 116.
32 TsDAVOU f. 2. op. 7, spr. 3731, ark. 111.
33 Memuary N. S. "Hrushheva", 38.
34 Memuary N. S. "Hrushheva", 38.
35 TsDAHOU f. 1, op. 6, spr. 1103, ark. 63–66, 67–73, 74–77, 78–80, 80–82, 82–86, 87–90, 90–92, 92–93, 93–94, 94–95, 96–97, 98–99; spr. 1108 ark. 57–59 ob.
36 TsDAHOU f. 1, op. 6, spr. 1108, ark. 68–72.
37 TsDAHOU f. 2. op. 7, spr. 4871, ark. 156.
38 TsDAHOU f. 2. op. 7, spr. 4871, ark. 156.
39 *Holod v Ukraïni, 1946-1947. Dokumenty i materialy*, 10–11.
40 V. Danylenko, et. al. *Ukraïna v epitsentri protystoiannia svitovykh system (1939–1990).* Kyiv Akademperiodyka, 2021, 284.
41 Kaganovich was also operating under new laws against theft, which increased the penalties for theft of state property (grain). See Yoram Gorlizki, "Rules, Incentives and Soviet Campaign Justice after World War II", *Europe-Asia Studies*, vol. 51, no. 7 (1999).
42 R. A. Medvedev, *Okruzhenie Stalina* (Moscow: Molodaia gvardiia, 2006), 197 and E. A. Rees, *Iron Lazar: A Political Biography* (Anthem Press, 2012), 241.
43 Iu. Shapoval, *Ukraïna 20-50-kh rokiv: Storinky nenapisanoï istoriï* (Kyïv: Naukova dumka, 1993), 266–267.
44 O. Kornijchuk, "Literatura Radyans 'koi Ukraïny pered velykym yuvileyem", *Radyans'ka Ukrayina.* 1947, 2 veresnya.
45 *XXII s'ezd KPSS, 17-31 oktiabria, 1947, Stenograficheskii otchet* (Moscow: Politizdat, 1962), vol. 1, 280.
46 *Povidomlennya pro plenum TsK KP(b)U, Radians'ka Ukraïna 1947,* 27 *grudnia.*
47 Typhus continued throughout the famine with differing severity. See a 1947 report in National Agency for Archives, (Agenția Națională a Arhivelor, hereafter ANA), f. 51, op. 51S, d. 82, ll. 48–54.
48 The 1st secretary of the Central Committee of the C(b)PM, Coval, was removed from his post in 1950 not for his failure in dealing with the famine but for his failures in dealing with 'nationalism' in MSSR. See more, Igor Cașu, "Patterns of Succession: Top Party Elite recruitment in Soviet Moldavia and Centre-Periphery Relation, 1940-1991", in Li Bennich-Bjökman, Saulius Grybkauskas, eds., *Moscow and the non-Russian Republics in the Soviet Union. Nomenklatura, Intelligentsia and Centre-Periphery Relations*, London& New York: Routledge, 2022, p. 75–77.
49 For more on this term, see Rebecca Manley, 'Nutritional Dystrophy: The Science and Semantics of Starvation in World War II', in Wendy Z. Goldman and Donald A. Filtzer, eds., *Hunger and War: Food Provisioning in the Soviet Union during World War II* (Bloomington: Indiana University Press, 2015).
50 The Russian State Archive of Socio-Political History (RGASPI) f. 17 op. 122, d. 220, ll. 69–75. See more, Igor Cașu, "Police vs. Party? Institutional Hierarchies and Agency in Soviet Moldavia, 1944–1952", in Contemporary European History, Volume 32, Issue 1, February 2023, pp. 79–96.
51 State Archive of the Russian Federation (GARF) f. 5446, op. 499, d. 2965, ll. 24–25.
52 Note difficulties in delivery/corruption and other food sources, that is, vegetables coming in April.
53 V. Pasat, RSS Moldovenească în epoca stalinistă (1940–1953) (Chisinau: Cartier, 2011), 257.
54 Zima, *Golod v SSSR*, 139–140.
55 ANA, F. A-51, inv. 4, d. 68.
56 For the minutes of his meeting of the Bureau of CC of C(b)PM held on February 24 with the participation of Kosygin, see *Golod v Moldove,* 498–512.
57 O. Khlevniuk ed., *TsK VKP(b) i regional'nye partiinye komitety,1945–1953* (Moscow: 2004), *6, 123* and Cynthia Hooper, 'A Darker Big Deal: Concealing Party Crimes in the Post-Second World War

Era', in J. Fürst ed. *Late Stalinist Russia: Society between Reconstruction and Reinvention* (Routledge, 2000), 142–64.

58 Anatol Țăranu, Mihai Gribincea, Ion Şişcanu et al., eds., *Golod v Moldove. Sbornik dokumentov* (Chişinău: Ştiința, 1993), 624, 650–651, 659.

59 For mortality numbers across the USSR, see Ellman, "The 1947 Soviet Famine" p. 611–612. Our estimates are partly based on figures in TsDAVOU f. r-582, op. 11, spr. 80.

References

Baran, V. K. and Danylenko, V. M. *Ukraïna v umovah systemnoi kryzy (1946–1980)*. Kyiv: Al'ternatyvy, 1999.

Danylenko, V. et. al. *Ukraïna v epitsentri protystoiannia svitovykh system* (1939–1990). Kyiv Akademperiodyka, 2021.

Ellman, M. 'The 1947 Soviet Famine and the Entitlement Approach to Famines', *Cambridge Journal of Economics,* vol. 24, no. 5 (2000).

Fürst, J. ed. Late Stalinist, *Late Stalinist Russia: Society between Reconstruction and Reinvention.* Routledge, 2000.

Ganson, N. *The Soviet Famine of 1946-47 in Global & Historical Perspective*. New York, Palgrave, 2009.

Goldman. W. Z. and Filtzer, D. A. eds. *Hunger and War: Food Provisioning in the Soviet Union during World War II.* Bloomington: Indiana University Press, 2015.

Gorlizki, Y. 'Rules, Incentives and Soviet Campaign Justice after World War II', *Europe-Asia Studies*, vol. 51, no. 7 (1999).

Kaganovych, L. M. *Pamiatnye zapiski rabochego, kommunista-bol'shevika, profsoiuznogo, partiinogo i sovetsko-gosudarstvennogo rabotnika*. Moscow, 1996.

Khlevniuk, O. ed., *TsK VKP(b) i regional'nye partiinye komitety,1945–1953.* Moscow, 2004.

Krivosheev, G. F. ed. *Rossiia i SSSR v voinakh XX veka. Poteri vooruzhennykh sil: Istoriko-statisticheskoe issledovanie*. Moscow: Olma-Press, 2001.

Kyrychenko, V. M. and Tymchenko, S. M. *Holodne povoienne lykholittia*. Zaporizhzhia, 1996.

Makoviĭchuk I. M. and Pyliavets', Iu. H. 'Holod na Ukraïni u 1946–1947 rr.', *Ukraïns'kyĭ istorychnyĭ zhurnal* no. 8 (1990).

Medvedev, R. A. *Okruzhenie Stalina*. Moscow: Molodaia gvardiia, 2006.

Memuary, N. S. 'Hrushheva', *Voprosy Istorii*, 11 (1991).

Pasat, V. *RSS Moldovenească în epoca stalinistă (1940–1953)*. Chisinau: Cartier, 2011.

Qualls, K. D. *From Ruins to Reconstruction: Urban Identity in Soviet Sevastopol after World War II.* Ithaca: Cornell University Press, 2009.

Raleigh, D. J. ed. *Provincial Landscapes: Local Dimensions of Soviet Power, 1917–1953.* Pittsburgh: University of Pittsburgh Press, 2001.

Rees, E. A., *Iron Lazar: A Political Biography* of Lazar Kaganovich. London: Anthem Press, 2012.

Shapoval, Iu. *Ukraïna 20-50-kh rokiv: Storinky nenapisanoï istoriï.* Kyïv: Naukova dumka, 1993.

Shapoval, Iu. 'Holod 1946–1947 rokiv v Rosiyi ta v Ukraïni: potreba porivnyal'noho analizu', in *Ukrayina XX st.: kul'tura, ideolohiya, polityka*: *Zb. St.* Kyiv, 2008.

Shevelev, V. N. *N. S. Khrushchev*. Rostov-on-Don, 1999.

Slaveski, F. *Remaking Ukraine after World War II: The Clash of Local and Central Soviet Power.* Cambridge: Cambridge University Press, 2021.

Vasilev, V. and Shapoval, Iu. eds. *Komandiry velikogo goloda: Poezdki V. Molotova i L. Kaganovicha v Ukrainu i na Severnyi Kavkaz, 1931–1933 gg*. Kyiv: Heneza, 2001.

Veselova, O., Marochko, O and Movchan, O. *Holodomory v Ukraïne, 1921–1923, 1932–1933, 1946–1947: Zlochyny Proty Narodu.* Kyiv, 2000.

Zima, V. F. *Golod v SSSR 1946–1947 godov: proiskozhdenie i posledstviya*. Moscow, 1996.

Part II

The international politics of famine and relief

5 The Allied blockade and British politics of food and famine during World War II

Ingrid de Zwarte and Miguel Ángel del Arco Blanco

Introduction

In August 1940, Winston Churchill delivered a famous speech on the Allied naval blockade, in which the prime minister outlined what would remain the British approach to famine in occupied Europe throughout the war:

> The only thing that can create famine in any part of Europe now or during the coming winter will be German looting or German failure to distribute the supplies which they command. [...] Reserves of food will be built up all over the world and held in trust for the free Europe of tomorrow. These supplies shall go in when, but only when, Hitler's armies go out. Bread and Freedom shall go in together.[1]

The Allied blockade during World War II (WWII) aimed to cut off German-controlled Europe from overseas markets and sources of supply, including foodstuffs, forcing Germany to rely on accumulated stocks and on the production of raw materials available in occupied territory.[2] The blockade, which lasted from 1939 to 1945, consisted of a naval blockade, the bombing of economically important targets, and the pre-emptive purchase of war materials from neutral countries to prevent their sale to the Axis powers. Churchill's speech demonstrated that the British approach to food aid for civilians within the blockaded area would be completely different from that during World War I (WWI). According to the Ministry of Economic Warfare (MEW), led by Hugh Dalton, the experience with Herbert Hoover's Commission for Relief in Belgium, which had provided food to 7.3 million civilians in Belgium and 2 million in northern France under the Allied blockade and German occupation of WWI, had demonstrated that humanitarian aid would significantly 'prolong and strengthen German resistance' and that it was practically impossible 'to turn off the tap once it has been turned on'. In addition, the scale of relief required and the area involved was far greater than in the last war.[3] Based on the 'successes' of the naval blockade during WWI,[4] both Churchill and Dalton believed in maintaining a ruthless and rigid blockade policy. Relief should follow liberation and not the other way around.

This chapter examines the role of the Allied blockade and British economic warfare in European famines during WWII. While existing historical studies primarily focus on famines within their national contexts and examine domestic political factors, particularly enemy occupation, this chapter shifts the focus to international wartime food politics. It does so by comparatively investigating the effects of the Allied blockade on famines in three different contexts: (1) the Spanish famine under Franco's dictatorship (1939–42), (2) the famine in Axis-occupied Greece (1941–44), and (3) the 'Hunger Winter' in the German-occupied Netherlands (1944–45). Although excellent studies have been written on all three famines,[5] they have not yet been

DOI: 10.4324/9781003465805-8

comparatively examined. This comparison is particularly relevant because, despite the vastly different contexts, the same state institutions and key political actors were largely involved, thus linking Allied responses to the famines. Drawing on extensive archival research in multiple countries, our study reveals the pivotal role of geopolitical interests in causing and/or exacerbating these famines. Our main aim is to bring to the fore the global political dynamics underlying modern wartime famines.

The Spanish famine and the Allied 'carrot and stick' approach

The Spanish famine occurred between 1939 and 1942, with a second stage in 1946. The main cause of the famine lay in the irrational and disastrous economic policy adopted at the end of the Spanish Civil War (1936–39) inspired by other fascist models: autarky (see Chapter 2 of this volume). The adoption of this policy was aimed at forcing Spanish industrialisation, achieving the country's economic independence and thus guaranteeing its imperial destiny. The autarkic policy had implications that extended far beyond the economic sphere, promoting an ultranationalist ideology that envisioned a new Spanish empire. Scholars estimate that in the first three years after the civil war alone, around 200,000 people lost their lives due to starvation or infectious diseases caused by undernourishment.[6]

The ultra-nationalism of Franco's dictatorship was deeply inspired by other fascist models in Europe at the time. The Franco-led 'New State's' alignment with the Axis powers was a consequence of the Spanish Civil War. The conspirators against the democratic Second Republic had established contact with Italy and Germany as early as the spring of 1936. Subsequently, when the insurgents staged the *coup d'état* on July 18th, Italy and Germany offered crucial military assistance to ensure the success of the uprising. German and Italian aid to Franco would continue throughout the civil war, contributing to the Republic's suffering and eventual demise.[7] With the civil war won, Franco's 'New State' openly displayed its friendship with the Axis. The signing of a cultural agreement with Germany (24 January 1939), Spain's adherence to the Anti-Comintern Pact (27 March 1939), and the Spanish-German treaty of friendship (31 March 1939) reciprocated this aid and offered beneficial conditions for Nazi Germany. The continued presence of German and Italian troops in Spain after the end of the civil war (until May and June 1939, respectively) and Spain's withdrawal from the League of Nations (8 May 1939) were clear signs of Francoist Spain's political orientation.[8]

Notwithstanding Spain's declaration of neutrality at the start of WWII in September 1939, the Allies had no doubt about Franco's Axis sympathies. They were also aware of Spain's crucial strategic importance in any future war. The existence of naval or air bases on the Spanish Mediterranean coast or the Balearic Islands posed a significant danger to the passage of British military and commercial traffic through the Mediterranean, threatening supply routes to and from the overseas colonies. The British position was clear, as military theorist Captain Liddell Hart stated in 1939: 'a friendly Spain is desirable, a neutral Spain is vital'.[9] To that end, and to keep Spain out of the approaching conflict, in May 1939, the British government decided to impose a strictly managed economic blockade on Spain, adopting a policy of 'carrot and stick'. This economic dependence would keep Spain out of the coming war while ensuring that it could not supply Britain's enemies. This dual-sided strategy consisted, on the one hand, of rigid control of trade and, on the other, of extending to Spain the possibility of financial aid to support reconstruction and promote friendly relations.[10]

From the first months of WWII, it was clear to the British and the French that Franco's regime was helping the Germans in any way it could. Franco permitted the supply of German warships and submarines in Spain. Spanish collaboration with the German navy had massive consequences for the maritime war, as it contributed to the isolation of France from Britain. Following the fall of France, the *Kriegsmarine* intensified the blockade over the British Isles. An active programme of cooperation between Spain and Germany was established, through which 23 German submarines were refuelled in Vigo, El Ferrol, Cádiz, and Las Palmas (Canary Islands) between 1940 and 1942.[11] Spain was also one of the most important sources of raw materials and foodstuffs for Germany as a repayment for the assistance offered during the Spanish Civil War. The Third Reich exponentially increased its demand for Spanish products following the outbreak of war, leading to an increasingly favourable balance of imports and exports *vis-à-vis* Germany. This imbalance damaged Spain's post-civil war recovery and hampered the regime's ability to improve the food supply for a starving population.[12]

These collaborations between Spain and Nazi Germany coincided with the first phase of the Allied blockade, which would have damaging consequences for Spain's food supply. From 1 December 1939 onwards, the Royal Navy blocked the arrival of vessels bound for Germany and detained any vessel travelling to Spain without a 'navicert' (document approved by the British authorities which authorised exports and imports between neutral countries) until it could be inspected. Spain's Ambassador in London, the Duke of Alba, wrote to the Foreign Ministry in Madrid that Britain had '[presently] more than 700 vessels under detention'. The blockade intensified the disastrous economic legacies of the Spanish Civil War and Franco's calamitous economic policy of autarky. In the winter of 1940, deaths from starvation were reported in the southern region of Andalusia.[13]

As the winter of 1939–40 approached, Britain showed itself open to a trade agreement with Spain, hoping that this would distance it from Germany. Spain initially proved reluctant to negotiate, but Britain applied pressure by detaining merchant vessels, thus further restricting supplies. Facing an exhausted economy, Franco reluctantly authorised negotiations. Even though talks began in November 1939, the Anglo-Spanish Clearing Agreement was not signed until 18 March 1940. Britain offered a loan of £2 million, which had to be used to purchase British goods. Adopting the same strategy it used with neutral European countries during WW1, Britain would also permit the transit of essential goods to Spain, particularly food and raw materials. In exchange, Spain was not to allow their re-export to the enemy and was to provide detailed monthly reports of all exports and imports.[14] Through the blockade and carrot and stick approach, Britain had achieved its objectives: it had reduced Spanish exports to Germany, it had tied Spain's fate to that of Britain, and above all it had maintained Spain in its forced neutrality, notwithstanding its sympathy for the German cause.[15]

This situation would not last for long. After the fall of France and Italy's entry into the war in June 1940, Spain was tempted to join the war on the Axis side. Despite the terrible state of the country, Franco and his most loyal acolytes toyed with the idea of entering the war at the last moment, hoping to benefit from the victory of Nazism. On 12 June 1940, Spain moved from 'neutrality' to 'non-belligerence', imitating the moves of Italy and hinting at its future entry into the World War. The following day, taking advantage of Nazi entry into Paris, Spain occupied the international city of Tangier.[16] Collaboration with the Axis also accelerated in Spain. For example, the highest rate of refuelling Nazi submarines from Spanish ports occurred between June 1940 and July 1941, including the provision of food and water. Between 18 July 1940 and 3 June 1943, Italian warplanes conducted 15 air raids on Gibraltar with Spanish cooperation. At least five Italian submarines were also refuelled in Spanish ports during the war.[17]

In response, Britain tightened economic pressure on Spain by reducing deliveries, thus limiting the chance of re-exporting to its enemies, and insisted that Spain step back from its belligerent intentions. On 17 June, 1940, in agreement with the United States, Britain suspended its supply of petroleum. The economic blockade was intensified, and Britain declared that 'navicerts' would be obligatory for any commerce with the 'neutral' countries, including Spain.[18] The impact on Spanish imports was immediate. As British searches and detentions of vessels increased, the Spanish Foreign Minister Beigbeder and the Ambassador in London complained to British authorities about the difficulties that the navicert system was creating for supply.[19] In Murcia, one Falange report sent in July termed the situation 'very grave'. In that month alone, the ration had been 'shared out twice over'. The amounts were 'so meagre and so partial' that it was impossible to feed the population of the province.[20]

Spain faced a dilemma: food or empire. Spain could ask for assistance from the hated Britain to guarantee the survival of the population or enter the war alongside Germany to achieve its territorial claims on Gibraltar, Oran, and French Morocco. Facing an exhausted nation, Franco authorised renewed negotiations with the British. The mechanism of the British policy of economic appeasement resumed. On 30 August 1940, the British made their offer in an attempt to appease Spain's belligerent moods. The supply of petroleum would be renewed, a monthly quota of imports would be agreed upon for a couple of months, and Spain would agree not to re-export goods to enemy countries.[21]

Despite his dependence on the Allies, the critical socioeconomic situation of the country and the worsening of the famine among the poorest classes, Franco continued to make his support for the Axis cause very clear. On 3 June 1940, Franco sent an adulatory letter to Hitler, in which he offered 'services which you regard as most valuable'. On 16 September, Serrano Súñer visited Berlin to meet the *Führer* and negotiate Spain's entry into the war. The corollary of this pro-Axis escalation came on 23 October 1940, with the meeting between the *Führer* and the Caudillo in Hendaye (France). The aim was to remove the stumbling blocks in the negotiations for Spain's entry into the war. Hitler sought the immediate participation of Spain in the war through a joint offensive against Gibraltar (Operation Felix). Franco showed a willingness to fight alongside the Nazis, but pointed to difficulties in food supplies and fuel, and sought German economic support to enter the war in exchange for Gibraltar, all of French Morocco, and even Oran. Hitler promised that Spain would receive all the economic and material support from Germany, but only after it had entered the war. In truth, the key question centred on Spanish claims in North Africa, since it could pose a problem for Germany in its alliance with Vichy France and Fascist Italy. Spain's lack of entry into the war was not due to the dire socio-economic situation, nor to Franco or his wishes, but in truth to the imperial ambitions of Nazi Germany, which were incompatible with Spanish claims in North Africa.[22]

The Allies returned to the policy of carrot and stick. They understood that hunger was their best weapon in keeping Spain out of the war. Winston Churchill stated on 3 November 1940: 'We have in our hands a very powerful lever in the form of our economic blockade and I think that Spain's desire to obtain provisions from the United States and from this country will be the most powerful factor in keeping them out of the war'.[23] Considering the possibility that Spain would enter the war, the Allies made military preparations and suspended deliveries of cereals. The principal victims of the belligerent whims of the 'New State' would be the Spanish people. After the punishment came the carrot. With Britain's resources increasingly exhausted, it turned to the United States and convinced them to supply Spain with raw materials and foodstuffs, resulting in the signing of new agreements in the autumn of 1940, by obtaining credits and shipping wheat.[24]

Nonetheless, the Franco regime was far from embracing strict neutrality. On 12 February 1941, Franco met with Mussolini in Bordighera, Italy, the latter dictator was prodded by Hitler to see if he could convince Spain to enter the war. The German invasion of the Soviet Union on 22 June 1941 emboldened the imperialist discourses of leaders of Francoist Spain. On 24 June, Serrano Súñer delivered a fiery speech, followed by the march of a crowd of Falangists to the British embassy in Madrid, where they threw rocks at the building and shouted 'Gibraltar for Spain. British assassins' in front of authorities who barely reacted. Franco approved then the creation of the *División Azul* (Blue Division), a body of 18,801 volunteers under Army command, which would go off 'to fight against Communism'. The grand finale to all of this was a markedly Falangist-sounding speech by Franco on 17 July in which he declared, 'The Allies are on the wrong side in this war and they have lost it'. Once again, the thirst for an empire came before feeding the country.[25]

Spain's pro-Axis policy and the ensuing British policy of 'carrot and stick' continued throughout 1941. However, one factor changed the landscape: the entry of the United States into the war in December 1941. The new context hardened the stance of the Allies towards Spain, with the US consistently advocating harsher measures with Franco's Spain than the British, stretching the nation's supply problems to their limit. The detention of Spanish boats was sped up, stopping the arrival of essential products like potatoes, wheat, flour, and pyrites.[26]

It is important to reiterate that the main aims of the Allied blockade were to prevent Spain from entering the war and to ensure that Spain could not re-export the goods it received to Axis countries. Thus, the entry of the United States into the war meant the employment of a powerful new weapon. In addition to blockade and trade restrictions, a massive programme of pre-emptive purchases began of Spanish products that had wartime value – wolfram, iron, mercury, cork – with the aim of preventing them from reaching the Third Reich. In January 1942, a desperate Spain accepted the conditions imposed by the Allies. Spain agreed to send coveted products for inspection of petroleum supplies and prohibition of its re-export to Germany, Italy, Japan, or occupied nations. The dictatorship was forced to accept the presence of American and British observers. Franco began to understand that the entry of the US had signalled an important change in the fortunes of the conflict.[27]

Franco's distancing of Spain from the Axis and its belligerent ambitions, and consequently the improvement of food supply to the population from August onwards, was due to two factors. First, the emergence of an internal crisis within the regime. On 16 August 1942, at the Basilica in Begoña (Bilbao), Falangists threw two grenades into a crowd attending a Mass in honour of Carlists who had fallen in the civil war. On 2 September, Franco reshuffled his cabinet, dismissing pro-fascist Serrano Súñer and replacing him with ex-Minister (and General) Gómez Jordana, who favoured neutrality. The second factor was the favourable course of the war for the Allies. From September 1942, while *Wehrmacht* soldiers were fighting the Soviets in Stalingrad and Germany and its allies were in retreat in North Africa following the Allied landings of Operation Torch (November 1942), Spain began to shift its political posture.[28]

In this new context, 1943 proved to be a good year for Spain in terms of foreign trade. The momentum in the war had shifted, as did the Franco regime's explicit political position in favour of the Axis. Spain officially declared its neutrality on 1 October 1943. Accordingly, the supply of food to the country, although far from ideal, improved.[29] The worst of the famine had passed, even if Spain continued to be plagued by scarcity, rationing, and deprivation throughout the rest of the 'hunger years'. The worst of the rigid economic blockade was also over, albeit not for German-occupied Europe, where difficulties persisted.

The special case of Greece

In the spring of 1941, the British Foreign Office became increasingly concerned by the deteriorating food situation in Greece, which was occupied by German, Italian, and Bulgarian forces. The triple Axis occupation had split the import-dependent country up into patchwork pieces and imposed tough controls on markets, as well as restrictions upon population movement, shipping, and fishing. A lack of reliable information and government authority in imposing laws further contributed to the difficult food situation, as did – of course – the Allied blockade of occupied Greece, which stopped outside foodstuffs from entering the country. As a result of all of these factors, food supplies in Greece dwindled fast, and prices on the black market rose exponentially, leading to widespread hunger conditions affecting both urban areas and multiple islands under German and Italian occupation. The 1941–44 Greek famine led to an estimated 400,000 excess deaths.[30]

Already in late April 1941, the Greek prime minister Emmanouil Tsouderos made a request to the Allies for food and medical supplies. In line with the blockade policy, the British Foreign Office responded to the prime minister – who had fled with the Greek King George II and his cabinet to Crete – that they regarded all foodstuffs as contraband and could not agree to food relief for Greece without doing so for other occupied territories.[31] From the terminology used in internal correspondence, referring to the 'genuinely starving Greeks', the British administration seemed to take the Greek case seriously. In light of 'the heroic example set by the Greeks to other nations' in their resistance against Italy and Germany, and the known insufficiency of local food production, the Foreign Office pushed for immediate relief plans; however, not just because of humanitarian concerns. Similar to the situation in Spain, the British attached great importance to Greece's strategic position, in this case in the Eastern Mediterranean, positioned favourably within Britain's sea communications with India and to supplies of oil in the Middle East. A friendly post-war Greece was also vital to the British, with the Foreign Office aiming for a constitutional monarchy under the pro-British King George II.[32]

The British War Cabinet initially concurred that the most convenient solution was to purchase wheat in 'neutral' Soviet Russia, but when this option was pushed off the table in late June 1941, the focus shifted to Turkey. Minister of Economic Warfare Dalton argued that, as they could not prevent Turkish produce from reaching the Germans, it may as well go to the Greeks. Naval forces operating in the Aegean would protect the Turkish vessels from attacks, but the arrangement needed to remain strictly secret as these sea transports still involved a technical breach of the blockade, which officially did not allow food imports into occupied countries, and could therefore possibly lead to difficulties with the other Allied governments.[33] The MEW explained to the US government that the Greek claim to relief was the strongest they had yet encountered: 'Their gallant fight has earned them exceptional sympathy, and there are reports that their present distress is exceptionally severe'.[34] All credits for the relief scheme nevertheless had to go to the Greek leaders, who by then had relocated to London: a policy that the Foreign Office described as 'selling the King to his people',[35] which underwrites the strong political dimension to British support for food aid for Greece.

In August 1941, the Turkish government agreed to the relief scheme, and the first Turkish vessels set sail to Greece two months later.[36] However, it soon became clear that this scheme would hardly suffice in providing for the basic needs of the Greeks, who needed wheat more than anything; something that Turkey could not supply. Mortality levels in Greece were rising rapidly, which increased pressure on the British administration to relax the blockade. In late 1941, the Greek-American community and Prime Minister Tsouderos sent urgent letters to Churchill and Roosevelt to allow a cargo of 8,000 tons of wheat to be sent to Greece, which Minister of State in the Middle East, Oliver Lyttelton, had already concurred to release from the Middle East Supply Centre.[37] Lyttelton wrote to London:

> I cannot believe that at the worst our blockade would be seriously impaired if even one full cargo found its way into German bellies, nor can I believe in the long run that to allow the Greeks to die in the streets is going to help us to win the war on their behalf.[38]

The Foreign Office anxiously agreed that the suffering might be attributed to British action, thereby 'producing a permanent anti-British feeling in those countries which may well dictate the post-war policies of their Governments'.[39] At the same time, the Greeks might look more favourably towards the Americans, who had persistently offered help. Yet, in the War Cabinet meeting on 24 December 1941, Dalton's view still prevailed – any supply of wheat to Greece through the blockade would open the way to demands from the other Allies and make it 'impossible to deny similar treatment to the peoples of other European countries overrun by the enemy'.[40]

Within a couple of weeks, the MEW and War Cabinet also shifted to the Foreign Office's stance. This shift was surely related to the US entering the war in December 1941, who were committed to winning the war through an internationalist foreign policy.[41] Additionally, in Britain, public criticism of the blockade was being voiced on an unprecedented scale. Yet perhaps even more decisive was the mounting internal opposition. In addition to high-ranking officials in Turkey and Egypt, the Foreign Office began openly opposing the War Cabinet's decision, stating that 'the Greek relief issue is one in which arguments of economic warfare cannot be allowed to outweigh arguments of political warfare'.[42] Foreign Secretary Anthony Eden warned about British public opinion and embarrassment in the event of future military operations in Greece, even explicitly stating that their policy was 'partially responsible for starving the most gallant of our Allies'.[43] Lyttelton similarly wrote to Churchill:

> I must recount my opinion that we shall undermine resistance of ally and lose a possible centre of successful insurrection against Axis if we continue starving the Greeks [...] I have no doubt where balance of advantage to win war lies.[44]

It became impossible for the War Cabinet to ignore this broad-based opposition, which clearly voiced British responsibility for exacerbating the famine.

In a meeting on 7 January 1942 with the Foreign Office, Dalton reluctantly agreed with Eden to allow an immediate 'token' shipment of 8,000 tons of wheat from Egypt to be sent under the auspices of the International Red Cross Committee (ICRC), provided the US and Soviet Union concurred. Furthermore, it would be made publicly known that this was an exceptional case and no further concessions would be made. Five days later, the War Cabinet approved this proposal. The Foreign Office's suggestion to keep the plan secret was firmly rejected, as Dalton considered it vital to 'get the maximum propaganda value' from the concession, suggesting it was more about the appearance of relief than actually relieving the famine.[45]

Significantly, Lord Privy Seal and soon-to-be Deputy Prime Minister Clement Attlee wrote to Churchill, who was not present during the meeting, that the War Cabinet's decision was made in view of the effect upon Greek crews serving with them and Greek public opinion.[46] Foreign Secretary Eden, on the other hand, explained to the prime minister that it was imperative to win public support for the Greek government, whose resigning would 'create a most damaging situation for us both at home and abroad'. He added:

> If [the] Greek population is seriously reduced it may take generations to restore the Greek state to healthy condition and a healthy Greece is essential to us in [the] Eastern Mediterranean. Three is a danger too that Italians might successfully infiltrate into and establish themselves in a half-populated Greece.[47]

Churchill briefly responded to both of them: 'I agree with your decision. Impossible [to] resist Minister of State'.[48] This suggests that the most significant breach of the blockade policy may not have been prompted by humanitarian considerations, but because of public opinion and, perhaps even more so, post-war geopolitical considerations. All considerations by the British War Cabinet were clearly influenced by the role Greece could play to their benefit in the new post-war world order.

This did not conclude the discussions on Greece, as it was evident that sending just one cargo would not suffice. On Dalton's initiative, further concessions were drafted on very strict conditions, which while 'perfectly reasonable on the face of it' would be unlikely for the Germans to meet.[49] He suggested that the Germans would allow 'neutral' Swedish ships to carry imports from overseas to Greece, with all belligerents giving safe conduct and that a neutral commission consisting of 'reliable' Swedish nationals would be established in Greece to control the distribution under the auspices of the ICRC. The advantage of the Swedish scheme was that the British would not have to assume any commitment and that benevolent Swedes could inform the British on what was happening in Greece. Furthermore, neither wheat nor flour was considered a major factor in the blockade, as it was wrongly estimated that Germany was not short of cereals.[50] Both acceptance and rejection of the offer would work in favour of the Allies: in case of rejection, the Germans could be publicly and undeniably blamed for the famine in Greece. This indicates that, as was the case for the Axis, both hunger and food aid functioned as weapons of warfare for the British. It also demonstrates that Swedish 'neutrality' during the war was exploited and violated by both Allied and Axis powers, as well as by the Swedes themselves.

On 16 February 1942, Churchill chaired the War Cabinet meeting that approved the proposal and, in the following two months, the scheme was respectively approved by the US, Swedish, Canadian, Italian, and German governments. The Swedish scheme would aim at shipping 15,000 tons of wheat per month from Canada with the money for shipping coming from the Greek government and the wheat being a gift from the Canadians.[51] While the scheme was completely London-born, to the outside world – including the British House of Commons – it was presented as a Swedish plan.[52] The British interference and dominance in the scheme became even clearer in the following months when the composition of the commission was discussed and the MEW delayed the scheme until all their wishes for 'neutral' Swedish supervision were met.[53]

The scheme was inaugurated in August 1942 and continued well into 1944.[54] The experience of establishing a humanitarian corridor to provide food for the Greek population established an important model for addressing hunger in subsequent armed conflicts.[55] However, during WWII, after Greece, the War Cabinet turned down all proposals for allowing foodstuffs to pass through the blockade to relieve the populations in enemy-occupied territory, thereby reaffirming British dominance in wartime European military and economic matters.[56] Yet, in reality, the relief scheme was largely run by the US. In addition to Canadian wheat, the shipments eventually included pulses, dried fish, powdered milk, and vitamins: mostly produced in the US and largely paid for with US Lend-Lease money. After liberation, Greece would become one of the main United Nations Relief and Rehabilitation Administration (UNRRA) beneficiaries, which was similarly largely US-dominated.[57] Relief for wartime and post-war Greece thereby marked the shift in transatlantic relations that the British had been fearing all along.

Liberation before relief: The Netherlands, 1944–45

The tightening of the Allied blockade after the Greek exemption would play a central role during another European famine: the Dutch 'Hunger Winter' of 1944–45. The Dutch famine resulted from the cumulative effect of several transportation and distribution difficulties following the Allied liberation of the south of the Netherlands. In September 1944, the Allied advance under Operation Market Garden stagnated at the Rhine River following the loss of the Battle of Arnhem. The northern part of the Netherlands remained occupied by the German forces until the spring of 1945, separating the western Netherlands from three major food-producing provinces as well as from the Dutch mining area in the south. The further impact of a national railway strike, a temporary German embargo on inland shipping, a heavy frost period, severe fuel shortages, and the German requisitioning of transportation means resulted in increased food shortages and ultimately led to famine in the urbanised western Netherlands between November 1944 and May 1945, costing approximately 20,000 lives.[58]

On the very day that the Allies lost the Battle of Arnhem on 25 September 1944, Dutch Queen Wilhelmina summoned prime minister of the Dutch government-in-exile in London Pieter S. Gerbrandy to approach Churchill to discuss relief for the occupied Netherlands.[59] After numerous requests, on 5 October 1944, the prime ministers finally met. Based on estimations of the food supply, Gerbrandy warned that people in the western Netherlands could survive only until 1 December of that year. But Churchill did not consider breaching the blockade policy again; he was adamant that any food admitted would directly or indirectly benefit the Germans and therefore prolong their resistance. Moreover, he also believed that there was a good chance that the Netherlands would be liberated before 1 December.[60]

In the meantime, the Dutch cabinet had already approached the neutral Swedish and Swiss governments to enquire about relief opportunities from their countries and, as early as 2 October 1944, Sweden declared to be agreeable to this idea.[61] Provided that the Dutch government made full arrangements with the Swedes, the British War Cabinet saw no objections from the blockade point of view. Since 1941, they had allowed this kind of foreign exchange within the blockaded area, enabling occupied territories to purchase food from neutral countries.[62] US General and Commander of the Supreme Headquarters Allied Expeditionary Force (SHAEF) Dwight D. Eisenhower also approved of the plan. In late October, he stated: 'I recognize [that] part of relief supplies will fall into German hands, but I accept this risk. Any assistance to the Dutch civil population that can be provided before liberation will ease the relief problem subsequent to liberation'.[63]

On 6 November 1944, the British Chiefs of Staff discussed four possible relief schemes: (1) A Swedish ship would bring relief supplies from Gothenburg to a Dutch port, most likely Amsterdam, (2) an ICRC ship would bring cargo from Lisbon, (3) supplies would be dropped by air onto three principle towns in the western Netherlands, and (4) a Red Cross barge would ship supplies from Basel down the Rhine.[64] In the following negotiations between the Allies and Germans, military considerations proved to be of prime importance. Germany quite clearly favoured the last plan: according to the SHAEF, this was only because they wanted the Rhine navigable for their own benefit. The Allied Headquarters dismissed the idea of airdrops, since there was no guarantee that the supplies would actually reach the civil population. The Allies did, however, regard an initial symbolic airdrop of supplies after liberation to be 'essential' in terms of 'psychological warfare'.[65] The first two plans seemed agreeable, but the British War Cabinet considered Red Cross shipments from Lisbon less desirable in view of the many requests from other occupied countries.[66] Thus, the only proposition left at this point to consider seriously was relief from neutral Sweden.

Despite the promising outlook, no progress was made in the following weeks. Shortly after SHAEF refused to open the Rhine for transportation, the Germans denied observers from the ICRC to distribute the Swedish supplies on grounds that the Netherlands was now a combat zone and any relief permitted needed to be distributed by the German and Dutch Red Cross. Although this would mean an enormous concession from the Allied side, Secretary of State Anthony Eden initially endorsed this change of plans. However, soon after, a secret report from the Netherlands was received that stated that all lorries and petrol belonging to the Dutch Red Cross had been confiscated and its officers were resigning, as a protest against the forcible appointment of a Dutch Germanic SS official as its new chief.[67] While food relief ships in Sweden and Lisbon lay ready with German approval, the Allies immediately put the plans for Swedish relief on hold.[68]

By December 1944, the food shortage in the western Netherlands had turned into famine, but all relief negotiations seemed stranded. On 16 December, Dutch prime minister Gerbrandy wrote to General Eisenhower: 'Relief for the occupied Netherlands at the time of the liberation must have priority above everything, even above the slogan: first of all, defeat of Germany. The Netherlands government cannot accept the liberation of corpses'.[69] The Supreme Commander himself also grew anxious to get supplies into the Netherlands: 'a ton sent before starvation is worth five sent too late'.[70] But Churchill was not convinced about the severity of the situation and delayed approval of new relief plans:

> Before the liberation of Western Europe, we used to be told that most of the inhabitants would be starving. When we got to France and found the inhabitants alive, we were told that it was the Belgians who were short of food, and now that we are in Belgium, the Dutch are proclaimed as the principal sufferers. Where will it stop?[71]

Churchill was convinced that any relief shipments would compromise the principles of economic warfare, according to which principles of no foodstuffs were allowed to pass the blockade to enemy-occupied territories, except for the benefit of prisoners of war.[72] Other considerations also played a role. During the war, the question of food aid became intertwined with the British import programme, as diverting shipping and food supplies meant less capacity for domestic imports. Food imports in Britain had halved from an average of 22 million tons before the war to between 10.6 and 11.5 million tons in the years 1942–44. The British government had to account for the declining food supplies, and allocating shipping for food aid thus came with significant risks, including popular discontent and loss of British support for the war effort.[73] There was also the domestic aspect of the Channel Islands, where, following the blockade by the British Royal Navy after the invasion of Normandy, food shortages in the autumn of 1944 also evolved into a severe food crisis. The Channel Island's last winter also became known as the 'hunger winter' and diverted British attention from the pleas from the Dutch and many other occupied countries in this same period.[74]

Finally, on 19 January 1945 – over three months after the initial Swedish promise – an agreement was reached. In the months of February to April 1945, a total of five Red Cross shipments – three from Sweden, one from Switzerland, and one from the ICRC – arrived in the occupied Netherlands, bringing a total of approximately 14,000 tons of food into the country. In terms of measurable effects, the supplies meant eight weeks of daily rations increased by 200–400 kcal with greater allowances for the specific needs of different age groups, infants in particular. Nevertheless, the Red Cross shipments could certainly not bring an end to the famine. In total, the people in the occupied western Netherlands received less than 5 kg of food relief per capita during the Hunger Winter. In comparison, during the months of December 1944–May 1945, the still-occupied Channel Islands received 70 kg per capita from neutral sources.[75]

Meanwhile, negotiations about Allied relief also continued, in particular talks concerning the possibility of deploying aircrafts to drop food supplies onto the principal urban areas. The use of airplanes to drop food had been dismissed by the Combined Chiefs of Staff in the autumn of 1944 but was again re-examined in March 1945. One reason was that estimations of the Dutch food supply indicated that it would be completely exhausted by 28 April: after this point, famine mortality would occur 'on a considerable scale'.[76] Another factor was that, from a military standpoint, SHAEF considered it far from advisable to undertake military operations in the western Netherlands, thus favouring preparations to enable relief.[77]

The British Chiefs of Staff agreed with SHAEF that an immediate attempt to drop suitable supplies ought to be made, in spite of the risk that these supplies might fall into German hands – a shift in mindset that was surely related to the imminent Allied invasion of Nazi Germany and the risks of liberating a half-starved country, for which they would partly be held responsible. Yet this time, it was the US Joint Chiefs of Staff who delayed the initiative, remaining adamant about not sending supplies through the blockade.[78] Despite this opposition, on 17 April, Chief of Staff of SHAEF Walter Bedell Smith summoned Air Commodore Andrew Geddes, the mastermind behind Operation Overlord and Operation Market Garden, to commence planning for an air operation with heavy bombers that would provide relief to the Dutch.[79] Six days later, the Combined Chiefs of Staff formally authorised Eisenhower to negotiate a truce with the German authorities in the Netherlands that enabled the introduction of relief, on the condition that it did not prejudice the principle of unconditional surrender.

While both the British and the Americans were apprehensive about upsetting Anglo-Soviet relations over the question of food aid for the Dutch, both sides did concede that the Russians should simply be informed and not consulted, as Roosevelt had proposed. Churchill warned: 'I have already made it clear [...] that I am not prepared to let the Russians veto the plan'.[80] The Soviet command was, however, invited to be present at all discussions with German representatives. In response, Soviet Liaison Officer General Antonov added one more condition to the list; namely, that the local German command was obliged not to transfer its troops to other parts of the front during the armistice period, including to the Eastern Soviet-German front.[81]

Eisenhower assigned two strategic bomber forces – the RAF Bomber Command and the Eighth US Air Force.[82] The German authorities agreed to the airdrops and accepted the invitation to meet with Allied representatives on 28 and 30 April in the small village of Achterveld to negotiate matters directly connected with the introduction of food supplies into Western Holland. Following these negotiations, from 29 April until 8 May 1945, RAF Lancasters and USAAF B-17 heavy bombers dropped food onto the western Netherlands, in a total of 5,294 flights.[83] In the meanwhile, on 5 May, the German troops in the Netherlands officially surrendered. While the entire operation was impressive, the outcome for the population was somewhat less extraordinary: the total amount of the drops (7.8 million kg) equalled a mere 3 kg of food per head of population in the starving urban west. The true Allied contribution to relieving the crisis followed more than a week after liberation, predominantly through land and sea supply. In the end, the contribution of the famous airdrops was mostly symbolic, which was exactly how the Allies had intended it. For them, the food drops were a political instrument, important for their legitimacy and post-war power relations as it contributed to verifying an end to the war in a visible and spectacular fashion.

Conclusion

The Allied economic blockade was a powerful weapon of warfare during WWII. While the blockade was aimed at weakening the Axis powers by depriving them of resources and forcing neutral countries to align with Allied interests, it had devastating effects on civilian populations and even contributed to famines in Europe. This chapter has revealed the major differences in the British political decision-making process and approach to three of these wartime famines. In Spain, restrictive trade policies were a response to the Franco regime's pro-Axis stance, and leveraging food supplies and other vital resources was aimed at keeping Spain from entering the war on the Axis' side. In Greece, the blockade contributed to famine conditions by reducing foodstuffs in the country, and then hampering large-scale relief operations, although public and political pressure eventually led to an exceptional relaxation of these measures to secure Greece as a post-war ally. By contrast, during the Dutch famine, the Allied blockade was strictly maintained until only a few days before the end of the war, as Churchill firmly believed that relief should follow liberation and any relief supplies sent through the blockade would only prolong German resistance.

Ultimately, the Allied approach to famine in wartime Europe was mostly dictated by political motivations – whether to force neutrality, defeat the enemy, or secure post-war alliances. At times, political pressures, unfavourable public opinion, and strategic interests led to adjustments in these tactics, as seen in the example of Greece. However, in other instances, such as in the Netherlands, psychological warfare tactics and propaganda were deployed to shape the post-war narrative of wartime deprivation and absolve the Allies of all responsibility for hunger and famine. Thus, the use of food and hunger as weapons of warfare comprised of a complex interplay of military strategies and political objectives, often with little regard for the long-lasting effects on the affected civilian populations.

Notes

1 The National Archives Kew, London [TNA], FO 837/1218, Statement for the Prime Minister's speech, 15 August 1940.

2 British Library [BL], IOR/M/3/939, *Handbook of Economic Warfare* (London 1939); BL, IOR/M/3/939, 'Three Years of Economic Warfare', 18 August 1942.

3 TNA, FO 837/1218, Minutes MEW, 15 and 24 June 1940; Ibid., Leith Ross to Cadogan, 1 July 1940; TNA, FO 837/1218, Draft minute MEW, August 1940; J. Beaumont, 'Starving for Democracy: Britain's Blockade of and Relief for Occupied Europe, 1939-1945', *War & Society,* 8 (1990): 58. On the WWI blockade: Clotilde Druelle, *Feeding Occupied France during World War I: Herbert Hoover and the Blockade* (Switzerland: Palgrave Macmillan, 2019); and George H. Nash, *The Life of Herbert Hoover: The Humanitarian, 1914–1917* (New York: W. W. Norton, 1988).

4 While the impact of the blockade upon German civilians had been severe, the British saw the military measure as the key driver behind the Allied Victory, as it had forced the Germans into submarine warfare, which ultimately brought the Americans into the war. M.E. Cox, *Hunger in War & Peace: Women and Children in Germany, 1914–1924* (Oxford, 2019). See also: N.A. Lambert, *Planning Armageddon: British Economic Warfare and the First World War* (Cambridge, MA 2012), Ch 2–3.

5 On Spain: M. A. Del Arco Blanco, 'Famine in Spain during Franco's Dictatorship (1939-1952)', *Journal of Contemporary History*, 56:1 (2021), 3–27; M. A. Del Arco Blanco and P. Anderson, eds., *Franco's Famine: Malnutrition, Disease and Starvation in Post-Civil War Spain* (London: Bloomsbury, 2021). On Greece: M. Mazower, *Inside Hitler's Greece: The Experience of Occupation 1941–1944* (New Haven, 1993); G.A. Kazamias, 'The Politics of Famine Relief for Occupied Greece', in R. Clogg (ed.) *Bearing Gifts for Greeks: Humanitarian Aid to Greece in the 1940s* (Basingstoke, 2008), 39–57; V. Hionidou, *Famine and Death in Occupied Greece, 1941-44* (Cambridge, 2006). On the Netherlands: B. Moore, "The Western Allies and Food Relief to the Occupied Netherlands, 1944–1945," *War & Society* 10 (1992): 91–118; I. De Zwarte, *The Hunger Winter: Fighting Famine in the Occupied Netherlands, 1944–1945* (Cambridge, 2020).

6 Del Arco Blanco, 'Famine'; Del Arco Blanco and Anderson, *Franco's Famine*.

7 A. Viñas, *¿Quién quiso la guerra civil?: historia de una conspiración* (Barcelona: Crítica, 2019). P. Preston, *The Spanish Civil War: Reaction, Revolution and Revenge* (London: Harper, 2006).

8 J. A. Durango, 'España y la política internacional del fin de la guerra civil al comienzo de la mundial', *Espacio, Tiempo y Forma, Serie V, Historia Contemporánea*, 5 (1992), 261.

9 Axis Plans in the Mediterranean. *An Analysis of German Geopolitical Ideas on Italy, France, the Balearic Islands, Gibraltar, Catalonia and Spain, with a Preface by Captain Liddell Hart* (London: General Press, 1939), 3–4.
10 D. W. Pike, *Franco and the Axis Stigma* (Basingstoke: Palgrave, 2014). E. Moradiellos, *Franco frente a Churchill: España y Gran Bretaña en la Segunda Guerra Mundial, 1939–1945* (Barcelona: Península, 2005), 71–75.
11 J. J. Díaz Benítez, 'The Etappe Kanaren: A Case Study of the Secret Supply of the German Navy in Spain during the Second World War', *The International Journal of Maritime History*, 30:3 (2018), 477–478.
12 A. Viñas, *Guerra, dinero, dictadura. Ayuda fascista y autarquía en la España de Franco* (Barcelona: Crítica, 1984), 255–256; R. García Pérez, *Franquismo y tercer Reich. Las relaciones económicas hispano-alemanas durante la segunda guerra mundial* (Madrid: CEC, 1994).
13 W. N. Medlicott, *The Economic Blockade*, vol. 1 (London: HMSO, 1952), 94–101. Archivo General de la Administración [AGA], Asuntos Exteriores [AE], 82/5692, October 30, 1939. AGA, Presidencia del Gobierno [PG], 20495, February 5, 1940.
14 The experience of Sweden in the Great War may have prompted the British to adopt a more expedient approach towards Spain. See: Cox, *Hunger in War & Peace*, 31–33.
15 AGA, AE, 82/03975, folder 1, December 12, 1939. R. Wigg, *Churchill and Spain. The Survival of the Franco Regime, 1940–1945* (New York: Routledge, 2005), 9–10.
16 J. Tusell, *Franco, España y la II Guerra Mundial: entre el eje y la neutralidad* (Madrid: Temas de Hoy, 1995), 71–72. *Boletín Oficial del Estado*, June 13, 1940.
17 Moradiellos, *Franco*, 117; Tusell, *Franco*, 237–239.
18 Medlicott, *The Economic Blockade*, vol. 1, 96, 431–434, 436–437, 509–510; A. Viñas, J. Viñuela, F. Eguidazu, C. Fernández, and F. Senen, *Política comercial exterior en España, 1931–1975, vol. 1* (Madrid: Banco Exterior de España, 1979), 331.
19 AGA, AE, 54/7293, 9 August 1940.
20 AGA, PG, 20557, *Informe de la Secretaría Local de FET y de las JONS*, June 1940.
21 Moradiellos, *Franco*, 159, 164–167.
22 P. Preston, *Franco: Caudillo de España* (Barcelona: Grijalbo, 1994), 487–490; N. J. W. Goda, *Y mañana... el mundo: Hitler, África noroccidental y el cambio hacia América* (Alianza: Madrid, 2002), 129–134, 149–156, 201–202 y 206–208.
23 E. Moradiellos, *Quo vadis, Hispania? Winston Churchill y la guerra civil española (1936–1939)* (Madrid: Real Academia de la Historia, 2021), 164.
24 Viñas, *Política*, 334–335; Wigg, *Churchill*, 20–21; J. M. Thomàs, *Roosevelt y Franco: de la Guerra Civil española a Pearl Harbor* (Barcelona: Edhasa, 2007), 348–351.
25 S. Hoare, *Ambassador on a Special Mission* (London: Collins, 1946), 114–115. *La Vanguardia Española*, 18 July 1941, 5–6.
26 Examples: AGA, AE, 82/5444, folder 4, telegram, December 21, 1941. AGA, AE, 82/05444, folder 5, Gibraltar, salida 1941, December 28, 1941.
27 Moradiellos, *Franco*, 259–261.
28 M. Peña Díaz and F. Contreras Pérez, 'Carceller Segura y el origen del sector petrolero español', in Raúl Molina Recio, ed., *Pioneros. Empresas y empresarios en el primer tercio del siglo XX en España* (Granada: Comares, 2019), 93–94.
29 AGA, AE, 54/6940, Discurso del Duque de Alba, June 1943.
30 Hionidou, 'Famine in Occupied Greece: Causes and Consequences', in *Bearing Gifts to Greeks*, 25–26.
31 TNA, FO 837/1230, Memorandum Royal Greek Legation, 25 April 1941; TNA, FO 837/1230, FO to Canea, 1 May 1941.
32 TNA, FO 837/1230, Ronald to Stirling, 8 May 1941; TNA, FO 837/1230, FO to Lampson, May 1941; Clogg, 'The Greek Government-in-Exile 1941-4', *The International History Review*, 1, 3 (1979), 378; Hionidou, *Famine and Death in Occupied Greece*, 236; Kazamias, 'The Politics of Famine Relief', 50. See also: P. Papastratis, *British Policy towards Greece during the Second World War, 1941–1944* (Cambridge 1984).

33 TNA, FO 837/1230, Eden to Dalton, 28 June 1941; Ibid., Dalton to Eden, 3 July 1941; Ibid., FO to Angora, 14 July 1941.

34 TNA, FO 837/1230, MEW to Washington, 14 July 1941.

35 TNA, FO 371/33187, Memorandum on position King of Greece, without date; Clogg, 'The Greek Government-in-Exile', 379–380; Hionidou, *Famine and Death in Occupied Greece,* 18.

36 TNA, FO 837/1239, Summary Statement of the Greek Relief Program, 16 August 1944. From October 1941 until August 1942, a total of almost 20,000 tons of food was sent from Turkey to Greece. TNA, FO 837/1217, Lists of food sent to Greece by Embassy London, 6 December 1943; Kazamias, 'Turks, Swedes and Famished Greeks: Some Aspects of Famine Relief in Occupied Greece, 1941–44', *Balkan Studies,* 33, 2 (1992), 294–298.

37 TNA, FO 837/1232, Appeal Greek Relief Committee of America, 10 November 1941; TNA., FO 837/1233, Tsouderos to Churchill, 14 December 1941; TNA, FO 837/1233, FO to Dalton, 22 December 1941; A. Kyrou, 'The Greek-American Community and the Famine in Axis-occupied Greece', in *Bearing Gifts to Greeks*, 58–84.

38 TNA, FO 837/1233, Lampson to FO and MEW, 9 December 1941.

39 TNA, FO 837/1233, Memorandum on Greek relief by FO, 22 December 1941. See also: Kazamias, 'The Politics of Famine Relief', 48.

40 TNA, CAB 65/20/26b, W.M. 134 (41) Conclusions, 24 December 1941. Dalton suggested three other ways of helping the Greeks: (1) expanding the Turkish scheme, (2) a child emigration scheme, and (3) a scheme to allow free and safe passage to Axis vessels carrying food from Trieste. Earlier, they had also seriously considered retaliating against the Italian civil population in East Africa. TNA, PREM 3/74/5; TNA, FO 837/1231; Kazamias, 'The Politics of Famine Relief', 47–48.

41 S.A. Brewer, *Why America Fights: Patriotism and War Propaganda from the Philippines to Iraq* (Oxford 2009), 80–126.

42 FO 371/32455, Hoare to Sargent, 2 January 1945.

43 TNA, CAB 66/20/37, Memorandum Eden 'Greece: The Blockade', 3 January 1942. See also: TNA, PREM 3/74/5.

44 TNA, PREM 3/74/5, Lampson to Churchill, 9 January 1942. See also: Hionidou, *Famine and Death in Occupied Greece,* 17–18.

45 TNA, FO 837/1231, Minutes Dalton on meeting with FO, 7 January 1942; TNA, FO 837/1231, Note on position Dalton, 8 January 1942; TNA, FO 837/1231, CAB 65/25/4, W.M. 4 (42) Conclusions, 12 January 1942.

46 TNA, PREM 3/74/5, Attlee to Churchill, without date.

47 TNA, PREM 3/74/5, Eden to Churchill, without date. See also: 'The Politics of Famine Relief', 50.

48 TNA, PREM 3/74/5, Churchill to Attlee and Eden, without date.

49 TNA, FO 837/1235, Draft conditions MEW for admission of further relief foodstuffs into Greece, 2 February 1942; TNA, FO 837/1235, Minutes meeting MEW, 4 February 1942.

50 TNA, CAB 66/22/10, Memorandum Dalton 'Greece: The Blockade', 14 February 1942; TNA, FO 837/1235, Minute on Greek relief Camps, 15 February 1942. During WWI, neutral ships were also deployed to send food aid to warring Europe.

51 TNA, CAB 65/25/21, W.M. 21 (42), 16 February 1942; TNA, FO 837/1235, Sweden to FO, 18 April 1942; TNA, FO 837/1235, Canada H.C. to D.O., 12 April 1942.

52 TNA, FO 837/1235, FO to Stockholm, 27 February and 12 March 1942; Ibid., FO to British representatives in Stockholm, Washington, Ankara, Cairo, Berne and Vatican on statement House of Commons, 21 April 1942; TNA, FO 837/1235, FO 837/1237, Sargent to Tsouderos, 28 August 1942.

53 TNA, FO 837/1235, Minutes Camps on Swedish relief scheme, 17 May 1942; TNA, FO 837/1235, Agreements with notes Dalton, Selbourne and Morton, 19–22 May; Hionidou, *Famine and Death in Occupied Greece,* 131–34.

54 Kazamias, 'Turks, Swedes and Famished Greeks', 300–9.

55 Elisabeth Piller, 'The Blockade and the Making of Modern Food Aid in the Era of the Two World Wars', *The International History Review* (2024), 1–11.

56 TNA, CAB 66/53/46, W.M. 63 (43), Minute 5.

57 For more on the politics of relief in occupied Greece, see: A. Laiou-Thomadakis, 'The Politics of Hunger: Economic Aid to Greece, 1943–1945', *Journal of the Hellenic Diaspora,* 7, 2 (1980), 47–62; Hionidou, 'Relief and Politics in Occupied Greece, 1941-4', *Journal of Contemporary History* 48, 4 (2013), 761–783. Kazamias similarly calls the Swedish relief scheme an 'early precursor of the shape of the post-war world under American dominance'. Kazamias, 'The Politics of Famine Relief', 50–53.
58 De Zwarte, *The Hunger Winter*. This section is largely based on Ch5 of that book.
59 Louis De Jong, *Het Koninkrijk der Nederlanden in de Tweede Wereldoorlog* (Amsterdam: NIOD, 2011), 10b, 1083; Moore, "The Western Allies," 96.
60 TNA, PREM 3/221/11, Minutes interview Churchill and Gerbrandy, 5 October 1944; NARA, 331, Entry 2, Box 117, Letter Morton to Bedell Smith, 12 October 1944.
61 NARA, 331, Entry 2, Box 117, Letter Foreign Office to Chiefs of Staff, 5 October 1944; NIOD, 233b, inv.no 28, Telegram Van Kleffens to Bern, 11 October 1944; Letter C.H.C. Flugi van Aspermont Genève to Dutch government, 19 October 1944. See also: Pieter Sjoerds Gerbrandy, *Eenige Hoofdpunten van Het Regeeringsbeleid in Londen Gedurende de Oorlogsjaren 1940–1945* (The Hage: Rijksuitgeverij, 1946), 128–129.
62 TNA, WO 220/668, AMSSO to SHAEF Forward, 6 October 1944; TNA, FO 238/303, Telegram FO to Stockholm, 19 October 1944; Beamont, "Starving for Democracy," 65–66.
63 National Archives and Record Administration, Maryland [NARA], 331, Entry 2, Box 117, Letter SHAEF Main signed Eisenhower to British Chiefs of Staff, 29 October 1944. Also cited in: Moore, "The Western Allies," 98.
64 NARA, 331, Entry 2, Box 117, Message SHAEF Main signed Eisenhower to British Chiefs of Staff, 6 November 1944.
65 NARA, 331, Entry 2, Box 117, Message SHAEF Main G-5 signed Eisenhower to War Office, 15 November 1944.
66 TNA, FO 238/303, Message FO signed W.G. Hayter to Ambassador Sir Neville Bland, 9 November 1944; TNA, CAB 119/140, COS meeting 27 October-7 November 1944; TNA, Letter Foreign Office to Secretary Chiefs of Staff Committee, 30 October 1944; TNA, WO 220/668, Admiralty to FO, 26 October 1944; TNA, PREM 3 221 11, AMSSO to SHAEF Main, 3 November 1944.
67 TNA, FO 238/303, Letter R.A. Gallop to Sir Nevil Bland, 7 December 1944; Aart W. Wassenaar. *Van Winterhulp via Oost-Compagnie en Marseille naar Rode Kruis: De Loopbaan van Carel Piek Voor, Tijdens, en Na de Bezettingstijd 1940–1945. Een Geschiedenis van Idealisme en Collaboratie* (Soesterberg: Aspekt, 2016), 139–145.
68 Bundesarchiv Berlin [BA], NS19/3403, Telegram Rauter to Berlin, 14 December 1944.
69 Cited in: De Jong, *Het Koninkrijk* 10b, 1115.
70 TNA, PREM 3/221/11, Message Eden to Churchill, 17 December 1944. See also: TNA, CAB 66/57, Report War Cabinet, 4 November 1944; Henri A. Van der Zee, *The Hunger Winter: occupied Holland, 1944–45* (Lincoln: Nebraska University Press, 1998), 170–172.
71 TNA, PREM 4/29/12, Cherwell to Churchill, without date.
72 TNA, FO 837/1223, Camps to Markbreiter, 20 January 1942. See also: TNA, FO 837/1232, Letter Dalton to Maitland, 8 October 1941.
73 Ina Zweiniger-Bargielowska, *Austerity in Britain: Rationing, Controls, and Consumption, 1939–1955* (Oxford: Oxford University Press, 2023), 32–44.
74 Charles Cruickshank, *The German Occupation of the Channel Islands* (London: Oxford University Press, 1975), 259–286.
75 De Jong, *Het Koninkrijk* 10b, 1103.
76 NARA, 331, Entry 2, Box 118, SHAEF Forward signed Eisenhower to AGWAR and AMSSO; NARA, 331, Entry 2, Box 118, Message to Blaskowitz, 23 March 1945. See also: TNA, PREM 3/221/12.
77 NARA, 331, Entry 2, Box 118, Report SHAEF FWD to AGWAR and AMSSO, 27 March 1945. Eisenhower, *Crusade in Europe* (London: William Heinemann Limited, 1948), 449.
78 TNA, WO 220/668, JSM Washington to AMSSO, 7 April 1945.
79 NIOD, 458, inv.no. 27, Hearing Schwebel, 14 June 1946, 11708–11709; Stephen Dando-Collins, *Operation Chowhound: The Most Risky, Most Glorious US Bomber Mission of WWII* (New York: Palgrave, 2015), 89–94.

80 TNA, CAB 122/993, Telegram Churchill to British Chiefs of Staff, 21 April 1945.
81 TNA, CAB 122/993, Message SHAEF Forward to War Department, 24 April 1945; NARA, 331, Entry 2, Box 118, Message Military Mission Moscow to Combined Chiefs of Staff and Eisenhower, 27 April 1945.
82 NARA, 331, Entry 2, Box 118, Message Air Staff SHAEF to USSTAF Main, 24 April 1945.
83 On two days, the RAF and USAAF had to cancel one of their missions due to bad weather. For more on these missions, see also: Onderwater, Hans. *Operatie "Manna": De Geallieerde Voedseldroppings April/Mei 1945* (Weesp: Romen Luchtvaart, n.d.), 60–85; 128–130; De Jong, *Het Koninkrijk* 10b, 1344–1351.

References

Axis Plans in the Mediterranean. *An Analysis of German Geopolitical Ideas on Italy, France, the Balearic Islands, Gibraltar, Catalonia and Spain, with a Preface by Captain Liddell Hart*. London: General Press, 1939.

Beaumont, Joan. 'Starving for Democracy: Britain's Blockade of and Relief for Occupied Europe, 1939-1945'. *War & Society*, 8 (1990): 57–82.

Brewer, Susan A. *Why America Fights: Patriotism and War Propaganda from the Philippines to Iraq*. Oxford: Oxford University Press, 2009.

Clogg, Richard. 'The Greek Government-in-Exile 1941-4'. *The International History Review*, 1, 3 (1979): 376–398.

Cox, Mary Elisabeth. *Hunger in War & Peace: Women and Children in Germany, 1914–1924*. Oxford: Oxford University Press, 2019.

Cruickshank, Charles. *The German Occupation of the Channel Islands*. London: Oxford University Press, 1975.

Dando-Collins, Stephen. *Operation Chowhound: The Most Risky, Most Glorious US Bomber Mission of WWII*. New York: Palgrave, 2015.

De Jong, Louis. *Het Koninkrijk der Nederlanden in de Tweede Wereldoorlog*. Amsterdam: NIOD, 2011.

De Zwarte, Ingrid, *The Hunger Winter: Fighting Famine in the Occupied Netherlands, 1944–1945*. Cambridge: Cambridge University Press, 2020.

Del Arco Blanco, Miguel Ángel. 'Famine in Spain during Franco's Dictatorship (1939–1952)'. *Journal of Contemporary History*, 56, 1 (2021): 3–27.

Del Arco Blanco, Miguel Ángel and Peter Anderson, eds., *Franco's Famine: Malnutrition, Disease and Starvation in Post-Civil War Spain*. London: Bloomsbury, 2021.

Díaz Benítez, Juan J., 'The Etappe Kanaren: A Case Study of the Secret Supply of the German Navy in Spain during the Second World War'. *The International Journal of Maritime History*, 30, 3 (2018): 472–487.

Druelle, Clotilde, *Feeding Occupied France during World War I: Herbert Hoover and the Blockade*. Switzerland: Palgrave Macmillan, 2019.

Durango, José Alfonso. 'España y la política internacional del fin de la guerra civil al comienzo de la mundial'. *Espacio, Tiempo y Forma, Serie V, Historia Contemporánea*, 5 (1992): 257–272.

Eisenhower, Dwight D. *Crusade in Europe*. London: W. Heinemann Limited, 1948.

García Pérez, Rafael. *Franquismo y tercer Reich. Las relaciones económicas hispano-alemanas durante la segunda guerra mundial*. Madrid: CEC, 1994.

Gerbrandy, Pieter Sjoerds. *Eenige Hoofdpunten van Het Regeeringsbeleid in Londen Gedurende de Oorlogsjaren 1940–1945*. The Hage: Rijksuitgeverij, 1946.

Goda, Norman J. W. *Y mañana…el mundo: Hitler, África noroccidental y el cambio hacia América*. Alianza: Madrid, 2002.

Hionidou, Violetta. *Famine and Death in Occupied Greece, 1941–44*. Cambridge: Cambridge University Press, 2006.

Hionidou, Violetta. 'Relief and Politics in Occupied Greece, 1941-4'. *Journal of Contemporary History* 48, 4 (2013): 761–783.

Hoare, Samuel. *Ambassador on a Special Mission*. London: Collins, 1946.

Kazamias, Georgios A. 'Turks, Swedes and Famished Greeks: Some Aspects of Famine Relief in Occupied Greece, 1941-44', *Balkan Studies*, 33, 2 (1992): 293–307.
Kazamias, Georgios A. 'The Politics of Famine Relief for Occupied Greece', in Richard Clogg, ed., *Bearing Gifts for Greeks: Humanitarian Aid to Greece in the 1940s.* Basingstoke: Palgrave, 2008.
Kyrou, Alexander. 'The Greek-American Community and the Famine in Axis-occupied Greece', in Richard Clogg, ed., *Bearing Gifts for Greeks: Humanitarian Aid to Greece in the 1940s.* Basingstoke: Palgrave, 2008.
Laiou-Thomadakis, Angeliki. 'The Politics of Hunger: Economic Aid to Greece, 1943–1945'. *Journal of the Hellenic Diaspora,* 7, 2 (1980): 47–62.
Lambert, Nicholas A. Lambert. *Planning Armageddon: British Economic Warfare and the First World War.* Cambridge: Harvard University Press, 2012.
Mazower, Mark. *Inside Hitler's Greece: The Experience of Occupation 1941–1944.* New Haven: Yale University Press, 1993.
Medlicott, William N. *The Economic Blockade*, vol. 1. London: HMSO, 1952.
Moore, Bob, 'The Western Allies and Food Relief to the Occupied Netherlands, 1944–1945'. *War & Society*, 10 (1992): 91–118.
Moradiellos, Enrique. *Franco frente a Churchill: España y Gran Bretaña en la Segunda Guerra Mundial, 1939–1945.* Barcelona: Península, 2005.
Moradiellos, Enrique. *Quo vadis, Hispania? Winston Churchill y la guerra civil española (1936–1939).* Madrid: Real Academia de la Historia, 2021.
Nash, George H., *The Life of Herbert Hoover: The Humanitarian, 1914–1917.* New York: W. W. Norton, 1988.
Onderwater, Hans. *Operatie "Manna": De Geallieerde Voedseldroppings April/Mei 1945*. Weesp: Romen Luchtvaart, n.d.
Papastratis, Procopis. *British Policy towards Greece during the Second World War, 1941–1944.* Cambridge: Cambridge University Press, 1984.
Peña Díaz, Manuel and Francisco Contreras Pérez. 'Carceller Segura y el origen del sector petrolero español', in Raúl Molina Recio, ed., *Pioneros. Empresas y empresarios en el primer tercio del siglo XX en España.* Granada: Comares, 2019.
Pike, David W. *Franco and the Axis Stigma*. Basingstoke: Palgrave, 2014.
Piller, Elisabeth. 'The Blockade and the Making of Modern Food Aid in the Era of the Two World Wars', *The International History Review*, May (2024), 1–17.
Preston, Paul. *Franco: Caudillo de España.* Barcelona: Grijalbo, 1994.
Preston, Paul. *The Spanish Civil War: Reaction, Revolution and Revenge*. London: Harper, 2006.
Thomàs, Joan Maria. *Roosevelt y Franco: de la Guerra Civil española a Pearl Harbor*. Barcelona: Edhasa, 2007.
Tusell, Javier. *Franco, España y la II Guerra Mundial: entre el eje y la neutralidad.* Madrid: Temas de Hoy, 1995.
Van der Zee, Henri A. *The Hunger Winter: Occupied Holland, 1944-45.* Lincoln: Nebraska University Press, 1998.
Viñas, Ángel. *Guerra, dinero, dictadura. Ayuda fascista y autarquía en la España de Franco.* Barcelona: Crítica, 1984.
Viñas, Ángel, *¿Quién quiso la guerra civil?: historia de una conspiración*. Barcelona: Crítica, 2019.
Viñas, Ángel, Julio Viñuela, Fernando Eguidazu. Carlos Fernández Pulgar and Florensa Senen, *Política comercial exterior en España, 1931–1975, vol. 1.* Madrid: Banco Exterior de España, 1979.
Wassenaar, Aart W. *Van Winterhulp via Oost-Compagnie en Marseille naar Rode Kruis: De Loopbaan van Carel Piek Voor, Tijdens, en Na de Bezettingstijd 1940–1945. Een Geschiedenis van Idealisme en Collaboratie*. Soesterberg: Aspekt, 2016.
Wigg, Richard. *Churchill and Spain. The Survival of the Franco Regime, 1940–1945*. New York: Routledge, 2005.
Zweiniger-Bargielowska, Ina. *Austerity in Britain: Rationing, Controls, and Consumption, 1939–1955.* Oxford: Oxford University Press, 2023.

6 Humanitarian action

A moral economic periodization of famine relief

Norbert Götz, Georgina Brewis and Steffen Werther

Although the history of humanitarian efforts has become a vibrant field of academic study, there have been few attempts to delineate chronological patterns of humanitarianism. A few overviews offer suggestions on how to understand humanitarian action as a succession of characteristic periods or turning points that encapsulate prevailing conditions and trends. This chapter seeks to contribute to this discussion by emphasizing societal factors (including culture, media structures, and economics) to a greater extent than research has hitherto done.[1]

We propose a new periodic outline of humanitarianism based on moral economic developments and their socio-political consequences, rather than a history of events.[2] This implies a shift from the question of "what" to that of "how," and a shift of focus from the imperatives of crisis management in the outside world to the mechanisms of relief efforts themselves. We realize that periodization can be problematic if imposed too rigidly. Our aim is to offer a heuristic device that will help researchers improve their understanding of humanitarian efforts, particularly in relation to famine relief. We illustrate our temporal suggestions with three episodes of transnational famine relief: the Great Irish Famine in the 1840s, the famine in Soviet Russia and Ukraine in 1921–1922, and the Ethiopian famine of the mid-1980s.

A revisionist periodization

The years 1945 and 1989 appear in Michael Barnett's *Empire of Humanity* as turning points for humanitarian action. They illustrate the prominence of geopolitical explanations in humanitarian studies, such as the process of decolonization and the Cold War, and mirror the presentism that governs relief agencies and academic discourse alike. Practically all studies identify 1989 as a watershed.[3] Our economic and cultural approach to the history of humanitarian action deviates from such geopolitically determined perspectives, although some histories of humanitarianism do blend geopolitical and societal perspectives. A consistently cultural and socio-economical approach such as ours challenges the dominant paradigm that rests on issues of war and intervention, and government perspectives.

We identify three phases of humanitarian action, each with widely differing societal, political, and international circumstances: (a) nineteenth-century ad-hoc efforts, (b) twentieth-century organized relief based on planning and economics of scale, and (c) expressive humanitarianism characteristic of the half century from 1968 to the present. These periods correlate with (a) the politico-economic regimes of elitist laissez-faire liberalism, (b) Taylorism and mass society, and (c) an ambivalent blend of individualized post-material lifestyles, flexible production and communication regimes, and neoliberal public management. They are also connected with three distinct industrial revolutions (circa 1800, 1900, and 1970). The characterization of our first two periods as "ad hoc" and "organized" humanitarianism builds on the work of Curti.[4] Our

DOI: 10.4324/9781003465805-9

framework also resonates with that of those who challenge the notion of a "short" twentieth century extending from 1914 to 1989 and who advocate an alternative narrative of a "long" century from the 1890s until the present, with the 1970s as a decisive transformative period.[5]

The term "organized humanitarianism" reflects the proliferation of "organization" as a guiding principle in the early twentieth century. While the First World War raised relief efforts to a magnitude previously unimagined, this represents a high point in an ongoing transformation of philanthropic endeavors that started in the 1890s.[6] This transition involved physicians, social workers, engineers, and later public relations specialists and accountants who actively promoted scientific and technological innovations, new media, and business methods. An expansive humanitarian vigor surfaced in the merging of Protestant missionary zeal and liberal civilizational aspirations during the Russian Famine of 1890–1891, when a reluctant US government agreed to lend logistical support to relief efforts, heralding the transition from "non-interventionism" to a "missionary humanitarianism."[7] Curti emphasized the correlation between voluntary and government action and the institutionalization of relief, both of which had manifested themselves in the run-up to the Spanish–American War of 1898. According to this analysis, the bureaucratic-rational and semi-official approach of the American Red Cross (ARC) marginalized earlier popular relief efforts.

The advancement of organizational structures, mass appeals, and government intervention brought about a sea change in humanitarian action.[8] Ian Tyrrell calls attention to the 'historical experience of organized giving' in response to the geographically distant calamities of the 1890s. He also points to the gradual displacement of idiosyncratic human-interest endeavors by the more systematic work of foundations, which facilitated the emergence of philanthropy as a coherent epistemic community in the decade after 1900.[9] Georgina Brewis has traced the transition from religious philanthropy to organized social service in relief efforts during the Indian famines in the last years of the nineteenth century.[10] Such developments coincided with the systematic employment of photographs in the fundraising campaigns for India in 1896–1897 and the Second Boer War (1899–1902), creating an enhanced sense of the authenticity of aid causes in an unholy alliance "with the sensationalistic mass culture that intensified after the turn of the century."[11]

The period after the First World War, with its collapsing empires, civil and border wars, expulsions, and waves of refugees created a vast humanitarian crisis. The war became a node for organized humanitarianism that displaced earlier ad-hoc charity efforts.[12] Here though, the rise of international organizations after the war resumed an ongoing trend the conflict had interrupted.[13] The turn-of-the-century economic globalization, including new communication and transport technologies, enabled global civil society and encouraged philanthropy.[14] Moreover, pre-war imperialism had a profound impact on British humanitarianism, including the "ethics of relief," aid practice, and staffing. Administrators and relief workers with experience from colonial institutions or religious organizations remained an integral part of the humanitarian "mixed economy" of voluntary and official relief. Newly established organizations including the Save the Children Fund (SCF) and the American Relief Administration (ARA) "utilized the expert knowledge and techniques of famine relief first elaborated by the liberal imperialism of the late nineteenth century."[15] The period is also characterized by an increased emphasis on the hunger and suffering of children;[16] a group of beneficiaries that required specialized relief.

In contrast to the views of Curti and others, we concur with Johannes Paulmann that the Second World War was not the watershed in the history of humanitarian action that it is often proclaimed to be, since ideas and procedures that marked this period drew strongly on previous developments.[17] Paulmann suggests, instead, the late 1960s and early 1970s as a turning point, and this is one with which other researchers also agree.[18] The international famine relief effort during the Biafran Civil War at this time is widely recognized as a rupture in the history of humanitarianism. It effected the split of the Red Cross movement with the formation of *Médecins Sans Frontières* (MSF), molded a generation of relief workers, and brought civil society organizations to center stage as mediators between Western audiences and the "Third World."[19]

The concept of "expressive humanitarianism" that we propose pertains to post-material values of self-expression, an increasing fusion of relief with advocacy strategies, the notion of rights, utilization of media, spectacles of various kinds, commercial branding, populism, and the aggressive conduct of humanitarian intervention. These tendencies emerge from what economic analysts and contemporary historians identify as a caesura around 1970 that was the origin of many formative developments for society.[20] Therefore, just as the names we have chosen for the first two periods correlate with ad hoc or more systematic humanitarian logistics and ways of engendering compassion, the third refers to dramatized humanitarian choreography and to spectacular forms of intervention.

The truism that the end of the Cold War transformed the world has led many to assume that a new period of humanitarianism began after 1989. However, there is little evidence that there has been a major shift in the culture of humanitarianism parallel to the geopolitical change.[21] Paulmann leaves open the question of whether we have witnessed "a new departure" or merely an emphasis on emergency aid containing conflicts at low cost. At the same time, in underscoring the global nature of modern media pertinent to the present, Paulmann points to satellite transmissions and the BBC report on famine in Ethiopia that led to the Live Aid benefit concert in 1985, that is, events that pre-date the end of the Cold War.[22] He has also questioned the significance of the geopolitical shift of 1989 for humanitarian "so-called complexities" in general.[23]

Lilie Chouliaraki, who contrasts examples from the 1970s and 1980s with those of recent years, characterizes the whole period since the 1970s as an "age of global spectacle" typified by three transformations: the market-compliant instrumentalization of aid, the decline of the grand political narrative of solidarity, and the technologically fueled rise of self-expressive spectatorship. Taken together, she suggests they effect an epistemic shift toward an emotional, subjective humanitarianism correlated to narcissistic morality and an emergent "neoliberal lifestyle of 'feel good' altruism."[24] Our concept of expressive humanitarianism encapsulates these trends, which are also summarized in Alain Finkielkraut's formula of the "sentimental alienation" that has characterized humanitarian efforts since the late 1960s.[25]

A focus on plateaus achieved guided our selection of episodes by which to illustrate the three periods we term (a) ad-hoc, (b) organized, and (c) expressive humanitarianism. We present a brief overview of relief efforts during the Great Irish Famine of the 1840s, the Soviet Famine of 1921–1922, and the Ethiopian Famine of 1984–1985, rather than dwelling on forerunners.[26]

Ad hoc humanitarianism and the Great Irish Famine

Curti has explained that nineteenth-century ad hoc humanitarianism lacked formal and institutional connections between different relief efforts, emphasized voluntary initiatives, and relied on a fundraising repertoire that had emerged from the philhellenic movement of the 1820s. It involved the formation of ad hoc committees to oversee the collection of money and the transportation of foodstuffs, the holding of public meetings, church fund drives, charity events, ladies' bazaars, and newspaper campaigns.[27]

In the UK, building upon the long-distance imperial charity of the eighteenth century, ad hoc humanitarianism emerged during the Napoleonic Wars. Despite the war context, humanitarian activities were then entirely civilian endeavors with links to the British and Foreign Bible

Society, the evangelical and anti-slavery movement, and domestic charity. In addition to Curti's points, there were patterns for committee procedures and for the documentation of subscriptions and disbursements. However, there were no agencies for the continuous monitoring of food insecurity or other disasters, nor was there any permanent infrastructure for fundraising or aid distribution. Governments were also unprepared to manage foreign aid.

While famines had occurred periodically in Ireland, the first significant British relief effort to address an Irish famine emerged in 1822. The Irish famine that followed in 1831 was aided by the fundraising of a Catholic newspaper in Paris.[28] However, the "Hungry Forties" represented a difficult time for transnational relief. Throughout Europe, they were years marked by bad harvests, an economic downturn, and political unrest. Both the Vatican State and the Ottoman Empire banned the export of grain, although Pope Pius IX and Sultan Abdulmejid I made significant personal donations in 1847.[29] In France, only when domestic food scarcity abated at the beginning of the harvest season did relief efforts take on a broader scale. Disaffection with the Age of Metternich, culminating in the revolutions of 1848, minimized the concern of European elites with the Irish disaster.

The first distant group to provide relief in 1845 was the Irish community in Boston. In 1846, the British imperial forces in Bengal, which included Irish soldiers, initiated another long-distance effort. When the famine intensified at the end of that year, Catholic parishes and proselytizing societies in England, as well as Irish organizations in the US and transnational Quaker networks began raising funds.[30] The Society of St. Vincent de Paul (SVP) expanded its model of local Catholic charity in major Irish cities.[31]

However, before the establishment of the British Association for the Relief of Extreme Distress in the Remote Parishes of Ireland and Scotland on 1 January 1847, transnational activity was low. While this initiative was managed by the financial elite of London, it was directed by the same officials responsible for inadequate government relief. Politically, the association served to showcase charitable leadership to the Irish and British, allowing for a slightly less bureaucratic distribution of aid alongside the stringent public relief work system. One-sixth of the total fund was reserved for Scotland, where some districts had also experienced poor harvests, though the situation was far less severe than the famine in Ireland. The £390,000 collected for Ireland, which included donations from across the empire and the wider world, was depicted as a success, although it barely exceeded funds raised during the more minor famine of 1822.[32]

This major British campaign encouraged the nascent relief efforts of Irish communities in the US and Catholics around the world. Thus, a considerable, although short-lived, international voluntary effort came about in 1847, and for some time alleviated Irish distress. In England, Catholic districts organized collections, and the Catholic weekly, *The Tablet*, became a conduit of news to the British public. It continued to serve famine relief long after that cause was fashionable. The newly inaugurated Pope Pius IX mandated collections for Ireland in mid-January 1847. His second encyclical in March 1847 extended the call for famine relief to the wider Catholic world. Prelates from Italy and elsewhere forwarded the offertories of their districts to the Vatican's Sacred Congregation for the Propagation of the Faith, which distributed the sums among two dozen Irish bishops and archbishops.

French fundraising was also carried out by dioceses but was ultimately coordinated by the voluntary *Comité de secours pour l'Irlande*, which conveyed the proceeds to the Irish clergy. The committee's first action, taken at a time when the Pope's sphere of activity was still limited to Rome, was to ask him to address the world at large.[33] The key figure behind the petition was Jules Gossin, the president of SVP.[34] Gossin's circular to SVP chapters, issued in February 1847, resulted in funds that helped establish SVP branches in a number of Irish cities.[35] These groups and their transnational network transcended the ad hoc humanitarianism of the nineteenth century, although the sum they raised did not exceed £6106, and their *raison d'être* was local charity. SVP branches continued their work throughout the years of famine, even after external sources had dried up.

In contrast to Europe, conditions for providing famine relief to Ireland were propitious in the US, where a populous community in close touch with its homeland existed. Irish-American organizations became the nucleus for broader civic engagement and a nationwide campaign. At the same time, plentiful US harvests enabled great profits in undersupplied European markets, facilitating generosity and even giving rise to the notion of a moral obligation to compensate those who suffered most under the anomalous terms of trade. Moreover, opposition to US aggression against Mexico at the time inclined many people toward humanitarian action.[36] The isolated relief initiatives in the US were coordinated and expanded by a national fundraising meeting that took place in Washington, D.C., in February 1847. Principal collection committees were established in major cities, sending relief ships to Ireland. There, local agents, primarily from the Society of Friends (Quakers), distributed the provisions to the populace.[37] Overall, contributions from the US amounted to roughly £200,000.

Thus, the Irish Famine of 1847 saw a broad, well-coordinated network of fundraising bodies, aid providers, and local distributors working together on a hitherto unknown scale. Irish aid recipients frequently exaggerated aid received from abroad, while downplaying the British efforts. Nevertheless, there was no preparedness for a sustained effort in any quarter. By the summer of 1847, relief committees in the US and elsewhere began to disband, church bodies turned their attention to other issues, and volunteers on the ground who had distributed aid were exhausted. Famine raged for another three years with no significant voluntary or official relief efforts. The number of victims amounted to one million people and another million emigrated, reducing the population of Ireland by one-fourth. Although some Catholic and Irish American collections exhibited anti-British sentiments, few abroad could have anticipated that a powerful government like the UK would remain largely passive in view of such an ongoing domestic calamity. When, in the autumn of 1847, civil servants in London declared the situation in Ireland under control, it was generally assumed that this was in fact the case. Thus, after a single season, almost all efforts ceased, showing that ad-hoc humanitarianism was a weak and unreliable source of aid. This is also evident when one considers that direct remittances from Irish people abroad to family and friends dwarfed humanitarian efforts, even at the height of voluntary action.[38]

Despite the trust in public authorities, by the mid-nineteenth century, a European, trans-Atlantic, imperial disposition to engage in far-reaching humanitarian projects had emerged. It surpassed the bilateral endeavors of the Napoleonic era and the limited chiefly military philhellenic activism of the 1820s. The SVP illustrates the potential of charitable structures that are more enduring than the temporary committees of the nineteenth century, and even more than religious organizations with their multiplicity of obligations. While other relief initiatives slackened, the SVP spread its net of auxiliaries throughout Ireland providing an infrastructure for the local middle class to engage with their suffering compatriots.

Organized humanitarianism and the Russian famine of 1921–1923

Historians and contemporary witnesses cite the Russian Famine of 1921–1923 as a defining moment in the history of humanitarian aid.[39] The extensive international relief efforts it called forth illustrate trends that originated in the years around 1900 and that were reinforced, refined, and in part redirected during and after the First World War. Those efforts provide a paradigm for what we term organized humanitarianism. The era is characterized by the professionalization of humanitarian practice, including business-like fundraising, purchasing, and accounting procedures, the active role of experts, and the impact of scientific methods. A "mixed economy" of voluntary and state efforts, as well as the systematic use of photographs and film footage in fundraising campaigns, became more common.

With origins in the late nineteenth century, the model of organized humanitarianism gained considerable momentum in 1914 when Herbert Hoover created the Commission for Relief in Belgium (CRB), the blueprint for US relief efforts after the war. Between 1914 and 1919, the CRB managed an aid operation of unprecedented scale, sustaining an entire nation that was suffering under German occupation and the Allied blockade. After the war, Hoover continued his work with the American Relief Administration (ARA), first in Central Europe and then during the famine in Soviet Russia. Mainly a government-sponsored organization, it was also supported by tens of thousands of private donors and spent $5 billion between the armistice of 1918 and 1924.[40] The principal US goals were unloading an agricultural surplus, boosting the US economy, and securing future markets. In addition, the ARA and affiliated organizations like the American Red Cross (ARC) were tools to contain communism and influence the nation- and institution-building process in Europe.[41]

Whereas the CRB and the ARA were examples of twentieth-century relief efforts that were state-financed and partly state-led, the British SCF combined service with advocacy, and it functioned as a corrective to government policy. Eglantyne Jebb, who co-founded the SCF in 1919, saw her organization's role as a counterforce to nationalist politics and consciously chose "enemy children" (first German and Austrian, then Russian) as primary beneficiaries of famine relief.[42] American and British Quakers were another significant group during the Russian Famine. Quakers had already set up humanitarian missions during the Russian famine of the 1890s in the city of Buzuluk, which became the center of their famine relief. They returned in 1916 and 1917 and were later engaged by both the ARA and the International Committee of the Red Cross (ICRC) to channel relief.[43] During World War I, transnational Quaker relief was professionalized, and the British Friends Emergency and War Victims Relief Committee (FEWVRC) and the American Friends Service Committee (AFSC) were established in 1915 and 1917, respectively. Initially, both organizations cooperated closely.[44] Generally, the organization and professionalization of efforts elevated famine relief to a new level.

The famine in parts of Soviet Russia in 1921 followed a bad harvest, a harsh winter, and subsequent drought, especially in the Volga Valley. The White armies were still active, and the methods of war communism, including confiscation and collectivization, had made rural communities vulnerable. Twenty million people were threatened by starvation; an estimated two million died.[45] Nevertheless, to avoid acknowledging political weakness, the Bolshevik government did not officially recognize the famine until mid-1921. At that time, the renowned Russian author Maxim Gorky dramatically appealed for aid, immediately triggering a relief campaign for starving Russia and Ukraine.

The Western public was now facing an ethical and political dilemma: would famine relief benefit or undermine the Soviet regime? Moreover, was the answer of any relevance in the decision to help a starving population? In the end, some one million metric tons of relief goods reached the famine regions between late 1921 and early 1923. By the time operations peaked in August 1922, more than eleven million people were receiving food aid through foreign organizations.[46] The extent of the assistance is even more remarkable as the Soviet government was not recognized by any Western power at this time. Moreover, Soviet officials showed a distrust of any foreign interference often bordering on paranoia. While conservative politicians and Russian exiles warned that famine relief would keep a weakened regime alive, Soviet officials feared a counterrevolution in humanitarian disguise. One way to circumvent such tensions was to frame humanitarian aid as (partly) self-interested action when lobbying and fundraising for aid.[47]

Relief was mainly delivered by two umbrella agencies, both of which signed treaties with the Bolshevik government, namely, Hoover's ARA and the International Committee for Russian Relief (ICRR) led by Norwegian explorer Fridtjof Nansen.[48] The ARA drew on the experience of its vast relief efforts in post-war Europe and provided more than four-fifths of all foreign relief. The ICRR was a creation of the ICRC, in cooperation with the Secretariat of the League of Nations. Most US relief agencies, including the ARC, worked under the ARA heading, while Nansen represented organizations from two dozen primarily European countries. Most of these organizations were exclusively fundraising bodies. However, the SCF established its own distribution system in the province of Saratov. British and American Quakers also worked on the ground, although they did not join forces. The FEWVRC became part of Nansen's coalition, whereas the AFSC initially opted for ARA, favoring a national affiliation and access to governmental funds over a transnational collaboration.[49]

Nansen struggled with the fact that few governments supported the ICRR; participating humanitarian organizations were unwilling or unable to commit themselves financially. Only the SCF gave an advance pledge to feed 10,000 children. While Hoover drew on the functioning machinery of the ARA and ample financial means when bargaining with suspicious Russian authorities, Nansen's position was weak as he negotiated the conditions under which relief would be provided. When Nansen arrived, Hoover's representative had just successfully secured far-reaching US control over distribution and had obliged the Russian government to fund much of the relief work with its gold reserves.[50] Nansen's agreement was less favorable, particularly regarding distribution. However, his major problem remained funding.[51] The ICRR continued its work as a private charity, supported by minor sums from a few governments such as Norway, Sweden, and the Baltic states. The principal affiliated organizations like the SCF, the British Quakers, or the Swedish Red Cross, remained largely independent in their fundraising and relief work, but in many cases became distributing agencies for ICRR provisions.

The development of humanitarianism after 1900 culminated in the relief efforts during the Russian Famine. Foreshadowing the label we have chosen for this humanitarian era, the SCF proclaimed in 1922 that "whatever is not organized is dead."[52] While ARA officials praised the centralized relief work under a national umbrella in alignment with official policies, they showed little understanding of the wishes of affiliated organizations to preserve independent operations or their own culture of altruism. With regard to efficiency, the ARA suggested that "all these organizations would be greatly benefitted if their funds were donated outright to the ARA."[53] SCF adopted a similar position suggesting that there was no longer room for "the amateur philanthropist."[54] Professionalization also meant that experts would handle logistics of relief, procurement of food and other supplies, accounting, as well as marketing and public relations – the latter an area that especially engendered conflicts.[55] Photography had begun to be used for fundraising before the war, and during the Russian Famine various organizations produced films. The SCF appropriated the slogan "Seeing is believing" and attempted to settle public controversies by claiming their documentaries provided "incontrovertible evidence of the ravages of the famine."[56] As was to become a common refrain among fundraisers, they believed the ends justified the means of using such famine imagery.

A symbiotic mixed economy, with private relief organizations and the state, was a necessity if comprehensive relief was to be provided for millions threatened by starvation. The success of the ARA illustrates this. It was possible because Hoover's goals and those of his government were generally the same.[57] Nansen and the SCF were equally quick to declare governmental support indispensable, and they put great effort into lobbying for state-financed relief missions. Other than symbolic success, however, they failed, because they were unable to persuade European governments that a joint commitment was justified. In view of the self-image as a government corrective, the SFC's attempts to gain state support illustrate the inevitability of the humanitarian mixed economy. Even the Quakers, with their storied incorruptible relief philosophy, considered it necessary to adapt to the new development during the Russian Famine, and so the AFSC reluctantly engaged in a pragmatic relationship with the ARA, not least of all because of Hoover's access to government funding.

Expressive humanitarianism and the Ethiopian famine of 1984–1985

The famine in Ethiopia has been widely cited as another landmark in the history of humanitarianism.[58] It signifies what we term expressive humanitarianism. The Ethiopian disaster relief effort saw the culmination of several trends that originated in the late 1960s and became prominent during the famine in Biafra 1967–1970, which claimed the lives of at least one million people. Expressive humanitarianism included a media-driven understanding of disasters and relief efforts and an emphasis on celebrity, spectacle, and mass participation in relief.[59] It was marked by the emergence of new groups of donors and spontaneous organizations, typified by the Band Aid and Live Aid movements, which became conduits between donor governments, the charitable public, and recipients.[60] There was also increased emphasis on humanitarian concerns for witnessing.[61] In 1968, a group of French doctors denounced the Red Cross principles of silence and neutrality in Biafra. On returning home, they organized marches and media events to raise awareness of Nigerian atrocities against civilians. Their activism, followed by similar experiences in Bangladesh, led to the formation of *Médecins Sans Frontières* (MSF) in 1971. The new organization propagated the idea of *témoignage* (outspoken witnessing), heralding a new humanitarian style.[62]

The role played by voluntary organizations in disaster relief attracted public attention more than long-term development efforts. Toward the end of the twentieth century, it became increasingly clear that "association with high profile disasters was good for business."[63] Various relief operations of the 1970s saw voluntary agencies build a reputation for efficiency, in part based on a perceived ability to work with grass-roots communities.[64] From the 1960s, global musicians and pop stars became increasingly involved with humanitarian efforts, a development that was exemplified in George Harrison's 1971 Concert for Bangladesh and the 1979 Concerts for the People of Kampuchea (Cambodia).

In January 1985, Bob Geldof launched a new UK charity, *The Band Aid Trust*, to disperse the funds raised by the recorded single "Do They Know It's Christmas?" The Trust also arranged additional fundraising efforts, of which the Live Aid concerts were the most significant. The success of the original recording encouraged the production of Michael Jackson and Lionel Ritchie's song "We Are the World" and at least twenty other charity singles in many languages.[65] The West German "*Nackt im Wind*" [Naked in the Wind] addressed the gravity of the situation and lack of political consciousness, while the chorus of the Austria für Afrika song "*Warum*?" [Why?] stated that "we" were sending money in order not to feel so bad, providing an ironic commentary on the Western response to the famine.[66]

The famine had been developing since December 1982. By late 1984, it was affecting wide swaths of Sahelian Africa and acutely threatened more than seven million people in Ethiopia – approximately one-fifth of the total population. Ethiopia was a Marxist state, ruled by military officers who had assumed power after a coup d'état in 1974. The causes of the famine are disputed, but civil war with secessionist militias, years of drought, compulsory land reform, and forced collective farming all played a part.[67] In addition, food aid was late in coming and when it did arrive, problems with relief to rebel-held areas and the regime's program of forced resettlement for famine-affected people from Northern Ethiopia added to the death toll. Estimates vary, but between 400,000 and one million people are believed to have died from 1984 to 1986.[68]

Famine in Ethiopia was initially covered only to a limited extent by the international media. Approaching its tenth anniversary in power in August 1984, the Ethiopian government did not wish to draw attention to either famine or civil war. The US, for its part, had suspended development assistance to Ethiopia in 1979 and was reluctant to participate in a relief effort for a Soviet-aligned country.[69] It was not until 23 October 1984, in a now-famous BBC television news broadcast, that reporter Michael Buerk and video-journalist Mohamed Amin raised the world's awareness of the "biblical famine" affecting large portions of Ethiopia. In the days that followed, their announcement was rebroadcast by 425 stations, reaching a global audience of 470 million and sparking an enormous international response.[70]

In the expressive, media-driven humanitarianism of the late twentieth century, "an emergency begins and ends when the BBC says so," noted one commentator.[71] International donors began to mobilize in earnest, and Finnish diplomat Kurt Jansson was appointed UN Assistant Secretary General for Emergency Operations in Ethiopia.[72] The European Economic Community (EEC) development ministers pledged the equivalent of £19 million. Recalling the approach in Soviet Russia sixty years earlier, food aid was a political means to win the "hearts and minds" of a demoralized recipient population. The director of USAID visited Ethiopia, followed by legislators who helped secure support for relief in the US Congress. In early November 1984, an emergency airlift began that, however, transcended the Cold War and the North–South divide. It was a cooperative effort of the US, UK, France, Poland, Libya, and both German states.[73]

Around 1.5 million metric tons of emergency food aid reached Ethiopia. Food and non-food aid provided to Ethiopia between 1984 and 1986 was valued at $1.5 billion to $2 billion.[74] In early 1985, an estimated 600,000 of the most vulnerable people received cooked food and supplementary nutrition in relief camps. While most food aid was funded by governments, it was voluntary agencies that were largely responsible for distribution and allocation. The US government became the largest single donor, contributing more than $500 million to a USAID program, masking the Cold War geopolitics of such relief under the slogan "a hungry child knows no politics."[75] The largest bilateral donor of food aid in the EEC in 1985 was the Federal Republic of Germany, followed by the UK.[76] Other donors included Canada, Australia, the Scandinavian countries, Japan, China, and Zimbabwe. The creation of a special fund illustrates the stimulus the famine had on aid policy in Italy – the former colonial ruler of Eritrea and also briefly of Ethiopia, where Prime Minister Bettino Craxi developed one of the largest aid programs in the Horn of Africa, although one marred by corruption and misallocation.[77] Alongside its ongoing military support, the USSR's main contribution was the provision of transport for the government's resettlement program, the latter framed as a famine relief measure.[78]

Jansson judged that the role played by non-governmental organizations in this famine was greater than in any earlier emergency relief program. Although some agencies had long been active in Ethiopia, there was a rush to get into the country following the heavy media coverage after October 1984.[79] The number of organizations working on the ground in Ethiopia went from 21 at the beginning of 1984 to 48 by the middle of 1985.[80] An organization's presence during a world crisis had become essential to the humanitarian system by the mid-1980s.[81] The political reluctance of some donor nations to work with the Ethiopian Relief and Rehabilitation Commission had the effect of strengthening the position of voluntary agencies, which distributed 95 percent of the food aid the US provided.[82] The EEC was more willing to work with the Ethiopian government, although 29 percent of its food aid in 1985 was still given out via voluntary organizations. Many smaller donor countries like Australia, Japan, and Finland directed all relief through civil society organizations.[83]

Food distribution was complicated by the fact that many of those affected by the famine were living in areas that were outside the control of the Ethiopian government, such as Eritrea, Tigray, and northern Wollo. There, quasi-autonomous aid organizations linked to rebel forces worked with supportive organizations abroad.[84] Both the Ethiopian government and the rebel groups tried to manipulate aid for their own ends. MSF was the only aid agency to publicly criticize the regime and its resettlement program and was ultimately expelled for doing so. MSF's refusal to "renounce our moral responsibilities or cooperate blindly in a perversion of the very meaning of international aid" is a hallmark of the era of expressive humanitarianism that developed after the Biafran crisis.[85] However, MSF's position was vigorously denounced by other aid organizations, who held that it left vulnerable famine survivors at greater risk.

The famine in Ethiopia catalyzed the formation of aid structures embodying what we call expressive humanitarianism: involvement of high-profile figures, large-scale televised spectacles, and engagement of the public (particularly young people). Musicians and celebrities across the world initiated fundraising activities. For the first time in the history of Germany, a joint campaign of voluntary organizations held a fundraising spectacular known as the *Tag für Afrika* (Day for Africa) in January 1985.[86] Aid organizations raised significant sums and benefitted from unsolicited donations from individuals outside their traditional support base.

Celebrity activism had played a role in earlier relief efforts but assumed far greater significance in the era of expressive humanitarianism. It reached its height when Band Aid and other groups capitalized on participatory enthusiasm but also contributed to a shared desire to downplay the political context of relief. Moreover, while the Ethiopian crisis in some ways marked the continuation of a process of professionalization of humanitarian action,[87] the Band Aid Trust, as a self-styled newcomer, stood in opposition to the professional aid industry with its high overhead and salaries. Geldof later suggested that the legacy of Band Aid was as much in mobilizing the public to believe that anything was possible, in contrast to experts telling them "it is hopeless," as in delivering on its relief and rehabilitation projects.[88] Even in the age of expressive humanitarianism, then, we see the incorporation of older forms of ad hoc humanitarianism, such as in Band Aid's critique of an aid industry that had emerged over decades of increasing professionalization and the marginalization of amateur philanthropy.

Conclusions

Unlike most forms of voluntary action, humanitarianism is a transnational phenomenon that is directly affected by geopolitics and international affairs. Suggested turning points and periods of humanitarian action show that the dominant narrative regards such factors as decisive. The power-political configuration of the international system and the famines and other emergencies resulting from the major wars of the twentieth century appear as formative for humanitarianism. Scholars thus emphasize landmarks such as the world wars or the breakdown of the Soviet Bloc around 1989. This is a convenient perspective for relief agencies, which tend to present themselves as neutral problem-solvers, rather than as intrinsically driven organizations that do a great deal more than simply respond to the emergency needs of distant strangers.

We have attempted to show that cultural and economic factors play an underestimated role in how humanitarians work, particularly in the field of famine relief, and that those factors may outweigh the power politics of international relations. Whether the West reasonably expected to achieve any of its geopolitical aims when providing large-scale relief to the Soviet Union in the

1920s or Ethiopia in the 1980s, cultural and economic dynamics of morality and capacity were embedded in those decisions and gave rise to specific moral economies in which donors and relief agencies endowed their allocations with altruistic meaning.[89]

Claims of periodization are inevitably simplifications. As analytical tools, they are frequently criticized for missing significant processes and details, or risk imposing limits on our understanding.[90] However, we hope that the periods of humanitarianism derived from this framework – nineteenth-century ad hoc humanitarianism, organized humanitarianism until the 1960s, and expressive humanitarianism in the decades thereafter – may assist future researchers in better understanding voluntary famine relief at large and, above all, the working conditions and challenges confronting humanitarian agencies.

Notes

1 Merle Curti, *American Philanthropy Abroad: A History* (New Brunswick: Rutgers University Press, 1963); Michael Barnett, *Empire of Humanity: A History of Humanitarianism* (Ithaca: Cornell University Press, 2011); Eleanor Davey, John Borton, and Matthew Foley, *A History of the Humanitarian System: Western Origins and Foundations* (London: Overseas Development Institute, 2013); Johannes Paulmann, "Conjunctures in the History of International Humanitarian Aid during the Twentieth Century," *Humanity* 4, no. 2 (2013): 215–38; Kevin O'Sullivan, Matthew Hilton, and Juliano Fiori, "Humanitarianism in Context," *European Review of History* 23, no. 1–2 (2016): 1–15; Silvia Salvatici, *A History of Humanitarianism, 1755–1989: In the Name of Others* (Manchester: University Press, 2019).

2 See Norbert Götz, Georgina Brewis, and Steffen Werther, *Humanitarianism in the Modern World: The Moral Economy of Famine Relief* (Cambridge: Cambridge University Press, 2020).

3 For obvious reasons, this does not apply to Curti, *American Philanthropy Abroad*, published in 1963.

4 Curti, *American Philanthropy Abroad*, 619–23.

5 Mary Nolan, *The Transatlantic Century: Europe and America, 1890–2010* (Cambridge: University Press, 2012).

6 Curti, *American Philanthropy Abroad*, 621f.

7 Jeff Bloodworth, "A Complicated Kindness: The Iowa Famine Relief Movement and the Myth of Midwestern (and American) Isolationism," *The Historian* 73, no. 3 (2011): 480–502, 482–5.

8 Curti, *American Philanthropy Abroad*, 199–223, 258, 621f. For the UK, see Rebecca Gill, *Calculating Compassion: Humanity and Relief in War, Britain 1870–1914* (Manchester: University Press, 2013), 179.

9 Ian Tyrrell, *Reforming the World: The Creation of America's Moral Empire* (Princeton: University Press, 2010), 98, 118.

10 Georgina Brewis, " 'Fill Full the Mouth of Famine:' Voluntary Action in Famine Relief in India 1896–1901," *Modern Asian Studies* 44, no. 4 (2010): 887–918.

11 Heather Curtis, "Depicting Distant Suffering: Evangelicals and the Politics of Pictorial Humanitarianism in the Age of American Empire," *Material Religion* 8, no. 2 (2012): 153–82, 155 (quotation there); Valérie Gorin, "L'enfance comme figure compassionnelle: Étude transversale de l'iconographie de la famine aux dix-neuvième et vingtième siècles," *European Review of History* 2, no. 6 (2015): 940–62, 944.

12 Branden Little, "An Explosion of New Endeavours: Global Humanitarian Responses to Industrialized Warfare in the First World War Era," *First World War Studies* 5, no. 1 (2014): 1–16; Barnett, *Empire of Humanity*, 86; Paulmann, "Conjunctures," 225f.

13 Akira Iriye, *Global Community: The Role of International Organizations in the Making of the Contemporary World* (Berkeley: University of California Press, 2002), 20.

14 Andrew Arsan, Su Lin Lewis, and Anne-Isabelle Richard, "Editorial: The Roots of Global Civil Society and the Interwar Moment," *Journal of Global History* 7, no. 2 (2012): 157–65, 158; Iriye, *Global Community*, 11.

15 Tehila Sasson, "From Empire to Humanity: The Russian Famine and the Imperial Origins of International Humanitarianism," *Journal of British Studies* 53, no. 3 (2016): 519–37.
16 Gill, *Calculating Compassion*, 201, 210.
17 Paulmann, "Conjunctures," 226–7.
18 Eleanor Davey, *Idealism Beyond Borders: The French Revolutionary Left and the Rise of Humanitarianism, 1954–1988* (Cambridge: University Press, 2015), 3, 21; O'Sullivan, Hilton, and Fiori, "Humanitarianism in Context."
19 Norbert Götz and Irène Herrmann, "Universalism in Emergency Aid before and after 1970: Ambivalences and Contradictions," in *Nationalism and Internationalism Intertwined: A European History of Concepts Beyond the Nation State*, ed. Pasi Ihalainen and Antero Holmila (New York: Berghahn, 2022), 247–269.
20 Luc Boltanski and Eve Chiapello, *The New Spirit of Capitalism* (London: Verso, 2005); Anselm Doering-Manteuffel and Lutz Raphael, *Nach dem Boom: Perspektiven auf die Zeitgeschichte seit 1970* (Göttingen: Vandenhoeck & Ruprecht, 2010); Thomas Borstelmann, *The 1970s: A New Global History from Civil Rights to Economic Inequality* (Princeton: University Press, 2012).
21 A work that does not see 1989 as a watershed is Davies, *NGOs*.
22 Paulmann, "Conjunctures," 229 (see quotation there), 221, 230.
23 Johannes Paulmann, "The Dilemmas of Humanitarian Aid: Historical Perspectives," in *Dilemmas of Humanitarian Aid in the Twentieth Century*, ed. Johannes Paulmann (Oxford: University Press, 2016), 1–31, 3.
24 Lilie Chouliaraki, *The Ironic Spectator: Solidarity in the Age of Post-Humanitarianism* (Cambridge: Polity, 2013), 52, 4 (quotations there), 1–21.
25 Alain Finkielkraut, *In the Name of Humanity: Reflections on the Twentieth Century* (New York: Columbia University Press, 2000), 93.
26 For case studies on turning points, see Norbert Götz, "Rationales of Humanitarianism: The Case of British Relief to Germany, 1805–1815," *Journal of Modern European History* 12, no. 2 (2014): 186–99; Norbert Götz, "Towards Expressive Humanitarianism: The Formative Experience of Biafra," *An Era of Value Change: The Seventies in Europe*, ed. Fiammetta Balestracci, Christina von Hodenberg and Isabel Richter (Oxford: Oxford University Press, 2024), 207–232.
27 Curti, *American Philanthropy Abroad*, 619–21.
28 For 1822, see Cormac Ó Gráda, *Famine: A Short History* (Princeton: University Press, 2009), 218; for 1831, see Donal A. Kerr, *A Nation of Beggars? Priests, People, and Politics in Famine Ireland, 1846–1852* (Oxford: Clarendon, 1994), 54.
29 "Intelligence of the Week," *Roman Advertiser*, Jan 9, 1847; Semih Çelik, "Between History of Humanitarianism and Humanitarianization of History: A Discussion on Ottoman Help for the Victims of the Great Irish Famine, 1845–1852," *Werkstatt Geschichte*, no. 68 (2015): 13–27, 25.
30 Christine Kinealy, *Charity and the Great Hunger in Ireland: The Kindness of Strangers* (London: Bloomsbury, 2013).
31 *First Annual Report of the Society of Saint Vincent de Paul, Cork* (Cork: O'Brien, 1846).
32 Norbert Götz, "Lionel de Rothschild and the Great Irish Famine: The Origins of the British Relief Association," *History Ireland* 30 (2022) 5; on 1822: *Transactions of the Central Relief Committee of the Society of Friends during the Famine in Ireland in 1846 and 1847* (Dublin: Hodges and Smith, 1852), 27.
33 *Comité de secours pour l'Irlande* (Paris: A. Sirou et Desquers, 1847).
34 Bruno Belhoste, *Augustin-Louis Cauchy: A Biography* (New York: Springer, 1991), 189.
35 "Rapport général pour l'année 1847," *Bulletin de la Société de Saint-Vincent de Paul* 1, no. 2 (1848): 45–60, 47.
36 H.A. Crosby Forbes and Henry Lee, *Massachusetts Help to Ireland during the Great Famine* (Milton: Captain Robert Bennet Forbes House, 1967), 22–5.
37 Curti, *American Philanthropy Abroad*, 41–64.
38 For statistics, see "Thirteenth General Report of the Colonial Land and Emigration Commissioners," here cited from: *Justice of the Peace, and County, Borough, Poor Law Union, and Parish Law Recorder* 17 (1853): 582.

39 *Report on Economic Conditions in Russia: With Special Reference to the Famine of 1921–1922 and the State of Agriculture* (Geneva: League of Nations, 1923); Sasson, "From Empire to Humanity," 520; Daniel Maul, "Appell an das Gewissen: Fridtjof Nansen und die Russische Hungerhilfe 1921–23," Themenportal Europäische Geschichte (Berlin: Humboldt Universität, 2011), available at www.europa.clio-online.de/essay/id/artikel-3604 (accessed 17 Feb 2024).

40 Charles E. Noyes, "American Relief of Famine in Europe," in *Editorial Research Reports*, vol. 2 (Washington DC: CQ Press, 1940).

41 Friederike Kind-Kovács, "The Great War, the Child's Body and the American Red Cross," *European Review of History* 23, no. 1–2 (2016): 33–62, 41.

42 Linda Mahood and Vic Satzewich, "The Save the Children Fund and the Russian Famine of 1921–23: Claims and Counter-claims about Feeding 'Bolshevik' Children," *Journal of Historical Sociology* 22, no. 1 (2009): 55–83; Rodney Breen, "Saving Enemy Children: Save the Children's Russian Relief Operation, 1921–1923," *Disasters* 18, no. 3 (1994): 221–38.

43 David McFadden and Claire Gorfinkel, *Constructive Spirit: Quakers in Revolutionary Russia* (Pasadena: International Productions, 2004), 9, 27.

44 James E. Miles and Meaburn Tatham, *The Ambulance Unit, 1914–1919: A Record* (London: Swarthmore Press, 1919). See also Daniel Maul, "American Quakers, the Emergence of International Humanitarianism, and the Foundation of the American Friends Service Committee, 1890–1920," in *Dilemmas of Humanitarian Aid in the Twentieth Century*, ed. Johannes Paulmann (Oxford: University Press, 2016), 63–87.

45 Bruno Cabanes, *The Great War and the Origins of Humanitarianism, 1918–1924* (Cambridge: University Press, 2014), 239f; Bertrand M. Patenaude, *Big Show in Bololand: The American Relief Expedition to Soviet Russia in the Famine of 1921* (Stanford: University Press, 2002), 197.

46 "Feeding of the Starving Russian Population on August 1st 1922: Organisations Working under the Nansen Agreement," *International Committee for Russian Relief – Information* 30 (30 Aug 1922), 20.

47 Steffen Werther, "Help Yourself by Helping Others: Self-interest in Appeals for Russian Famine Relief, 1921–23." *Disasters* 46, no. 3 (2022): 700–719.

48 Patenaude, *Big Show*; Carl Emil Vogt, *Nansens kamp mot hungersnøden i Russland 1921–23* (Oslo: Aschehoug, 2007).

49 Maul, "American Quakers."

50 Patenaude, *Big Show*, 745–8.

51 Vogt, *Nansens kamp*, 145ff.

52 "The New Charity," *Record* 2, no. 8, Jan 1, 1922.

53 Haskell to London, Mar 20, 1922, Hoover Archive, Russian operational records, reel 115.

54 "Of Giving Way to Others: A Word to Workers and Friends," *Record* 2, no. 4, Nov 1, 1921.

55 Breen, "Saving Enemy Children."

56 "Seeing is believing," *Record*, 2, no. 10, Feb 1, 1922.

57 Hoover led the ARA as private citizen, but was secretary of commerce in the Harding administration.

58 Davey et al, *A History;* Barnett, *Empire of Humanity*, 133; Alexander Poster, "The Gentle War: Famine Relief, Politics and Privatization in Ethiopia, 1938–86," *Diplomatic History* 26, no. 2 (2012): 399–425; Kurt Jansson "The Emergency Relief Operation: The Inside View," in *The Ethiopian Famine*, ed. Michael Harris and Angela Penrose (London: Zed Books, 1987).

59 Susanne Franks, *Reporting Disasters: Famine, Aid, Politics and the Media* (London: Hurst, 2013); Norbert Götz and Carl Marklund (eds), *Biafra and the Nordic Media* (Huddinge: Södertörn University, 2024).

60 Kevin O'Sullivan, "Biafra's Legacy: NGO Humanitarianism and the Nigerian Civil War," in *Learning from the Past to Shape the Future: Lessons from the History of Humanitarian Action in Africa* (London: Overseas Development Institute, 2016), 5–13; Tanja R. Müller, "'The Ethiopian Famine' Revisited: Band Aid and the Antipolitics of Celebrity Humanitarian Action," *Disasters* 37, no. 1 (2013): 61–79.

61 Franks, *Reporting Disasters*; Kevin O'Sullivan, "Biafra's Legacy"; Eleanor Davey, "Famine, Aid, and Ideology: The Political Activism of Médicins sans Frontières in the 1980s," *French Historical Studies* 34, no. 3 (2011): 531–58.

62 Davey, *Idealism beyond Borders*, 31–6; Bertrand Taithe, "Reinventing (French) Universalism: Religion, Humanitarianism and the 'French doctors,'" *Modern & Contemporary France* 12, no. 2 (2004): 147–58.
63 Barnett, *Empire of Humanity*, 132.
64 Alex de Waal, *Famine Crimes: Politics and the Disaster Relief Industry in Africa* (Oxford: Currey, 1997), 78.
65 *Food and Trucks and Rock 'n' Roll: The Band Aid Story*, directed by Ian McMillan (London: Band Aid, 1985).
66 See Werther, "Help yourself," 710–2.
67 De Waal, *Famine Crimes,* 115.
68 Alex de Waal, *Evil Days: 30 Years of War and Famine* (New York: Human Rights Watch, 1991), 173–6; Peter Gill, *Famine and Foreigners: Ethiopia since Live Aid* (Oxford: University Press, 2012), 43.
69 Peter Gill, *A Year in the Death of Africa: Politics, Bureaucracy and the Famine* (London: Palladin, 1986), 4–6; Harold G. Marcus, *A History of Ethiopia*, 3rd ed. (Oakland: University of California Press, 2002), 205–7; Poster, "Gentle War," 404; US General Accounting Office, "The United States Response to the Ethiopian Food Crisis," Apr 1985, 2–3, available at http://pdf.usaid.gov/pdf_docs/Pcaaa061.pdf (accessed June 20, 2024).
70 Angela Penrose, "Before and After," in *The Ethiopian Famine*, 154; Greg Philo, "From Buerk to Band Aid: The Media and the 1984 Ethiopian Famine," in *Getting the Message: News, Truth and Power*, ed. John Eldridge (London: Routledge, 1993), 73–103, 121.
71 *Report on the African Emergency Relief Operation 1984–1986 with Particular Reference to the Contributions of Non-Governmental Organisations, and at the Request of the UN Office for Emergency Operations in Africa* (London: International Institute for Environment and Development, 1986), 39.
72 Jansson, "Emergency Relief," 1.
73 *Final Disaster Report Ethiopia Drought / Famine FY 1985 1986* (Washington: USAID, 1987), 5, 11, http://pdf.usaid.gov/pdf_docs/PNABG233.pdf (accessed June 20, 2024).
74 *Evaluation of Band Aid Funded Projects in Ethiopia: Country Annex to Final Report,* (PAID, 1991), 7; *Final Disaster Report*, 36.
75 Poster, "Gentle War," 399.
76 *Final Disaster Report*, 38.
77 Paola Bollina and Michael R. Reich, "The Italian Fight against World Hunger: A Critical Analysis of Italian Aid for Development in the 1980s," *Social Science of Medicine* 39, no, 5 (1994): 607–20.
78 Central Intelligence Agency, *Ethiopia: A Political and Security Assessment of the Drought*, Apr 1985, 4, available at www.cia.gov/readingroom/docs/CIA-RDP86T00589R000200160006-3.pdf (accessed Mar 4, 2024); de Waal, *Evil Days*, 211.
79 Jansson, "Emergency Relief," 22.
80 Dawit Wolde Giorgis, *Red Tears: War, Famine and Revolution in Ethiopia* (Trenton: Red Sea Press, 1989), 228.
81 de Waal, *Famine Crimes*, 80; Alex de Waal, "The Humanitarian Carnival: A Celebrity Vogue," *World Affairs* 171, no. 2 (2008): 43–55.
82 Poster, "Gentle War," 415; Jansson, "Emergency Relief," 47.
83 *Final Disaster Report*, 38.
84 De Waal, *Famine Crimes*, 129; Max Peberdy, *Tigray: Ethiopia's Untold Story* (London: Relief Society of Tigray UK Support Committee, 1985).
85 Bertrand Desmoulins and Michael Fiszbin, "An Open Letter to NGOs in Ethiopia," Dec 13, 1985, Box 1220, File 17 (CARE Archives, New York Public Library).
86 "Hungerhilfe: Schokolade für Zuckerkranke?," *Der Spiegel*, Jan 21, 1985.
87 Andrew Jones, "Band Aid Revisited: Humanitarianism, Consumption and Philanthropy in the 1980s," *Contemporary British History* 31, no. 2 (2017): 189–209, 195.
88 *With Love from Band Aid: Report of 7 Years Work* (London: Band Aid Trust, [1992]), 3.
89 Norbert Götz, " 'Moral Economy': Its Conceptual History and Analytical Prospects," *Journal of Global Ethics* 11, no. 2 (2015): 147–62, 158; see also Götz, Brewis, and Werther, *Humanitarianism in the Modern World.*

90 For an extended discussion of issues of periodization, see Norbert Götz, Georgina Brewis and Steffen Werther, "Humanitäre Hilfe: Eine Braudel'sche Perspektive," *Freiwilligenarbeit und gemeinnützige Organisationen im Wandel: Neue Perspektiven auf das 19. und 20. Jahrhundert*, ed. Nicole Kramer and Christine Krüger (Berlin: de Gruyter, 2019), 117f.

References

Arsan, Andrew, Su Lin Lewis, and Anne-Isabelle Richard, "Editorial: The Roots of Global Civil Society and the Interwar Moment," *Journal of Global History* 7, no. 2 (2012): 157–65.

Barnett, Michael, *Empire of Humanity: A History of Humanitarianism* (Ithaca: Cornell University Press, 2011).

Belhoste, Bruno, *Augustin-Louis Cauchy: A Biography* (New York: Springer, 1991), 189.

Bloodworth, Jeff, "A Complicated Kindness: The Iowa Famine Relief Movement and the Myth of Midwestern (and American) Isolationism," *The Historian* 73, no. 3 (2011): 480–502.

Bollina, Paola and Michael R. Reich, "The Italian Fight against World Hunger: A Critical Analysis of Italian Aid for Development in the 1980s," *Social Science of Medicine* 39, no. 5 (1994): 607–20.

Boltanski, Luc and Eve Chiapello, *The New Spirit of Capitalism* (London: Verso, 2005).

Borstelmann, Thomas, *The 1970s: A New Global History from Civil Rights to Economic Inequality* (Princeton: University Press, 2012).

Breen, Rodney, "Saving Enemy Children: Save the Children's Russian Relief Operation, 1921–1923," *Disasters* 18, no. 3 (1994): 221–38.

Brewis, Georgina, "'Fill Full the Mouth of Famine': Voluntary Action in Famine Relief in India 1896–1901," *Modern Asian Studies* 44, no. 4 (2010): 887–918.

Cabanes, Bruno, *The Great War and the Origins of Humanitarianism, 1918–1924* (Cambridge: University Press, 2014).

Çelik, Semih, "Between History of Humanitarianism and Humanitarianization of History: A Discussion on Ottoman Help for the Victims of the Great Irish Famine, 1845–1852," *Werkstatt Geschichte*, 68 (2015): 13–27.

Central Intelligence Agency, *Ethiopia: A Political and Security Assessment of the Drought*, Apr 1985, 4, available at www.cia.gov/readingroom/docs/CIA-RDP86T00589R000200160006-3.pdf (accessed Mar 4, 2024).

Chouliaraki, Lilie, *The Ironic Spectator: Solidarity in the Age of Post-Humanitarianism* (Cambridge: Polity, 2013).

Comité de secours pour l'Irlande (Paris: A. Sirou et Desquers, 1847).

Curti, Merle, *American Philanthropy Abroad: A History* (New Brunswick: Rutgers University Press, 1963).

Curtis, Heather, "Depicting Distant Suffering: Evangelicals and the Politics of Pictorial Humanitarianism in the Age of American Empire," *Material Religion* 8, no. 2 (2012): 153–82.

Davey, Eleanor, "Famine, Aid, and Ideology: The Political Activism of Médicins sans Frontières in the 1980s," *French Historical Studies* 34, no. 3 (2011): 531–58.

Davey, Eleanor, *Idealism Beyond Borders: The French Revolutionary Left and the Rise of Humanitarianism, 1954–1988* (Cambridge: University Press, 2015).

Davey, Eleanor, John Borton, and Matthew Foley, *A History of the Humanitarian System: Western Origins and Foundations* (London: Overseas Development Institute, 2013).

De Waal, Alex, *Evil Days: 30 Years of War and Famine* (New York: Human Rights Watch, 1991).

De Waal, Alex, *Famine Crimes: Politics and the Disaster Relief Industry in Africa* (Oxford: Currey, 1997).

De Waal, Alex, "The Humanitarian Carnival: A Celebrity Vogue," *World Affairs* 171, no. 2 (2008): 43–55.

Doering-Manteuffel, Anselm and Lutz Raphael, *Nach dem Boom: Perspektiven auf die Zeitgeschichte seit 1970* (Göttingen: Vandenhoeck & Ruprecht, 2010).

Evaluation of Band Aid Funded Projects in Ethiopia: Country Annex to Final Report, (PAID, 1991).

"Feeding of the Starving Russian Population on August 1st 1922: Organisations Working under the Nansen Agreement," *International Committee for Russian Relief – Information* 30 (30 Aug 1922).

Final Disaster Report Ethiopia Drought / Famine FY 1985 1986 (Washington: USAID, 1987), 5, 11, http://pdf.usaid.gov/pdf_docs/PNABG233.pdf (accessed June 20, 2024).
Finkielkraut, Alain, *In the Name of Humanity: Reflections on the Twentieth Century* (New York: Columbia University Press, 2000).
First Annual Report of the Society of Saint Vincent de Paul, Cork (Cork: O'Brien, 1846).
Forbes, H.A. Crosby and Henry Lee, *Massachusetts Help to Ireland during the Great Famine* (Milton: Captain Robert Bennet Forbes House, 1967).
Franks, Susanne, *Reporting Disasters: Famine, Aid, Politics and the Media* (London: Hurst, 2013).
Gill, Peter, *A Year in the Death of Africa: Politics, Bureaucracy and the Famine* (London: Palladin, 1986).
Gill, Peter, *Famine and Foreigners: Ethiopia since Live Aid* (Oxford: University Press, 2012).
Gill, Rebecca, *Calculating Compassion: Humanity and Relief in War, Britain 1870–1914* (Manchester: University Press, 2013).
Giorgis, Dawit Wolde, *Red Tears: War, Famine and Revolution in Ethiopia* (Trenton: Red Sea Press, 1989).
Gorin, Valérie, "L'enfance comme figure compassionnelle: Étude transversale de l'iconographie de la famine aux dix-neuvième et vingtième siècles," *European Review of History* 2, no. 6 (2015): 940–62.
Götz, Norbert, "Rationales of Humanitarianism: The Case of British Relief to Germany, 1805–1815," *Journal of Modern European History* 12, no. 2 (2014): 186–99.
Götz, Norbert, "'Moral Economy': Its Conceptual History and Analytical Prospects," *Journal of Global Ethics* 11, no. 2 (2015): 147–62.
Götz, Norbert, "Lionel de Rothschild and the Great Irish Famine: The Origins of the British Relief Association," *History Ireland* 30, no. 5 (2022): 24–27.
Götz, Norbert, "Towards Expressive Humanitarianism: The Formative Experience of Biafra," *An Era of Value Change: The Seventies in Europe*, eds. Fiammetta Balestracci, Christina von Hodenberg, and Isabel Richter (Oxford: Oxford University Press, 2024), 207–232.
Götz, Norbert, Georgina Brewis and Steffen Werther, "Humanitäre Hilfe: Eine Braudel'sche Perspektive," *Freiwilligenarbeit und gemeinnützige Organisationen im Wandel: Neue Perspektiven auf das 19. und 20. Jahrhundert*, ed. Nicole Kramer and Christine Krüger (Berlin: de Gruyter, 2019), 89–120.
Götz, Norbert, Georgina Brewis and Steffen Werther, *Humanitarianism in the Modern World: The Moral Economy of Famine Relief* (Cambridge: Cambridge University Press, 2020).
Götz, Norbert and Irène Herrmann, "Universalism in Emergency Aid before and after 1970: Ambivalences and Contradictions," in *Nationalism and Internationalism Intertwined: A European History of Concepts Beyond the Nation State*, ed. Pasi Ihalainen and Antero Holmila (New York: Berghahn, 2022), 247–269.
Götz, Norbert and Carl Marklund (eds), *Biafra and the Nordic Media: Witness Seminar with Uno Grönkvist, Lasse Jensen, Pierre Mens, and Pekka Peltola* (Huddinge: Södertörn University, 2024).
"Hungerhilfe: Schokolade für Zuckerkranke?" *Der Spiegel*, Jan 21, 1985.
"Intelligence of the Week," *Roman Advertiser*, Jan 9, 1847.
Iriye, Akira, *Global Community: The Role of International Organizations in the Making of the Contemporary World* (Berkeley: University of California Press, 2002).
Jansson, Kurt, "The Emergency Relief Operation: The Inside View," in *The Ethiopian Famine*, ed. Michael Harris and Angela Penrose (London: Zed Books, 1987).
Jones, Andrew, "Band Aid Revisited: Humanitarianism, Consumption and Philanthropy in the 1980s," *Contemporary British History* 31, no. 2 (2017): 189–209.
Kerr, Donal A., *A Nation of Beggars? Priests, People, and Politics in Famine Ireland, 1846–1852* (Oxford: Clarendon, 1994).
Kind-Kovács, Friederike, "The Great War, the Child's Body and the American Red Cross," *European Review of History* 23, no. 1–2 (2016): 33–62.
Kinealy, Christine, *Charity and the Great Hunger in Ireland: The Kindness of Strangers* (London: Bloomsbury, 2013).
Little, Branden, "An Explosion of New Endeavours: Global Humanitarian Responses to Industrialized Warfare in the First World War Era," *First World War Studies* 5, no. 1 (2014): 1–16.

Mahood, Linda and Vic Satzewich, "The Save the Children Fund and the Russian Famine of 1921–23: Claims and Counter-claims about Feeding 'Bolshevik' Children," *Journal of Historical Sociology* 22, no. 1 (2009): 55–83.
Marcus, Harold G., *A History of Ethiopia*, 3rd ed. (Oakland: University of California Press, 2002).
Maul, Daniel, "Appell an das Gewissen: Fridtjof Nansen und die Russische Hungerhilfe 1921–23," Themenportal Europäische Geschichte (Berlin: Humboldt Universität, 2011), available at www.europa.clio-online.de/essay/id/artikel-3604 (accessed 17 Feb 2024).
Maul, Daniel, "American Quakers, the Emergence of International Humanitarianism, and the Foundation of the American Friends Service Committee, 1890–1920," in *Dilemmas of Humanitarian Aid in the Twentieth Century*, ed. Johannes Paulmann (Oxford: University Press, 2016), 63–87.
McFadden, David and Claire Gorfinkel, *Constructive Spirit: Quakers in Revolutionary Russia* (Pasadena: International Productions, 2004).
Miles, James E. and Meaburn Tatham, *The Ambulance Unit, 1914–1919: A Record* (London: Swarthmore Press, 1919).
Müller, Tanja R., "'The Ethiopian Famine' Revisited: Band Aid and the Antipolitics of Celebrity Humanitarian Action," *Disasters* 37, no. 1 (2013): 61–79.
"The New Charity," *Record* 2, no. 8, Jan 1, 1922.
Nolan, Mary, *The Transatlantic Century: Europe and America, 1890–2010* (Cambridge: University Press, 2012).
Noyes, Charles E., "American Relief of Famine in Europe," in *Editorial Research Reports*, vol. 2 (Washington DC: CQ Press, 1940).
"Of Giving Way to Others: A Word to Workers and Friends," *Record* 2, no. 4, Nov 1, 1921.
Ó Gráda, Cormac, *Famine: A Short History* (Princeton: University Press, 2009).
O'Sullivan, Kevin, "Biafra's Legacy: NGO Humanitarianism and the Nigerian Civil War," in *Learning from the Past to Shape the Future: Lessons from the History of Humanitarian Action in Africa* (London: Overseas Development Institute, 2016), 5–13.
O'Sullivan, Kevin, Matthew Hilton, and Juliano Fiori, "Humanitarianism in Context," *European Review of History* 23, no. 1–2 (2016): 1–15.
Patenaude, Bertrand M., *Big Show in Bololand: The American Relief Expedition to Soviet Russia in the Famine of 1921* (Stanford: University Press, 2002).
Paulmann, Johannes, "Conjunctures in the History of International Humanitarian Aid during the Twentieth Century," *Humanity* 4, no. 2 (2013): 215–38.
Paulmann, Johannes, "The Dilemmas of Humanitarian Aid: Historical Perspectives," in *Dilemmas of Humanitarian Aid in the Twentieth Century*, ed. Johannes Paulmann (Oxford: University Press, 2016), 1–31.
Peberdy, Max, *Tigray: Ethiopia's Untold Story* (London: Relief Society of Tigray UK Support Committee, 1985).
Penrose, Angela, "Before and After," in *The Ethiopian Famine*, ed. Michael Harris and Angela Penrose (London: Zed Books, 1987).
Philo, Greg, "From Buerk to Band Aid: The Media and the 1984 Ethiopian Famine," in *Getting the Message: News, Truth and Power*, ed. John Eldridge (London: Routledge, 1993), 73–103.
Poster, Alexander, "The Gentle War: Famine Relief, Politics and Privatization in Ethiopia, 1938–86," *Diplomatic History* 26, no. 2 (2012): 399–425.
"Rapport général pour l'année 1847," *Bulletin de la Société de Saint-Vincent de Paul* 1, no. 2 (1848): 45–60.
Report on Economic Conditions in Russia: With Special Reference to the Famine of 1921–1922 and the State of Agriculture (Geneva: League of Nations, 1923).
Report on the African Emergency Relief Operation 1984–1986 with Particular Reference to the Contributions of Non-Governmental Organisations, and at the Request of the UN Office for Emergency Operations in Africa (London: International Institute for Environment and Development, 1986).
Salvatici, Silvia, *A History of Humanitarianism, 1755–1989: In the Name of Others* (Manchester: University Press, 2019).

Sasson, Tehila. "From Empire to Humanity: The Russian Famine and the Imperial Origins of International Humanitarianism," *Journal of British Studies* 53, no. 3 (2016): 519–37.
"Seeing is believing," *Record*, 2, no. 10, Feb 1, 1922.
Taithe, Bertrand, "Reinventing (French) Universalism: Religion, Humanitarianism and the 'French doctors,'" *Modern & Contemporary France* 12, no. 2 (2004): 147–58.
"Thirteenth General Report of the Colonial Land and Emigration Commissioners," *Justice of the Peace, and County, Borough, Poor Law Union, and Parish Law Recorder* 17 (1853): 582.
Transactions of the Central Relief Committee of the Society of Friends during the Famine in Ireland in 1846 and 1847 (Dublin: Hodges and Smith, 1852).
Tyrrell, Ian, *Reforming the World: The Creation of America's Moral Empire* (Princeton: University Press, 2010).
US General Accounting Office, "The United States Response to the Ethiopian Food Crisis," Apr 1985, 2–3, available at http://pdf.usaid.gov/pdf_docs/Pcaaa061.pdf (accessed June 20, 2024).
Vogt, Carl Emil, *Nansens kamp mot hungersnøden i Russland 1921–23* (Oslo: Aschehoug, 2007).
Werther, Steffen, "Help Yourself by Helping Others: Self-interest in Appeals for Russian Famine Relief, 1921-23." *Disasters* 46, no. 3 (2022): 700–719.
With Love from Band Aid: Report of 7 Years Work (London: Band Aid Trust, [1992]).

7 Fight the famine

American Quakers and child feeding in Germany after the First World War[1]

Daniel Maul

In the immediate aftermath of the First World War American, and to a lesser degree British, Quaker organizations took a crucial part in the large-scale US-led feeding program directed at German children.[2] During two-and-a-half years (1919–1922) of the *Quäkerspeisung* (Quaker feeding), as the operation came to be known, a handful of representatives of the American Friends Service Committee (AFSC), the central relief organization of the US Society of Friends, along with hundreds of thousands of German helpers organized the distribution of daily meals to nearly a quarter of the German children across the entire territory of the young Weimar Republic.[3] By doing so, the AFSC significantly contributed in establishing the image of the United States as a 'humanitarian superpower' during the inter-war period.[4]

In this chapter, I will use the Quakers' humanitarian effort in Germany as a model case in a dual sense. Firstly, the Quakers will serve as an example of the challenges non-state actors like the AFSC faced against the backdrop of an emerging and expanding international humanitarian 'system', in which state, non-state, and international actors interacted on an unprecedented scale. Secondly, and more specifically, through the lens of the AFSC's child feeding operation in Germany, this contribution will put a spotlight on the highly politically charged terrain the field of food aid constituted in the immediate aftermath of the First World War and it will highlight the complex web of interests that humanitarian actors like the Quakers had to navigate. My overarching argument is that while the approach the AFSC took to German child feeding was heavily informed by their specific religious background and aims, both the tensions they faced within this web of interests and the answers they found to mitigate those tensions were by no means unique to them, but rather representative of the very tensions that shaped the emerging humanitarian system at large.

The chapter will start with following the AFSC through the two phases of the German child feeding operation. Initially, as part of the mobilization against the ongoing Allied blockade of Germany in the period between the armistice of 1918 and the signing of the Versailles Treaty, the Quakers' activities turned into large-scale child-feeding programs – heavily supported and partly commissioned by official state agencies like the American Relief Administration, led by future US president Herbert Hoover. In the second part, the chapter will map out the web of relationships the AFSC food aid operation to Germany was embedded in – between British Friends, American donors, and German partners and recipients – before ending with a reflection on the AFSC representation of the *Quäkerspeisung* to various target audiences.

DOI: 10.4324/9781003465805-10

Quakers oppose the Allied blockade

The AFSC was founded in 1917. It was established on the occasion of the US entry into the war, and its initial main purpose was to provide young Friends in the US with an opportunity to render what the committee termed 'constructive service'. This was a kind of service that could be promoted to Quakers and the general public alike as being patriotic while remaining true to fundamental Quaker beliefs, of which the so-called 'peace testimony' was under particular pressure during times of mobilization for the war. On the basis of this strategy, the AFSC trained and dispatched around 500 young men to France, who served in Reconstruction and Ambulance Units together with their British co-religionists, behind the front lines of the war.

While this work received positive acknowledgment from government authorities and Quaker communities, there had also been critical voices among the latter. Some Quakers thought that 'constructive service' had brought the AFSC dangerously close to direct involvement in the war effort. They saw it accordingly in a principal conflict with the Quaker spirit of peace and reconciliation.[5] In this sense, the end of hostilities in late 1918 and its aftermath gave Friends a chance to redefine their role. In the meanwhile, the Allied powers had maintained a blockade against the vanquished middle powers in the months between the armistice in October 1918 and the conclusion of the Treaty of Versailles in June 1919 in order to force the German government into acceptance of the Allied peace terms.[6] In the end, it was this very policy that offered the Friends an occasion to turn to a service that was more in line with Quaker's religious values. When the Allies subjected the flow of food and other essential goods into Germany to severe restrictions and thereby exacerbated a situation already strained by the shortages of the last years of the war, Quakers on both sides of the Atlantic began to rally behind the idea of a possible relief operation in Germany.

While the Allied blockade policy was initially met with little opposition from the general public in the US, it acted as a wake-up call to pacifist circles. Debates over the blockade reached the AFSC at the very moment when many among its constituency considered the Committee's task accomplished – as the war and the immediate pressure on young Quaker men had ended – and consequently argued for its dissolution. For others, not the least a good part of the members of the AFSC itself, the German situation opened up an entirely new perspective. They saw the end of the war as an opportunity for a genuine new beginning, in which the AFSC, freed from the necessities of wartime, could continue the spiritual and practical renewal of the Society of Friends through constructive humanitarian service. From this point of view, the young German Republic, suffering from hunger imposed not to the least by short-sighted political considerations on the part of the victors of the war, offered an ideal place for action. Reaching out to former enemies was undoubtedly in line with Quaker ideals of peace and reconciliation and thus appeared to open the path to re-align their religious and pacifist aims.

Germany also seemed particularly well-suited for such a new endeavor because some leading American and British Quakers had entertained close personal relationships in Germany before the war, in particular through pacifist and social reform networks. Plans by American and British Quakers to strengthen their cooperation with each other after the end of the war also played an important role. Placing reconciliation with wartime enemies at the center of future relief work directly echoed the thinking of some British Quakers, who already during the last phase of the war had campaigned for a decidedly spiritually oriented peace service after the cessation of hostilities.[7] Their ambitions found expression in the first All Friends Conference in London in early 1920, which was attended by Quakers from both sides of the Atlantic and all corners of the

British Empire. The idea of an international Quaker service also had many supporters within the AFSC, among whom Wilbur Thomas, the Committee's Executive Secretary between 1918 and 1929, was one of the most outspoken ones.[8]

One of the first Quakers to advocate in favor of making Germany the target for a humanitarian relief operation countering the effects of the blockade was the New York social reformer Carolena Wood. As early as October 1918, she addressed Thomas to express her 'concern for service among the people of Germany'. 'I believe', Wood wrote, 'that Friends have, awaiting them in that country, an important service in spiritual healing and reconstruction'[9] Quaker women like Wood played a crucial role in drawing attention to Germany's suffering in this early phase, partly because of their connections to the larger pacifist-oriented women's rights movement in the United States.

The relationship that the AFSC maintained with social reformer and peace activist Jane Addams is an important example. During the war, Addams' opposition to American entry into the war in 1917 had made her the target of sometimes savage hostility in the United States. At the same time, her pacifist stance had solidified her status as an icon of the American peace movement. Through the feminist-pacifist Women's International League for Peace and Freedom (WILPF), which Addams helped to launch in 1915 and in which she took a leading position, she had opened a channel for women pacifists to reach out to like-minded women across the trenches of war.[10] Addams, who was born a Quaker but did not practice the faith in her adult years, would also become a key figure for the AFSC in the context of the German relief effort – not least through her close interaction with American Friends such as Wood and women's rights activist Lucy Biddle Lewis as well as British Quakers such as Dorothy Buxton, one of the co-founders of the British child aid organization Save the Children.[11] Through all connections, Quakers on both sides of the Atlantic were well-positioned to take a leading part in opposing the Allied blockade and early relief efforts directed to Germany.

Initially, the initiative to mobilize against the Allied blockade policy and in favor of providing relief to the starving Germans came primarily from England. In response to the British government's intransigent attitude toward all initiatives to relieve German suffering, various critics of the Allied blockade policy joined together in January 1919 to form the Fight the Famine Council (FFC). The FFC provided a platform for the British peace movement as well as for parts of the liberal and moderate left public, including figures like the economist John Maynard Keynes. British Quaker activists such as Ruth Fry played a crucial role in the FFC. The Council's work largely built on networks established during the war by the 'Emergency Committee for the Assistance of Germans, Austrians and Hungarians in Distress', a group of private citizens, many of whom were Quakers who aimed to care for so-called 'enemy aliens': foreign nationals stranded and subsequently interned after the outbreak of the war. Similar groups were established on both sides of the war front. For some, the Emergency Committee had already served as a significant channel for maintaining connections with like-minded people in enemy countries during the war. It provided a niche for many Quakers and pacifists, allowing a modest amount of peace work and exchange across the front lines to remain tolerated and possible, even in times of total war.[12]

The work of the Emergency Committee during the war thus represented an important starting point for the first humanitarian activities of British Quakers after the Armistice. In an even broader sense, the work for the civilian internees would turn out to be the main starting point for a rapprochement with Germany after the war. Especially consequential were the contacts that the Emergency Committee maintained with its counterpart in Germany, the *Auskunfts- und Hilfsstelle für Deutsche im Ausland und Ausländer in Deutschland* (Agency for Information and Aid for Germans abroad and foreigners in Germany).[13] As in England, the *Hilfsstelle* was a private initiative, which was headed by the Swiss-German educational reformer Elisabeth Rotten, who had maintained close contact with British Quakers since before the war.[14] Rotten and others provided a link to the pacifist Fellowship of Reconciliation, which was founded after the outbreak of war in 1914 by the German Lutheran theologian Friedrich Siegmund-Schultze and the British Quaker Henry Hodgkin. Thus, Rotten, Siegmund-Schultze, and a circle of like-minded people became important facilitators of a German relief effort.

For Quaker organizations on both sides of the Atlantic, Rotten in particular served as a central contact person on all matters pertaining to the situation on the ground in Germany and the need for relief during the period from the armistice to the end of the child feeding operation in 1922.[15] As chairwoman of the *Deutsche Wohlfahrtsstelle* (German Welfare Office: DWS), an institution that sought to coordinate the influx of foreign aid beginning in March 1919, Rotten was well-positioned to act as a door-opener to official agencies and social service and welfare organizations throughout Germany. Rotten was also active within the Women's International League for Peace and Freedom and knew Jane Addams from before the war. Taken together, these reformist and pacifist networks that had maintained and even strengthened their ties across the divisions of the war formed the backbone of the German relief effort.[16]

From the beginning of 1919, there was a division of labor between the WILPF and the Quaker relief organizations in Philadelphia and London. The Women's League took action against the Allied blockade at the political level, by publishing appeals and lobbying governments. Yet it was up to the Quakers together with the Save the Children Fund, which had been founded that April out of the Fight the Famine movement by the social reformer Eglantyne Jebb and her sister Dorothy Buxton (who had joined the Society of Friends during the War), to prepare a relief campaign in Germany. The success of this cooperation, however, remained modest. In the end, it was not until the Weimar Republic delegation had accepted the peace terms in the Treaty of Versailles on June 28 that the way was cleared for a small delegation led by Jane Addams to enter Germany.[17]

The reports produced by the members of the group conveyed a vivid picture of conditions in Germany, which Addams described as a 'shipwreck of a nation'. Based on the delegation's visits of mainly child welfare institutions all over Germany, they confirmed widespread severe malnutrition and a sharp rise of deficiency diseases such as rickets and tuberculosis after the end of the war because of the shortages resulting from the Allied blockade policy. At least one in three children in Germany, if not two-thirds of those under fourteen in urban areas, suffered from severe malnutrition according to the reports, with growth and weight everywhere far below the age standard. As Carolena Wood pointed out, any further delay in aid would result in the present generation of children in Germany facing an 'early death or a handicapped life'. Although children were the focus of attention, the reports made clear that the problem was by no means limited to them alone and that Germany's population as a whole was experiencing a severe famine.[18]

Relief to Germany

Before long, these conclusions formed the basis for the first joint Quaker relief effort to Germany. In the late summer of 1919, the stage was finally set for an Anglo-American aid program in Germany, which positioned the AFSC essentially in the role of a junior partner to the British Quakers. However, this order of things changed completely when, in November of the same year, the AFSC received an offer from Herbert Hoover to conduct a large-scale child-feeding program in Germany. Hoover, who had made a name for himself during the First World War as an organizer of private and government relief efforts, in particular in German-occupied

Belgium, approached the Quakers in his capacity as head of the American Relief Administration (ARA), a semi-governmental organization which had been responsible in the immediate postwar period for ensuring the supply of food and other essential goods to European civilians in the Allied states.[19] Hoover now wanted to extend this aid to Germany and offered the Quakers the role to act as a 'repository of any funds which may be subscribed in the US for this purpose'.[20]

Hoover had been an opponent of the Allied blockade of Germany and was convinced that the ARA should extend its activities to Germany for humanitarian as well as political reasons. What Hoover feared most was that starvation might ultimately contribute to a revolutionary overthrow of the country's new democratic order. For Hoover, hunger and deprivation bred revolution. From his point of view, American aid was the prime weapon to fight this danger; a conviction that he would apply to many theaters of humanitarian engagement throughout his public life.[21]

Providing aid to the very country against which American soldiers had recently fought and died in the trenches and which war propaganda had relentlessly portrayed as blood-thirsty 'huns' was not a popular project immediately after the war. Hoover's original plan to include Germany in the ARA's relief planning thus had been frustrated early on by the US Congress, which had approved the ARA's $100 million endowment in February 1919 on the explicit condition that former enemy states would be excluded from its funds. Although the conclusion of the Paris Treaties half a year later led to the dissolution of the Allied blockade, this restriction continued unchanged. Yet around that same time, the ARA was transferred to a private corporation under the name European Children's Fund (ECF), for which the name 'ARA' remained in common use. This initially gave Hoover more room to maneuver. However, since all government grants remained subject to congressional legislation, the ECF had to find money outside official channels with regard to Germany (and Austria).[22] This clearly shows that aid to former enemies, whatever rational political considerations it followed, was a political minefield that Hoover had to skillfully navigate in order to not alienate the public.

Precisely because of these political strains, Hoover reached out to the Quakers, among all possible groups, to become his representatives in Germany. His choice was due to a couple of different reasons. As one of only a few American organizations, the AFSC already maintained a small aid program in Germany and had a network on which to build. The fact that Hoover was a Quaker by birth certainly also played a role as he had no reservations about Friends and their goals.[23] Most importantly, however, Hoover hoped that with the help of the Quakers, the American public would be more amenable, or at least less hostile, to an aid mission in Germany. In this sense, the Friends and their reputation as a community driven by purely Christian and humanitarian motives were to serve as a kind of protective shield against expected attacks from various quarters against aiding former enemies.[24]

There was another reason why Hoover saw the AFSC as a suitable partner. Due to opposition from the US Congress, it was foreseeable early on that the bulk of the funds required to fulfill the German relief effort would have to come from private sources. From Hoover's point of view, this was where the millions of US citizens of German descendant came into play. Hoover's goal vis-à-vis the German-American associations, which had a broad network, especially on the East Coast and in the Midwest, went beyond simply collecting donations. Rather, Hoover wanted to neutralize the German-Americans politically and, in particular, to prevent parallel channels of aid from developing, for example, through the German-Americans' potential cooperation with German institutions such as the German Red Cross, which were beyond the control of the United States.[25]

The problem with mobilizing the German-American community was that a majority harbored strong reservations about Hoover, who had taken clear positions against Germany during the war. Many German-Americans considered Hoover to be one of the main contributors to the aggressive anti-German sentiment that took hold in the United States after the country's entry into the war. Against this background, Hoover hoped that the participation of the Quakers in the relief operation might ease the mistrust against him. 'American Quakers, who are beyond all questions of political interest', Hoover wrote in his letter of invitation to the AFSC, were to become the filter for a relief effort that would be perceived credibly as an 'effort in sheer humanity'.[26]

An AFSC memorandum titled 'Hoover opens a door' reflected the overall positive and partly enthusiastic response with which the offer was received by the Committee. 'The fate of the child life of a great nation', suffering from hunger and deprivation, would be placed in the hands of Quakers. The opportunity 'to put our hand of healing on the sorest spot in suffering Europe' and to be able to extend this hand – equipped with Hoover's superior resources – to precisely those who were among the 'most helpless and blameless of those who were recently our enemies' was euphorically welcomed.[27]

At the same time, the collaboration with Hoover also raised questions, and one in particular: would the AFSC's profile lose its contours in cooperation with Hoover? The offer was tied to several conditions, some of which touched the core of the Quakers' religious and humanitarian identity and called into question the very character of the relief action. Two demands in particular aroused doubts: first, the Quakers had to refrain from any missionary or other overtly religious activity in and second, the relief had to be carried out according to ECF specifications as a purely American operation. This first demand was a delicate issue because, while the AFSC had always emphasized the humanitarian nature of food aid, there was widespread agreement that this aid should, in Wilbur Thomas's words, be associated with 'some special Friendly message'. Although the main goal of the campaign was to fight hunger, Thomas pointed out in 1919, 'we do not want it to be done in a soulless way'.[28] If Quakers had to set aside their religious identity, this unquestionably diminished the AFSC's integrative role toward their own Quaker community.

Hoover's second requirement that child feeding should be an 'American' enterprise also presented difficulties for the AFSC. From Hoover's perspective, if American aid was to serve its diplomatic purpose, it had to be clearly identifiable as such. In a practical sense, this meant an organizational separation from the British Quakers. Yet an aid campaign in Germany was precisely seen as an opportunity to deepen the cooperation with British Friends that had begun during the war. In this sense, the AFSC initially expressed to Hoover its intention to cooperate with British Quakers 'in every possible way' in Germany.[29] Still, to most AFSC officials, a temporary separation from the British Friends seemed in order for the higher good. After all, as the memorandum 'Hoover opens a door' read, the effort to ensure the survival of the new generation in Germany and to exert influence on German society 'at its most impressionable period' was an opportunity second only to the founding of the Quaker colony of Pennsylvania in 1682.[30] After a short debate, the AFSC accordingly decided to cooperate with the ECF, greeting with enthusiasm the 'great responsibility and wonderful opportunity involved'. Surely, the AFSC did not ignore the political overtones and aims of Hoover's offer, but those seemed a small price to pay.[31]

Although the AFSC was responsible for the daily management of the operation, it was Hoover who was in charge of preparing the diplomatic and logistical conditions for the child-feeding campaign in Germany. Representatives of the ARA and the ECF, respectively, conducted negotiations with the German government in November and December 1919, which laid the groundwork for the relief operation. The German authorities determined the needs and paid for the cost of transporting and distributing the relief supplies; they also paid Hoover (from the Reich's gold reserves) for much of the relief.[32] Hoover initially provided about $14 million worth of goods to the AFSC through the ECF, some of which went to purchasing grain surpluses from American farmers (the fact that aid to Germany and later to Soviet Russia was in the best interest of the US politically and economically had been an argument used by Hoover vis-à-vis the American public from the start). The ECF also organized a European Relief Council, which coordinated a joint appeal for donations ('Hoover Drive') in the United States and served as a focal point for several private relief organizations – from the YMCA to the Jewish Joint Distribution Committee – to bring their relief funds to Germany.

At the same time, the AFSC itself served as a conduit for donations from German-American organizations, by establishing a fundraising campaign aimed specifically at this group, which would raise another million dollars by the summer of 1920. The AFSC, in turn, was given the role of aid organizer in Germany in its agreement with Hoover. The Quakers would oversee the entire operation, from landing supplies at German ports to storage and the distribution of the aid by German volunteers. Representatives of the AFSC also took over the bookkeeping and all communication with German agencies from the top level down to the welfare groups, which, in turn, managed the bulk of the German aid workers. All German agencies were required to report only to the AFSC, which for its part reported to Hoover and the ECF, which points to the highly centralized character of the operation under the premise of a strictly American aid effort.

To meet the extensive responsibilities of being the institution primarily responsible for aid distribution, the agreement with Hoover provided that the AFSC would rapidly increase its staff in Germany. It was thus also clear that the relief operation would be difficult to reconcile with the original goal attached to aid in Germany, which was to serve as a field of experience for young Quakers to consolidate their faith and their membership in the Quaker community. Rather, what was needed was professional experience and training in organizational and practical matters. The first people the AFSC sent to Germany were therefore mainly established professionals, who were only later in the operation supplemented by younger volunteers without relevant experience. As a case in point, the head of the German mission Alfred Scattergood, a Quaker from Philadelphia, took a leave of absence as Vice President of the Provident Trust Company in order to join the German assignment.

In January 1920, the AFSC began the first phase of its child-feeding program, in which the Committee for the first six months (January–June 1920) acted as the (unofficial) agent of the ARA-ECF. During the second phase (July 1920–July 1922), the AFSC nominally operated the relief effort on its own. During this period, the Hoover organization continued to turn over all donations raised by the ECF for Germany to the AFSC. German Americans also directed their donations to the Quakers during this second phase, in what was known as the '3 Million Dollar Drive'.

At the beginning of the child-feeding program, the AFSC had contracted the *Deutscher Zentralausschuss für die Auslandshilfe* (German Central Committee for Foreign Aid: DZA), a newly established agency under the umbrella of the Reich Ministry of Nutrition. For its part, the DZA served as the AFSC's liaison to the German Red Cross as well as to the *German Welfare Office* (DWS) led by Elisabeth Rotten, which united under its umbrella a variety of charitable organizations throughout the Reich.[33] One of the main tasks of the DZA was to organize relief committees of German volunteers at regional and local levels, into whose hands the actual distribution of food aid was placed. The DZA's associated members represented a cross-section of the entire religious and secular social and welfare spectrum in Germany. Beyond this, associations of teachers and physicians played a key role in determining the neediest children.[34]

The food was cooked throughout the country based on uniform recipes, determined by their nutritional value, in central kitchens and distributed to the children in school buildings and kindergartens. Need was determined based on a medical test conducted in schools and other public institutions according to fixed criteria based on the measurement of height and weight, first by teachers and then by specially assigned medical doctors. Children were divided into four categories according to their physical condition: as a rule, Quakers focused on feeding the most severely malnourished children. Everything – from the procedures involved to the equipment required, the arrangement of locations in which the children would be fed (food was to be eaten while seated and with sufficient time) to the composition of the menus – followed a meticulous plan drawn up by the AFSC in cooperation with the ARA or ECF and the American Red Cross, incorporating their experiences of relief during the war and immediate postwar years. In the expression of the leaders of the operation as well as their German partners, it was precisely this 'scientific' approach that constituted the specifically American character of the aid. Evidence of its success may be seen in the fact that the Quaker program was continued for several years by German school authorities as a school feeding program, whose socio-medical benefits were widely recognized.[35]

Tensions of Quaker aid

The eulogies the AFSC representatives received from all sides as they left Germany in 1922, when the child feeding operation was dissolved, could not hide the fact that for most of its duration the mission had been fraught with quite severe tensions, stemming from the complex web of interests the feeding program was working within. Indeed, during the child-feeding mission, the AFSC became positioned between German recipients and the American sponsors, as well as between the quest for fellowship in an 'international' relief operation uniting British and American Quakers and the contradicting demands for the mission to project a decidedly American profile.

Although the AFSC's relations with its German partners were, on the whole, harmonious, frictions emerged in this relationship as well, essentially because the AFSC operated in a gray area as a private aid organization acting, as it were, on a quasi-governmental mandate. For the German government, aid from the United States was particularly important since the Weimar government was not only concerned with fighting hunger. Rather, American aid was intrinsically linked to the hope of gaining the attention of the US public vis-à-vis the precarious situation of the Weimar Republic in a much broader sense. This served a larger goal: the revision of the Treaty of Versailles and the reparations stipulated therein.[36] As part of a deliberately pursued 'diplomacy of pity' tailored to the United States, the DZA undertook the task of painting a picture of German suffering for its American partners in the darkest possible colors.[37]

The Quakers assumed a key role in this strategy pursued by the DZA. First of all, their position as Hoover's representatives in Germany gave the AFSC mission in Germany a quasi-diplomatic role. Second, from the German government's perspective, the Quakers could be counted on for general goodwill and for understanding Germany's difficult situation, not least against the background of their position within the 'Fight the Famine Campaign'. The German government consequently made every effort to show its gratitude and repeatedly issued public expressions of its appreciation to the American benefactors. *Reichspräsident* Friedrich Ebert received leaders of the AFSC mission both at the beginning of the relief effort in January 1920 and again in 1922 after the official end of the child-feeding program; the DZA and local authorities were especially active in organizing local meetings at which German notables and often school children extended gratitude to the Quakers.

It should hardly come as a surprise that the Friends' relations with the DZA and the DWS, headed by Elisabeth Rotten, were marked by mutual trust. These contacts were built on a long-established network of contacts between mainly British Quakers and reformist circles in Germany. After the start of the child-feeding program this close cooperation continued, in particular, through the many regional committees in which AFSC representatives met with members of the welfare associations coordinated by the DWS, the medical profession, and local authorities. The DWS also served as a channel through which Quakers came into contact with progressive, internationalist, and pacifist circles throughout Germany. Elisabeth Rotten's own wide network, which included among others the progressive-liberal *Bund Neues Vaterland* (The New Fatherland Union), the German Society for the League of Nations, and various associations from the women's and peace movements, may serve as an illustration of its reach. In addition, the DWS opened contacts with educational reformers, as well as with physicians and nutritionists. The latter, and in particular those who worked with the medical advisory board convened by the DZA and its many local sub-councils, often saw the AFSC as an ally with regard to their own reformist concerns.[38]

In contrast, relations between the Quakers and the German Red Cross (DRK) were often marked by tension. Many disputes were related to the close relationship that the DRK had built up since the end of the war with German-American associations such as the Central Relief Committee of New York. After the establishment of the DZA, which was to serve as the AFSC's sole point of contact, the Red Cross receded into the background without, however, relinquishing its role as an advocate and privileged contact for the German-Americans, who maintained a liaison office with the German Red Cross in Berlin. The resulting parallel structures, as well as the politically more conservative orientation of the Red Cross, which had in its ranks many of the elites from the former *Kaiserreich*, compared to the much more liberal and pro-republic DZA and DWS, led time and again to conflicts and jealousies.[39]

Relations between the AFSC and British Quakers were in turn fraught by tensions of a different sort. When aid began in Germany in the fall of 1919, there were still high hopes that this work could form the starting point for a joint relief effort with the ultimate goal to unite Quakers across the Atlantic in a joint 'Friends International Service'.[40] Quite naturally, the agreement with Hoover, which provided for the separation of existing Anglo-American cooperation, acted as a brake on such plans and strained the relationship between the British and Americans. Initially, the British Quakers accepted the AFSC's request for a temporary separation until the end of the child-feeding operation without complaint. This, however, was on the understanding that this separation would last for half a year, until the summer of 1920, when the first agreement with Hoover would terminate.

The disappointment among the British Quakers became even greater when the AFSC decided to maintain the separation between the two missions even after direct cooperation with the ECF ended, and there was no longer an immediate need to uphold it. From the American point of view, cooperation with the German-American associations and the fact that the AFSC had established itself as the face of American aid in Germany made it necessary to continue to present a distinct American profile. The AFSC's head of mission in Germany Alfred Scattergood argued along the same lines: what had been started as an American relief effort could not now simply be called an 'international' activity. Private donor groups such as the German-Americans would rightly interpret the consolidation of Quaker aid as an attempt 'to cash in for the sake of Quakerism the child feeding work' – work that had been presented to them as an American relief effort.[41] Pragmatic considerations – without ARA money there would have been simply no room for a large-scale child-feeding operation – in this sense pushed the project of an international Quaker service into a more distant future.

That there might have been other reasons that justified continued separation from the British Quakers from the AFSC's point of view and that in fact many of them were quite satisfied with being and staying part of an All-American aid operation instead of an Anglo-British Quaker one, becomes clear when looking at the case of Austria. Like Germany, Austria, as the political center and heartland of the former Habsburg Empire, had been among the vanquished of the Great War. The Austrian state that had emerged from the ruins of the dual monarchy that had perished in the war found itself in an even more precarious food situation after 1918 than the German Reich. Cut off from large parts of its traditional supply areas in Hungary, Bohemia, Poland, and Galicia, the capital Vienna in particular faced a desperate situation, with hunger and deprivation widespread and affecting large parts of the population. Unlike in Germany, however, the victors of the war prepared early on to allow humanitarian relief to enter the country. As early as the spring of 1919 and at a point in time when the Paris peace negotiations were still ongoing, the ARA initiated a child-feeding program, which was successively expanded until 1921.

At the same time, the British Quakers also established a small-scale aid mission in Vienna in May 1919, headed by Hilda Clark, who followed up immediately on her work with the Friends War Victim Relief Committee in France. The AFSC participated in this relief mission in July with some aid workers who also had been relocated from the reconstruction units in France. Heading the AFSC contingent was Alfred Scattergood's brother Henry, himself a veteran of the Anglo-American relief contingents in France, who was at the same time serving as the AFSC's European director. Until the spring of 1920, a division of labor existed in Vienna between the large and financially strong ARA relief organization that provided school-age children with a daily meal, and the small Anglo-American mission that concentrated on feeding children under six and, as in Germany, maintained a smaller student-feeding program. Funds for this work came from private donations, with the AFSC providing a disproportionately large share.[42]

When Hoover briefly considered in May 1920 that the ARA-ECF might end its operation in Austria and transfer all aid to a joint German-Polish-Austrian relief organization under the direction of the AFSC, the question of the 'Americanization' of Quaker aid and consequently a separation of the Anglo-American mission was once again raised. That it did not come to this was mainly due to the resistance of the ARA representatives in Vienna. Their leader, Gilchrist Stockton, was bothered not only by the religious orientation of the Quakers but also by their general approach to aid, which in his view differed from the consistently rational and efficient one of the ARA. Stockton observed that the Quakers, whom he seemed to associate with the British leadership, placed too much emphasis on personal encounters as part of the relief effort. As a result, they had a comparatively large staff, unlike the ARA, which operated with few American aid workers and relied primarily on local personnel to carry out the actual work. Finally, according to Stockton, the Anglo-American mission in Vienna was perceived by Austrians as primarily a British enterprise. Indeed, forty British cooperated with fourteen Americans, which was incompatible with the goal of a purely American relief effort.[43]

Unlike Stockton, AFSC representatives were delighted with Hoover's initial idea of placing the child-feeding operation in Vienna under Quaker's direction. Henry Scattergood immediately made it clear that the AFSC was available and that, if this required separation from the British Quakers and the temporary dissolution of the 'international' mission, the Committee was prepared to take this step immediately and without hesitation. In the end, things turned out differently, and the ARA-ECF decided to continue the operation on its own until June 1922. After 1921, the ARA did integrate the AFSC into parts of the child-feeding operation as a purely American enterprise, under the American flag and thus without any British participation.[44] What became clear once again was that, when in doubt, the AFSC representatives in Vienna also preferred cooperation with the ARA to practising the pure doctrine of Quaker relief in cooperation with their British co-religionists.[45] The pattern established here was to repeat itself on many future occasions, from the famine in Soviet Russia (1921–1923) to the Spanish Civil War (1936–1939). When presented with a choice between working in a joint Anglo-American Quaker mission with small resources or an All-American aid operation with greater possibilities, the AFSC invariably went for the latter option.[46]

What makes all these cases even more striking is the fact that the British Quakers in all cases argued against a separation of a joint Anglo-American effort and of what they saw as a 'nationalization' of aid efforts. They would have preferred a continuation of the 'international' Quaker work even if that would have implied to work with much lesser resources. In Germany, the British Quakers were particularly bitter about the American decision for separation, as they could rightly claim to have served as a door-opener for the US Quakers in Germany. Almost all of the contacts that the AFSC used within the social reformist milieu in Germany originally came from the British side. Many of them now felt that they were pushed to the sidelines, without sufficient funding, having to work on small-scale projects. Nevertheless, a separation continued de facto beyond the winter of 1921–1922, when ECF aid ended and the AFSC assumed sole responsibility for the administration of German-American funds. It was not until the summer of 1922, with the conclusion of the child-feeding operations, that the AFSC and the British resumed their cooperation, for example through the joint work at the Quaker International Center in Berlin, which was to continue the work for peace and reconciliation and reach out to like-minded pacifist, reformist, and other groups in Germany. What can be taken from these episodes then is that the US Quakers were by and large prepared to serve as agents of 'American aid' as well as to accept and partly even embrace the idea of the openly political aims attached to it.

While the AFSC's position as a representative of American aid in Germany turned into a problem for relations with their British co-religionists, conversely, the Committee's relationship with American aid sponsors was by no means free of ambivalence and conflict either. On the contrary, many American Quakers reacted with mixed feelings to the growing perception of the AFSC as an American aid organization, whose decidedly national character was reinforced by the demands of the funders to show a clear American profile. In reality, however, very few in the AFSC saw a contradiction in assuming the role of representatives of their country on the one hand, and as Quakers and partners of their German hosts on the other. Rather, they saw their efforts as part of a historic mission that was by no means limited to the religious aspect and in which the idea of 'constructive service' carried once again a promise to reconcile patriotism with the claim to perform Quaker-specific work of reconciliation.

In practice, however, this very promise turned out to be a fragile one, and points of friction continued to rise due to the specific constellation and context of the relief action in Germany. Representatives of the ECF, such as its European director Walter Lyman Brown, distrusted the AFSC and considered its approach naive and unprofessional. Lyman Brown was, in Wilbur Thomas's view, one of many who displayed a 'rather hostile attitude to our whole work' over the long duration of the mission.[47] Most of the time, the conflicts simmered below the surface or were masked by Hoover's essentially positive attitude toward the AFSC. Occasionally, however, they broke out and led to open disagreement. Controversies arose mostly around the issue of the degree to which the Quakers should feel obliged to emphasize the American origin of the goods they were distributing among German children. In early 1921, for example, Lyman Brown asked the AFSC to display the Star-Spangled Banner in all child-feeding stations in Germany. The Quakers refused because, as Alfred Scattergood sarcastically noted, this would inevitably arouse suspicion that the United States was concerned with more than purely humanitarian goals.

Scattergood and his colleagues were of course well aware of the political aims attached to Hoover's campaign in Germany and were not generally opposed to them either.[48] Dealing with demands for a distinct 'American profile' to the child-feeding program nevertheless remained a constant balancing act, and the attempts of the AFSC in Philadelphia to subject the flow of information about relief operations in Germany to tight control can be interpreted as an indicator of this. Already at the beginning of 1921, Wilbur Thomas admonished Scattergood to avoid as a matter of principle certain words like 'international' in connection with Quaker aid in Germany, since this was a 'bugbear to some people, especially Hoover and some of the members of his Committee', as it run counter to the ARA's aim to convey the clear message that American aid would be delivered and be fully recognizable as such for the recipients, in order to fulfill its political and diplomatic function.[49]

Another source of controversy turned out to be the cooperation with the German-American associations, in which the AFSC repeatedly threatened to get caught between the different parties. The main catalyst was the German Americans' distrust of cooperation with Hoover, especially because he initially tried, out of deference to public opinion, to avoid anything that might make him appear 'pro-German'. This plunged the Quakers into a dilemma because, after all, Hoover had wanted to get the German-Americans to use the AFSC as the sole channel for their donations without first making a public commitment to this work. Hoover relied entirely on the diplomatic skills of the AFSC here, and it was his stated goal to make it appear that the initiative for German aid came solely from the Quakers. If in doubt, he would have been prepared, at least as AFSC representatives understood it, to deny a connection.[50]

Selling German aid

Precisely because the AFSC's work in Germany took place against the backdrop of the conflicting interests outlined above, from the very beginning great importance was attached to the external and internal presentation of the mission. In this sense, the German aid mission served as a big push for the professionalization of the AFSC's public relations work. The AFSC was primarily concerned with gaining control over varying, sometimes contradictory, messages to be sent to specific target groups. The AFSC's public relations work had to reflect both its claim to be a patriotic and decidedly American organization performing 'constructive service' on behalf of and in the interest of the United States and its desire to emphasize its own Quaker-specific profile. Sending out the 'right message' was even more significant because the AFSC, aside from during the initial phase of the relief effort when money came also from public sources, relied to an overwhelming degree on donations. At the same time, material considerations were not the only, and possibly not even the most important, driver behind the construction of the AFSC's public relations machinery. Rather, it expressed to a significant degree the desire – evident in a plethora of memoranda, reports from aid workers, letters, and diary entries – to lend meaning to one's actions. Part of the public relations work, and not only the part directly addressed to the Quaker community, served to construct and consolidate a Quaker identity renewed and expanded in the spirit of humanitarian aid.

The early days with Hoover had already trained the AFSC leadership to craft a nuanced message that was able to accommodate these different sensitivities. A case in point was the focus on 'innocent' children as the exclusive recipients of aid in line with Hoover and the European Children's Funds' demands and a means to depoliticize the aid. While this focus permeated all fundraising campaigns and all AFSC publications and pronouncements directed to the broader public from the summer of 1919 onward, it played only a minor role vis-à-vis the

Quaker audience. Instead, Quaker publications focused on the reconciliation aspect, in both its religious pacifist and its political implications.[51]

Another prominent element in public relations work was to bring the gratitude of the recipients to the fore. This concerned the German government, which was consistently portrayed as both cooperative and appreciative of aid from the United States. For example, the AFSC's Annual Report of 1920 included excerpts of a letter of thanks from *Reichskanzler* Hermann Müller, which was described as 'typical of thousands of expressions of appreciation from the German people'.[52] Beyond that, the focus was primarily on the gratitude of the children, and often that of the parents and teachers of those children as well. The core of the message was always that the Quaker method 'worked'. Gratitude thereby signaled, on the one hand, the worthiness of the victims, which was an established topos of aid since the nineteenth century. On the other hand, it served as a marker that the recipients showed themselves open to the reconciliatory approach, which carried in itself the promise of a peaceful future. The AFSC's Annual Report for 1920 also quoted a Hamburg newspaper in this vein:

> Many a memory of childhood will vanish, but never will the children forget the memory of the delicious meals, which were once given them by kind people, strangers to them in language and customs, from whom, however, they gained a deep impression, because they felt the real love for mankind, which actuated this whole relief work [...] And these children about whose early childhood so many war passions raged and whose child-life had witnessed so much distress of war, have an inkling of the meaning of this message, and will perhaps save something of its truth for their later life.[53]

Generally, the AFSC took pains to always emphasize to the broader public the professionalism of the aid over the religious motivation. This, in turn, could have adverse effects, fueling the concerns of those who questioned whether the AFSC's relief work in Germany was carried out in a sufficiently Quakerly spirit – a concern that intensified just as the AFSC gained recognition for the 'professional' quality of its work. The AFSC's many attempts to convey an image of the aid as being both professional and 'Friendly' in nature can serve as indicators for the dilemma.

The reputation for providing efficient and targeted aid according to scientific standards lent credibility to the AFSC and helped to reduce reservations about Quakers and thus also to increase the willingness to donate, especially with regard to the general public. In line with this, the AFSC's publications were full of reports highlighting the number of meals distributed and the rationality of the distribution system, as well as the positive and measurable impact of the feeding campaign on children's growth and general health.[54] At the same time, the strategy of emphasizing the professionalism of Quaker aid also produced undesirable side effects. In the view of many AFSC activists being professional alone did not provide sufficient legitimacy for the humanitarian endeavour. For this, the aid needed a clear Quaker profile, which would justify the collective commitment of a primarily religious community.

A way out of the dilemma and a response to critics who saw the AFSC's Quaker-specific profile as blurred was offered by putting emphasis on the neutrality of Quaker aid. Those who gave their money to the AFSC could be assured that their donations would be used

> to save lives, to alleviate suffering, to rehabilitate homes, to fortify human spirits and not to further political schemes, nor to propagate social theories nor to make converts to a sect. It will be made the bearer of love and good-will, of hope and healing.[55]

In this sense, under the notion of neutrality, religious and secular contents were merged such that Quakers of all directions could identify with it. In this sense, neutrality provided an ideal foundation on which to base the AFSC's work, not only in Germany but also in all future missions.

In the course of the relief operation in Germany, a strategy crystallized in the AFSC's public relations work that would become formative. At its heart, it propagated humanitarian professionalism as well as rigorously practiced neutrality fed precisely by a specific religious foundation as the unique selling point of Quaker aid. Highlighting this specific humanitarian identity of Quaker aid through the AFSC was first recognized in the years of the German child-feeding campaign as a means of consolidating the Committee's position in various directions. Increasingly centralized public relations thus reflected the acknowledgment in the light of the German experience that effective 'branding' was a necessity and an asset both internally vis-à-vis the Quaker community and externally in an increasingly competitive humanitarian marketplace.

As part of this emerging strategy, once the child-feeding program began, the AFSC ensured that the food was accompanied by a note or a small pamphlet featuring the red and black Quaker star – symbolizing the AFSC (and other Quaker aid organizations) – as well as a brief statement. While the content of the statement varied, it always included the same three elements: a reference to American origins, to Quakers as the deliverers of aid, and an emphasis on the reconciliation aspect of the feeding operation.[56] Apart from strategy, it can serve as a perfect expression of the tensions the *Quäkerspeisung* had to overcome between a commitment to an 'All-American' aid operation and the quest to deliver a clearly recognizable 'Friendly' message to the recipients.

Conclusion

To conclude, the German child-feeding campaign proved to be transformative for the AFSC in several ways. While the First World War had provided patriotic credibility to the Quakers, the relief effort in a defeated and starving Germany, imbued with a spirit of reconciliation, seemed to many Friends like a return to authentic Quakerly service after the compromises made necessary by the war. However, the German operation had not been free of frictions either, mostly because of the AFSC's cooperation with Herbert Hoover's American Relief Administration (ARA). True, the role the AFSC had played in the pursuit of American foreign policy goals in Germany was considered by many as perfectly in line with Quaker values. But, at the same time, the tensions the AFSC encountered in its humanitarian work for German children and the answers it found in mitigating them would set a precedence for the future and would accompany the Quaker relief operations from Soviet Russia to the Spanish Civil War and into another World War.

It was even true for Germany, for neither there nor in Austria did the story of Quaker humanitarian involvement finish with the end of the child feeding campaigns. In 1923, the AFSC returned for a short episode during the French occupation of the Ruhr.[57] Later in the 1920s, American and British Friends opened so-called Quaker 'embassies',[58] among other places, in Vienna and Berlin to serve as centers of exchange and spiritual renewal. Those centers kept their doors open until far into the Second World War. During the 1930s, both worked as hubs for aid efforts for the victims of Nazi persecution and important knots in the net of refugee work for those fleeing from Germany and later from Austria after the '*Anschluss*' in 1938. Eventually, the Quakers would return to Germany after the Second World War to launch yet another feeding program – this time not restricted to children – in the defeated and occupied country, now freed from Nazi terror.

It was this latter case where the lessons taken from the earlier child-feeding campaign in Germany became most tangible. When a group of AFSC officials met in 1943 to discuss possible future venues for Quaker aid operations, Germany was on top of the list. This was not despite, but rather because of, the fact that, in light of the monstrous atrocities committed by Nazi Germany, any future feeding operation there would be even less popular than after the First World War; A memorandum produced on the occasion made a claim for the Quakers to become once again the ones to bring help to 'unpopular groups'. By doing so, it was argued, they did not merely follow a moral imperative in line with Friends religious conviction: by providing aid to a defeated Germany, the Quakers would play a crucial role in preventing hunger and the social and political unrest that would necessarily follow in its footsteps. Based on their history, they would therefore be able to offer a service to the occupational forces that no one organization was better equipped for and very few were willing to perform. In rendering aid to (future) former enemies, the Quakers thus would not only be true to 'an important tradition' but also serve a 'specific function'.[59] This demonstrates that the ability to bridge and ultimately embrace one of the fundamental tensions inherent to food aid to former enemy states – transforming it from a politically contagious issue into an asset for humanitarian action – was largely based on the experience of the *Quäkerspeisung*. In this light, it stands out as one of the most important legacies of humanitarian action after the First World War, not only for the Friends but for the humanitarian system as a whole.

Notes

1 The following contribution is based on two chapters from my monography Daniel Maul, "The Politics of Service. American Quakers and International Humanitarian Relief 1917–1945" (Berlin/Boston: DeGruyter, 2024). The parts this article is based on are ch.3: A New Pennsylvania. The Quäkerspeisung in Germany 1919–1923 (pp.72–114) and the sub-chapter in ch.4: The AFSC in Poland and Austria (pp.150–154).

2 In the following, I use the terms "Quaker" and "Friends" as synonyms, as well as "Quakerism" and Religious Society of Friends as descriptions of the totality of Quakers/Friends in a country. On Quaker history, see Stephen W. Angell, Pink Dandelion, and David Harrington Watt (eds.), *The Creation of Modern Quaker Diversity, 1830–1937* (Philadelphia: Penn State Press, 2023); Pink Dandelion, *An Introduction to Quakerism* (Cambridge: Cambridge University Press, 2007).

3 The most detailed treatment of the German *Quäkerspeisungen* to date is Guy Aiken, "Feeding Germany: American Quakers in the Weimar Republic", *Diplomatic History* 43, 4 (2019), 597–617, which focuses primarily on the operation itself from an American perspective. For a concise introduction, see Hans A. Schmitt, *Quakers and Nazis: Inner Light in Outer Darkness* (Columbia, MI: University of Missouri Press, 1997), 11–37. On the AFSC history and its humanitarian work, see Maul, *Politics of Service* and from the rich literature on the broader humanitarian field Silvia Salvatici, *A History of Humanitarianism*, 1755–1989: In the Name of Others, (Manchester: Manchester University Press, 2019); Michael Barnett, *Empire of Humanity: A History of Humanitarianism* (Ithaca, NY: Cornell University Press, 2011); Johannes Paulmann, "Conjunctures in the History of Humanitarian Aid during the Twentieth Century", *Humanity* 4, 2 (2013), 215–238.

4 For the numbers: see AFSC Annual Report 1920, 5–6; the numbers for June 1921: Jones, *Quakers in Action*, 55, quoted in Aiken, "Feeding Germany", 610.

5 On the idea of constructive service, see Maul, *The Politics of Service*, 38–71; J. William Frost, "Our Deeds Carry our Message: The Early History of the American Friends Service Committee", *Quaker History* 81, 1 (1992), 1–51.

6 Mary Elisabeth Cox, *Hunger in War and Peace: Women and Children in Germany, 1914–1924* (Oxford: Oxford University Press, 2019).

7 On the idea and practice of Quaker "embassies" that opened during the 1920 as Anglo-American Centers in Berlin, Vienna, Moscow, Warsaw, Paris and some smaller places the British brochure, *Quaker Embassies: A Survey of Friends Service in Europe since 1919* (London: Friends House, 1933).

8 John T. Elliott to Wilbur Thomas 14/4/1919, in: American Friends Service Committee Historical Archives (in the following AFSCA), General Administration, Foreign Service, Country: Germany 1919 (*Letters to and from*).

9 Carolena Wood to Wilbur Thomas 15/10/1918, in: AFSCA, Personnel Files Win-Z, 1917–1927; quoted in Aiken, "Feeding Germany", 597.

10 On Jane Addams, see Patricia M. Shields, *Jane Addams: Progressive Pioneer of Peace, Philosophy, Sociology, Social Work and Public Administration* (New York: Springer, 2017). On her role in the WILPF, see also several chapters in Mona L. Siegel, *Peace on Our Terms: the Global Battle for Women's Rights after the First World War* (New York City: Columbia University Press, 2020).

11 Glenda Sluga, "Women, Feminisms and Twentieth-Century Internationalisms", in: Glenda Sluga and Patricia Clavin (eds.), *Internationalisms: A Twentieth Century History* (Cambridge: Cambridge University Press, 2016), pp. 61–84; Siegel, *Peace on Our Terms*; Quaker women such as Edith Pye, Hilda Clark, and Ruth Fry also played a significant role in the history of Save the Children. On Save the children, see Emily Baughan, *Saving the Children: Humanitarianism, Internationalism and Empire, 1915–1970*. Berkeley: University of California Press, 2021; Linda Mahood,. 'Feminist, Politics and Children's Charity: The Formation of the Save the Children Fund', *Voluntary Action* 4, 1 (2008): 1–18.

12 Tammy Proctor, *Civilians in a World at War, 1914–1918* (New York: New York University Press, 2010), 203–238.

13 For the broader context of civilian internment, see Matthew Stibbe, *Civilian Internment during the First World War: A European and Global History, 1914–1920* (London: Palgrave Macmillan, 2019).

14 Elisabeth Rotten (1882–1964) had studied at Cambridge and had come into contact with the Quakers there. Prior to World War I she had spent time at the Quaker Education Study Centre at Woodbroke (Birmingham). Dietmar Haubfleisch, "Elisabeth Rotten (1882–1964) – Eine (Fast) Vergessene Reformpädagogin", in: Inge Hansen-Schaberg (ed.), *"Etwas Erzählen": Die Lebensgeschichtliche Dimension in der Pädagogik* (Baltmannsweiler: Schneider Hohengehren, 1997), 114–131., on her role in the Auskunftsstelle during WWI, Matthew Stibbe. 'Elisabeth Rotten and the Auskunfts- und Hilfsstelle für Deutsche im Ausland und Ausländer in Deutschland', 1914–1919', in: Alison S. Fell and Ingrid Sharp, eds., *The Women's Movement in Wartime*. Basingstoke/New York: Palgrave Macmillan, 2007. On the broader network of reformers' significance for the aid operation see also the forthcoming Ph.D. thesis by Laura Viktoria.Huth, *To Make the World a Better Place to Live in. US-Relief nach dem Ersten Weltkrieg und die Bedeutung von transatlantischen Frauennetzwerken*.

15 Letters from Rotten were translated by the British and forwarded to Philadelphia in the hope "that this may be the beginning of a new spirit of cooperation in the relief of distress". John T. Elliott to Wilbur Thomas 14/4/1919, in: AFSCA, General Administration, Foreign Service, Country: Germany 1919 (*Letters to and from*).

16 On the Fellowship of Reconciliation: David Cortright, *Peace: A History of Movements and Ideas* (Cambridge: Cambridge University Press, 2008).

17 In this delegation, Carolena Wood represented the AFSC. Also included were some British Quakers, and the Dutch women's rights activist Aletta Jacobs. Report Jane Addams and Alice Hamilton, 12/8/1919, in: AFSCA, General Administration, Foreign Service, Country: Germany 1919 (*Friends Delegation to Germany*).

18 Report Jane Addams and Alice Hamilton 10/8/1919, in: AFSCA, General Administration, Foreign Service, Country: Germany 1919 (*Friends Delegation to Germany*); Report Carolena Wood 4/7/1919, in: AFSCA, General Administration, Foreign Service, Country: Germany 1919 (*Friends Delegation to Germany*).

19 Kendrick Clements, *The Life of Herbert Hoover: Imperfect Visionary, 1918–1928* (New York: Palgrave Macmillan, 2010); Nash, *The Life of Herbert Hoover*.

20 Herbert Hoover to Rufus Jones 6/11/1919, in: AFSC Minutes 1919 (*Executive Board*).

21 Portions of the funds with which English Quakers traveled to Germany in July came from the Hoover Commission. Charles Rhoads to Carolena Wood 20/6/1919, in: AFSCA, General Administration, Foreign Service, Country: Germany 1919 (*Letters to and from*).

22 Merle Curti, *American Philanthropy Abroad* (New Brunswick, NJ: Rutgers University Press, 1963), 274–275.

23 On Herbert Hoover's role Aiken, "Feeding Germany", 605–606.
24 Curti, *American Philanthropy Abroad*, 274.
25 On the role of German Americans in the German action, see Charles E. Strickland, "American Aid to Germany, 1919 to 1921", *The Wisconsin Magazine of History* 45, 4 (1962), 256–270.
26 Herbert Hoover to Rufus Jones 6/11/1919, in: AFSCA, AFSC Minutes 1919 (*Executive Board*).
27 Memorandum "Hoover Opens a Door" 15/11/1919, in: AFSCA, AFSC Minutes 1919 (*Executive Board*).
28 Wilbur Thomas (Philadelphia) to Vincent Nicholson 3/7/1919, in: AFSC Minutes 1919 (*Executive Board*).
29 Commentary on Hoover's letter of invitation 7/11/1919, in: AFSCA, AFSC Minutes 1919 (*Executive Board*).
30 Memorandum "Hoover Opens a Door" 15/11/1919, in: AFSCA, AFSC Minutes 1919 (*Executive Board*).
31 Commentary on Hoover's letter of invitation 7/11/1919, in: AFSCA, AFSC Minutes 1919 (*Executive Board*).
32 Guy Aiken estimates the German contribution at about $200 million (compared to about $14 million from ARA funds). Aiken, "Feeding Germany".
33 Bericht über Auslandshilfe des DRK und des DZA, November 1918–Juni 1920, Cecilienhaus July 1920, in: AFSCA, General Administration, Foreign Service, Country: Germany 1920 (*Deutscher Zentralausschuss General*). A short overview of the entire operation in: AFSC Annual Report 1923, 7.
34 *DZA Korrespondenzblatt 6* (17/10/1921), in: AFSCA, General Administration, Foreign Service, Country: Germany 1921 (*Deutscher Zentralausschuss*).
35 *DZA Korrespondenzblatt* 6, 17/10/1921, in: AFSCA, General Administration, Foreign Service, Country: Germany 1921 (*Deutscher Zentralausschuss*); for the broader context Cox, Hunger in War and Peace, and with a focus on the post-war situation Mary Elisabeth Cox, 'Hunger Games: Or How the Allied Blockade in the First World War Deprived German Children of Nutrition and Allied Food Aid Subsequently Saved Them', *The Economic History Review* 68, 2 (2015): 600–631.
36 Elisabeth Piller, *Selling Weimar? German Public Diplomacy and the United States, 1918–1933* (Stuttgart: Steiner, 2021).
37 Elisabeth Piller, "German Child Distress, US Humanitarian Aid and Revisionist Politics, 1918–24", *Journal of Contemporary History* 51, 3 (2016), 453–486.
38 The central advisory board was composed of the "most eminent German scholars in the fields of public nutrition and pediatrics". Czerny to AFSC 31/7/1922, in: AFSCA, Foreign Service, Country: Germany 1922.
39 For many Quakers on the ground, the German Red Cross mode of operation was 'in direct contradiction' to the 'spirit of love and reconciliation' of the Quaker mission and the conviction was as one Quaker aid worker put it 'that the Red Cross is not an organization which should gain increased influence here'. Julia Branson to Wilbur Thomas 10/4/1922, in: AFSCA, General Administration, Foreign Service, Country: Germany 1922 (*Berlin-Reports 1922*).
40 Memorandum "Cooperation with British Friends", 24/12/1919, in: AFSCA, AFSC Minutes 1919 (*Executive Board*).
41 Meeting 30/9/1920, in: AFSCA, AFSC Minutes 1920 (*Executive Board*).
42 On hunger relief in Austria, see Franz Adlgasser, *American Individualism Abroad: Herbert Hoover, Die American Relief Administration Und Österreich, 1919–1923* (Vienna: VWGÖ, 1993); Franz Adlgasser, "Today America Feeds Austria's Children: Food, Supplies and Propaganda – Austria and the United States after the Great War", in: Waldemar Zacharsiewicz and Siegfried Beer (eds.), Cultural Politics, Transfer, and Propaganda: Mediated Narratives and Images in Austrian-American Relation (Vienna: Verlagder Österreichischen Akademie der Wissenschaften, 2021), 79–103.
43 For the ARA campaign in particular, Adlgasser, *American Individualism Abroad*. Adlgasser emphasizes the decidedly American tone of the campaign, which was even more pronounced than in Germany. The so-called Hyphenate-Americans, in this case Austro-Americans, were also involved here – but in this case through the ARA itself.

44 The exchange between Gilchrist Stockton and Henry Scattergood is documented by Adlgasser, *American Individualism Abroad*, 135–141.

45 An overview of the Work of the Friends Relief Mission in Austria, *AFSC-Bulletin* 32 (1920); Quaker Relief Work in Vienna, 1922–1923, *AFSC-Bulletin* 55 (1923).

46 On the huge relief operation in Soviet Russia, see Bertrand M. Patenaude, *The Big Show in Bololand: The American Relief Expedition to Soviet Russia in the Famine of 1921* (Stanford, CA: Stanford University Press, 2002); More specifically on the Quakers: David McFadden and Claire Gorfinkel, *Constructive Spirit: Quakers in Revolutionary Russia* (Pasadena, CA: Intentional Productions, 2004).

47 Wilbur Thomas to Francis Bacon 25/11/1921, in: AFSCA, General Administration, Foreign Service, Country: Germany 1921 (*Correspondence Berlin-Philadelphia from/to*).

48 Alfred Scattergood to Walter Lyman Brown (ARA) 10/2/1921, in: AFSCA, General Administration, Foreign Service, Country: Germany 1921 (*American Relief Administration – London Office, European Children's Fund*).

49 Wilbur Thomas to Alfred Scattergood 18/2/1921, in: AFSCA, General Administration, Foreign Service, Country: Germany 1921 (*Correspondence Berlin-Philadelphia from/to*).

50 Wilbur Thomas to Jane Addams 28/11/1919, in: AFSCA, Foreign Service, Country: Germany 1919. Jane Addams then urged that there must be a written confession from Hoover for this. The German Americans would otherwise trust the German Red Cross more. Jane Addams to Wilbur Thomas, 1/12/1919, in: AFSCA General Administration, Foreign Service, Country: Germany 1919 (*Individuals: Jane Addams*).

51 $3,000,000 Campaign German Child Feeding, *AFSC-Bulletin* 39 (1921). From the rich literature highlighting the longer tradition of putting children at the center of humanitarian campaigns, see Laura Suski. 'Children, Suffering, and the Humanitarian Appeal', in: Richard Ashby Wilson and Richard D. Brown, eds., *Humanitarianism and Suffering. The Mobilization of Empathy* (Cambridge: Cambridge University Press, 2008); Dominique Marshall, 'International Child Saving', in: Paula Fass, ed., *The Routledge History of Childhood in the Western World* (London: Routledge, 2013).

52 AFSC Annual Report 1920, 6.

53 AFSC Annual Report 1920, 7.

54 For example in: "Feeding 600,000 Undernourished Children in Germany", *AFSC-Bulletin* 35 (1920).

55 An Interpretation of Quaker Service 24/3/1921, in: AFSCA, AFSC Minutes 1921 (*Executive Board*).

56 On example often used was: "To those who suffer in Germany with a message of good will from the American Society of Friends who already for 250 years and all through the great war have believed that those who were called enemies were really friends separated by a great misunderstanding". The first mention could be detected in: Carolena Wood to Wilbur Thomas 18/8/1919 in: AFSCA, General Administration, Foreign Service, Country: Germany 1919 (*Friends Delegation to Germany*).

57 For an overview, see Aiken, "Feeding Germany", 610–612 and Maul, The Politics of Service, 111–114.

58 The history of the idea and the institution is told in the British brochure, *Quaker Embassies: A Survey of Friends Service in Europe since 1919* (London: Friends House, 1933).

59 Confidential memorandum: Debate among foreign service staff of the AFSC with Friends on post-war planning 4 and 5/6/1943, in: AFSCA, AFSC minutes 1943.

References

Adlgasser, Franz. *American Individualism Abroad: Herbert Hoover, Die American Relief Administration und Österreich, 1919–1923*. Vienna: VWGÖ, 1993.

Adlgasser, Franz. 'Today America Feeds Austria's Children: Food, Supplies and Propaganda – Austria and the United States after the Great War', in: Waldemar Zacharsiewicz and Siegfried Beer, eds., *Cultural Politics, Transfer, and Propaganda: Mediated Narratives and Images in Austrian-American Relation*, Vienna: Verlag der Österreichischen Akademie der Wissenschaften, 2021.

Aiken, Guy. 'Feeding Germany: American Quakers in the Weimar Republic', *Diplomatic History* 43, no. 4 (2019): 597–617.

Angell, Stephen W., Pink Dandelion, and David Harrington Watt, eds., *The Creation of Modern Quaker Diversity, 1830–1937*. Philadelphia: Penn State Press, 2023.

Barnett, Michael. *Empire of Humanity: A History of Humanitarianism.* Ithaca: Cornell University Press, 2011.

Baughan, Emily. *Saving the Children: Humanitarianism, Internationalism and Empire, 1915–1970.* Berkeley: University of California Press, 2021.

Clements, Kendrick. *The Life of Herbert Hoover: Imperfect Visionary, 1918–1928*. New York: Palgrave Macmillan, 2010.

Cortright, David. *Peace: A History of Movements and Ideas*. Cambridge: Cambridge University Press, 2008.

Cox, Mary Elisabeth. 'Hunger Games: Or How the Allied Blockade in the First World War Deprived German Children of Nutrition and Allied Food Aid Subsequently Saved Them', *The Economic History Review* 68, no. 2 (2015): 600–631.

Cox, Mary Elisabeth. *Hunger in War and Peace: Women and Children in Germany, 1914–1924.* Oxford: Oxford University Press, 2019.

Curti, Merle. *American Philanthropy Abroad.* New Brunswick, NJ: Rutgers University Press, 1963.

Dandelion, Pink. *An Introduction to Quakerism*. Cambridge: Cambridge University Press, 2007.

Frost, J. William. 'Our Deeds Carry Our Message: The Early History of the American Friends Service Committee', *Quaker History* 81, no. 1 (1992): 1–51.

Haubfleisch, Dietmar. 'Elisabeth Rotten, (1882–1964) – Eine fast vergessene Reformpädagogin', in: Inge Hansen-Schaberg, ed., *Etwas Erzählen': Die lebensgeschichtliche Dimension in der Pädagogik.* Baltmannsweiler: Schneider Hohengehren, 1997.

Mahood, Linda. 'Feminist, Politics and Children's Charity: The Formation of the Save the Children Fund', *Voluntary Action* 4, no. 1 (2008): 1–18.

Marshall, Dominique. 'International Child Saving', in: Paula Fass, ed., *The Routledge History of Childhood in the Western World.* London: Routledge, 2013.

Maul, Daniel. 'The Rise of a Humanitarian Superpower: American NGOs and International Relief, 1917–1945. The Pasts of the Present', in: Miguel Bandeira Jerónimo and José Pedro Monteiro, eds., *Internationalism, Imperialism and the Formation of the Contemporary World.* Basingstoke: Palgrave Macmillan, 2018.

Maul, Daniel. *The Politics of Service. American Quakers and the Emergence of International Humanitarian Aid.* Boston/Berlin: DeGruyterBrill, 2024.

McFadden, David and Claire Gorfinkel. *Constructive Spirit: Quakers in Revolutionary Russia. Pasadena*: Intentional Productions, 2004.

Nash, George H. *The Life of Herbert Hoover: The Humanitarian, 1914–1917*. New York: Norton, 1983.

Patenaude, Bertrand M. *The Big Show in Bololand: The American Relief Expedition to Soviet Russia in the Famine of 1921*. Stanford: Stanford University Press, 2002.

Paulmann, Johannes. 'Conjunctures in the History of Humanitarian Aid during the Twentieth Century', *Humanity* 4, no. 2 (2013): 215–238.

Piller, Elisabeth. 'German Child Distress, US Humanitarian Aid and Revisionist Politics, 1918–24', *Journal of Contemporary History* 51, no. 3 (2016): 453–486.

Piller, Elisabeth. *Selling Weimar? German Public Diplomacy and the United States, 1918–1933.* Stuttgart: Steiner, 2021.

Proctor, Tammy. *Civilians in a World at War, 1914–1918*. New York: New York University Press, 2010.

Schmitt, Hans A. *Quakers and Nazis: Inner Light in Outer Darkness*. Columbia: University of Missouri Press, 1997.

Shields, Patricia M. *Jane Addams: Progressive Pioneer of Peace, Philosophy, Sociology, Social Work and Public Administration*. New York: Springer, 2017.

Siegel, Mona L. *Peace on Our Terms: The Global Battle for Women's Rights after the First World War.* New York City: Columbia University Press, 2020.

Sluga, Glenda. 'Women, Feminisms and Twentieth-Century Internationalisms', in: Glenda Sluga and Patricia Clavin, eds., *Internationalisms: A Twentieth-Century History*. Cambridge: Cambridge University Press, 2016.

Stibbe, Matthew. 'Elisabeth Rotten and the "Auskunfts- und Hilfsstelle für Deutsche im Ausland und Ausländer in Deutschland", 1914–1919', in: Alison S. Fell and Ingrid Sharp, eds., *The Women's Movement in Wartime*. Basingstoke/New York: Palgrave Macmillan, 2007.

Stibbe, Matthew. *Civilian Internment during the First World War: A European and Global History, 1914–1920*. London: Palgrave Macmillan, 2019.

Strickland, Charles E. 'American Aid to Germany, 1919 to 1921', *The Wisconsin Magazine of History* 45, no. 4 (1962): 256–270.

Suski, Laura. 'Children, Suffering, and the Humanitarian Appeal', in: Richard Ashby Wilson and Richard D. Brown, eds., *Humanitarianism and Suffering. The Mobilization of Empathy*. Cambridge: Cambridge University Press, 2008.

Part III

Politicization of famine legacies

8 Famine, trauma and memory

Commemorating the Great Irish famine in the 1990s[1]

Cormac Ó Gráda

1947 was a bleak year in Ireland. At some point during that year, the country faced a rash of what the media described as 'famines', including a 'glass famine', an 'egg famine', a 'turf famine', a 'petrol famine' and a 'bread famine'. Meanwhile, several parts of the globe were at risk of literal, biblical famine. It was not a propitious time to mark the centenary of Black '47, as the worst year of the Great Irish Famine of the 1840s was widely known. Commemorations were low-key, and there was little official recognition of the anniversary.

How different it was in the mid-1990s when the sesquicentennial of the Great Irish Famine was commemorated enthusiastically in almost every corner of the country and further afield.[2] It helped in the mid-1990s that Irish people everywhere shared a collective or communal memory of that catastrophe. In speeches to the *Oireachtas* (the Irish Houses of Parliament), at Grosse Île in Quebec (where thousands of famine emigrants died in 1847), at the opening of the Irish famine museum at Strokestown (county Roscommon), and elsewhere, President Mary Robinson led the way, arguing that the Famine had defined Irish people's 'will to survive' and their 'sense of human vulnerability'. For Robinson, the commemoration was a 'moral act', a means of strengthening bonds between present-day Ireland and its 'diaspora', and of increasing goodwill towards, and concern for, 'Third World Famines'.[3] There was also a flip-side to this collective memory. For some at least, the trauma caused by the Famine had long been repressed, whence the need to 'recover' the memory of what had been 'forgotten' since the 1840s.

Much of the commentary by politicians, journalists, and poets embodied an understanding of the famine which bears comparison with the historical record, as understood by historians. Historical scholarship suggests that the impact of the Irish Famine was unequal and divisive. A disaster that struck the poor more than the rich and that pitted neighbour against neighbour is hardly promising material for a communal, collective memory. But surely folklore or the oral tradition represents memory? Such may well have been the belief of the Irish Folklore Commission which began to assemble material on the famine and on much else in the 1930s.[4]

I will show, however, that specific features of famine suffering, which might leave their mark on the oral tradition – such reminiscences of the workhouse or employment works – are reflected only faintly or at a safe distance in archives. I then turn to collective memory as commemorations and show the tension between folklore records, on the one hand, and 'memory' reflected in speeches and publications, on the other. I will argue that famine history the 'collective memory' commemoration is in large part artefact or myth. This conclusion is informed by a reading of some psychotherapy and the historiography of collective memory.

DOI: 10.4324/9781003465805-12

A catastrophe unequally shared

The Great Irish Famine brought the era of major famines in Ireland to a brutal end.[5] In terms of the proportion of the population killed, if not in absolute terms, this was a big famine by world historical standards. The human cost of the famine is often captured in two numbers: a million dead and a million emigrated.[6] When set against a population of about 8.5 million, the resonance of these numbers is very powerful. The numbers who received relief of some kind or another also underline the scope of the disaster: nearly one in twelve of the population relied on the public works at their peak in the spring of 1847; more than one in three on daily soup rations at their peak in July 1847; a year later over 140,000 were in the workhouses and another 800,000 on outdoor relief. The sheer scale of these numbers would seem to suggest a disaster that affected the entire population. However, the famine's impact was very uneven; poverty and death were closely correlated, both at the local level and in cross-section. In some areas, particularly along the east coast, mortality was low and mainly confined to the first half of 'Black '47'; in others, the famine removed one-quarter or one-third of the entire population and normality had still not been restored by 1851.

In considering the collective memory of the Irish famine a crucial aspect is that, like all famines, it produced a hierarchy of suffering. As is usually the case when famine strikes, the first to succumb were elderly beggars and vagrants.[7] However, one-third or so of the population which was made up of farm labourers and mini-farmers and their dependants accounted for most of the famine's dead. These were overwhelmingly the people forced onto the public works and the soup kitchens and into the workhouses by the failure of the potato.

As noted above, there is a tendency to aggregate as victims those who perished and those who emigrated. Such 'adding up' must not be allowed to obscure the point that dying was a much worse fate than emigrating-unless, as on the so-called 'coffin ships' plying the Canadian route in 1847, a significant proportion of those who left died en route. Considering famine emigration as a whole the striking point is how, despite the evidence of overcrowding and undernourishment, relatively so few perished en route or on arrival. Nor did the migrants fare worse after arrival than those more numerous survivors who remained at home. Moreover, far from being a disaster, emigration relieved what would have been a much worse disaster in its absence. Without the safety valve of North America, far more would have been forced either to remain at home or to move to Great Britain. The consequences may be imagined.[8]

Most emigrants relied on their own savings or on other assets, such as a tenancy or livestock, which could be readily transferred into liquid funds. This implies that only those with some capital could afford the move. So, while not denying that emigrants were also famine casualties, it is also clear were more fortunate than the hundreds of thousands locked in poverty. And yet it is the emigrant rather than the labourer at home who has become 'the archetypal figure of the famine'.[9]

Those who perished and those who emigrated were obvious victims of the famine. For the rest, landlords fared badly, though not as badly as implied by the historiography. Farmers faced reduced rent bills, but most were hurt by the failure of and the increase in the efficiency wage or effective cost labour. Outside of agriculture workers, suffering varied according to their dependence on the potato for their food and on markets for their output. In sum, in rural Ireland, there were few 'winners' in the late 1840s. It is more difficult to gauge the impact of the famine on small traders, village usurers, and the like. In famines everywhere, such people always incur the resentment and wrath of those most at risk. Yet an analysis of the Great Famine's impact on pawnbroking, one activity perhaps representative of such people, suggests that the famine produced an initial rush of business, soon followed, however, by an increasing burden of unredeemed pledges and forced sales. So, it is not easy to see any winners there either.[10]

Because they apply broadly similar occupational categories, the population census reports of 1841 and 1851 offer an indication of how different occupations and occupational groups were affected. Given that the population is likely to have grown somewhat between 1841 and 1846, the true impact of the famine is not fully captured in the data. Some of the main features are summarised in Tables 8.1 and 8.2. Table 8.1 shows that the overall decline in the labour force in the island was 19.1 per cent. There were 14.4 per cent fewer farmers and 24.2 per cent fewer farm labourers. The shift in the diet is reflected in the increase in the number of millers and bakers, one group of possible 'winners'. The figures suggest that most trading categories were affected, though the number has held its own. The number of servants dropped by one-fifth. Not surprisingly, given their vulnerability, there were also fewer medical practitioners and doctors, which offers a reminder that, though famine mortality was quite class-specific, it was less so than in modern famines. Not only medical personnel but workhouse officials and clergymen of all denominations succumbed, mainly from typhus. The impact of the legal profession is less expected. The decline in spinning was part exogenous shock, part consequence of the famine. The small number of coffin-makers (eight in 1841, twenty-two in 1851) is a reminder that during the famine most coffins were not made by specialist coffin-makers. The mass evictions of the period probably explain why there were more bailiffs in 1851, and the demands on the poor law why there were more rate-collectors. The increase in the paupers and beggars group is

Table 8.1 Occupational change, Ireland 1841–51

OCCUPATION	*1841*	*1851*	*% CHANGE*
Farmers	471,398	403,638	−14.4
Farm labourers, herds, ploughmen, gardeners	1,362,756	1,032,845	−24.2
Domestic servants	328,889	260,522	−20.8
Millers, bakers	11,007	14,490	+31.6
Tavern-keepers, vintners, wine and spirit merchants	7,484	6.070	−18.9
Huxters, provision dealers, tobacconists	6,515	5,425	−16.7
Butchers, poulterers, victuallers	9,169	9,115	−0.6
Dealers (unspecified)	15,347	15,920	+13.7
Shopkeepers (do.)	10,732	12,176	+13.5
Merchants (do.)	3,257	2,133	−34.5
Bailiffs	1,398	1,902	+36.1
Rate collectors	182	587	+222.5
Ministering to charity	253	1,898	+650.2
Coffin-makers	8	23	+187.5
Barristers, attorneys	3,326	3,268	−1.7
Physicians, surgeons	2,850	2,439	−14.4
Spinners	516,424	112,275	−78.3
Weavers	122,631	118,559	−3.3
Shoemakers	55,728	42,742	−23.3
Sailors, boatmen, pilots	8,756	23,724	+170.9
Paupers, beggars	36,137	41,808	+15.7
All others	537,613	730,064	+35.8
Total	**3,511,860**	**2,841,623**	**−19.1**

Sources: British Parliamentary Papers, *Report of the Commissioners Appointed to Take the Census of Ireland for the Year 1841* [504], H.C. 1843, xxiv, 440; *The Census of Ireland for the Year 1851, part vi: General Report* [2134] 1856, xxxi, 634–636.

Table 8.2 Occupational change, Connacht 1841–51

OCCUPATION	*1841*	*1851*	*% CHANGE*
Farmers	80,278	69,212	−13.8
Farm labourers, herds, ploughmen, gardeners	288,206	193,798	−32.8
Domestic servants	35,484	27,882	−21.4
Millers, bakers	1,090	1,514	+38.9
Tavern-keepers, vintners, wine and spirit merchants	564	527	−6.6
Huxters, provision dealers, tobacconists	630	594	−5.7
Butchers, poulterers, victuallers	1,131	1,027	−9.2
Dealers (unspecified)	2,558	1,211	−52.7
Shopkeepers (do.)	1,103	1,022	−7.3
Merchants (do.)	231	168	−27.3
Bailiffs	255	311	+22.0
Rate collectors	1	101	+10100
Ministering to charity	10	372	+3620
Coffin-makers	0	0	–
Barristers, attorneys	83	184	+121.7
Physicians, surgeons	245	183	−25.3
Spinners	113,998	25,433	−77.7
Weavers	8,982	3,285	−63.4
Shoemakers	5,800	3,927	−32.3
Sailors, boatmen, pilots	1,019	1,404	+44.5
Paupers, beggars	8,183	11,825	+44.5
All others	55,276	58,394	+5.6
Total	**605,127**	**403,374**	**−33.5**

Sources: British Parliamentary Papers, *Report of the Commissioners Appointed to Take the Census of Ireland for the Year 1841* [504], H.C. 1843, xxiv, 430; *The Census of Ireland for the Year 1851, part vi: General Report* [2134] 1856, xxxi, 616–618.

as expected, that in sailors and boatmen less so. Note the significant increase in the 'all other' category, consisting mainly of non-agricultural and more urban occupations.

Table 8.2 replicates Table 8.1 for Connacht, the worst affected of Ireland's four provinces. Broadly speaking, the pattern is the same but magnified. The number of farm labourers fell by one-third over the decade, and the huge drop in the number of spinners is also noteworthy. In Connacht, the 'all other' category also increased but only by eight per cent. These census tables corroborate the point that while it is not easy to identify any significant group of winners in the famine, the suffering was by no means evenly shared. Some historians would go further. W. E. Vaughan insisted that 'for many life went on normally' during the famine and that 'any local study of the famine should, therefore, keep an eye on that large section who were unaffected by starvation'.[11] Vaughan mentioned as examples 'not only those who went to the Curragh races in 1847 but those who consumed six million gallons of whiskey in the same year and the thousands of farmers who reorganised their farming to cope with the permanent loss of over two-thirds of their potato crop'. He also pointed to the big increase in the number of second-class houses between 1841 and 1851 ('more than in any subsequent the nineteenth century'), the rise in the number of children at national schools from 456,410 in 1846 to 507,469 in 1848, and the 'slight' decline in the number of houses between (558,000 to 522,000). The point about housing is well taken, even if the increase was greatest in Ulster and in urban areas where the impact of the famine was the least. But the rise in the number of children, which was greatest in the south and west, 'may be ascribed, to a considerable degree, to the fact of food having been distributed by the British Relief Association, to the children attending a large number of the National Schools, especially south and west of Ireland'.[12] Perversely, that reflects the gravity of the famine, not its 'invisibility'.

Vaughan's revisionism was supported by L. M. Cullen in a *bravura* address to the Douglas Hyde Summer School in 1996:

> There was no central menace to existence at large. Comfortable people lived their normal lives [...] Church building [...] reflected the perspective that life remained quite normal for many and for institutions [...] The 1847 general election was conducted normally and on the basis of normal political issues. One Waterford paper reported in relation to the conditions in one area that 'we since had not room, owing to parliamentary and other reports, to return to the subject as promised'. The priorities were clear.[13]

This may exaggerate the degree to which people were fully insulated from the disaster, but it is also a reminder that for some the famine did not last long and was not life-threatening.

Not only are famines uneven: but they are also, always and everywhere, deeply divisive tragedies. The charity and solidarity that bind communities together are strengthened for a while but break as the crisis worsens: hospitality declines, crime and cruelty increase, as do child abandonment and infanticide. Examples abound in the literature of appalling inhumanity and heartlessness. A chronicler wrote of a famine in the Russian city of Novgorod in the year 1230: 'There was no kindness among us, but misery and unhappiness; in the streets, unkindness to one another, at home anguish, seeing children crying for bread and others dying'. At the height of the French famine of 1693–94, Louis Jacquelin, a haberdasher on his way to a fair, was killed in a forest near Poitiers by a gang of soldiers, 'who stole his trunk and his money and beat him to death'. In Lyons, in 1709, a note attached to an abandoned child read, 'This girl is called Claudine, aged three years. Necessity obliges me to expose her. I hope when the times change to get her back'. In Burgessbeg, near Nenagh in county Tipperary, on the night of 19 January 1848, farmer Denis Gorman bludgeoned to death Mary Ryan, a destitute woman, for stealing 'a few sheaves of wheat' from his haggard. A survivor of the Great Finnish Famine of 1866–68 reminisced how 'the flow of beggars was so great that the farmers became quite tired of them' and how they have themselves 'only scraps of food'. On the streets of besieged Leningrad in 1941–42, 'deadly criminals attacked people for their ration cards'. In Somalia, in the early 1990s, the notorious 'technicals', heavily armed thugs in trucks terrorised the poor. There is much more in the same vein from Ireland in the 1840s. All too often hospitality was abandoned and private charity dwindled as the crisis was prolonged. Instead of *ar scáth a chéile a mhaireann na daoine* (people rely on each other) – as the saying goes – it 'became a question of everyone for himself'.[14]

Folklore and memory

The prospect of the Great Famine centennial in 1945–47 led the Irish Folklore Commission to circulate a questionnaire on famine folklore, which provided the raw material for a series of lectures by UCD academic Roger McHugh and a chapter in an important book on the famine, published much later.[15] Asking for folklore or oral memory to bridge a gap of a century or more and generate reliable evidence on the famine was asking a lot. The long gap between the event and the evidence allowed ample time for confusion, forgetting, and obfuscation. It also virtually guaranteed the contamination of extraneous data. The variable quality of this source and some of its pitfalls were noted long ago, rather crudely by myself, and with considerably greater sophistication by Niall Ó Ciosáin.[16] And just as the questions posed of the archive by modern scholarship are shaped by current intellectual and ideological concerns, the material on the famine collected by the Irish Folklore Commission in its heyday in the 1930s and 1940s reveals as much about the concerns of the 1940s as it does about the 1840s. Such considerations inform the U.S. historian Peter Novick's scepticism of memoirs of the Holocaust collected, for example, by Steven Spielberg and others.[17]

An added consideration, given the subject matter, is the memory loss possibly caused by the famine itself. Psychiatric research suggests that adult survivors of catastrophes such as earthquakes 'often show considerable memory impairment'. Memories of more protracted catastrophes such as war or famine may be weighted towards their early phases. Moreover, some traumatised victims may be reluctant to talk, while more may be silenced by the reluctance of non-victims to listen.[18] These are serious problems. And yet the folklore record at its best is vivid, harrowing, telling and, sometimes, intriguing and puzzling. Rejecting what it has to offer would be going too far.[19]

Half a century after the material was collected, it provided the raw material for Patricia Lysaght's pioneering studies on the impact of the famine on women.[20] Lysaght's strategy was to draw from the archive at large in order to flesh out a storyline or generalisation. Inevitably, perhaps, the outcome was a somewhat clichéd collage of Irishwomen as models of compassion and 'heroic self-sacrifice', with the twist that they were also 'women of power' who cursed evildoers such as evicting landlords and land grabbers.[21] But given the unequal and divisive character of famine, should the archive be expected to yield an archetypal famine woman? And if it did, would this not be a worrying weakness? Or is it that the quest for such an identity has conditioned the reading of the evidence? While Lysaght's focus on a sub-group rather than on the nation is a step in the right direction,[22] the implicit double assumption in her approach that Irishwomen were similarly affected in the 1840s and similarly remembered a century or so later is questionable.

An alternative approach is to seek out the *range* or *kaleidoscope* of memories or evidence on particular topics. I deal here with how three aspects of the famine are represented in the Irish folklore archive: (i) experiences on the public works, (ii) theft and its perpetrators and victims, and (iii) workhouse inmates during the famine years. I rely mainly on a simple analysis of Cathal Póirtéir's two *compendia* of famine material.[23]

The public works

As noted earlier, at their peak the public works employed nearly 700,000 people, or one-twelfth of the entire population. In the poorer parts of the island, over-represented in the folklore archive holdings, they employed a higher proportion and, of course, a higher proportion still of the adult male population. Over forty accounts (I counted nineteen in Irish, twenty-four in English) in Póirtéir's selection refer to the public works. Some of them are striking and rich in detail; most are critical of the authorities. However, only *three* narrators in Póirtéir's selection refer to an ancestor who participated in the works. One, Martin Manning from Carrowholly near Westport in county Mayo, was the son of a ganger or foreman on the local works. The other two refer to labourers. The second, Mick Kelly's father, worked on a relief scheme near Castletowngeoghegan in county Westmeath, and the third, John Doyle's grandfather, worked for four pence a day building 'the straight mile' near Aughrim in south county Wicklow.[24] A Béara woman's father-in-law also worked on the works as a young but somebody complained that he did not need relief – *go bhféadfadh sé sin mairiúint sa bhaile'* ['that that fellow could survive at home'] – so he lost his place.[25]

In all other instances, 'memory' of the public works as reflected in these accounts is not only distanced in time but vicarious also in the sense that the memory was not autobiographical even a few generations back. I do not know why this was so. Perhaps 'silence' or 'denial' had something to do with it. Hidden selection bias in the collectors and questionnaire respondents of the 1930s and 1940s is another possible reason: insofar as they may have resorted to the most articulate in the local community, they may have also inadvertently missed the descendants of those worst affected by the disaster.

Thieves and their victims

Taken as a whole, the material on thieves and thieving in the archive is less distanced. Here, several accounts are by the descendants of perpetrators, victims, or potential victims. The narrators include a county Wicklow woman whose grandfather stole a leg of mutton from the pot of a well-to-do farmer in Slievenamoe and a county Roscommon woman whose father stole some oatmeal. Representing the victims, an old man from Tullaghan, county Leitrim, lamented the theft of his parents' potatoes, a 'cruel wrong', while Colm Ó Caoidheáin related how his granduncle was robbed of oatmeal in county Galway by a woman who cut a hole in the sack he was carrying. We learn how Galwayman Pádraig Ó Discín's grandfather let a thief away with a meal, while Wicklowman's grandfather, who drove a horse and car for the local landlord, was protected by guards. Mairéad Ní Mhionacháin's mother, then only a little girl, spent many nights guarding the family potato plot in Béara against thieves. A striking, if understandable, feature is that the descendants' victims never name the perpetrators.[26] The accounts are divided in their perspectives on the morality of the majority showing some sympathy for the thief.

The workhouse

Memories of the workhouse have the same vicarious quality as those describing the public works. This may come as a surprise, given how large the workhouse looms in both contemporary commentary and the historiography of the Irish famine. And so it should loom large: over one in five of those who perished from the famine died in a workhouse or in a workhouse hospital.[27] Moreover, workhouse deaths represented only a fraction of those admitted and workhouse survivors were unlikely to have had the resources to emigrate afterwards. Therefore, a significant number of the famine survivors in Ireland must have had personal experience of the workhouse. It is curious to find, then, how distanced archives are folklore archive accounts of the workhouse. The following excerpts are typical:

> Patrick Reilly, Culleagh, tells of people found along the roads weak with hunger, grass on their mouths and who were brought to the poorhouse (Belturbet, county Cavan).
>
> Auld Mrs Corcoran, the wife of Peter Corcoran, who went into Granard workhouse and took three children out of it (county Longford).
>
> *Ní babhta nó dhó* ... ['More than once I heard my grandfather, who lived down here in Magh Adhair and who was a married man during the Famine, say that there were so many making for the poorhouses that there wasn't accommodation for half of them.'] (Luogh, County Clare).
>
> *Bhí seanchapall ag Beait* ... ['Bat had an old horse, and when the opportunity arose, it was Foxy Bat's horse that would convey people to the Beathach workhouse.'] (Caherdaniel, county Kerry).
>
> Anthony O'Dwyer's father told him that he saw people dead, dying and staggering about at a rest house at Knockroe, a short distance on the Cashel side of Golden (county Tipperary).

> To be buried in a workhouse coffin was regarded as a slur on the friend and on the deceased (Ballymoe, county Galway).
>
> 'Tá *brand* an *Union ort', adéarfaí le duine* ['You have the brand of the Union on you', is what people would be told.'] (Caherdaniel, county Kerry).[28]

Literally, none of these accounts conveys a real sense of 'having been there'. There is virtually nothing about living conditions inside the workhouse walls. Even when the account is specific, it is always about somebody outside the narrator's family. Not a single informant refers to an ancestor who was a pauper inmate during the famine, the closest being one Johnny Callaghan, whose father worked as a baker in Castlerea workhouse during the famine.[29] This 'silence' may in part reflect the enduring shame associated with the workhouse. Once again, however, an unintended bias in the selection of informants may also be responsible. For whatever reason, the memories of those who suffered most are simply not represented in these folklore accounts.

A collective famine memory?

The material collected by the Irish Folklore Commission in the 1930s and 1940s – distanced, fractious and individual – is quite distinct in theme from 'memory' as represented in much of the famine commemoration of the 1990s. As noted earlier, a collective memory of the famine was a key feature of the commemorations. Popularised by President Mary Robinson, it was echoed repeatedly by Minister of State Avril Doyle, by academics such as Kevin Whelan and David Lloyd, and by representatives of charity operations in the Global South. *Irish Times* journalist John Waters, California state senator Tom Hayden, pop singer Sinéad O'Connor and others identified with a bleaker version of stressing repressed memory and communal trauma.

When asked by a CBS reporter in Somalia in 1992 'why there were so many Irish aid workers on the ground, and such an Irish interest in Somalia', Mary Robinson replied with 'the story of the Choctaw Indians: how they as a poor dispossessed raised over seven hundred dollars for the relief victims in the 1840s, and how Irish people had a folk memory of famine which helped us identify with countries like Somalia'.[30] Elsewhere President Robinson proclaimed that than any other event 'shaped us as a people. It defined our will to survive. It defined our sense of human vulnerability. It remains one of the strongest, most poignant links of memory and feeling that connects us to our diaspora. It involves us still in an act of remembrance which increasingly, is neither tribal nor narrow'. The late Aengus Finucane of *Concern* saw the anniversary as 'provid[ing] us with an opportunity to reach across the centuries and, in the name of our own Famine dead, try to heal the hurts of history'.[31]

'We are a First World country with a Third World famine, dislocation, and exile . . . Our own Famine echoes are constantly with us', proclaimed Minister of State Avril Doyle in 1996. Indeed, the phrase 'a First World country with Third World memory' became one of Minister of State Doyle's key phrases. Elsewhere she talked of the famine as 'an event which traumatised this country', echoing Kevin Whelan's claim that 'the famine experience burned itself into the Irish character'. And, again, Kevin Whelan:

> The frail Famine voices now reach us across an aching void. We need to amplify that acoustic; in hearing them attentively, we might reclaim our Famine ghosts from their enforced silence and invisibility. In doing so, we can rescue them from the enormous condescension of posterity, paying them the respect which their lonely deaths so signally lacked. That very gesture of reconnection may alleviate a cultural loneliness we do not even know we have and liberate

> us into a fuller and more honest sense of ourselves, showing us how we got to be where we are, even as we leave it behind.[32]

In 1997, Tom Hayden dedicated a collection of commemorative essays on the Irish famine 'to all those who have had to live with their deepest story denied'. One of his contributors, literary critic David Lloyd, referred to 'our memory of hunger' and 'its psychic and corporeal costs'. Another poet Nuala Ní Dhomhnaill, referred to 'our recovery from the collective trauma of the Famine', while novelist Sean Kenny wrote of 'restoring our memory of the Famine'.[33] Elsewhere, historian Christine Kinealy has referred approvingly to ongoing work on the 'healing process' and 'post-colonial traumatic stress' by Irish-Californian psychotherapist, Dr Garrett O'Connor.[34] Sinead O'Connor's 1995 rap poem offers an extreme case of this approach to collective famine memory. For O'Connor, 'all the old men in the pubs' and 'all our young people on drugs' were the product of the famine and the resultant post-traumatic stress disorder. The Irish were like 'a child that got itself bashed in the face' and 'if there ever is gonna (sic) be healing there has to be remembering'. Philosopher Richard Kearney's focus in 2014 on 'the inheritance of historical traumas by Irish Americans and Irish Australians' which are ingenerationally 'acted out – very often though violence, through alcoholism, through depression, through suicide' is very much in the same vein.[35]

I have quoted these statements to give a flavour of the discourse on collective memory. Note throughout the collective rhetoric of 'we', 'us', 'all those', 'ourselves', 'Irish character', 'Irish people', 'this country', 'a country with a memory', 'our own', 'our memory'. This is collective or communal memory with a vengeance. But such inclusive, collective language occludes the uneven and divisive character of the famine.

The view that their shared famine suffering sensitised Irish people, taken as a whole, to suffering in the Global South or, more prescriptively, should spur them to greater generosity was also a constant echo during the sesquicentennial commemoration of the 1990s. 'Inherited values trigger our sympathy for anyone, anywhere facing starvation', according to Michael Callopy of the Cobh Heritage Centre. A Dublin nurse told a Boston physician that 'she came to Rwanda because her grandmother never let her forget'. Foreign Minister David Andrews has described the 'Irish people's generosity of thought and action' as 'one of the few positive legacies we gained from our terrible experiences during the Great Famine of the last century'. In the same vein, Stephen Jackson, director of University College Cork's International Famine Centre, claimed that Ireland's bond with famine-afflicted places stems from 'the sense we were as they are'.[36] In Avril Doyle's rendition, 'As such, we as a people have contributed significantly on both a personal and a national level to relieving global hunger'. On a more prescriptive note, junior minister Doyle urged, in the rather excessive style typical of her commemorative speeches, that 'commemoration of the Famine should equally sensitise us to current social inequality and injustice, notably our travellers and urban underclass, whose marginalised positions so eerily replicate that of the rural famine underclass of pre-famine Ireland'. A year later, no longer junior minister, Doyle would say: 'We are now giving back what we received during our darkest hour ... The migration of families to relief centres in Korea and other areas of famine is similar to our people's emigration to the workhouses'.[37] In more sober tones, a 1993 Department of Foreign Affairs policy document states that 'our historical experience, the absence of colonial or exploitative interest, the fact that we experienced famine within the relatively recent past [...] have made us especially aware of and sensitive to the economic and social needs of developing countries'.

Whether the famine commemorations spurred the public at large into greater generosity towards 'Third World' NGOs remains a moot point.[38] Moreover, it bears noting, given all the claims to the contrary, that the supposed link between famine memory and generosity in the face of 'Third World hunger' is really for the most part a tradition invented in the 1970s and 1980s.[39] If a historical link is required, a century-long tradition of Irish missionary activity far afield, particularly in sub-Saharan Africa, has a stronger claim. However, such a 'collective memory' would be out of place in a modern, outward-looking Ireland.[40]

The rhetoric of famine memory today, such as it is (or was in the wake of the commemorations), is all-inclusive. It is as if virtually all those living in Ireland during the famine were forced to die or emigrate, with knock-on effects on their traumatised descendants. But how could the memory of such an uneven and divisive disaster famine be truly collective? How could such a range of experiences have spawned a common memory? Surely, only by glossing over and filtering out much of the history of the famine?

Nor is the correlation between the intensity of memory of the famine and the injury suffered by any means straightforward. As argued earlier, those who managed to emigrate were *relatively* fortunate, yet it is their 'descendants' – real or vicarious – who 'remember' the most. But this is as much a reflection of modern American culture as it is of the sufferings of these people's ancestors in Black '47. In their campaigns for compulsory Irish famine studies some American-Irish activists are now competing with Black and Jewish activists in a sordid victimhood stakes.[41]

When French sociologist Maurice Halbwachs coined the term 'collective memory' in the 1920s, he was interested in how the present conditions a community's understanding of its past. Modern historians' fascination with memory and tradition owes much to his insights.[42] For Halbwachs, there was something inherently ahistorical about shared group memories. They lasted only insofar as they adapted to what the American psychologist John Kotre calls 'the needs of changing times'.[43] Typically, such shared memories gloss over complexities and awkward evidence, they are prone to being highly partisan, and they make events in the distant past seem like they happened just yesterday. Collective memory, informed by a simplistic understanding of the past, always tells us more about the present than the past. Historical scholarship, by contrast, is complex and multifaceted and ambiguous, though hardly value-free either. One has only to compare collective memories in the Irelands of, say, William of Orange or Oliver Cromwell or Charles Trevelyan with the ambivalent verdicts of historians.

'Collective trauma' is a concept of more recent vintage. In the hands of John Waters, Tom Hayden and others cited earlier, it acquired a particular meaning: the transfer of the early Freudian notion of repressed memory from a micro to a macro context. John Waters justified this transfer by declaring that when he had asked psychoanalysts whether the trauma and repression that affected individual people 'might also be true of peoples, of societies, nations ... [t]he answer ... ha[d] invariably been yes'.[44] This understanding of collective trauma misses an important aspect emphasised elsewhere in the literature: that is, communal trauma as a blow 'that damages the bonds attaching people together impairs the prevailing sense of community'.[45] Analyses of disasters such as Chernobyl (1986), Hurricane Katrina in New Orleans (2005), and the Haiti earthquakes of 2010 and 2021 focus on the resultant disarticulation of the cultural systems of the affected communities.[46]

But these are all recent disasters; so perhaps it comes as a surprise that in the Irish case, the focus is on the 'repressed' memory of an event that took place long ago. Nobody doubts the psychic scars inflicted by an event like Chernobyl or the Great Famine on those who had to live through them. Arguing that Ireland in the mid-1990s was in need of 'recovered memory therapy' (RMT), a 'cure' that has since been largely discredited,[47] because of the famine is another matter, however. What, one may wonder, is the life span of a collective trauma? How does one measure its intensity? Were Irishmen and Irishwomen in the mid-1840s still emotionally affected by the massive famine that struck the country in 1740–41?[48] When did the French stop suffering the trauma of famines of 1693–94 and 1709?

But the argument suffers from several other weaknesses. First, it forgets that RMT has been subjected to a vigorous critique over the past decades. In the course of the high-profile 'memory wars' critics have cast serious doubt on the empirical both the original Josef Breuer/ Sigmund Freud version and its re-incarnation (as represented in, say, the *Courage to Heal* by Ellen Bass and Laura Davis). Critics have also accused the RMT approach of simply ignoring the biological component of mental illness. Instead of what UCLA sociologist and psycho-analyst Jeffrey Prager (a sympathetic critic) dubs 'the extraordinary complexity of individual subjectivity', trauma therapy 'tend[ed] to reduce all understanding of the human psyche to external material conditions that impinge on the person'. Prager deems trauma diagnosis and RMT clumsy tools against the complexity of the individual character. They over-emphasise 'the effects of the external world ... and dispute memory's subjectivity'.[49]

Another more fundamental problem is the transfer from the individual to some national or communal psyche. When a whole group is subject to precisely the same shock this might make sense, though it is not easy to think of examples. In an interesting contribution, urban sociologist and historian Richard Sennett offers a microstudy of a group of white-collar workers dismissed by IBM in upstate New York, treating them as 'people who have shared common injuries at the hands of the modern economy and are seeking to interpret them' when they meet for coffee.[50] Fair enough, perhaps. But one of the points at issue here is that the Irish famine did *not* inflict 'common injuries' at the time, never mind across the generations.

And even supposing, for the sake of argument, that the famine inflicted the same shock on everybody, we are still left with the problem that the concept of communal trauma leaves no room for the subjectivity of the individual psyche. A given shock is supposed to influence everybody, and thus be remembered by everybody, in the essentially same way.

Conclusion

Peter Novick's reminder that collective memory is subject to 'memory spasms' that coincide with anniversaries certainly rings a bell regarding the Irish famine sesquicentennial commemorations of the mid-1990s. Equally apposite is his denial that 'the flurry of commemorations on such occasions doesn't signify that we're in the presence of important collective memory'.[51] The famine commemorations of the 1990s and the collective memory they articulated even got the chronology of the famine wrong. They began too soon, in 1995, and came to an abrupt end in 1997, glossing over the awkward historical reality that people were still dying of famine-related causes in some parts of Ireland into 1850 and even 1851. As a friend put it at the time, a new form of famine fever in 1995 gave way to a new form of famine fatigue a year or two later. Then it was on to the next collective memory. If mentions in articles in *The Irish Times* or books published on the topic are any indication, the collective memory of the Irish famine has been in semi-hibernation since.[52] If it re-awakens in 2045 or so, its concerns will be different and so will its interpretation of the past.

Notes

1 This is an amended version of a paper read to a meeting of An Cumann le Béaloideas Éireann/The Folklore of Ireland Society, 6 November 2000 and published in *Béaloideas: Journal of the Irish Folklore Society* in 2001. An earlier draft was presented at the Dublin City University Conference on Cultural Trauma and National Identity, 28–29 April 2000. My thanks to Guy Beiner, Michael Laffan,

Sarah Maza, Niall Ó Ciosáin, Tim O'Neill, Máire Ní Chiosáin, Brendan Walsh, and Nicholas Williams for helpful comments and to the Head of the Department of Irish Folklore, University College Dublin, for permission to cite manuscript material in the care of the Department.

2 *Dáil Éireann debates*, 22 Jan 1997, 473(4), Written Answers. Commemorative events (www.oireachtas.ie/en/debates/debate/dail/1997-01-22/72/); Emily Mark-Fitzgerald, *Commemorating the Irish Famine: Memory and the Monument*. Liverpool: Liverpool University Press, 2015.

3 Two of Mary Robinson's keynote addresses on famine commemoration and the diaspora are available online: www.oireachtas.ie/en/debates/debate/dail/1995-02-02/2/; https://president.ie/en/media-library/speeches/international-conference-on-hunger (last accessed 18 February 2025).

4 Niall Ó Ciosáin, 'Famine memory and the popular representation of scarcity', in McBride, ed., *History and Memory in Early Modern Ireland*, 95–117 (Cambridge: Cambridge University Press), 2001, Ch. 3.

5 On the issue of post-famine famines see Tim O'Neill, 'The persistence Ireland', in C. Póirtéir, ed., *The Great Irish Famine* (Cork: Merciel Press, 1995), 204–18.

6 E.g. Stephen Devereux, 'Famine in the twentieth century', IDS Working Paper No. 105 (2005), 7.

7 Cormac Ó Gráda, *Black '47 and Beyond: The Great Irish Famine in History, Economy, and Memory* (Princeton: Princeton University Press, 1999), 39; see too Marcel Lachiver, *Les années de misère* (Paris: Fayard, 1991) 82–8.

8 Cormac Ó Gráda and Kevin O'Rourke, 'Mass migration as disaster relief: lessons from the Great Irish Famine', *European Review of Economic History* 1(1) (1997), 3–26.

9 Boyce, David George. *Nineteenth Century Ireland: The Search for Stability* (Dublin: Gill & Macmillan, 2005), 120.

10 Ó Gráda, *Black '47*, Ch. 4.

11 William Edward Vaughan, 'Reflections on the Great Famine', *Ulster Local Studies* (1995), 7–8.

12 British Parliamentary Papers, 'Fifteenth report of the commissioners of national education for Ireland (for the year 1848)', [1066.] XXIII (1849), 3.

13 Louis M. Cullen, 'The politics of the famine and famine historiography', in *Comhdháil an Chraoibhín 1996*, Roscommon 1997, 24.

14 Eric, Christiansen, *The Northern Crusades* (London: Penguin, 1997); Lachiver, op. cit., 53; W. Gregory W. Monahan, *Year of Sorrows: The Great Famine 1709 in Lyon* (Columbus: Ohio State University, 1993), 90; A. Häkkinen, 'On attitudes and living strategies in the Finnish countryside in the years of famine 1867–68', in id. (ed.), *Just a Sack of Potatoes? Crisis Experiences in European Societies, Past and Present*, Helsinki 1992, 156; Harrison Salisbury, *The 900 Days: The Siege of Leningrad* (London: Secker & Warburg, 1969), 482; Freeman's Journal, 24 January 1848; C. Ó Gráda, *An Drochshaol: Béaloideas agus Amhráin (The Famine: Folklore and Songs)*, Dublin, 1994; Ó Gráda, *Black '47*, Ch. 6.

15 Roger McHugh, 'The famine in folklore', in Ruth D. Edwards and T. D. Williams, eds., *The Great Famine: Studies in Irish History* (Dublin: Lilliput Press, 1992), 391–406. According to its Annual Report for 1945–1946, the Irish Folklore Commission was asked by the committee behind the publication of this volume to undertake the collection of oral tradition about the Great Famine. [*D'iarr an Choiste atá i mbun an leabhair ar an nGorta (atá le foillsiú an bhliain seo chughainn) ar an gCoimisiún cabhrú leo san obair le heolas agus seanchas i dtaobh an Ghorta a mhaireann fós ar bhéalaibh na ndaoine a chruinniú. Dob oiriúnach an ócáid chuige sin é, agus do thoiligh an Coimisiún ar thabhairt fé cheistiúchán den tsaghas san* (The Committee in charge of the book on the Famine (which is to be published next year) asked the Commission for help in this work by collecting information and folklore about the Famine that still survives in the mouths of the people. It would be a good occasion for doing this, and the Commission agreed to undertake a questionnaire of that kind).]

16 Ó Gráda, *An Drochshaol* (1994); Ó Ciosáin, *Famine memory* (2001).

17 Peter Novick, *The Holocaust and Collective Memory* (London: Bloomsbury, 1999), 180–3, 275–7.

18 Novick, *The Holocaust*, 83-4, 274-5; John Kotre, *White Gloves: How We Create Ourselves through Memory* (New York: Norton, 1996), 137.

19 Compare Ó Gráda, *An Drochshaol*; G. Beiner, '*Bodhaire Uí Laoghaire*: oral history and contemporary Irish historiography', *Pages: Postgraduate Research in Progress*, 6 (1999), 9–21.

20 Patricia Lysaght, 'Perspectives on women during the Great Irish Famine from the oral tradition', *Béaloideas* 64/65 (1996/7), 63–130; Lysaght, 'Women and the Great Famine', in A. Gribben, *The Great Famine and the Irish Diaspora in America*, Amherst 1999, 21–47.
21 Lysaght, 'Women and the Great Famine', 43–4.
22 Compare J. Fentress and C. Wickham, *Social Memory*, Oxford, 1992.
23 Cathal Póirtéir. *Famine Echoes* (Dublin: Gill & Macmillan, 1995); same author, *Glórtha ón Ghorta* (Dublin: Coiscéim, 1996).
24 Póirtéir, *Famine Echoes*, 151, 155.
25 M. Verling, *Béarach Mná ag Caint: Seanchas Mhairéad Ní Mhionacháin (An Elderly Woman from Beara Speaking: the Folklore of Mairéad Ní Mhionacháin)*, Indreabhán 1999, 50.
26 Póirtéir, *Famine Echoes*, 68–9, 71, 72, 78–9, 82; Póirtéir, *Glórtha ón Ghorta*, 97; Verling, *Béarach Mná*, 49.
27 T. Guinnane and C. Ó Gráda, 'The workhouses and Irish famine mortality', in T. Dyson and C. Ó Gráda (eds.), *Famine Demography: Evidence from the Past and the Present*, Oxford, 2002.
28 See Póirtéir, *Famine Echoes*, 116–31; Póirtéir, *Glórtha ón Ghorta*, 157–62.
29 Póirtéir, *Famine Echoes*, 128.
30 Mary Robinson, *A Voice for Somalia*, Dublin 1992, 23.
31 Mullan, Don, and Concern (Organisation). *A Glimmer of Light: An Overview of Great Hunger Commemorative Events in Ireland and throughout the World* (Dublin: CONCERN Worldwide, 1995), 2.
32 A. Doyle, in European Community Humanitarian Office, *Ireland's Famine: Commemoration and Awareness*, Brussels 1996, 3, 7; id., 'Caint an Aire (The Minister's Speech)', in *Comhdháil an Chraoibhín 1996*, 6; *The Detroit News*, 20 August 1995; Kevin Whelan, 'Frail voices of the Famine: *Famine Diary* by Brendan O Cathaoir', *Irish Times*, 16 January 1999.
33 T. Hayden (ed.), *Irish Hunger: Personal Reflections on the Legacy of the Famine*, Boulder 1997, 9, 46, 69, 190.
34 C. Kinealy, 'The Great Irish Famine: a dangerous memory?', in Gribben, op. cit., 244, 252.
35 O'Connor's song and its lyrics are available here: https://oldtimemusic.com/w2/the-meaning-behind-the-song-famine-by-sinead-oconnor/ (last accessed May 7, 2024). On Kearney, see S. Lynch, 'Philosopher to address Abbey symposium on the national 'traumas that were never named': Richard Kearney reveals how trauma of Famine affects us even today', *The Irish Times*, January 16, 2014.
36 *The Detroit News*, 20 August 1995 (Michael Collopy); *Parliamentary Debates Seanad Éireann* (*PDSE*), vol. 152, no. 16, 27 November 1997 (David Andrews); *Boston Herald*, 7 May 2000 (Stephen Jackson).
37 Doyle, op. cit., 7; id., EC Humanitarian Office, 8; *Parliamentary Debates Seanad Éireann*, vol. 152, no. 16, 27 November 1997.
38 Department of Foreign Affairs, *Irish Aid: Consolidation and Growth: A Strategy Plan*, Dublin 1993, 10 (I am grateful to Monica O'Connor of the Department for a photocopy). The sums (in £1,000s) received by Trócaire and Concern in donations and church door collections, as given in their annual reports, were as follows:

Trócaire		*Concern*	
Year	*Collected*	*Year*	*Collected*
1993/4	4,937	1990	4,430
1994/5	5,299	1991	7,368
1995/6	4,920	1992	16,434
1996/7	4,936	1993	9,013
1997/8	6,377	1994	13,491
1998/9	7,541	1995	6,764
		1996	7,478
		1997	8,190

Note: accounting years end on 28/29 February

39 Note, however, how in November 1963 Muintir Mhuigheo organised Cecil Woodham-Smith about her experiences in writing *The Great Hunger* the Irish Freedom from Hunger Campaign (see Ó Gráda, 'Making history in the 1940s and 1950s: the saga of The Great Famine', *The Irish Review*, [1992], 97).

40 Ó Gráda, 'The Great Famine and other famines', in Ó Gráda, ed., *Famine 150: Commemorative Lecture Series*, Dublin, 1997, 129–31.

41 J. S. Donnelly, 'The construction of the memory of the famine Irish diaspora, 1850–1900', *Éire-Ireland*, XXXI (1996), 26–61; compare www.irishholocaust.org/.

42 See, e. g., Pierre Nora, 'Between memory and history: *les lieux de mémoire*', *Representations*, no. 26 (1989); Eric Hobsbawm and Terence Ranger, *The Invention of Tradition*, Cambridge 1983; Fentress & Wickham, op. cit.; John R. Gillis, ed. *Commemorations: The Politics of National Identity*, Princeton, 1994; O'Carroll, Paddy, 'Re-membering 1798', in E. Slater & M. Peillon (eds.), *Memories of the Present: Sociological Chronicle of Ireland, 1997–1998* (Dublin: Institute of Public Admnistration, 2000), 15–23.

43 Kotre, *White Gloves*, 238–9; Novick, *The Holocaust*, 4–5.

44 Cited in Hayden, *Irish Hunger*, 27.

45 Kai Erickson, *A New Species of Trouble: The Human Experience of Modern Disasters* (New York: Norton, 1994), 23.

46 Nel, Philip, and M. Righarts, 'Natural Disasters and the Risk of Violent Civil Conflict', *International Studies Quarterly*, 52(1) (2008), 159–185; Arcaya, Mariana, E. J. Raker, and M. C. Waters, 'The social consequences of disasters: individual and community change', *Annual Reviews of Sociology*, 46 (2020), 671–91.

47 See e.g. Richard J., 'Dispelling confusion about traumatic dissociative amnesia', *Mayo Clinic Proceedings*, 82(9) (2007), 1083–87.

48 D. Dickson, *Arctic Ireland: The Extraordinary Story of the Great Frost Forgotten Famine of 1740-1*, Belfast 1997.

49 Elaine Showalter, *Hysteries: Hysterical Epidemics and Modern Culture* (London: Picador, 2013), 155–8; Jeffrey Prager, *Presenting the Past* (Cambridge: Harvard University Press, 1988), 131–3; F. Frederick Crews. *Unauthorized Freud: Doubters Confront a Legend* (New York: Penguin, 2000); Borch-Jacobsen, Mikkel. "How a fabrication differs from a lie." *London Rev Books* 22.8 (2000): 3–7.

50 Richard Sennett, 'Disturbing memories', in Patricia Fara and Karalyn Patterson, eds. *Memory: The Darwin College Lectures* (Cambridge 1998) 15, 22.

51 Novick, *The Holocaust*, 4.

52 The number articles mentioning "Great Famine" in *The Irish Times* rose from 4 in 1990 and 25 in 1994 to 142 in 1995; between 2014 and 2023 it averaged 14. Books in UCD's library with "Great Famine" in the title peaked at ten published in 1995; in 2014–2023 they averaged 2.

References

Arcaya, Mariana, E. J. Raker, and M. C. Waters, 'The social consequences of disasters: individual and community change', *Annual Reviews of Sociology*, 46 (2020), 671–91.

Beiner, Guy, '*Bodhaire Uí Laoghaire*: oral history and contemporary Irish historiography', *Pages: Postgraduate Research in Progress*, 6 (1999), 9–21.

Borch-Jacobsen, Mikkel. 'How a fabrication differs from a lie', *London Review Books* 22.8 (2000), 3–7.

Boyce, David George. *Nineteenth Century Ireland: The Search for Stability*. Dublin: Gill & Macmillan, 2005.

Christiansen, Eric. *The Northern Crusades*. London: Penguin, 1997.

Crews, Frederick C. *Unauthorized Freud: Doubters Confront a Legend*. New York: Penguin, 2000.

Cullen, Louis M., 'The politics of the famine and famine historiography', in *Comhdháil an Chraoibhín 1996*, Roscommon 1997.

Department of Foreign Affairs, *Irish Aid: Consolidation and Growth: A Strategy Plan*. Dublin: Department of Foreign Affairs, 1993.

Devereux, Stephen, *Famine in the Twentieth Century*. Working Paper 105. Brighton: Institute of Development Studies, 2000.

Dickson, David, *Arctic Ireland: The Extraordinary Story of the Great Frost Forgotten Famine of 1740-1*, Belfast: White Row Press, 1997.

Donnelly Jr, James S, 'The construction of the memory of the famine in Ireland and the Irish Diaspora, 1850–1900', *Éire-Ireland*, 31.1 (1996), 26–61.

Donnelly, James S., 'The construction of the memory of the famine Irish diaspora, 1850–1900', *Éire-Ireland*, 31.1 (1996), 26–61.

Doyle, Andrew, 'Caint an Aire (The Minister's Speech)', in *ComhdhaiL an ChraoibhíN: Conference Proceedings 1996: An Gorta MóR (2)*. Comhairle Chontae Roscomáin, 1997.

Erickson, Kai, *A New Species of Trouble: The Human Experience of Modern Disasters*. New York: Norton, 1994.

Famine Commemoration Committee. *Ireland's Famine: Commemoration and Awareness*. Brussels: The Famine Commemoration Committee, 1995.

Fentress, James, and Chris Wickham. *Social Memory: New Perspectives on the Past*. Blackwell, 1992.

Gillis, John R., ed. *Commemorations: The Politics of National Identity*. Princeton: Princeton University Press, 1994.

Giolláin, Diarmuid Ó. *Locating Irish Folklore: Tradition, Modernity, Identity*. Cork: University Press, University College, 2000.

Guinnane, Timothy and C. Ó Gráda, 'The workhouses and Irish famine mortality', in Tim Dyson and Cormac Ó Gráda, eds., *Famine Demography: Evidence from the Past and the Present*. Oxford: Oxford Academic, 2002.

Häkkinen, Antti J., 'On attitudes and living strategies in the Finnish countryside in the years of famine 1867-68', in Antti J. Häkkinen, ed, *Just a Sack of Potatoes? Crisis Experiences in European Societies, Past and Present*. Helsinki: Societas Historica Finlandiae, 1992.

Hayden, Thomas (ed.), *Irish Hunger: Personal Reflections on the Legacy of the Famine*. Boulder: Roberts Rinehart Publishers, 1997.

Hobsbawm, Eric John, and Terence Ranger, eds. *The Invention of Tradition*. Cambridge: Cambridge University Press, 1983.

Kinealy, Christine, 'The Great Irish Famine: a dangerous memory?', in A. Gribben, ed, *The Great Famine and the Irish Diaspora in America*. Amherst: University of Massachusetts Press, 1999, 239–53.

Kotre, John, *White Gloves: How We Create Ourselves through Memory*. New York: Norton, 1996.

Lachiver, Marcel, *Les Années de Misère: La Famine Au Temps Du Grand Roi 1680–1720*. Paris: Fayard, 1991.

Lysaght, Patricia, 'Perspectives on women during the Great Irish Famine from the oral tradition', *Béaloideas* 64/65 (1996/7), 63–130.

Lysaght, Patricia, 'Women and the Great Famine', in A. Gribben, *The Great Famine and the Irish Diaspora in America*. Amherst: University of Massachusetts Press, 1999, 21–47.

Mark-Fitzgerald, Emily, *Commemorating the Irish Famine: Memory and the Monument*. Liverpool: Liverpool University Press, 2015.

McHugh, Roger, 'The famine in folklore', in Ruth D. Edwards and T. D. Williams, eds, *The Great Famine: Studies in Irish History*, 391–406. Dublin: Lilliput Press, 1992.

McNally, Richard J., 'Dispelling confusion about traumatic dissociative amnesia', *Mayo Clinic Proceedings*, 82.9 (2007), 1083–1087.

Monahan, W. Gregory. *Year of Sorrows: The Great Famine 1709 in Lyon*. Columbus: Ohio State University, 1993.

Mullan, Don, and Concern (Organisation). *A Glimmer of Light: An Overview of Great Hunger Commemorative Events in Ireland and throughout the World*. Dublin: CONCERN Worldwide, 1995.

Nel, Philip, and M. Righarts, 'Natural disasters and the risk of violent civil conflict', *International Studies Quarterly*, 52.1 (2008), 159–185.

Nora, Pierre. 'Between memory and history: Les lieux de mémoire', *Representations*, 26 (1989), 7–24.

Novick, Peter. *The Holocaust and Collective Memory*, London: Bloomsbury, 2000.

O'Carroll, Paddy, 'Re-membering 1798', in E. Slater and M. Peillon, eds, *Memories of the Present: Sociological Chronicle of Ireland, 1997–1998*. Dublin: Institute of Public Admnistration, 2000, 15–23.

Ó Ciosáin, Niall, 'Famine memory and the popular representation of scarcity', in McBride, ed, *History and Memory in Early Modern Ireland*, 95–117. Cambridge: Cambridge University Press, 2001.

Ó Gráda, Cormac, *An Drochshaol: Béaloideas agus Amhráin (The Famine: Folklore and Songs)*, Dublin: Coiscéim, 1994.

Ó Gráda, Cormac, 'The Great Famine and other famines', in Ó Gráda, ed., *Famine 150: Commemorative Lecture Series.* Dublin: University College Dublin, 1997.

Ó Gráda, Cormac, *Black '47 and Beyond: The Great Irish Famine in History, Economy, and Memory.* Princeton: Princeton University Press, 1999.

Ó Gráda, Cormac and Kevin O'Rourke, 'Mass migration as disaster relief: lessons from the Great Irish Famine', *European Review of Economic History* 1.1 (1997), 3–26.

O'Neill, Tim, 'The persistence Ireland', in Cathal Póirtéir, ed, *The Great Irish Famine,* 204–218. Cork: Merciel Press, 1995.

Póirtéir, Cathal, *Famine Echoes*. Dublin: Gill & Macmillan, 1995.

Póirtéir, Cathal, *Glórtha ón Ghorta.* Dublin: Coiscéim, 1996.

Prager, Jeffrey, *Presenting the Past.* Cambridge: Harvard University Press, 1998.

Robinson, Mary, *A Voice for Somalia.* Dublin: O'Brien Press, 1992.

Salisbury, Harrison E, *The 900 Days: The Siege of Leningrad.* London: Secker & Warburg, 1969.

Sennett, Richard, 'Disturbing memories', in Patricia Fara and Karalyn Patterson, eds, *Memory: The Darwin College Lectures*, Cambridge: Cambridge University Press, 1998.

Showalter, Elaine, *Hysteries: Hysterical Epidemics and Modern Culture.* London: Picador, 2013.

Vaughan, William Edward, 'Reflections on the Great Famine', *Ulster Local Studies* 17.2 (1995), 7–18.

Verling, M. *Béarach Mná ag Caint: Seanchas Mhairéad Ní Mhionacháin (An Elderly Woman from Beara Speaking: the Folklore of Mairéad Ní Mhionacháin)*, Indreabhán: Mercier Press, 1999.

9 "I haven't eaten so well for so long!"

Representations of the Allied blockade of Germany in German textbooks and film, 1914–32

Mary Elisabeth Cox and Anne van Mourik

The Allied blockade of Germany during WWI had a long legacy. Started by the English at the outset of the conflict, yet dependent on the support of the Allies and reluctant acceptance of neutral countries, the blockade eventually aimed to prevent all goods, including food, from flowing in and out of Germany and other members of the Central Powers. From the very beginning, the blockade was tangled with legal and moral implications because of the 1909 Declaration of London which had confirmed, among other things, that food could not be blockaded unless it was headed for the military, and that neutrals had the right to free trade so long as certain practices were followed. By the war's end, an estimated 424,000–750,000 German civilians had died because of the blockade. Germans responded to these circumstances with frustration and despair, especially as the blockade remained during the armistice period from the fall of 1918 through the winter of 1919.[1]

When the blockade was discussed in the German media during the war, it was often portrayed as something that the Germans would survive as they pulled together, and as inhumane actions from a terrible enemy. Research on the afterlife of the Allied blockade against Germany primarily focuses on lessons that the Nazi regime drew from it.[2] The Nazi party used hunger memories and the promise to vanquish it to win elections. Furthermore, the blockade played a significant role in shaping Nazi economic policies, particularly the drive for autarky.[3] Some historians link the excessive nature of German violence, including deliberate starvation policies, to lingering memories of hunger in WWI, arguing that to prevent a recurrence of the events of 1918, Nazi authorities pursued everything deemed vital for the conduct of war (*kriegsnotwendig*).[4] This included prioritizing the establishment of a cohesive home front with the elimination of Jewry and preventing food shortages. Moreover, memories of the blockade were also used to invoke Nazi identities and garner continued public support.[5] Beyond policy and identity, the Nazis also used the WWI blockade as a propaganda tool, claiming that England won the war not 'through bravery or democracy, but through destroying women and children and the German race'.[6] Memories of the blockade and hunger thus had a huge impact on Nazi identity, planning, politics, and propaganda.

This chapter explores uses and understandings of the Allied Blockade and hunger in Germany *before* the Nazis came into power, from 1914 to 1932. We focus on how those who directly lived through and experienced hunger and blockade understood and expressed those experiences in textbooks and film, using some thirty secondary education textbooks, and two films. Textbooks and films both serve as valuable 'indicators of historical culture',[7] offering insights into the interpretations and communication surrounding the blockade. Peoples' understanding of the past is shaped by a 'kaleidoscopic mass of fragments' including media like radio, newspapers, novels, photography, textbooks, and films. Through interaction with this diverse 'mass of fragments', people construct their own interpretations as they try to comprehend their world.[8] By analysing

DOI: 10.4324/9781003465805-13

textbooks and films, we show how both popular and more official narratives surrounding hunger were present during the Great War and in Weimar Germany.

Michael Wintle, Nanci Adler, and Remco Ensel define narratives as: ‘a self-image, a story told, a sequence of experienced events, an explanation and framing of how something came into being, and where it is going’.[9] Narratives are often self-reflective, serving as a rationale for one’s own standpoint. They endow events with cultural significance, serving as political tools and imbuing the past with purpose by framing it within specific contexts. Whether official or unofficial, narratives essentially convey ‘this is what occurred’ or ‘this is its significance’ or ‘this is how we (or I) interpret it’.[10] They reconstruct reality by selecting focal points, determining significance, and establishing causal relationships between events. In this context, focusing on narratives used in school textbooks and films makes it possible to reflect on how the history of the blockade was interpreted and represented.

Narratives shape the content and structure of societies, and societies in turn shape narratives. In this context, films and textbooks both transmit and perpetuate narratives within a society and are shaped by the societies they exist in. Textbooks examined in this chapter are primarily history textbooks, designed for children aged nine to nineteen. They offer valuable insights into the prevailing narratives and educational contexts of two distinct political periods. The textbooks studied are thus not neutral; they reflect political biases present in these two periods.

Like textbooks, films are also narratives. They transmit information, opinions, stories, and even feelings. Yet they have additional tools to shape those narratives such as cinematography, sound, costumes, sets, props, and actors and actresses themselves. Within cinematography alone a variety of camera angles, sequencing and cuts, the use of light and darkness, closeups and distant shots, longer vs short scenes, and so on can create, emphasize, or diminish multiple narratives. This is complicated further by scripts, instructions from the directors and others, actors and actresses themselves, and the objects around them. Similar to textbooks, narratives presented in film are influenced by the cultural, social, and political contexts in which they are created, reflecting the perspectives and ideologies of the filmmakers and producers.[11]

The rest of the chapter is outlined as follows: first, we examine the representation of the Allied Blockade in textbooks published between 1914 and 1932. Here we focus on temporal shifts, exploring the initial representation of the blockade (1914–18) and subsequent changes, expansions (1919–32), or alterations to the narratives within the evolving political-cultural landscape of Weimar Germany. Finally, we analyse the blockade and hunger period’s portrayal in two very different films, a propaganda/documentary and a feature film. These sources illuminate varied perspectives on the Allied blockade and served a variety of different political agendas. Narratives surrounding the Allied Blockade in Germany were more than singular issues of victimhood and outside enemies later weaponized by the Nazis. While many narratives were aimed at fostering unity and obedience to authority, others portrayed hunger and poverty with humor.

The blockade in textbooks 1914–18: ‘starvation of women and children’

During WWI, from 1914 to 1918, German textbooks were tightly controlled by the state under the regime of Wilhelm II and reflected a centralized narrative that emphasized national resilience.[12] The overarching messages presented in WWI textbooks thus largely aligned with the state’s agenda. In regard to hunger narratives, the Wilhelmine government used them for at least two purposes: first, as a means to remind German youth that Germany would prevail over the blockade and the food-related challenges, and second, to cultivate popular support for governmental interventions in the food economy.

Secondary school textbooks started addressing events surrounding what Germans began calling 'British hunger blockade' from 1915 onward. Textbook authors put great emphasis on the inhumanity and illegality of economic warfare, arguing that, 'according to international law', hunger 'may only be waged against the armed power of the enemy, not against women and children'.[13] Here, the authors are quoting part of the 1909 Declaration of London. However, the authors of the textbook made slight modifications. While Article 33 of the Declaration of London declares that 'Conditional contraband is liable to capture if it is shown to be destined for the use of the armed forces or of a government department of the enemy State', women and children are nowhere mentioned. Indeed, hunger is not mentioned anywhere in the Declaration of London, although the food was denoted as 'conditional contraband', a good that could only be captured under specific circumstances, as outlined in Article 33.[14] WWI textbooks misrepresented international law to garner sympathy and cast Germany's enemies as immoral. It was not until after the Second World War that hunger as a weapon of war was explicitly addressed in the legal community,[15] making the textbook commentary on the use of hunger in war as illegal all the more remarkable.

History textbooks during 1915–16 also emphasized that despite the severity of the situation for civilians, 'British arch-enemies' would not be capable to 'crush German economic life'[16] and assured students 'that no one suffered from hunger'.[17] *Kriegslesebuch fürs Vaterland* (War reader for the Fatherland) (1915) ensured students that 'we have so much food in Germany that we do not need to worry about human nutrition'.[18] In this way, textbooks played a crucial role in the government's aim to boost morale and foster a sense of resilience in the face of food-related adversities.

Some textbooks in the first half of the war also went so far as to assert that the reduced food supply situation was actually beneficial for German health and society. *Erlebnisse und Darstellung aus dem Jahre 1915* (Experiences and Representations from 1915) (1916) stated that the current 'standard of living' was better as 'we had grown accustomed to lavish living and were wasteful in many aspects'.[19] This kind of language matches that used by some contemporary scientists of nutrition, who understood the blockade and the subsequent reduction in German food supplies to be part of an unprecedented 'experiment' on the effects of prolonged malnutrition on an entire population.[20] Ultimately, however, contemporary German scholars such as Eugen Schlessinger, who were interested in the impacts of the blockade on children's growth, reported that while the first two years of the war may have reduced unnecessary fat and sugar from children's diets that they did not need, after two years, the reduced food supplies available had become 'detrimental'.[21] Clearly, seeing the blockade as an opportunity to understand the impacts of an 'economic diet' on civilian population, at least by some scientists, was mirrored in history textbooks.[22] This highlights the use of education and hunger narratives as part of the government's propaganda tools.

Hunger narratives in textbooks were also used to foment popular commitment to the highly criticized governmental interventions in the food economy during the war.[23] In another textbook (1918), information about distribution that was more aspirational than factual was included:

> The authorities initially confiscated all grain stocks and introduced the bread card. When other foodstuffs became scarcer, fat, meat, butter and sugar cards were added. This meant that supplies were distributed evenly so that some did not live in abundance and others went hungry.[24]

Food supplies were not equally distributed in Germany during WWI. The greatest determinant in children's nutritional status in Germany, all things equal, was their socio-economic background.[25] Furthermore, food was not distributed evenly within single households that did not have enough food.[26] This misinformation found in textbooks was an attempt to garner popular support and commitment to the government's wartime policies. It aimed to legitimize the interventions in the food economy by portraying them as fair and effective.

War-time textbooks sought to instil confidence in governmental food policies. There were food riots and protests across Germany,[27] and the leader of the War Food Office (*Kriegsernährungsamt*), which was started in 1916, was mocked in the newspaper.[28] Amidst this growing distrust, the *Kriegsernährungsamt* was a recurring topic in post-1917 history textbooks.[29] The textbook *Der Weltkrieg* (The World War) (1918), for example, suggested that because the blockade caused severe food shortages, meticulous organization of consumption, distribution, and renewal of supplies was required. According to the textbook, this was why the *Kriegsernährungsamt* had been established. After this careful explanation, the textbook goes further and states that 'the population patiently complied with the measures [of the *Kriegsernährungsamt*], because every responsible citizen aimed to contribute to the service of the fatherland'.[30] Compliance with the dictates of the *Kriegsernährungsamt* was framed as a patriotic duty, and the office itself as a success. In this way, textbooks and hunger narratives functioned to foster a sense of unity and to mitigate existing distrust, dislike, and disregard for the government's food policies. Furthermore, this inclusion demonstrates that textbooks were sometimes updated during the war to address contemporary food-related issues, highlighting the importance the government placed on them for cementing popular commitment.

When read in isolation, these textbooks could create the impression that German hunger was solely attributed to the blockade, not far off from later statements given by the Nazis. Yet other history textbooks published during the war gave additional explanations for the growing food insecurity in Germany. The *Realienbuch* (Reference Book) (1918), for example, argued that 'especially after the poor potato harvest in 1916', German hardships grew, but 'the German people were determined to endure and persevere'.[31] This discourse continued in textbooks into Weimar Germany, demonstrating that even during the blockade, some textbook authors gave more nuanced explanations for hunger.

The blockade in textbooks 1919–32: 'battle for the annihilation' of the German people

A notable shift in educational policies occurred during the Weimar Republic. While government oversight over textbooks still existed, it was less restrictive compared to the preceding Imperial era. Various educational reformers, intellectuals, and political factions influenced the narratives presented in textbooks, reflecting the diverse ideological landscape of the Weimar period.[32] As education shifted from WWI to the Weimar Republic era, hunger in Germany persisted. Although the armistice was reached in November 1918, the Allied blockade of Germany continued into 1919, as the Allies aimed to maintain pressure during the peace negotiations. In this new context, textbook narratives represented the history of the blockade in still additional ways.

After 1918, textbooks began to depict hungry Germans no longer as resilient but as defenceless victims. The author of *Lehrbuch der Geschichte* (Textbook of History) (1922) summarized:

> The armistice was concluded on 11 November, and the Germans had to vacate not only the occupied enemy territories and Alsace-Lorraine, but also the left bank of the Rhine together with the 3 'bridgeheads' of Mainz, Koblenz and Cologne. The blockade remained in place; Germany was rendered defenceless; the powerless Germany then signed the disgraceful annihilation peace of Versailles 8 months later.[33]

According to many textbooks, not only the continued blockade during the armistice but also the 'dictate of Versailles' (*Versailler Diktat*) were unjust punitive measures imposed by the victorious Allied powers causing German dearth.

The focus on German victimhood and defencelessness in textbooks can be understood in the broader context of post-war economic conditions. Germany, still reeling from the aftermath of the Great War and the punitive measures imposed by the Treaty of Versailles, faced significant challenges. Coupled with hyperinflation and widespread economic instability, the nation was plunged into an economic crisis. The occupation of the Ruhr by French, Belgian, British, and American troops from 1923 to 1925 undermined German sovereignty and breadlines induced a widespread feeling of humiliation. It should be noted that historians have challenged these popular narratives that focus on this extreme German economic suffering, highlighting that reparations were not beyond Germany's capacity to pay.[34] Clearly, the exaggerated victimhood status was also incorporated in textbooks, with hunger being a central theme.

Textbooks not only echoed but actively fuelled Germany's victimization narrative. Narratives of hunger deliberately imposed by Germany's enemies played a significant role in this mobilization. Indeed, through the narrative of defencelessness, many history textbooks depicted the blockade and the Treaty of Versailles as evidence of a concerted campaign of annihilation against the German population. The author of the textbook *Schaffen und Schauen* (Creating and Observing) (1921), for example, wrote: 'The old, purely military war transformed into an economic war; the struggle between states turned into a battle for the annihilation of entire peoples' lives through hunger blockade and submarine warfare'.[35] The Allied Blockade gained new significance as additional evidence became available, alongside the Treaty of Versailles, of the exploitation and suffering of Germans within an international context of external enemies. This dominant narrative gained strength in Nazi Germany after 1932 and lasted up to 1945,[36] framing the blockade and the Treaty of Versailles as evidence of a campaign of annihilation against the German population.

In addition to the prevailing narratives of the assault on Germany's civilian population by its enemies, the democratic and inclusive approach in Weimar education allowed for other perspectives on the blockade in school textbooks. One textbook, for example, attributes the high number of deaths during the hunger period to German alcohol consumption. The author of *Vom Hunger zum Brot* (*From Hunger to Bread*) (1923), Gustav Klemm, wrote that: 'During the war, 500,000 people in Germany died of malnutrition. They could have stayed alive and been better nourished if alcohol had been banned and grain had only been used for food'.[37] While not overlooking the economic blockade, the author attributes meaning to the hunger period by connecting it with contemporary discussions on social reform, health, and public behaviour during the Weimar period.[38] Although the link between hunger and the use of alcohol was not widely used in other textbooks, this example nonetheless shows how memories of the Allied Blockade and hunger were utilized to construct meanings in Germany based on multiple political viewpoints.

The discourse surrounding alcohol use, as reflected in Klemm's cultural studies (*Kulturkunde*) textbook, can be contextualized within the emergence of prohibition movements in Weimar Germany, and indeed across the world.[39] These reached their nadir in the United States in 1920, when the manufacture, transportation, and sale of alcohol was made illegal across the entire country. While some groups in Germany advocated for the prohibition of alcohol for public health reasons, racial undertones were also present within many of the German movements.[40]

The emphasis on preserving public health intersected with ideologies of racial purity, something that is also visible in Klemm's textbook. Klemm distinguished German 'bread-eaters (*Brot-)*' from Asian 'rice-pudding (*Reisbrei*) people'. He argued that 'bread-eaters' were 'noble' and 'aspiring peoples' who were highly educated and the beacon of human progress.[41] Historian Robert Proctor refers to this larger climate as 'homeopathic paranoia' marked by apprehension over seemingly minor yet potent agents such as alcohol, tobacco, Jews, and 'Gypsies', believed to be detrimental to the German populace.[42] The inclusion of narratives on hunger, food, and race in this textbook underscores how alternative ideologies were integrated into educational materials of the time. Importantly, this narrative framework serves as a critical precursor to the ideological underpinnings of the Nazi regime. Here, similar themes of racial superiority and purity would dominate state propaganda and policies, as well as the idea of 'useless eaters' (*Nutzlose esser*) which the Nazis used to justify the murder of millions of people. Under the Hunger Plan, 30 million Ukrainian, Russian, and Slavic people would starve to death or move away, making way for German settlements.[43] Although it did not reach full effect as planned, some four million people died,[44] and millions of others died under the Nazis through deliberate starvation elsewhere.

Representations of the blockade in film

Experiences of the blockade and hunger were widespread. In addition to school curricula, hunger was also depicted in film, where the lines between propaganda, documentary, and entertainment were often blurred. Here we analyse two separate silent films: *Wirkung der Hungerblockade auf die Volksgesundheit* (The Effects of the Hunger Blockade on Public Health) (Ufa, 1921) and *Die Austernprinzessin* (*The Oyster Princess*) (Union, 1919).[45] Through analysing these two very different kinds of films, we demonstrate the pervasive presence of hunger-related symbols, language, and visuals in German society. While most German films did not refer to hunger or the blockade, those that did used shared visual or textual language. Contemporary audiences would have recognized these motifs from their own hunger memories and experiences, especially as many people in Germany were still experiencing hunger when the films were produced and shown. Together, these films demonstrate various ways that ideas of hunger, blockade, and relief were read and understood.

Die Wirkung der Hungerblockade auf die Volksgesundheit, produced in 1921 in Berlin (Ufa), most directly criticizes the Allied Blockade. This film uses footage from an earlier 17-minute film in English called *Hunger Blockade Germany* produced in 1919 by the amateur American film-maker William Held. The Ufa film is much longer (58 minutes) and adding changes and reversing the order of different scenes from Held's film. Whereas *Hunger Blockade Germany* was shown in private screenings to small audiences, *Die Wirkung der Hungerblockade auf die Volksgesundheit* was viewed by a much larger public.[46] *Die Wirkung der Hungerblockade auf die Volksgesundheit* portrays the reduced food supplies in Germany during the war and the associated hunger and deaths of civilians. It places the blame for this suffering squarely on the Allied Blockade. The film uses props to demonstrate the amount of food officially available through rationing. It depicts, for example, the daily and weekly rations of bread, butter, sugar, and dairy and meat (see Figure 9.1).

In addition to physical props, the film also used animations. One was directly lifted from Held's 1919 film. It shows a map of Germany surrounded by chains and bombs, emphasizing its isolation. Paris and London are included in the map and animations are used to cast blame for the blockade that has surrounded Germany. The film also used statistics, primarily from official sources, including the *Deutschen Reichsgesundheitsamt* (the German health office), inter-allied reports, neutral commissions, and scientific publications.[47] Even if the statistics presented were always in support of the argument that the blockade had negative impacts on the civilian population, they nonetheless were real, and the best available at the time. For example, the film

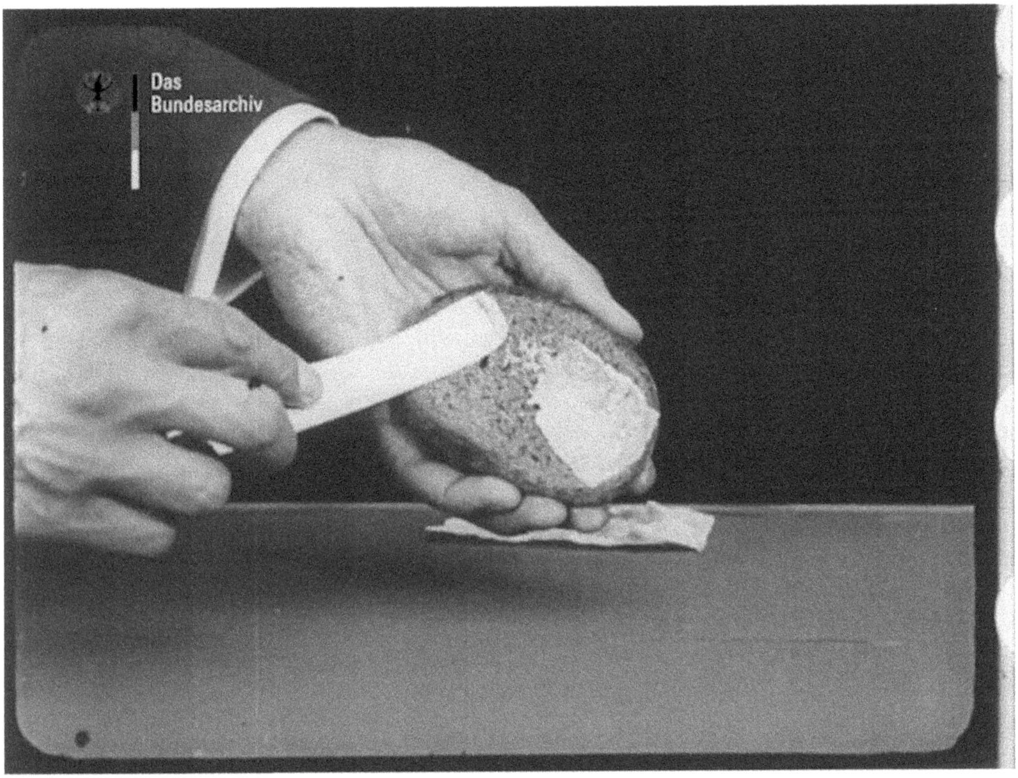

Figure 9.1 Daily butter ration.

Source: *Die Wirkung der Hungerblockade auf die Volksgesundheit* (1921). Daily butter ration. Image used by permission of Deutsches Filminstitut & Filmmuseum in Frankfurt am Main.

states that 70,000 tons of meat were sent by the United States during the armistice, which is close to the number reported for the same period by the American Relief Administration (ARA) (79,961.1 tons) some ten years later.[48] That the producers went to so much trouble to substantiate their claims of hunger and poor health in Germany through the use of official and scientific publications throughout the film gave strength to the narrative they were sharing about German suffering.

Die Wirkung der Hungerblockade auf die Volksgesundheit, similar to many German textbooks, also argued that the blockade of Germany during WWI was illegal. These claims of illegality were made by referring to the 1909 Declaration of London, just as they were in textbooks.[49] However, the film modified the language of the Declaration of London in a different way than textbooks had. In *Die Wirkung der Hungerblockade auf die Volksgesundheit*, the text specifies that the Declaration of London forbade blocking food into Germany. The way that the Declaration of London was written was in fact more general, stating that food could only be stopped from 'the military' uses of any belligerent. Signifying Germany rather than *any* belligerent, and omitting the Declaration of London's reference to allowing blocking food for enemy military use, created specificity in German victimization not contained in the document itself.

To illustrate the dire circumstances in Germany, the film often used scenes 'before' and 'during' the war and drew comparisons between Germany to the US, the Netherlands, and Denmark, with Germany always coming up short. The countries selected for comparison to Germany seem at best disingenuous. For example, the US was in a much stronger financial position than other countries during and especially after WWI. And, the Netherlands and Denmark had remained neutral. There is no mention of the millions of people who were also hungry during the war, particularly those who had been under German occupation. Furthermore, the millions of people in Russia and Ukraine experiencing famine when the film was being released were conveniently ignored. The disapproval depicted in the film that Germany received only 70,000 tons of meat during the armistice period is devoid of context.

One example of a misleading comparison includes healthy horses supposedly from Denmark compared to a horse from Germany with its ribs showing, struggling to move. The footage for these scenes originally came from Held's 1919 *Hunger Blockade Germany*, but the Ufa film reversed the ordering. Held's film showed the emaciated German horse first, followed by the healthy Danish horses. Starting with normal-looking horses in Denmark and then switching to a weak German horse, as Ufa does, increases the impact of Held's original scene.

The film also depicts many scenes of human suffering. While the use of children to foster empathy was not new, using moving footage rather than illustrations was an effective tool to create empathy. The message throughout these scenes was the same: babies, children, and adults before the war and the Allied Blockade were normal and healthy, and the Allied Blockade of Germany had greatly harmed them. Taken together, the film illustrates immense suffering and blames the Allied Blockade. These scenes put a human face to the statistics, medical facts, and legal arguments shown throughout the film with the same message of claiming German victimhood by the Allied Blockade.

Die Austernprinzessin took a far lighter approach to German suffering and hunger following the war. Directed by Ernst Lubitsch, it premiered in Berlin on 20 June 1919 and was immensely popular, prompting the production of an additional print run to meet exhibitor demand. Screenings were held across Germany to accommodate the high level of interest.[50] This 'bizarre comedy', (*Groteskes Lustspiel*), in four acts, stars a young, wealthy, American woman, Ossi Quaker (played by Ossi Oswalda), and her father Mr. Quaker (Victor Janson), the Oyster king from America. Ossi wishes to marry a European prince. Her extremely wealthy father, Mr. Quaker, agrees to her request, or rather, demand, and contacts a matchmaker for the arrangement.

The reference to Ossi's father as 'Mr. Quaker' may allude to the widespread relief sent to Germany following WWI by American Quakers through the auspices of the American Friend Service Committee (AFSC). While the AFSC was present in Germany through the summer and fall of 1919, the AFSC did not officially start operations in Germany until 26 February 1920.[51] Because AFSC relief in Germany was generally popular, it seems surprising that the film would poke fun at American Quakers. The timing of the production and release of *Die Austernprinzessin* in June 1919—before the AFSC had officially started operations—may explain why it was easy to place the Quakers and the AFSC at the centre of their comedy. Another possibility is that 'Mr Quaker' refers not to American Quakers as a group, but to one very specific Quaker, Herbert Hoover.[52]

Hoover had played a pivotal role in providing food aid relief to civilians in Belgium and Northern France during the War[53] and directed food aid relief for much of Europe, including Germany, during the armistice period just as the film was being released. Over 70,000 tons of meat alone had arrived from US organizations run by Herbert Hoover during the armistice period as also described and reported in *Die Wirkung der Hungerblockade auf die Volksgesundheit*. Hoover's efforts to supply Germany with food were widely reported and would have been known to a general audience. Finally, the use of the last name 'Quaker' for Ossie and her father may have simply been a more subtle reference to American wealth or abundance in general. The largesse of the Quaker-run AFSC and Herbert Hoover taken together could have led to 'Quaker' as a euphemism for American or foreign wealth. Whatever the motive, given the rarity of the use of 'Quaker' as a last name, its use was almost certainly deliberate. This shows that not only experiences of hunger but also of aid were narrativized in film, directly after the Great War.

Taken in the context of the hunger and blockade that millions of Germans were still living through when the film was released, the film, while a comedy, can also be read as a criticism of American excess wealth and wastefulness. It finds humour in ultra-rich American philanthropists, and plays off of the fantasy some Europeans supposedly held of having wealthy relatives in the United States who might assist them in their time of need. This usually took the form of an '*Onkel aus Amerika*' (*Uncle from America*).[54] The fantasy of having wealthy American relatives may have been popular because of widespread emigration to the United States leading up to the war, meaning that it was not uncommon for a person to have relatives there. And, of course, the fantasy may also have been popular because during the armistice period when the film was produced, the United States was responsible for the bulk of foreign food in Germany.

Yet the film also spares no criticism of the ridiculous wastefulness of Mr. Quaker and his daughter, Ossi Quaker, and their host of superfluous servants. In contrast to the excesses of these rich Americans, there are important signals, both visual and in the accompanying text, that point to the hunger and poor living conditions of the German people, especially of the former elite. Part of the humour lies not only in the ridiculousness of Mr. Quaker and his daughter, but also in the contrast between the lives of rich Americans and poor Germans.

The first scene of Prince Nucki is of him scrubbing his long underwear in a washtub, while Josef (his friend and possibly a former attendant) hangs up wet laundry in the background. Although Prince Nucki is well dressed, the attic he lives in is in disarray and contains broken furniture. That a prince was forced to live in an attic and scrub his own underwear may be an apt summation of the feelings and experiences of many Germans when the film was released in 1919. While inflation did not reach its peak in Germany until 1923, it had nonetheless destroyed the financial lives of many. When the matchmaker sent to procure Prince Nucki for Ossi Quaker knocks on his attic door, the Prince quickly takes off his watch and rings and hides them in the furnace, apparently afraid that the visitor may be a debt collector. After the visit, Prince Nucki sends Josef to check Ossi out for him first. When Josef enters the estate of the Quakers, he is mistaken for Prince Nucki and asked to wait. Josef grows bored and impatient as Mr. Quaker naps and Ossi prepares herself to meet him (or rather, her servants prepare her). Footage in this scene gives the most obvious visual reference to the American Friends Service Committee (AFSC) (see Figures 9.2 and 9.3). Its logo is huge and covers almost the entire entryway floor. This same symbol also shows up elsewhere in the film as wallpaper, including behind the foxtrot band at the dance after the wedding (Figure 9.4).

Food is central in the film. Once Ossi finally meets who she thinks is Prince Nucki (Josef), they get married, and a large party is given. Four chefs chop large lumps of beef and poultry in unison. Two women stand before a table piled high with lobster handing them and other food to cooks as they pass by. This abundance of food for the Quakers and their guests contrasts sharply with the German cooks and servants. There are more people preparing and serving food then there are guests eating. At one point in the kitchen a male youth hovers, hoping to charm someone into giving him something to eat. He is swatted away but is later successful in sneaking some pudding. Such contrasts between the abundance of food for the Quakers or Americans

Figure 9.2 Logo of the American Friend Service Committee (AFSC).

Source: Permission granted from the American Friends Service Committee Archives.

Figure 9.3 The marble floor resembles the American Friend Service Committee logo (AFSC).

Source: *Die Austernprinzessin* (1919). Image used by permission of the Friedrich-Wilhelm-Murnau-Stiftung in Wiesbaden, Germany.

Figure 9.4 Stage of the Fox-trot band. The wallcovering closely resembles the American Friend Service Committee logo.

Source: *Die Austernprinzessin* (1919). Image used by permission of the Friedrich-Wilhelm-Murnau-Stiftung in Wiesbaden, Germany.

with little thought for the Germans, match the widespread sentiment of German victimhood and loss.

The props used in these scenes are also telling. On close inspection, for example, the beef appears to be painted wood, and the lobsters look like they are made of plastic. Beef, poultry, and lobster were rare in Germany during the armistice period when the film was produced.[55] All goods would have been luxurious, but in this context of four years of fighting and an extended and expanded blockade, such large quantities of meat and lobster would have been absurd. Whether the filmmakers used wood and plastic props as their replacements to emphasize this absurdity, or as a substitute for the real thing because that was all they had, would have delivered the same narrative to audiences of the absurdity and excess of American consumerism during a time when Germany was suffering from severe shortages.

These contrasts of abundant luxury food for the Quakers to the servants and cooks (who are never shown eating anything, except for the youth when he steals some pudding) would have resonated with an audience still under a foreign blockade. Audiences may have also related to the individual hunger of Josef, Ossi's new husband. At the wedding dinner, Josef devours his food and wine, making Ossi uncomfortable. She tells him 'Don't be so greedy! Say a few words' (Sei doch nicht so verfressen! Sprich doch ein Paar Worte) to which he responds, 'I haven't eaten so well for so long' (Ich habe lange nicht so gut gegessen). Josef continues to eat and drink while the guests and his new bride move on to dance. Here too, in addition to props of food (fake beef and lobster) and text about food (I haven't eaten for so long), the film uses clever editing to emphasize the hunger felt by many Germans, even princes. As Josef burps and reaches for another glass of wine, the film then cuts to Prince Nucki in his crummy attic apartment, surrounded by his hanging laundry. In contrast to what guests at the wedding dinner ate, Prince Nucki holds up a solitary herring (Figure 9.5) 'Jeden Tag saurer Hering, das ist bitter' ('Sour herring every day—How bitter'). Many Germans did feel bitter about the quantity and quality of food available to them. The scene returns to Ossi and her father, who find Josef completely drunk and surrounded by bottles of alcohol. Mr. Quaker tells Josef that he should be ashamed of himself. Josef replies, ‚I am so happy!' (*Ich bin ja so glücklich!*). He was living the dream many Germans had of eating and drinking as much fine food and alcohol as he wanted to.

It is not only Prince Nucki who suffers. The film shows additional ways in which German elites more generally were in a reduced state. Other members of the aristocracy were also apparently persuaded by their poverty to marry wealthy American women. Indeed, Ossi's impetus to marry her own prince came after she read an announcement in the newspaper that the daughter of the shoe cream king married a count. The film shows additional ways in which German elites

Figure 9.5 Prince Nucki, in his poverty, eating herring.

Source: *Die Austernprinzessin* (1919). Image used by permission of the Friedrich-Wilhelm-Murnau-Stiftung in Wiesbaden, Germany.

more generally were in a reduced state. This representation of oversaturation might serve as a moral critique, questioning the ethics of such abundance in the face of German suffering.

The film also connected aid relief to larger discussions of the temperance movement, similar to the 1923 textbook which linked hunger to alcohol consumption and found humour in wealthy female international do-gooders[56]. The 'Fight against alcoholism' led by '*Der Verein der Milliardärstöchter*' (the Association of Billionaire's Daughters) is the best example of this. As Ossi ends her rousing speech with 'down with alcoholism!' the women all raise a glass of wine in her support. While *Die Austerprinzessin* does not blame Paris and London for German hunger and suffering as directly as *Wirkung der Hungerblockade auf die Volksgesundheit*, it still shows German hunger in sharp contrast to others, mocking Americans.

Conclusion

This chapter has demonstrated the evolution of narratives surrounding the Allied Blockade and hunger in Germany during WWI and into the Weimar period using secondary school textbooks and film. Textbooks initially emphasized resilience during the war, later framing it as collective suffering during the armistice period and after the war. The film *Wirkung der Hungerblockade auf die Volksgesundheit* (*The Effects of the Hunger Blockade on Public Health*) strengthened this narrative of victimhood and suffering, serving political agendas by assigning blame on Germany's enemies for hunger and defeat. In these materials, hunger narratives were further used to legitimize governmental food policies. Hunger, as such, proved to be a useful vehicle for fostering a sense of unity and obedience to authority among Germans in facing shared adversity.

Beyond overt political agendas, hunger narratives could also serve entertainment purposes as depicted in *Die Austerprinzessin* (The Oyster Princess), offering audiences a familiar depiction of German suffering and assistance from American Quakers. Both the film and textbooks reflected unofficial narratives prevalent in German society, revealing the influence of contemporary movements, particularly those advocating for temperance and alcohol prohibition, some tinged with racial undertones. The racial undertones connected to food and hunger in the cultural artefacts were later weaponized by the Nazi regime, where racialized food politics would be intensified and institutionalized. While racism in Weimar textbooks may have been marginal, these ideologies anticipate the propaganda and policies of the Nazi era, suggesting a developmental link between the interwar period and the atrocities of World War II and the Holocaust.

These sources demonstrate that the memory of the blockade was shaped not only by wartime context or political mandate but also by broader societal ideologies. Through both formal and informal media outlets, narratives on the blockade were strategically employed to serve various agendas, highlighting the rich and layered interpretation of this historical period in Germany.

Notes

1 Mary E. Cox, "The Blockade in the First World War," in *Harfleur to Hamburg: Five Centuries of English and British Violence in Europe* D.J.B. Trim and Brendan Simms (eds) (London: Hurst & Company, 2024), 185–200.

2 Lizzie Collingham, *Taste of War: World War II and the Battle for Food* (Penguin Books, 2011). Nicholas Mulder, *The Economic Weapon. The Rise of Sanctions as a Tool of Modern Warfare* (New Haven & London: Yale University Press, 2022), 227–47.

3 Dieter Petzina, *Autarkiepolitik Im Dritten Reich: Der Nationalsozialistische Vierjahresplan* (Stuttgart, 1968).Corinna Treitel, *Eating Nature in Modern Germany: Food, Agriculture, and Environment, c. 1870–2000* (Cambridge, 2017), 165. Jonas Scherner, "Germany, Blockade and Strategic Raw Materials in the Era of the Two World Wars," *The International History Review*, 2024, 3.

4 Christoph Dieckmann and Babette Quinkert, "»Kriegsnotwendigkeiten« und Die Eskalation Der Deutschen Massengewalt Im Totalen Krieg Einführende Bemerkungen," in *Kriegführung Und Hunger 1939–1945: Zum Verhältnis von Militärischen, Wirtschaftlichen Und Politischen Interessen* (Göttingen: Wallstein, 2015), 10.

5 Alice Weinreb, *Modern Hungers: Food and Power in Twentieth-Century Germany* (New York, 2017), 49–87. Gesine Gerhard, *Nazi Hunger Politics: A History of Food in the Third Reich* (Lanham, 2015), 42–48.

6 Werner Schaeffer, *The War Against Women and Children* (USA: Flanders hall, 1941). A Book-of-the-Hour Book. Translated by George Sylvester Viereck, Flanders Halls, USA, 1941. The book was also published in German and in Swedish. Werner Schaeffer, Krieg Gegen Frauen und Kinder. Englands Hungerblockade gegen Deutschland 1914–1920. Englands Verbrechen im Weltkrieg Nr. 1 (Berlin, Deutsche Informationsstelle, 1940); Werner Schaeffer, Englands krig mot kvinnor och barn: hungerblockaden mot Tyskland 1914–1920. Translated by Annie Åkerhielm. Svea rike, Stockholm, 1940.

7 Frank Van Vree, *Nederland En de Herinnering Aan de Jodenvervolging: 1945–2024* (Almere: Uitgeverij Verbum, 2024), 233.

8 Tessa Morris-Suzuki, *The Past Within Us: Media, Memory, History* (London, 2005), 2–3.

9 Michael Wintle, Nanci Adler, and Remco Ensel, "Narratives of War in the Twentieth Century: An Introduction," in *Narratives of War: Remembering and Chronicling Battle in Twentieth-Century Europe* (New York: Routledge, 2019), 6.

10 Wintle et al., "Narratives of War in the Twentieth Century", 5.

11 Frank van Vree, "The Imagery of War Screening the Battlefield in the Twentieth Century," in *Narratives of War: Remembering and Chronicling Battle in Twentieth-Century Europe* (New York and London: Routledge, 2019), 81–99.

12 Armin Kremer and Rieß Falk, "Mobilmachung Im Unterricht. Die Instrumentalisierung der Physikpädagogik Für Nation Und Krieg Im Kaiserreich," *Die Deutsche Schule* 98, no. 3 (2006): 270, 273.

13 Ludwig Kahnmeyer and Hermann Schulze, *Realienbuch Enthaltend Geschichte, Erdkunde, Naturgeschichte, Physik, Chemie Und Mineralogie. Mit Geschichte Des Weltkrieges* (Bielefeld: Velhagen & Klasing, 1918), 185.

14 "Declaration of London, Article 33" (International Humanitarian Law Databases), accessed May 14, 2024, https://ihl-databases.icrc.org/en/ihl-treaties/london-decl-1909.

15 Nicholas Mulder and Boyd Van Dijk, "Why Did Starvation Not Become the Paradigmatic War Crime in International Law?" in *Contingency in International Law*, ed. Ingo Venzke and Kevin Jon Heller (Oxford: Oxford University Press, 2021), 370–88.

16 Eduard Rothert, *Karten Und Skizzen Zum Weltkrieg 1914/15* (Düsseldorf: Bagel, 1915), 61.

17 Friedrich Baade, Emil Borchers, and Albert Gieseler, *Der Weltkrieg 1914–1915* (Leipzig and Bieleveld, 1915), 21.

18 Friedrich Lembke and Heinrich Sohnrey, *Fürs Vaterland* (Berlin: deutsche Landbuchhandlung, 1915), 220.

19 Unknown, *Erlebnisse Und Darstellungen Aus Dem Jahre 1915: Herausgegeben Für Lehrer Und Schüler Als Ergänzung Der Lesebücher* (Breslau: Hirt, 1916), 119. This form of stoicism of eating little and wasting less also fit into a national ideal conceived in a masculine and military tone, something that existed outside of Germany as well.

20 Kruse and Hintze, *Sparsame Ernährung Nach Erhebungen Im Krieg Und Frieden* (Dresden: Verlag des Deutschen Hygiene-Museum, C C. Meinhold & Söhne, n.d.), 5.

21 Eugen Schlessinger, "Wachstum, Gewicht Und Konstitution Der Kinder Und Der Herangewachsenen Jugend Während Des Krieges," *Zeitschrift Für Kinderheilkund* 22, no. 1 (1919). See also: Mary E. Cox, *Hunger in War and Peace: Women and Children in Germany, 1914–1924* (Oxford, 2019), 150–69.

22 This is literally the meaning of the title of one of the studies. Prof. Dr. Kruse and Prof. Dr. Hintze, *Sparsame Ernährung Nach Erhebungen im Krieg und Frieden.*

23 Weinreb, *Modern Hungers*, 23; Cox, *Hunger in War and Peace: Women and Children in Germany, 1914–1924*, 74.

24 Kahnmeyer and Schulze, *Realienbuch Enthaltend Geschichte, Erdkunde, Naturgeschichte, Physik, Chemie Und Mineralogie. Mit Geschichte Des Weltkrieges* (1918) 185.
25 Mary E. Cox, *Hunger in War and Peace: Women and Children in Germany, 1914–1924.* (Oxford University Press, 2019).
26 Cox, *Hunger in War and Peace*.
27 Ute Daniel, *The War from Within: German Women in the First World War* (Oxford: Berg Publishers, 1997). Belinda Davis, *Home Fires Burning: Food, Politics, and Everyday Life in World War I Berlin.* The University of North Carolina Press, 2000; Sean Dobson, *Authority and Upheaval in Leipzig, 1910–1920: The Story of a Relationship* (New York: Colombia University Press, 2001).
28 Cox, *Hunger in War & Peace*, p. 238.
29 Heinrich Kerp, *Ferdinand Hirts Neues Realienbuch Für Die Provinz Brandenburg* (Breslau: Hirt, 1917), 29; Friedrich Tromnau, *Geschichte Für Evangelische Schulen* (Breslau: Hirt, 1918), 29; Hermann Jaenicke, *Preußisch-Deutsche Geschichte* (Berlin: Weidmann, 1918), 57; Richard Seehaußen, *Der Weltkrieg* (Leipzig: Voigtländer, 1918), 43.
30 Seehaußen, *Der Weltkrieg*, 43.
31 Kahnmeyer and Schulze, *Realienbuch Enthaltend Geschichte, Erdkunde, Naturgeschichte, Physik, Chemie Und Mineralogie. Mit Geschichte Des Weltkrieges*, 186. Other textbook including bad harvest as a factor influencing the German food situation: Seehaußen, *Der Weltkrieg*, 43.
32 Marjorie Lamberti, *The Politics of Education. Teachers and School Reform in Weimar Germany* (New York, 2002) 1–3.
33 Friedrich Neubauer, *Lehrbuch Der Geschichte Für Höhere Lehranstalten.* (Halle: Verlag der Buchhandlung des Waisenhauses, 1922), 339–40.
34 For example: Sally Marks, "The Myths of Reparations," *Central Europan History* 11, no. 3 (1978): 231–55.
35 Alfred Giesecke Teubner, *Schaffen Und Schauen: Ein Führer Ins Leben. Volk Und Vaterland* (Leipzig and Berlin: B.G. Teubner, 1921), 234.
36 Mark Mazower, *Hitler's Empire: Nazi Rule in Occupied Europe* (London: Penguin Books, 2008), 259.
37 Gustav Klemm, *Kulturkunde: Vom Hunger Zum Brot* (Dresden: C. Heinrich, 1923), 79.
38 Treitel, *Eating Nature in Modern Germany: Food, Agriculture, and Environment, c. 1870–2000*, 132–33; Michael Hau, "The Dialectic of Medical Enlightenment: War,Alcohol Consumption and Public Hygiene inGermany, 1910–1925," *History* 104, no. 359 (2019): 149–68.
39 As elaborated upon by: Treitel, *Eating Nature in Modern Germany: Food, Agriculture, and Environment, c. 1870–2000*, 124–27.
40 Eric Kurlander, *Hitler's Monsters: A Supernatural History of the Third Reich* (New Haven & Londen: Yale University Press, 2017), 55.
41 Klemm, *Kulturkunde: Vom Hunger Zum Brot*, 88–89.
42 Robert N. Proctor, "The Nazi Campaign against Tobacco: Science in a Totalitarian State," in *Medicine and Medical Ethics in Nazi Germany*, ed. Jonathan Huener and Francis Nicosia (New York and Oxford: Berghahn Books, 2002), 42.
43 Stephen Wheatcroft and Cormac Ó Gráda, "The European Famines of World Wars I and II," in *Famine in European History*, ed. Guido Alfani and Cormac Ó Gráda (Cambridge: Cambridge University Press, 2017), 275.
44 Cormac Ó Gráda, "The Famines of WWII," *VoxEU Debate: The Economics of the Second World War: Eighty Years On*, September 2, 2019, https://cepr.org/voxeu/columns/famines-wwii.
45 Ernst Lubitsch, *Die Austernprinzessin*, 1919.
46 William Held, *Hunger Blockade Germany*, 1919, www2.landesarchiv-bw.de/ofs21/bild_zoom/zoom.php?bestand=52391&id=8740420&gewaehlteSeite=04_0004027197_0001_4-4027197-1.jpg&screenbreite=1512&screenhoehe=982.
47 The film itself makes this claim early on, and the point is substantiated throughout the many references made in the film. Often, full citations for scientific journals were used, making it possible to check.

48 Raymond L. Bland, *American Food in the World War and Reconstruction Period: Operations of the Organizations under the Direction of Herbert Hoover 1914–1924* (Stanford: Stanford University Press, 1931), 196.

49 Kahnmeyer and Schulze, *Realienbuch Enthaltend Geschichte, Erdkunde, Naturgeschichte, Physik, Chemie Und Mineralogie. Mit Geschichte Des Weltkrieges.*

50 Wayne Barker, "The Oyster Princess," in *Booklet: San Francisco Silent Film Festival* (San Francisco Silent Film Festival, 2019), 25–26.

51 Mary E. Cox, *Hunger in War and Peace: Women and Children in Germany, 1914–1924* (Oxford University Press, 2019), p. 304.

52 Rick McCormick, *Sex, Politics, and Comedy: The Transnational Cinema of Ernst Lubitsch* (Bloomington: Indiana University Press, 2020).

53 McCormick, *Sex, Politics, and Comedy.*

54 The hope of a wealthy uncle from America was sometimes published as children's fantasy, see Dörfler, "Wie Das Christkind in Der Hütte Wuchs," *Mülheimer Volkszeitung*, December, 359 edition; Fr. Lehne, "Vom Glück Vergessen," *The Tageszeitung: Amtliches Kreisblatt Für Den Kreis Arnsberg*, July 19, 1919; and for entertainment: Unknown, "Theater Und Musik: 'Die Armseligen Besenbinder' Karlruher Tagblatt," *Karlruher Tagblatt* 360 (December 29, 1918): 2.

55 Cox, *Hunger in War and Peace: Women and Children in Germany, 1914–1924*, 214–21.

56 Klemm, *Kulturkunde: Vom Hunger Zum Brot*, 79.

References

Baade, Friedrich, Emil Borchers, and Albert Gieseler. *Der Weltkrieg 1914–1915.* Leipzig and Bieleveld, 1915.

Barker, Wayne. "The Oyster Princess." In *Booklet: San Francisco Silent Film Festival*, 25–26. San Francisco Silent Film Festival, 2019.

Bland, Raymond L. *American Food in the World War and Reconstruction Period: Operations of the Organizations Under the Direction of Herbert Hoover 1914–1924.* Stanford: Stanford University Press, 1931.

Collingham, Lizzie. *Taste of War: World War II and the Battle for Food.* Penguin Books, 2011.

Cox, Mary E. *Hunger in War and Peace: Women and Children in Germany, 1914–1924.* Oxford, 2019.

Cox, Mary E., D.J.B. Trim, and Brendan Simms. "The Blockade in the First World War." In *Harfleur to Hamburg: Five Centuries of English and British Violence in Europe*, 185–200. London: Hurst & Company, 2024.

Daniel, Ute. *The War from Within: German Women in the First World War.* Oxford: Berg Publishers, 1997.

"Declaration of London, Article 33." International Humanitarian Law Databases. Accessed May 14, 2024. https://ihl-databases.icrc.org/en/ihl-treaties/london-decl-1909.

Dieckmann, Christoph, and Babette Quinkert. "»Kriegsnotwendigkeiten« und Die Eskalation Der Deutschen Massengewalt Im Totalen Krieg Einführende Bemerkungen." In *Kriegführung Und Hunger 1939–1945: Zum Verhältnis von Militärischen, Wirtschaftlichen Und Politischen Interessen*, 9–32. Göttingen: Wallstein, 2015.

Dobson, Sean. *Authority and Upheaval in Leipzig, 1910–1920: The Story of a Relationship.* New York: Colombia University Press, 2001.

Dörfler. "Wie Das Christkind in Der Hütte Wuchs." *Mülheimer Volkszeitung*, December, 359 edition.

Ernst, Lubitsch. *Die Austernprinzessin*, 1919.

Gerhard, Gesine. *Nazi Hunger Politics: A History of Food in the Third Reich.* Lanham, 2015.

Giesecke Teubner, Alfred. *Schaffen Und Schauen: Ein Führer Ins Leben. Volk Und Vaterland.* Leipzig and Berlin: B.G. Teubner, 1921.

Hau, Michael. "The Dialectic of Medical Enlightenment: War, Alcohol Consumption and Public Hygiene in Germany, 1910–1925." *History* 104, no. 359 (2019): 149–68.

Hunger Blockade Germany, 1919. www2.landesarchiv-bw.de/ofs21/bild_zoom/zoom.php?bestand=52391&id=8740420&gewaehlteSeite=04_0004027197_0001_4-4027197-1.jpg&screenbreite=1512&screenhoehe=982.

Jaenicke, Hermann. *Preußisch-Deutsche Geschichte*. Berlin: Weidmann, 1918.

Kahnmeyer, Ludwig, and Hermann Schulze. *Realienbuch Enthaltend Geschichte, Erdkunde, Naturgeschichte, Physik, Chemie Und Mineralogie. Mit Geschichte Des Weltkrieges*. Bielefeld: Velhagen & Klasing, 1918.

Kerp, Heinrich. *Ferdinand Hirts Neues Realienbuch Für Die Provinz Brandenburg*. Breslau: Hirt, 1917.

Klemm, Gustav. *Kulturkunde: Vom Hunger Zum Brot*. Dresden: C. Heinrich, 1923.

Kremer, Armin, and Rieß Falk. "Mobilmachung Im Unterricht. Die Instrumentalisierung Der Physikpädagogik Für Nation Und Krieg Im Kaiserreich." *Die Deutsche Schule* 98, no. 3 (2006): 270–84.

Kruse, and Hintze. *Sparsame Ernährung Nach Erhebungen Im Krieg Und Frieden*. Dresden: Verlag des Deutschen Hygiene-Museum, C C. Meinhold & Söhne, n.d.

Kurlander, Eric. *Hitler's Monsters: A Supernatural History of the Third Reich*. New Haven & Londen: Yale University Press, 2017.

Lamberti, Marjorie. *The Politics of Education. Teachers and School Reform in Weimar Germany*. New York, 2002.

Lehne, Fr. "Vom Glück Vergessen." *The Tageszeitung: Amtliches Kreisblatt Für Den Kreis Arnsberg*, July 19, 1919.

Lembke, Friedrich, and Heinrich Sohnrey. *Fürs Vaterland*. Berlin: deutsche Landbuchhandlung, 1915.

Marks, Sally. "The Myths of Reparations." *Central Europan History* 11, no. 3 (1978): 231–55.

Mazower, Mark. *Hitler's Empire: Nazi Rule in Occupied Europe*. London: Penguin Books, 2008.

McCormick, Rick. *Sex, Politics, and Comedy: The Transnational Cinema of Ernst Lubitsch*. Bloomington: Indiana University Press, 2020.

Morris-Suzuki, Tessa. *The Past Within Us: Media, Memory, History*. London, 2005.

Mulder, Nicholas. *The Economic Weapon. The Rise of Sanctions as a Tool of Modern Warfare*. New Haven & Londen: Yale University Press, 2022.

Mulder, Nicholas, and Boyd Van Dijk. "Why Did Starvation Not Become the Paradigmatic War Crime in International Law?" In *Contingency in International Law*, edited by Ingo Venzke and Kevin Jon Heller, 370–88. Oxford: Oxford University Press, 2021.

Neubauer, Friedrich. *Lehrbuch Der Geschichte Für Höhere Lehranstalten*. Halle: Verlag der Buchhandlung des Waisenhauses, 1922.

Ó Gráda, Cormac. "The Famines of WWII." *VoxEU Debate: The Economics of the Second World War: Eighty Years On*, September 2, 2019. https://cepr.org/voxeu/columns/famines-wwii.

Petzina, Dieter. *Autarkiepolitik Im Dritten Reich: Der Nationalsozialistische Vierjahresplan*. Stuttgart, 1968.

Proctor, Robert N. "The Nazi Campaign against Tobacco: Science in a Totalitarian State." In *Medicine and Medical Ethics in Nazi Germany*, edited by Jonathan Huener and Francis Nicosia, 40–58. New York and Oxford: Berghahn Books, 2002.

Rothert, Eduard. *Karten Und Skizzen Zum Weltkrieg 1914/15*. Düsseldorf: Bagel, 1915.

Schaeffer, Werner. *The War Against Women and Children*. USA: Flanders hall, 1941.

Scherner, Jonas. "Germany, Blockade and Strategic Raw Materials in the Era of the Two World Wars." *The International History Review*, 2024, 1–21.

Schlessinger, Eugen. "Wachstum, Gewicht Und Konstitution Der Kinder Und Der Herangewachsenen Jugend Während Des Krieges." *Zeitschrift Für Kinderheilkund* 22, no. 1 (1919).

Seehaußen, Richard. *Der Weltkrieg*. Leipzig: Voigtländer, 1918.

Treitel, Corinna. *Eating Nature in Modern Germany: Food, Agriculture, and Environment, c. 1870–2000*. Cambridge, 2017.

Tromnau, Friedrich. *Geschichte Für Evangelische Schulen*. Breslau: Hirt, 1918.

Unknown. *Erlebnisse Und Darstellungen Aus Dem Jahre 1915: Herausgegeben Für Lehrer Und Schüler Als Ergänzung Der Lesebücher*. Breslau: Hirt, 1916.

Unknown. "Theater Und Musik: 'Die Armseligen Besenbinder'." *Karlruher Tagblatt* 360 (December 29, 1918).

Van Vree, Frank. *Nederland En de Herinnering Aan de Jodenvervolging: 1945–2024*. Almere: Uitgeverij Verbum, 2024.

Vree, Frank van. "The Imagery of War Screening the Battlefield in the Twentieth Century." In *Narratives of War: Remembering and Chronicling Battle in Twentieth-Century Europe*, 81–99. New York and London: Routledge, 2019.

Weinreb, Alice. *Modern Hungers: Food and Power in Twentieth-Century Germany*. New York, 2017.

Wheatcroft, Stephen, and Cormac Ó Gráda. "The European Famines of World Wars I and II." In *Famine in European History*, edited by Guido Alfani and Cormac Ó Gráda. Cambridge: Cambridge University Press, 2017.

Wintle, Michael, Nanci Adler, and Remco Ensel. "Narratives of War in the Twentieth Century: An Introduction." In *Narratives of War: Remembering and Chronicling Battle in Twentieth-Century Europe*. New York: Routledge, 2019.

10 Heritages of hunger in Europe

Transnational matter for the present day

Marguérite Corporaal

Over recent years, the situation in Ukraine has rekindled international attention on to a historic event, the period of mass starvation under the Stalinist regime in 1932–33, known to Ukrainians as the Holodomor. The contemporary weaponization of food in Europe's breadbasket and the threat of starvation resonated in Ukraine and around the world. In the spring of 2022, Russia's 'Black Sea Blockade' generated fear that millions of people in Africa and the Middle East, which rely on Ukrainian grain for their food supplies, would be pushed 'towards famine'.[1] In an address on Holodomor Remembrance Day (2023), President Volodymyr Zelensky called on the world to recall the crimes of the past, as well as 'unite and stop today's crimes'.[2] Moreover, the heritage of the Ukrainian famine came to be reframed in relation to the ongoing conflict. Thus, a tweet by *Taoiseach* (prime minister of Ireland) Micheál Martín, posted on 6 July 2022, about his visit to the Holodomor Memorial in Kyiv, relates Stalin's mass starvation to Russia's current war politics, stating that 'Russia must not be allowed to use food as a weapon in this immoral and unjustified war', while also drawing analogies between Ukraine and Ireland as countries once subject to starvation: 'Ukraine and Ireland know the suffering and pain of famine'.[3]

The current concern with and reinterpretation of Holodomor monuments in the context of Putin's war in Ukraine illustrates a trend we may witness with regard to European famine heritages over the past years. Past famine legacies are recalled to give meaning to current problems, including not just food emergencies but also the refugee crisis and the COVID-19 pandemic. What Andreas Huyssen calls the 'politics of memory' applies to European famine pasts.[4] Indeed, current political events condition in what ways famines are remembered and what dimensions of these famine pasts are recollected or forgotten.

This chapter will go into these contemporary instrumentalizations of past European famines in light of current societal developments, discussing how present political agendas have led to a reinterpretation of these famine pasts. In so doing, it will examine recent heritage projects concerning European famines, addressing three major trends in the formation of new famine legacies. The first is the recovery of lost and often subaltern histories connected to these famines. The second is what I would like to call the transnational turn in European famine heritage, which is rooted in three phenomena: the increasing 'multidirectional' nature of these famine heritages, the intersections between the cultural memories of these famines in the homeland on the one hand and those of migrant communities on the other and the existence of transnational cultural repertoires of famine remembrance.[5] The third includes enactment and reconstruction as strategies to evoke what Laurence Gouriévidis has called 'vicarious empathy', that is, feelings of sympathy and understanding that are elicited through the emotions of others.[6]

DOI: 10.4324/9781003465805-14

European famine heritage: malleable legacies

As, amongst others, Astrid Erll has argued, memory is inherently fluid, as it can travel through time and space, 'across […] and also beyond cultures', and in that process attain new meanings that serve present agendas and future ambitions.[7] Indeed, in the case of the cultural legacies of European famines, we clearly see how they are often utilized and reframed in the context of recent societal issues and developments, for different aims.[8] For example, during his speech delivered on the occasion of the National Famine Commemoration on 21 May 2023, Ireland's president Michael D. Higgins called for solidarity with today's refugees—especially those fleeing hunger by seeking 'to enter Spanish territory from Africa', many of whom 'die before they make it to the coast'. As Higgins stated, the Irish 'have a moral duty to continue to honour our commitments to those vulnerable and displaced who seek asylum and refuge on our shores' in view of the 'parallels' between today's refugee crisis and 'An Gorta Mór [Ireland's Great Hunger] and the mass displacement it caused 175 years ago'.[9]

In a similar fashion, but with strikingly different political intent, the Dutch Farmers' Defence Force (FDF) has often recalled the Dutch Hunger Winter of 1944–45 in order to protest against national and EU policies which force them to shrink livestock as the means to help reduce nitrogen emissions. Thus, in late 2019 FDF's spokesman Marc van den Oever wondered whether Dutch society should refresh its memory of the Hunger Winter—then 75 years ago—to realize what farmers did to save their countrymen and women from starvation: sharing their own scanty supplies and secretly keeping back parts of their harvests and dairy. People must have forgotten, Van den Oever stated, for otherwise they would appreciate and support the farmers in their plight.[10] His statements were strongly criticized, amongst others, on the basis of historical accounts included in the Hunger Winter exhibition and website of the Resistance Museum in Amsterdam. These displayed personal histories suggest that some farmers also let people down, by demanding very valuable goods such as linen and table silver in exchange for money, or by refusing to barter food at all.[11]

Retrieved and recollected heritage

This latter example makes clear that recovered heritage can play a significant role in nuancing more radical politicizations of famine pasts by engaging with oral testimonies or historical data. In fact, one could argue that heritages of hunger, while shaped by ideological iconographies and 'narrative templates' themselves in processes of creation, preservation and canonization,[12] may also open up alternative or complementary perspectives in looking at European famine pasts. Often these heritage practices suggest a reassessment of commonly held perceptions of the past on the basis of the recuperation of famine legacies through hitherto underexplored texts, images and material artefacts. As Jefferson Singer and Martin Conway have argued, some pasts are not really forgotten, but less accessible in the public sphere: this happens when certain legacies are 'available' but may not be widely 'accessible' at any given time, because they remain hidden in archives, or because people have kept back testimonies of such a past for personal or political reasons. This implies, however, that such legacies 'can potentially be retrieved and through the retrieval process might enter consciousness and so influence experience and behaviour' as well.[13]

Especially regarding the famine pasts in Finland and Spain, we see such retrieval processes currently at work. While the famine of 1867–68 led to high mortality rates, until recently it received very little attention in Finland's public sphere. This is mainly, as Andrew Newby and Eliza Krataari have observed, because this famine took place under a devolved administration in Helsinki, even if Finland was part of Russia's empire at the time.[14] After the Civil War and

Finnish independence, for political reasons, the famine years therefore had to be framed as 'the inevitable economic birth pains of a new nation, pain that needed to be endured, or as one of several "building blocks" which helped to create a modern state' rather than as failure on part of the Snelmann government.[15] Andrew Newby's curation of the travelling exhibition 'Nälkä!: The Great Finnish Famine' (2019), which was hosted by, amongst others, the National Famine Museum Strokestown Park, the Irish Workhouse Famine in Portumna, the Culture Centre Valve in Oulu, and the University of Tampere, is a good example of how an almost neglected era of famine may receive renewed local, national and even international attention through heritage collection and construction. The exhibition displayed information panels in combination with images of news reports and engravings from the press and from the National Museum in Helsinki. These were brought together with local famine monuments photographed by Newby himself, and a few tangible objects. Furthermore, as Newby's pioneering research has revealed, one may discover more famine heritage than initially expected by adopting a regional focus. Newby's database of Finnish famine monuments reveals that on a local level, often in parish churchyards, one can find memorials that mark former mass graves or that generally remember past victims of hunger in these communities.[16] This dispersed famine heritage deserves an overarching narrative that roots Finland's years of hunger into the national collective memory.

More recently, Newby's exhibition has been followed up by the bilingual new main exhibition '*Yhteisvoimin*' ('United') at the Werstas Labour Museum (2023). This renewed gallery centralizes the question of how Finland has been 'built with joint efforts from a poor agricultural country to a welfare state' through a focus on 'the history of the working class from the 19th century to the present day from the perspective of an ordinary person'.[17] The exhibition presents the Hunger Years as the starting point of an era of common struggles ('Famine Knocking at the Door') commonly faced by the Finnish people. Displaying agricultural tools from the museum's collection along with reproductions of famine illustrations, '*Yhteisvoimin*' shifts away from the Civil War as the traditional focus of national identity formation, in favour of famine as a regional and national foundation myth (Figure 10.1).

In Spain, the memory laws passed in 2007 and 2022, the latter by a government coalition of Socialists and left-wing Unidas-Podemos, have at last led to the overall reassessment of the Franco dictatorship, as Miguel Ángel Del Arco Blanco and Deborah Madden argue.[18] The legacies of the Hunger Years have yet to be explicitly recognized by the state; nonetheless, the overall reassessment of the Franco dictatorship over the past decade has led to a stronger emphasis on the years of hunger that took place under his rule in general, and a more active use of the term '*hambre*' in relation to its repressed, but extant legacies. There are many resources—in the form of texts, art works and especially photographs—which document the Spanish Hunger Years, but which are dispersed over several archives.

Up till 2022, there had not been an exhibition yet which brought these legacies from the famine years and their aftermath together. However, on 26 October of that year '*La Hambruna Silenciada: El hambre durante la posguerra franquista, 1939–1952*' ('The Silenced Famine: Hunger in Post-War Spain'), curated by Miguel Ángel del Arco Blanco and Gloria Román Ruiz, opened at the Casa Molino de Ángel Ganivet in Granada. The travelling exhibition, subsidized by, amongst others, the Ministry Presidency, makes clear that societal impulses and top-down political support acknowledging long-repressed past suffering are often fundamental in helping to make accessible, collect and disseminate famine heritage. It shows samples of ration cards, propaganda posters of the Franco regime and photographs of living conditions, food queues, as well as quotes from eyewitnesses. Furthermore, the exhibition particularly highlights the role played by women and their resourcefulness as cooks and housewives during the famine years ('*El Papel de las Mujeres*'),[19] thereby bringing long-forgotten histories to light.

Figure 10.1 'Yhteisvoimin', The Finnish Labour Museum Werstas.
Courtesy: Anne Lahtinen.

Towards transnational famine heritages

At the same time, a top-down approach to famine heritage construction can also fuel controversy, rather than channelling it. This is demonstrated by the tensions surrounding the 2018 Glasgow Irish and Highland Famine Memorial. At first glance, the monument appears to integrate two colonial famine pasts occurring around the same time: the Great Irish Famine and the Highland Clearances and the 1846 Scottish famine. Featuring 'plants and stone native to Ireland and the Highlands, the memorial interprets the journey made by refugees, forced to flee home' and is a 'tribute and acknowledgement to those who experienced famine' and helped build the city, the Glasgow City council announced upon its dedication.[20]

Nonetheless, the ways in which the monument, in the shape of a boat, brings together Highland and Irish famine legacies has received critique from various sides, as Laurence Gouriévidis has also recently revealed: 'to some members of the city's Irish community, Glasgow City Council's memorial, was unsuitable in both aesthetic design and objective, notably with regard to its mingling the Irish and Highland experiences'.[21] Especially the local Great Hunger Memorial Committee felt frustrated that the Glasgow City council 'added on the Highland element, because they knew, or believed, that there were forces in Glasgow even today who would not accept a memorial which involved the Irish alone', as they stated to *The Guardian*. Furthermore, as representatives of this committee claimed,

> [t]he scale and extent of what happened to our people—one million dead and one million forced to emigrate out of a population of eight million made the notion of a 'Highland and Irish famine memorial' completely unacceptable to us and offensive in its very concept.[22]

The monument may seem an expression of 'multidirectional memory',[23] that is, the successful intersection of legacies kept alive by different communities. However, it is actually utilized as a futile way to overcome strongly competing memories that are furthermore reinforced by ethnic and religious differences.

The Glasgow Irish and Highland Famine Memorial may wrongly suggest that the formation of transnational famine legacies which could evoke sympathy and solidarity with victims of famine or other atrocities across borders may be a mission impossible. This is, however, not always the case. In what follows, I will show that we can witness the emergence of a transnational turn in the formation of famine heritage and that there is more potential for developing joint, comparative heritage initiatives. One example of such a '*lieu de mémoire*'[24] which is more effectively inscribed with transnational imperial legacies, perhaps because it resulted from a 'community-based' rather than top-down initiative,[25] is the famine graveyard at the back of Swinford Hospital Co. Mayo in Ireland (Figure 10.2).

The hospital was built around the remains of the Swinford Union Workhouse, which took in sick and starving people during the Great Famine (1845–50). The grave contains the remains of 564 inmates, and a simple plaque marks its site: 'Erected by the people of Swinford to the memory of 564 famine victims buried in this place. May they rest in peace'.[26] Close to the site, a monument was erected which was unveiled by Arun Gandhi, the grandson of the spiritual leader of India's independence movement Mahatma Gandhi in 1994. It portrays and quotes Michael Davitt, who 'visited the grave before he founded the National Land League',[27] and Gandhi, while referencing the buried famine victims: 'Here lie the remains of hundreds of poor people who died during Ireland's so-called Great Famine'. The monument also contains a text which encourages the visitor of the site to 'continue the struggle for a more just and equitable world' as an expression of respect to the memory of these victims; thereby voicing prospective memory, that is, a 'forward-looking, socially progressive and sustainable' form of remembrance that helps fashion future ways of living together.[28] Furthermore, in this way, the memorial site is truly heterochronic[29] and palimpsestic: it merges various 'slices in time'—the Great Irish Famine, the Irish Land Wars and the Indian struggle for independence—as well as involves 'an absolute break with traditional time', in that the boundaries between past, present and a wished-for future collapse in ways that enable a postcolonial critique on British imperial politics.[30] At the same time, the monument is essentially transnational in the past from different parts of the British empire that coalesced.

Recent examples of heritage in which European famine past interact and overlap in 'multi-directional' ways are, amongst others, the previously mentioned exhibition 'Nälkä!'. As it

Figure 10.2 Swinford Union Workhouse monument (1994).

Source: Photograph by the author.

toured Ireland, Northern Ireland as well as Finland, Newby incorporated a comparison between Finland's years of hunger and Ireland's Great Famine, pointing to shared experiences of receiving international charity, amongst others, by the Society of Friends, as well as the different political contexts in which both took place: a colonial territory governed from the centre of empire on the one hand and a devolved government in the colony's own capital on the other. As a result, the exhibition showed, 'Ireland's experience and memory of the famine are remarkably more national than those of Finland'.[31]

Contemporary literature has also suggested convergences between famine pasts. One such text is *For Freedom Alone* (2018), a novella by US author Lea Waite. It depicts how three siblings and their father Seumas Ross look for a new home in Edinburgh in late autumn 1846, after their eviction from their Highland home in Glencalvie. Like many other peasants, they have to 'leave' their 'land', because the landlords seek to replace agriculture by more profitable pasture: 'so they could fill Highland hills and glenns with fancy Cheviot sheep, and with red deer for English gentlemen to hunt'.[32] They arrive after a long journey on foot, and a period of severe destitution and hunger: Rab hopes to find 'food [...], thinking of his stomach, which had been empty so long'.[33] The city is already 'full of refugees from the Irish potato famine'.[34] Through the storyline that focuses on the friendship between 12-year-old Rab Ross and 9-year old Irish born Sully, the novella brings the legacies of the so-called Highland Clearances (1750–1860), and the

Highland Potato Famine (1846-50), and the widespread hunger and homelessness that ensued from them,[35] in dialogue with the Great Irish Famine and its diaspora. It is quite evident that Sully's family was badly afflicted by the Irish potato famine. Sully tells Rab that his 'family is from Ireland. The taters rotted and there was nothing left to eat there'. His mother died of fever, and his 'brother Patrick of the famine', while his father, having taken him to Edinburgh, became addicted to alcohol and abandoned Sully, who was forced to work as a chimney sweeper.[36]

The narratives of the Irish famine and Highland Clearances come together in the encounters between the two friends—a narrative intersection which is intensified by two narrative dimensions. First, this is the hunger and deprivation that both characters suffer in Edinburgh. Rab's family has hardly enough to eat and shares a cold, dark and ill-ventilated apartment with distant relatives. Sully, who succumbs to consumption as a result of his labour as a chimney sweeper, ends up slowly dying in his former employer's office, where Rab finds him 'in the rear of the shop, lying on a low pallet', 'in the office's shadows' so that it takes 'a moment' for Rab's 'eyes to adjust to the low light so he could see the boy'.[37]

This passage strongly resonates with the descriptions one finds in early accounts of the Irish Great Famine, which often portray famine victims as shrouded in darkness. For instance, in *The Widow O'Leary* (1847), the narrator visits the home of his former acquaintances, Jack and Mary O'Leary, and is shocked to witness the 'appearance of extreme poverty, disorder, and misery' that their house has attained since the outbreak of the blight.[38] Entering the dark cabin, the narrator can at first not 'distinguish' what kind of 'object' lies upon the bedstead, but, once accustomed to the darkness, perceives it to be 'a man, wasted to the greatest degree of emaciation, lying on a litter of straw, and covered only by a dirty ragged quilt'.[39]

The ways in which this extract from Wait's novella echoes early famine literature is endorsed by the emaciated state of Sully's body: 'Rab put his arm around the boy, whose bones he could feel through the thin fabric covering him'.[40] Second, Wait's narrative implies connections between the two experiences of dislocation that the two youngsters have experienced: both have lost their childhood home and share a dream of going to America, which only Rab manages to realize: as Sully tells Rab, 'You'll get to America with your family, and you'll take my dreams with you'.[41] Stating that '[m]emories are not owned by groups', and therefore do not run parallel with group boundaries, Michael Rothberg suggests that different sets of cultural memory exist 'in dynamic transfers'.[42] As memories overlap and become inscribed with other cultural recollections, an infinite, interactive space of transcultural recollection can come into existence. Wait's text stages such overlapping, multidirectional memories of eviction and famine from Scotland's and Ireland's colonial pasts.

These recent examples of comparative, transnational famine heritage bear witness to a growing awareness of analogous experiences of hunger in the past. This growing consciousness cannot only be explained by the increasing globalization through the media and migration but also by the expanding digitization of archives, newspapers and magazines. In fact, one may witness a transnational turn in famine heritage-making that can be connected to the general 'transcultural' trend in memory studies.[43] Two concrete examples illustrate this, which both concern a series of monuments that connect *lieux de mémoire* in the country of origin, where the famine took place, and in the diaspora. One example is the trilogy of bronze statues made by Rowan Gillespie, which connect the Custom House Quay in Dublin as the famine immigrants' point of departure with monuments at Toronto's Ireland Park, on Éireann Quay and Hobart's waterfront in Tasmania, former Van Diemen's Land. 'Famine' (1997) in Dublin represents evicted, starving peasants who have walked all the way to the emigrant vessel. 'Migrants' (2006) conveys the hope of the migrants—whose bronze images bear an exact likeness to the famishing throng in Dublin—as symbolized by the swollen belly of the expecting female passenger who has disembarked and the way in which one of the male figures stretches out his hands to the waterfront and the heart of the city.

While the monuments in Dublin and Toronto together constitute a narrative in a sense, 'Footsteps Towards Freedom' (2017) in Hobart (Tasmania, Australia) presents an alternative story related to Ireland's Great Famine. The four statues embody four convict women and serve to commemorate their plight:

> While many of these women left conditions of great poverty and, in Ireland, famine, on arrival they found themselves in an inhumane system where they were treated as little more than a commodity. Not only was their labour crucial to the fledgling colony, but they were considered breeding stock

reporter Dianne Snowden stated.[44] Although 'Footsteps towards Freedom' stands narratively more apart from the other two memorials, it further connects Ireland, once afflicted by the Great Famine, to two territories where some Famine Irish found new homes. The trilogy spans three continents and connects the legacies of three famine generation communities across the globe.

A similar dialogue between the homeland and various locations in diaspora exists in relation to the heritage of the Ukrainian famine. Petro Drozdovsky's iconic 'Bitter Memory of Childhood' (2008), the bronze image of a starving girl holding gleaned wheat which is integrated into the Holodomor Memorial in Kyiv, has its counterparts on several locations in Canada, a country which hosts a large Ukrainian diaspora. On 12 May 2015, a copy of 'made from the same cast as the one in Kyiv on the grounds of the National Holodomor Museum' was unveiled at the Saskatchewan Provincial Legislature in Regina.[45] A replica of also stands at the legislative building grounds in Manitoba—another site connected to law and justice, and perhaps a suitable location for that very reason: the five stalks of wheat symbolize 'the Soviet law that imposed death on anyone caught picking grain from collective farm fields'[46] and at the same time epitomize legalized human rights today. In that light, one could also see why a life-size statue after Drozdovsky's original found its place in Winnipeg's Canadian Museum for Human Rights (2016). More recently, a Toronto Holodomor memorial 'comprised of Ukrainian sculptor Petro Drozdovsky's iconic *Bitter Memory of Childhood* bronze monument, set on paving stones that suggest traditional embroidery' was revealed in 2018. Here the legacies of the Ukrainian famine are framed into a narrative of resilience and rebirth through the three millstone parkettes that are also present on site.[47]

All these sites in Canada and the monument near the Holodomor Museum in Kyiv geographically connect communities, forming a mnemonic network that transcends borders and reaches out to people of other descent as well. Moreover, the transnational heritage constellations in which these clusters of memorials are embedded and receive meaning suggest that monuments may be more 'portable' heritage than one would initially expect.[48] Photographs, illustrations and texts are even more transmissible heritage, especially in this digital age when virtual exhibitions and archives have the potential to make European famine legacies more accessible to broader audiences. The fact that these heritages of various European famines, separated by time and space, tap into very similar repertoires of representation, suggests the potential for further developing comparative approaches.

Can we speak of recurring transnational famine iconographies or narrative schemes? For this, we may take a comparative look at a set of images and texts concerning various European famines. Käte Kollwitz's charcoal sketch for an International Workers Aid Poster, 'Brot!' ('Bread', 1924) depicts a despairing mother struggling to divide a small piece of bread between her two begging children—an image which is not unlike Helmi Biese's illustration for Hilda Käkikoski's story '*Se Suuri Nälkävuosi*' ('The Great Hunger Year', 1902) which was published in the illustrated journal *Joulutervehdys* (*Christmas Greetings*).[49] Biese's drawing shows Koskela Kaisa and her children wandering by the roadside in quest for food, while she is unable to feed her infant, and has no drop of milk to offer to her famishing children. Both images portray mothers with averted and downcast faces, who are consumed by grief and anguish. These images related to post-WWI hunger in Germany, and the Finnish Hunger Years of 1866–67 are quite similar in testifying to the centrality of maternal figures to European famine iconographies.

What is more, plotlines focusing on infants and mothers, or parental figures, who are on the road, looking for food are very common in famine fiction. An example is Guus Luijters' Dutch Hunger Winter novel *De Hongergoochelaar* (2006), which is frequently read at secondary schools in the Netherlands. The novel tells the story of a former successful *varieté* artist Grote Mels, who takes in a young girl whom he encounters on the train and who refuses to give her name and whereabouts. As the narrate unfolds, several clues are given that the girl—whom he names Sientje—is in fact Jewish and has escaped Nazi deportation by fleeing Amsterdam.

Initially, Grote Mels can supply abundant food for the girl. The man has performed as an illusionist, and he seems able to magically conjure up the best of food, such as white bread, bacon and eggs. As of the autumn of 1944, when fuel is no longer available and hardly any food can be obtained, Grote Mels and Sientje have become destitute: they have to walk very long distances through heavy snow and frost in order to obtain something edible, in exchange for clothes. They only have a watery beet soup at their disposal, and we can read that their food supplies are decreasing by the day, while they suffer from physical weakness and constant famine: '*Sientje bleef in bed. Ze hadden de hele dag honger*' (Sientje stayed in bed. They suffered from hunger all day, translation mine).[50]

In describing the main characters' loss of the abundance of food they once had, Luijters' novel is similar to Irish famine narratives such as Mrs Hoare's 'Little Mary'. In this tale from *Shamrock Leaves* (1851), the protagonist's stepmother was once able to successfully grow 'cabbages, parsnips, and onions in it; and, to be sure, she got a fine crop out of it, enough to make us many a nice supper of vegetables stewed with pepper, and a small taste of bacon or a red herring'. This plenitude contrasts greatly with the destitution the family suffered during the famine so that the mother has become 'faint and weary' due to lack of food.[51] As becomes clear from these examples, European famine legacies tend to resort to similar narrative scripts in giving meaning to the painful past. As such, one can also speak of transnational famine legacies that are rooted in shared iconographies and narrative scripts.

Challenges for the future: absence and affect

The strong analogies between legacies of European famines in terms of themes, tropes and narratives call for future heritage projects that will take up the challenge of recollecting hunger comparatively. Creating a repository or virtual exhibition of famine heritage across Europe may therefore be a feasible manner to realize such a transnational vantage point on the hunger crises that were faced by Europe, and beyond.[52] At the same time, a purely digital format may make it difficult to engage today's citizens emotionally. In *Mediating Memory in the Museum* (2013), Silke Arnold-de Simine argues persuasively that

> the museum's representation of the past is intended to generate a sense of belonging which requires emotional investment and identification, sometimes to the extent that it generates the imaginative living through events in order to develop strong forms of affective engagement.[53]

Often, displaying artefacts is chosen as a method to draw audiences into distant pasts. This is what the Amsterdam-based Dutch Resistance Museum does in its renewed exhibition spaces, which opened in December 2022. These tell the story about the Hunger Winter during the Second World War through, amongst others, displayed containers of surrogate foods, such as sugar beets and tulip bulbs, as well as a yellow sign outlawing logging despite fuel rationing. Exhibiting these material objects behind railings furthermore adds to the sensation of restricted access to food and heat sources that marked the Hunger Winter.

Most museums, however, experience obstacles in representing European famine pasts due to the overall absence of material objects related to these hunger crises.[54] One strategy used by famine heritage makers to make the past come to life nonetheless is re-enactment. The website of the Dutch Resistance Museum in Amsterdam, for instance, incorporates the film *Naar de Boeren* ('To the Farmers', 2014) as part of a virtual exhibition about the children's transports during the Hunger Winter. While this film contains some rare original footage and interviews with people who as children were evacuated to the north and taken in by farmers, it also includes short dramatized clips re-enacting the evacuations.[55]

In her work on the Scottish Highland Clearances, Laurence Gouriévidis describes how museums increasingly convey dramatized experiences in the form of 'media-oriented displays' in order to trigger 'vicarious empathy' with past victims amongst audiences and to make up for the absence of material artefacts.[56] This appeal to 'emotionalism verging on the dramatic and sensational for visitors inured to television image' in the form of dramatic spectacle is a guiding principle in the representation of the Irish Famine past at the Doagh Famine village on the Inishowen peninsula. Amongst original thatched cabins which were inhabited until 1983, one can find tableaux featuring life-size manikins that express various dimensions of famine suffering: a burial of famished corpses, a mother and child looking for shelter near a scalp as well as a dramatic eviction scene representing a helpless family facing bailiffs holding out a battering ram. These staged scenes are accompanied by plates with some basic information about the practice of ejectments, emigration and estimated numbers of famine victims, but above all by plaques which voice emotive appeals to the visitors: 'If you woke up one morning, healthy with no illnesses, then you are not one of the million people who won't live to see next week'. The exhibits aim for experience rather than detailed historical data, for the interpretive signs provide minimal information about the famine past, while some are clearly aimed at generating awareness of present destitution and inequalities, especially those in the global south.

At the same time, the staged displays (Figure 10.3) hark back directly to a repertoire of famine images that visitors could already be familiar with. The displayed scene of bodies put on a cart is rooted in media representations of the famine era itself, such as Frederick James Smyth's 'Funeral in Skibbereen' from the *Illustrated London News* of 30 January 1847. The tableau of the famishing mother and child crouched near a scalp similarly reverberates with images from the *Illustrated London News*, such as 'Scalp of Brian O'Connor', published on 22 December 1849, and 'Life in a Scalp', published on 29 December 1849, to go with the article 'Conditions of Ireland: Illustrations of the New Poor Law'. The agonized mother figure in the museum display can furthermore be viewed as fitting in the earlier cited longstanding tradition of feminized images of famine suffering.[57] One such image is, for example, James Mahoney's 'Bridget O'Donnell and Her Children', printed in *Illustrated London News* on 22 February 1849, which depicts the emaciated figures of a mother and two children and is often interpreted as symptomatic of the tendency to focus on female characters—especially mothers—in early representations of the famine.

This strategy of dramatization to evoke affect may shift the balance away from educating visitors on the basis of historical data; at the same time, its resonance with past iconographies firmly situates these spectacles in the famine years themselves. What we may witness in the Doagh Famine village is what Astrid Erll would call 'transmedial remembrance',[58] in that

Figure 10.3 Doagh famine village.

Source: Photograph by the author.

images from one medium—visual art—are remembered through staged spectacle in a modern museum setting which moreover recontextualizes these scenes into references to present-day hunger.

A second strategy that museums use to overcome the lack of historical artefacts related to sustenance crises is the insertion of objects not dating from the famine eras but from slightly earlier or from later dates into famine narratives. This is what Andrew Newby did in curating the earlier mentioned exhibition 'Nälkä!': he chose to exhibit 'farm implements' used in the Finnish countryside during the larger nineteenth century as the few tangible objects that would bring Finland's famine past to life to today's visitors, as well as samples of newly baked pine or bark bread which Newby commissioned from 'a lady in the countryside' as a way to represent emergency food.[59] Likewise, the Museum of Country Life in Turlough presents turf and potato baskets as well as fishing nets to tell the story of rural Ireland in the 1840s. As Liam Doherty, director of the Irish Folklife Division, National Museum of Ireland, recently observed, these tangible objects are important because 'tables and tabulations' may enhance 'our understanding, but our empathy perhaps less so'. 'Numbers are bleak, chilling and difficult from which to elicit an appropriate emotional response', he stated.[60]

A risk of this approach, however, is losing historical accuracy. The reinterpretation of the Meenagarragh Cottage at the Ulster American Folk Park, built forty years after the famine but exhibited as a typical famine cottage, is a case in point. As this example of Meenagarragh's Cottier's House illustrates, famine heritage can take on the form of what Ann Rigney would call 'portable monuments', that is, transportable sites of memory.[61] The original cottage, representative of the single-room cabin typical for the era predating and during the famine, built in the 1880s 'in the townland of Meenagarragh, near to Plumbridge in County Tyrone' was 'dismantled and moved to the Folk Museum in 1974',[62] where it survives as a rare example of living conditions amongst the landless cottiers in the longer nineteenth century. Interestingly, built forty years after the famine, at the folk park the cottage is now framed in the context of the Great Famine, demonstrating that in heritage projects, different episodes of rural pasts are often represented as palimpsestic and heterochronic, in that demarcations between different decades become blurred.

A different, and quite effective, way of coping with the relative lack of material artefacts on famines employed by heritage institutes is the installation of newly created artworks which stress the absence and death that surround famine pasts. As Wiktoria Kudela-Świątek contends, the design of the new building of the Holodomor Genocide Museum in Kyiv, which is currently still under construction due to Russia's invasion, is meant to express the mass mortality which the famine caused, as well as to convey the hitherto often undisclosed truths about the brutalities suffered by Ukrainian famine victims, from the hand of the Stalinist regime. The interplay between light and darkness, she explains, plays a significant role in these museum spaces. Citing the architect Mirosław Nizio, Kudela-Świątek argues that the concept of the exhibition symbolizes the long-repressed, dark horrors of the crimes committed against the Ukrainian people during the Holodomor, as well as the resilience of the Ukrainians who feel strengthened by bringing to light this famine past. The museum itinerary takes visitors from brightly illuminated galleries down into a deepening darkness in the central galleries, which portray Holodomor atrocities; and then back into more illuminated spaces which are centred around eye-witness accounts of the famine which bring the past to light, as well as around global memory cultures of Holodomor today.[63]

A similar case study which involves the use of aesthetics to make up for the absence of historical artefacts, as well as to express death and loss effectively, is the installation '1845: Memento Mori' (2021) by Seattle-based Irish artist Paula Stokes (Figure 10.4). This installation, which consists of '1,845 handblown glass potatoes'[64] and which references the first year of blight and starvation, was displayed at four heritage sites which address the Great Famine: Strokestown Park in Co. Roscommon (May 2021), Johnstown Castle in Co. Wexford (July 2021), the Ulster American Folk Park in Co. Tyrone, Northern Ireland (September 2021) and Turlough Park in Co. Mayo (November 2021).[65] By combining techniques such as hand blowing and glass blasting, Stokes gave a 'white ghostly appearance to the potatoes' which, in her view, conveys 'the vulnerability and [...] the resilience of those who died and those who survived the famine'.[66] The glass potatoes are, moreover, presented in the form of a mound at the locations where they were displayed.

Figure 10.4 Paula Stokes: '1845: Memento Mori' (2021). Courtesy of Irish Heritage Trust.

This glass potatoes installation is interesting in various respects. First, the glass potatoes themselves express both a sense of materiality and the elusiveness of the famine past, in the absence of artefacts. The Great Famine is frequently identified with spectrality in nineteenth-century cultural expressions, namely as 'the "living dead", the ghastly, starving bodies of the Famine-stricken; figuratively, as the spirits of the deceased victims who claim retribution as well as remembrance in a post-Famine Ireland; and, third, as emblems of cultural memory itself'.[67] The latter can be interpreted as the haunting memories of the famine past, as well as the traces of famine histories that are, for instance, embodied by ruins of cottages abandoned during the famine and destroyed during evictions and that signify both presence and absence. The glass potatoes can be interpreted through this cultural repertoire of spectrality, in that they express their centrality to Ireland's rural past as well as their absence as food when struck by the blight.

Furthermore, they render a sense of concreteness that can evoke empathy when there is little material heritage from the era itself. As artist Stokes herself contends, the installation 'might elicit compassion'. Liam Corry, Curator of Emigration at Ulster American Folk Park, said they were 'delighted to host such a tangible symbol of the Irish Potato Famine'.[68] The installation is also adaptable to different contexts of presentation, and in the case of the Ulster American Folk Park, it was displayed in the single-room cabin, in such a way that the cottage was associated even more strongly with famine history. As Emily Mark-FitzGerald has noted, famine memorials often rely on figurative images that stem from the famine period itself, as it enables later generations to connect better to the famine past.[69] The combination of the cottage setting and the glass potatoes indeed offers a recognizable context to visitors, which moreover adds to a sense of tangibility of the famine past.

Conclusion

In her reflections on canon and heritage formation, Aleida Assmann distinguishes between active and passive forgetting. Certain pasts or certain dimensions of pasts may have been pushed into the realm of oblivion because they are inconvenient for present political agendas or regimes and have been actively forgotten through forms of repression. Yet pasts may also have unintentionally fallen 'out of frames of attention' through passive forgetting.[70] With regard to European famine pasts, active forgetting of hunger crises appears to have taken place during the Soviet regime (the Holodomor) and in Francoist Spain and its aftermath (the *años del hambre*), and processes of independence and political democratization have led to a recuperation of famine pasts as accessible memory. Political agendas furthermore frame and reframe European famine pasts: this becomes clear from, amongst others, the recent global engagements with Holodomor under the influence of Russia's aggressive invasion of Ukraine, as well as the gradual integration of the Finnish Hunger Years into national narratives. Heritage-making plays a central role in these processes of revisiting and reassessing European famine pasts, even if this brings along challenges. 'There is a fine line', Arnold-de Simine observes,

> between the historian's investment in the authentic object which can provide a wealth of information to the initiated and the fetishist belief that an object has somehow soaked up the events in which it has played a role and allows a spectator to feel that they are in the presence of the past.[71]

As we have seen, current heritage practices regarding European famines are marked by tensions between the absence of artefacts on the one hand and the need to bring the past to life to present and future generations on the other. However, dramatizing past events or telling the past through merely presenting material objects are less effective methods of transmitting heritage if not accompanied by proper historicization and contextualization.

International collaboration between famine heritage makers and academics will open up unique opportunities for combining impact with knowledge transfer and also for uncovering the transnational dimensions of European famine legacies, which intersect in manifold ways in today's reinterpretations of these hunger crises. Heritages of hunger presently have come to matter even more, through the recovery of previously hidden voices or objects, but also in relation to societal issues. How to engage especially younger audiences with these famine pasts? How to balance engagement and information, but also how to involve new European citizens—migrants and refugees—who may have experienced deprivation and hunger themselves? These important questions for future agendas of conserving, interpreting and disseminating European famine pasts will benefit from global exchanges of research data, learning strategies and curating practices.

Notes

1 Daniel Boffey, 'Russia's Black Sea Blockade Pushing Millions towards Famine, G7 says', *The Guardian*, 14 May 2022, www.theguardian.com/world/2022/may/14/ukraine-says-russian-forces-withdrawing-kharkiv, last accessed 7 Jan. 2024.

2 'On Holodomor Remembrance Day, Russia Unleashes Largest Drone Attack on Ukraine', *RadioFreeEurope*, 25 Nov. 2023, www.rferl.org/amp/ukraine-drone-strikes-holodomor-day/32699366.html, last accessed 8 Jan. 2024.

3 https://twitter.com/MichealMartinTD/status/1544653321939697668, last accessed 7 Jan. 2024.

4 Andreas Huyssen, *Present Pasts: Urban Palimpsests and the Politics of Memory* (Stanford, CA: Stanford UP, 2003), 15.
5 Michael Rothberg, *Multidirectional Memory* (Stanford: Stanford University Press, 2009), 19.
6 Laurence Gouriévidis, *The Dynamics of Heritage: History, Memory, and the Highland Clearances* (Farnham: Ashgate, 2010), 98.
7 Astrid Erll, 'From "District Six" to District 9 and Back: The Plurimedial Production of Travelling Schemata', in Chiara de Cesari and Ann Rigney, eds, *Transnational Memory: Circulation, Articulation, Scales* (Berlin/New York: De Gruyter, 2014), 29.
8 See also Marguérite Corporaal and Ingrid de Zwarte, 'Introduction: Famines and the Making of Heritage', in Marguérite Corporaal and Ingrid de Zwarte, eds, *Famines and the Making of Heritage* (London: Routledge, 2024), 1–3.
9 Michael D. Higgins, 'Speech by President Michael D. Higgins at the 2023 National Famine Commemoration', https://president.ie/en/media-library/speeches/speech-by-president-michael-d-higgins-at-the-2023-national-famine-commemoration, last accessed 7 Jan. 2024.
10 See www.bnnvara.nl/joop/artikelen/kritiek-op-borstklopperij-boeren-over-eigen-heldenrol-in-hongerwinter, last accessed 13 Sep. 2022.
11 'M'n linnengoed, al mijn tafelzilver, m'n vloerkleed, alles heb ik ingeruild voor eten. Op den duur wilden de boeren geen linnengoed meer. Sommigen hadden zelfs een bordje op hun deur: "Geen linnengoed meer"' ('My linen, all my table silver, my carpet, I have bartered everything for food. However, in the longer run the farmers would no longer trade these goods, and some even had a note on their door, stating "no more linen"'.) See www.verzetsmuseum.org/nl/kennisbank/hongerwinter, last accessed 13 Sep. 2022.
12 For the term, see James V. Wertsch, *Voices of Collective Remembering* (New York: Cambridge University Press, 2002), 57.
13 Jefferson A. Singer and Martin A. Conway, 'Should We Forget Forgetting', *Memory Studies*, 1, no. 3 (2018): 280.
14 See Andrew G. Newby and Eliza Krataari, 'Memory of the Great Hunger Years Revisited: Finland's 1860s Famine Memorials, Mass Graves and a Commemorative Craft Initiative', *Thanatos*, 7, no. 2 (2018): 96.
15 Newby and Krataari, 'Memory of the Great Hunger Years Revisited', 99.
16 See Andrew G. Newby, 'Finland's "Great Hunger Years" Memorials', https://katovuodet1860.wordpress.com/, last accessed 14 Sep. 2022. For further reading, see Andrew G. Newby, 'Finland's "Great Hunger Years" Memorials: A Sesquicentennial Report', *COLLeGIUM: Studies across Disciplines in the Humanities and Social Sciences* 22 (2017): 173–214. And Charley Boerman, 'Famine Landscapes: Finland's "Skeleton Track" in Memorials and Museums', in Marguérite Corporaal and Ingrid de Zwarte, eds, *Famines and the Making of Heritage* (London: Routledge, 2024a), 183–203.
17 See www.tyovaenmuseo.fi/nayttelyt/yhteisvoimin/, last accessed 7 Jan. 2024.
18 Miguel Ángel del Arco Blanco and Deborah Madden, 'Spain's "Hunger Years": A Lack of Musealisation of a Traumatic Past', in Marguérite Corporaal and Ingrid de Zwarte, eds, *Famines and the Making of Heritage* (London: Routledge, 2024), 204–226.
19 Many thanks to Gloria Román Ruiz for sharing the panels with me.
20 See https://glasgow.gov.uk/article/3496/Dedication-of-Glasgow-s-Irish-Highland-Famine-Memorialnd Famine Memorial - Glasgow City Council, last consulted on 2 Sep. 2022.
21 Laurence Gouriévidis, 'Commemorating Irish and Scottish Famine Migrants in Glasgow: Migration, Community Memories and the Social Uses of Heritage', *History and Memory*, 35, no. 2 (2023): 144.
22 See Kevin McKenna, 'Glasgow Is in Denial over Monument to Great Famine', *The Guardian*, 24 Sep. 2017, www.theguardian.com/commentisfree/2017/sep/24/glasgow-is-in-denial-over-monument-to-great-famine, last accessed 2 Sep. 2022.
23 Rothberg, *Multidirectional Memory*, 9.
24 For the term, see Pierre Nora, 'Between Memory and History: Les Lieux de Mémoire', *Representations*, 26 (1989): 7–25.

25 Chihei Suzuki, 'Sustainable Heritage through a Sustainable Community', in Kalliopi Fouseki et al. eds, *Routledge Handbook of Sustainable Heritage* (New York: Routledge, 2023), 164.
26 Brian Hoban, 'The Famine and Swinford Workhouse in Co. Mayo', www.mayo-ireland.ie/en/towns-villages/swinford/history/famine-and-swinford-workhouse.html, accessed 2 Sep. 2022.
27 Michael Davitt referred to the site in a speech before The Times-Parnell Commission in October 1889. See Brian Hoban, 'The Famine and Swinford Workhouse in Co. Mayo', www.mayo-ireland.ie/en/towns-villages/swinford/history/famine-and-swinford-workhouse.html, last consulted 5 Jan. 2024.
28 Astrid Erll, 'Foreword', in Andrea Hajek et al., eds, *Memory in a Mediated World: Remembrance and Reconstruction* (Basingstoke: Palgrave, 2016), x.
29 For the term coined by Mikhail Bakhtin, see, amongst others, Michael Holquist, *Dialogism: Bakhtin and His World* (London: Routledge, 1990), 107–10.
30 Michel Foucault, 'Of Other Spaces', *Diacritics*, 16 (1986): 26.
31 See https://finlandabroad.fi/web/irl/current-affairs/-/asset_publisher/h5w4iTUJhNne/content/nayttely-suomen-suurista-nalkavuosista-esilla-strokestownissa/384951, last accessed 5 Jan. 2024.
32 Lea Wait, *For Freedom Alone* (Edgecomb, Maine: Sheepscott River Press, 2018), unnumbered.
33 Wait, *For Freedom Alone*.
34 Wait, *For Freedom Alone*, blurb on the back cover.
35 See William Pulteney Allison, *Observations on the Famine of 1846–7, in the Highlands of Scotland and in Ireland* (Edinburgh and London: William Blackwood & Sons, 1847). See also Thomas M. Devine, *The Great Highland Famine* (Edinburgh: John Donald, 1988).
36 Wait, *For Freedom Alone*, 11.
37 Wait, *For Freedom Alone*, 56.
38 *The Widow O'Leary: A Story of the Present Famine* (Cork: G. Nash, 1847), 10.
39 *The Widow O'Leary*, 11–12.
40 Wait, *For Freedom Alone*, 76.
41 Wait, *For Freedom Alone*, 95.
42 Rothberg, *Multidirectional Memory*, 5.
43 See Lucy Bond and Jessica Rapson, 'Introduction', in Lucy Bond and Jessica Rapson, eds, *The Transcultural Turn: Interrogating Memory Between and Beyond Borders* (Berlin: De Gruyter, 2014), 1–26.
44 See Dianne Snowden, 'Shaping History: Rowan Gillespie's Statues', *FortySouth*, 29 Jul. 2017, www.fortysouth.com.au/people/shaping-history-rowan-gillespies-statues?amp=1, last accessed 14 Sep. 2022.
45 'Holodomor monument unveiled in Saskatchewan', *The Ukrainian Weekly*, 29 Jul. 2015, www.ukrweekly.com/uwwp/holodomor-monument-unveiled-in-saskatchewan/, last accessed 15 Sep. 2022.
46 'Manitoba Commemorates Holodomor with Ukrainian Community', 29 Nov. 2019, https://news.gov.mb.ca/news/index.html?item=46277&posted=2019-11-21, last accessed 15 Sep. 2022.
47 https://education.holodomor.ca/introduction/holodomor-monuments/, last accessed 16 Sep. 2022. See also Charley Boerman, Framing Famines: Memory, Museums, and Visual Culture, Unpublished PhD Diss. Radboud University Nijmegen, 2024b.
48 For the term, see Ann Rigney, 'Portable Monuments: Literature, Cultural Memory, and the Case of Jeanie Deans', *Poetics Today*, 25, no. 2 (2004): 361–96.
49 For Kollwitz's artwork, see wellesley.edu/davismuseum/friends-of-art/foa-artwork-of-the-month/node/194986. For Biese's illustration, see Andrew Newby's discussion on https://katovuodet1860.wordpress.com/tag/helmi/, last accessed 5 Jan. 2024.
50 Guus Luijters, *De Hongergoochelaar* (Amsterdam: Nieuw Amsterdam Uitgevers, 2006), 98.
51 Mrs Hoare, 'Little Mary', in *Shamrock Leaves; or Tales and Sketches from Ireland* (Dublin and London: J. M'Glashan, Patrick and Oakey, 1851), 82, 90.
52 The Heritages of Hunger project (PI Corporaal; funded by Dutch research council NWO, NWA 1160.18.197) is currenty developing such an educational repository. See hunger.rich.ru.nl. Moreover, under the curatorship of Charley Boerman and in collaboration with HOAX, the project team has created a digital exhibition (2024) that brings together a wide range of famine legacies. See www.heritagesofhunger.org.

53 Silke Arnold-de Simine, *Mediating Memory in the Museum: Trauma, Empathy, Nostalgia* (New York: Palgrave, 2013), 12.
54 See Marguérite Corporaal and Ingrid de Zwarte, 'Heritages of Hunger: European Famine legacies in Current Academic Debates', *International Journal of Heritage Studies* 28, no. 1 (2022): 30–43.
55 See www.verzetsmuseum.org/nl/kennisbank/introductie-4, last consulted 4 Jan. 2024.
56 Gouriévidis, *The Dynamics of Heritage*, 132, 98.
57 Margaret Kelleher, *The Feminization of Famine* (Durham, NC: Duke UP, 1997), 6.
58 Erll, 'From "District Six" to District 9 and Back', 29–50.
59 Niamh Loftus, 'Andrew Newby: Interview', www.rosfm.ie/dr-andrew-newby-interview/, last accessed 14 Sep. 2022.
60 www.museum.ie/en-IE/Museums/Country-Life/Exhibitions/Previous-Exhibitions/1845-Memento-Mori-by-Paula-Stokes, last consulted 11 June 2022.
61 Rigney, 'Portable Monuments', 362.
62 www.nmni.com/our-museums/Ulster-Folk-Museum/Things-to-see/Meenagarraghs-cottiers-house.aspx, last consulted 11 June 2022.
63 For further reading, see Wiktoria Kudela-Świątek, 'Holodomor Monuments on the Battlefield: Monuments and Memorials of the Great Famine 1932–1933 in Post-Maidan Ukraine', in Marguérite Corporaal and Ingrid de Zwarte, eds, *Famines and the Making of Heritage* (London: Routledge, 2024), 134-159.
64 www.tyronecon.co.uk/news/2021/09/21/gallery/new-famine-exhibition-featuring-1-845-glass-potatoes-arrives-at-ulster-american-folk-park-18534/, accessed 3 Jun. 2022.
65 www.1845mementomori.com/, accessed 3 Jun. 2022.
66 https://visitwaterford.com/vw_news/irish-potato-famine-exhibition/, accessed 7 Jun. 2022.
67 Marguérite Corporaal, *Relocated Memories: The Great Famine in Irish and Diaspora Fiction, 1846–1870* (Syracuse, NY: Syracuse UP, 2017), 108.
68 www.irishnews.com/news/northernirelandnews/2021/08/27/news/memorial-to-famine-to-arrive-at-ulster-american-folk-park-2429053/, accessed 3 Jun. 2022.
69 Emily Mark-FitzGerald, *Commemorating the Irish Famine: Memory and the Monument* (Liverpool: Liverpool UP, 2013), 102.
70 Aleida Assmann, 'Canon and Archive', in Astrid Erll and Ansgar Nünning, eds, *A Companion to Cultural Memory Studies* (Berlin: Walter de Gruyter, 2008), 97–98.
71 Arnold-de Simine, *Mediating Memory in the Museum*, 84.

References

Allison, William Pulteney. *Observations on the Famine of 1846–7, in the Highlands of Scotland and in Ireland.* Edinburgh and London: William Blackwood & Sons, 1847.

Arnold-de Simine, Silke. *Mediating Memory in the Museum: Trauma, Empathy, Nostalgia.* New York: Palgrave, 2013.

Assmann, Aleida. 'Canon and Archive', in Astrid Erll and Ansgar Nünning, eds., *A Companion to Cultural Memory Studies*, 97–108. Berlin: Walter de Gruyter, 2008.

Boerman, Charley. 'Famine Landscapes: Finland's "Skeleton Track" in Memorials and Museums', in Marguérite Corporaal and Ingrid de Zwarte, eds., *Famines and the Making of Heritage*, 183–203. London: Routledge, 2024a.

Boerman, Charley. Framing Famines: Memory, Museums, and Visual Culture. Unpublished PhD Diss. Radboud University Nijmegen, 2024b.

Boffey, Daniel. 'Russia's Black Sea Blockade Pushing Millions towards Famine, G7 Says'. *The Guardian*, 14 May 2022. www.theguardian.com/world/2022/may/14/ukraine-says-russian-forces-withdrawing-kharkiv.

Bond, Lucy and Jessica Rapson. 'Introduction', in Lucy Bond and Jessica Rapson, eds., *The Transcultural Turn: Interrogating Memory between and Beyond Borders*, 1–26. Berlin: De Gruyter, 2014.

Corporaal, Marguérite. *Relocated Memories: The Great Famine in Irish and Diaspora Fiction, 1846–1870.* Syracuse, NY: Syracuse UP, 2017.

Corporaal, Marguérite and Ingrid de Zwarte. 'Heritages of Hunger: European Famine Legacies in Current Academic Debates'. *International Journal of Heritage Studies* 28, no. 1 (2022): 30–43.

Corporaal, Marguérite and Ingrid de Zwarte. 'Introduction: Famines and the Making of Heritage', in Marguérite Corporaal and Ingrid de Zwarte, eds., *Famines and the Making of Heritage*, 1–18. London: Routledge, 2024.

'Dedication of Glasgow's Famine Memorial'. https://glasgow.gov.uk/article/3496/Dedication-of-Glasgow-s-Irish-Highland-Famine-Memorial

Del Arco Blanco, Miguel Ángel and Deborah Madden. 'Spain's "Hunger Years": A Lack of Musealisation of a Traumatic Past', in Marguérite Corporaal and Ingrid de Zwarte, eds, *Famines and the Making of Heritage*, 204–226. London: Routledge, 2024.

Devine, Thomas M. *The Great Highland Famine*. Edinburgh: John Donald, 1988.

Erll, Astrid. 'From "District Six" to District 9 and Back: The Plurimedial Production of Travelling Schemata', in Chiara de Cesari and Ann Rigney, eds, *Transnational Memory: Circulation, Articulation, Scales*, 29–50. Berlin/New York: de Gruyter 2014.

Erll, Astrid. 'Foreword', in Andrea Hajek et al., eds, *Memory in a Mediated World: Remembrance and Reconstruction*, x–xii. Basingstoke: Palgrave, 2016.

'Finlanda Abroad'. https://finlandabroad.fi/web/irl/current-affairs/-/asset_publisher/h5w4iTUJhNne/content/nayttely-suomen-suurista-nalkavuosista-esilla-strokestownissa/384951.

Foucault, Michel. 'Of Other Spaces: Utopias and Heterotopias'. Trans. Jay Miskowiec. *Diacritics* 16 (1986): 22–27.

'Glass Famine Memorial Wexford'. 2021. https://visitwaterford.com/vw_news/irish-potato-famine-exhibition/

Gouriévidis, Laurence. *The Dynamics of Heritage: History, Memory and the Highland Clearances*. Farnham: Ashgate, 2010.

Gouriévidis, Laurence. 'Commemorating Irish and Scottish Famine Migrants in Glasgow: Migration, Community Memories and the Social Uses of Heritage'. *History and Memory*, 35, no. 2 (2023): 143–68.

Higgins, Michael D. 'Speech by President Michael D. Higgins at the 2023 National Famine Commemoration'. 21 May 2023. https://president.ie/en/media-library/speeches/speech-by-president-michael-d-higgins-at-the-2023-national-famine-commemoration.

Hoare, Mrs. 'Little Mary', in *Shamrock Leaves; or Tales and Sketches from Ireland*, 80–94. Dublin and London: J. M'Glashan, Patrick and Oakey, 1851.

Hoban, Brian. 'The Famine and Swinford Workhouse in Co. Mayo'. www.mayo-ireland.ie/en/towns-villages/swinford/history/famine-and-swinford-workhouse.html

'Holodomor monument unveiled in Saskatchewan', *The Ukrainian Weekly*. 29 Jul. 2015. www.ukrweekly.com/uwwp/holodomor-monument-unveiled-in-saskatchewan/.

Holquist, Michael. *Dialogism: Bakhtin and His World*. London: Routledge, 1990.

'Hongerwinter'. www.verzetsmuseum.org/nl/kennisbank/hongerwinter.

HREC Education. 'Holodomor Monuments in Canada'. https://education.holodomor.ca/introduction/holodomor-monuments/.

Huyssen, Andreas. *Present Pasts: Urban Palimpsests and the Politics of Memory*. Stanford, CA: Stanford UP, 2003.

'Käte Kollwitz, Brot! (Bread!)'. www.wellesley.edu/davismuseum/friends-of-art/foa-artwork-of-the-month/node/194986.

Kelleher, Margaret. *The Feminization of Famine*. Durham, NC: Duke UP, 1997.

'Kinderevacuaties tijdens de Hongerwinter'. www.verzetsmuseum.org/nl/kennisbank/introductie-4.

'Kritiek op Borstklopperij Boeren over Eigen Heldenrol in Hongerwinter'. 2019. www.bnnvara.nl/joop/artikelen/kritiek-op-borstklopperij-boeren-over-eigen-heldenrol-in-hongerwinter

Kudela- Świątek, Wiktoria. 'Holodomor Monuments on the Battlefield: Monuments and Memorials of the Great Famine 1932–1933 in Post-Maidan Ukraine', in Marguérite Corporaal and Ingrid de Zwarte, eds, *Famines and the Making of Heritage*, 134–159. London: Routledge, 2024.

Loftus, Niamh. 'Andrew Newby: Interview'. www.rosfm.ie/dr-andrew-newby-interview/.

Luijters, Guus. *De Hongergoochelaar*. Amsterdam: Nieuw Amsterdam Uitgevers, 2006.

'Manitoba Commemorates Holodomor with Ukrainian Community'. 21 Nov. 2019. https://news.gov.mb.ca/news/index.html?item=46277&posted=2019-11-21

Mark-FitzGerald, Emily. *Commemorating the Irish Famine: Memory and the Monument.* Liverpool: Liverpool University Press, 2013.

McKenna, Kevin. 'Glasgow Is in Denial over Monument to Great Famine'. *The Guardian.* 24 Sep. 2017. www.theguardian.com/commentisfree/2017/sep/24/glasgow-is-in-denial-over-monument-to-great-famine,

'Meenagarragh's Cottiers House'. 2018. www.nmni.com/our-museums/Ulster-Folk-Museum/Things-to-see/Meenagarraghs-cottiers-house.aspx.

'Memento Mori by Paula Stokes'. 2021. www.museum.ie/en-IE/Museums/Country-Life/Exhibitions/Previous-Exhibitions/1845-Memento-Mori-by-Paula-Stokes

'New Famine Exhibition Arrives at Ulster-American Folk Park'. 21 Sep. 2021. www.tyronecon.co.uk/news/2021/09/21/gallery/new-famine-exhibition-featuring-1-845-glass-potatoes-arrives-at-ulster-american-folk-park-18534

Newby, Andrew. 'Katovuodet 1860'. https://katovuodet1860.wordpress.com.

Newby, Andrew. 'Finland's "Great Hunger Years" Memorials: A Sesquicentennial Report'. *COLLeGIUM: Studies across Disciplines in the Humanities and Social Sciences* 22 (2017): 173–214.

Newby, Andrew G. and Eliza Krataari. 'Memory of the Great Hunger Years Revisited: Finland's 1860s Famine Memorials, Mass Graves and a Commemorative Craft Initiative'. *Thanatos*, 7, no. 2 (2018): 90–126.

Nora, Pierre. 'Between Memory and History: Les Lieux de Mémoire'. *Representations*, 26 (1989): 7–25.

'On Holodomor Remembrance Day, Russia Unleashes Largest Drone Attack on Ukraine'. *RadioFreeEurope*, 25 Nov. 2023. www.rferl.org/amp/ukraine-drone-strikes-holodomor-day/32699366.html.

'Memorial to Famine to Arrive at Ulster-American Folk Park'. 27 Aug. 2021. www.irishnews.com/news/northernirelandnews/2021/08/27/news/memorial-to-famine-to-arrive-at-ulster-american-folk-park-2429053/Newry Democrat (6 Sep. 2021).

Rigney, Ann. 'Portable Monuments: Literature, Cultural Memory, and the Case of Jeanie Deans'. *Poetics Today*, 25, no. 2 (2004): 361–96.

Rothberg, Michael. *Multidirectional Memory*. Stanford: Stanford University Press, 2009.

Singer, Jefferson A. and Martin A. Conway. 'Should We Forget Forgetting'. *Memory Studies*, 1, no. 3 (2018): 279–85.

Snowden, Dianne. 'Shaping History: Rowan Gillespie's Statues'. *FortySouth*, 29 Jul. 2017, www.fortysouth.com.au/people/shaping-history-rowan-gillespies-statues?amp=1.

Suzuki, Chihei. 'Sustainable Heritage through a Sustainable Community', in Kalliopi Fouseki et al., eds, *Routledge Handbook of Sustainable Heritage*, 154–66. New York: Routledge, 2023.

The Widow O'Leary: A Story of the Present Famine. Cork: G. Nash, 1847. https://twitter.com/MichealMartinTD/status/1544653321939697668.

Wait, Lea. *For Freedom Alone*. Edgecomb, Maine: Sheepscott River Press, 2018.

Wertsch, James V. *Voices of Collective Remembering*. New York: Cambridge University Press, 2002.

'Yhteisvoimin'. 2023. www.tyovaenmuseo.fi/nayttelyt/yhteisvoimin/.

Afterword

Famines and power, past and present

Alex de Waal

Introduction

The Russian invasion of Ukraine, bringing in its wake the weaponization of food and the use of starvation as a military tactic, has vividly reminded Ukrainians—and Europeans more widely—of their continent's history of man-made famines. In the twentieth century, famines killed more Europeans than Africans.[1] But after the Second World War (WWII), for two generations of Europeans, famine was something that happened elsewhere. Ten years ago, a Google image search for the terms 'famine' or 'starvation' yielded mostly pictures of stick-thin African children, dry landscapes with withered crops, along with a smattering of 1840s engravings of Ireland and staged photographs of emaciated Indians from what Mike Davis has called 'Late Victorian Holocausts.'[2] Europe's recent memories of mass starvation have been largely buried, and famines—and its victims and survivors—have been othered. The dominant mode of humanitarian action became 'expressive' (in the terminology of Norbert Götz, Georgina Brewis and Steffen Werther),[3] a situation possible only when the sensibilities of the act of giving outweigh any welfare metrics of the outcome, which in turn demands that the people and places are distant.

Europe's modern famines are notable, but not atypical, in that none can primarily be attributed to the weather. The last calamity triggered by a climatic factor was in Finland in 1866–68. Drought was a secondary factor in the 1946–47 famines in Moldova, Ukraine and some other parts of the Soviet Union, but there is little doubt that the crop failures would not have caused famines that cost more than a million lives were it not for the devastation of the WWII and the Soviet state's policies of requisitioning and exporting grain.[4] Overwhelmingly, over the twentieth century, Europeans starved because war leaders and autocrats decided that their lives could be sacrificed for some higher good, and on several terrible occasions, because they should either be exterminated or rendered so desperate that their governments would be compelled to submit.

The recurring fact that contemporary journalists and policymakers use the term 'man-made famine' is a testament to the enduring power of denialist narratives and the victim-focused imagery of Western humanitarianism (of which more below). This has been unhelpful to scholarship on famine, because it has obliged historians and political scientists to return, time and again, to reiterating the rudimentary point that famines are always political-economic events.

This volume is a fine exemplar of the emerging generation of scholarship on famine that is moving the agenda on, exploring the more complex questions of how political structure and agency determine who eats and who goes hungry, who writes scripts that legitimize these power relations and decisions and how those scripts are contested. In this Afterword, I address three main questions, drawing on the chapters in this volume and bringing in contemporary controversies. The first question is whether we can make sense of famine denialism, both for specific

DOI: 10.4324/9781003465805-15

instances and for the wider neglect of European famines of the twentieth century. The second is how to understand more deeply the administrative, military, diplomatic and social politics of mass starvation. Third is how humanitarian interests and scripts have shaped how past famines are represented and how current and future famines may be permitted or designed.

Famine denialism

It is common for those responsible for famine to deny that they are happening, while they are raging and afterwards. This was notoriously the case for the world's largest-ever famine—China in 1959–62 and in Ethiopia and Sudan in the 1980s,[5] as well as in the Soviet Union in the 1930s.[6] Amartya Sen observed that a free press was crucial to famine prevention and response,[7] an insight subsequently explored by Olivier Rubin.[8]

In his seminal book *States of Denial*, Stanley Cohen analyzes the stratagems for denial used by perpetrators of and apologists for atrocities.[9] His framework readily transfers to famines. Cohen has a threefold schema: simple factual denial, 'interpretative denial' (accepting the facts but claiming that they are not what they appear to be) and 'implicatory denial' (giving a different meaning to atrocities and thereby justifying them). In this volume, Miguel Ángel del Arco Blanco describes how the Franco regime used exactly these strategies, 'to conceal the famine and evade its responsibility.'[10] Where simply denial was impossible, it deployed myths to blame 'a persistent drought,' the destructions of the civil war (1936–39) and to justify starvation by blaming the Allied blockade during WWII and economic isolation after the war.

It might appear odd to include Ireland's Great Hunger within this framework, because its existence was never covered up. However, important aspects of the harm of that famine have long been concealed. Cormac Ó Gráda's chapter shows how the memorialization of this catastrophe 150 years ago was an act of invention, constructed despite the uncomfortable reality 'that the Irish famine did not inflict "common injuries" at the time, never mind across the generations.'[11] Alongside the millions who starved were many Irish people who concurred with the English establishment's view that the hunger was an act of providence or who profited from the desperation. Ireland has acknowledged the famine but not its deeply divisive character.

During the Bengal famine of 1943, the British colonial authorities censored reports of starvation and refused to use the word 'famine,' in part because that would have required them to invoke relief measures under India's 'famine codes,' and in part because of the stigma of failure associated with the word.[12] Contemporary denialisms follow similar patterns. A striking instance of factual denial is the Ethiopian government's coverup of famine in Tigray in 2021 and subsequently. This has included preventing the Integrated Food Security Phase Classification (IPC) system from gathering data and concluding that the absence of evidence for famine is evidence for the absence of famine.[13]

Interpretative denial is practiced by those seeking to exonerate Israel from the horrors of Gaza. Thus, a group of Israeli nutritionists has argued that Gaza could not have suffered famine because enough food was delivered during certain months of 2024.[14] Presented as a work of academic rigour, the published pre-print was dismissed by a leading specialist as 'more like a political document than a scientific article.'[15] A vivid example of implicatory denial is the spokesman for the Sudan Armed Forces arguing that the only possible reason why the IPC might determine that Sudan is in famine would be as part of an international conspiracy 'to develop a narrative whereby famine could be from dictated from above [...][to] give a recipe for those ill-wishers to intervene in Sudan.'[16] Shortly after this, the Famine Review Committee of IPC determined that famine was indeed occurring in Sudan, on the basis of intense starvation in two camps for displaced people in Darfur, at the same time as national-level figures pointed to the largest-magnitude famine for decades. After a subsequent IPC report that found that famine conditions had intensified and widened, the Sudanese authorities expelled the IPC in December 2024.[17] This catastrophe is unfolding at the time of writing.

Negotiating starvation

A second theme emerging from the collection is how better to understand the administrative, military, diplomatic and social politics of mass starvation. The Nazi *Hungerplan* is an unambiguous instance of starvation as annihilation. We know little about the complexities of agency within the political and administrative systems responsible for its implementation. The chapter by Tatjana Tönsmeyer breaks new ground in its focus on how people tried to survive rather than exploring policies from above.[18] The stories of how women and children in occupied territories tried to feed the inmates of prisoner-of-war camps, despite their own hunger, point to hidden histories of solidarity amidst mass starvation.

Between the Hunger Plan and the instances in which a feckless national authority failed to prevent a famine lies a range of degrees of the political use of starvation. Famine has the characteristic of unfolding sufficiently slowly that authorities have the opportunity to evaluate what is unfolding and act accordingly. Soviet famines illustrate this. As Stephen Wheatcroft and Filip Slaveski show, all are complex.[19] Understanding their causes and trajectories requires a careful unpicking of political and administrative agencies at different levels, differing by geographical location and across the three waves of famines—in 1917–22, 1928–33 and 1941–47. The 1931–33 calamities demand special attention, when a set of Soviet policies intended to feed the northern cities and transform peasant agriculture led to a series of famines that in total killed about 6 million people,[20] half of whom were in Ukraine or Ukrainians in Kuban region in southern Russia. Wheatcroft and Slaveski describe how these calamities were set in motion by monumental policy errors, brutally enforced, compounded by 'the systematic process of exaggerating possibilities, denying inconvenient reality, and covering up their deadly mistakes.' Josef Stalin was certainly aware of what was happening. He was also preoccupied with the question of nationalities and resolute in repressing and punishing those he saw as actual or potential threats, including the Ukrainians.

Controversy surrounds the question of whether Stalin deliberately intensified starvation in Ukraine in the spring and summer of 1933, making the Holodomor an instance of genocidal mass starvation.[21] Wheatcroft and Slaveski argue that this is a rare crime for which Stalin is not guilty. Others contend that there is documentary evidence for Stalin's genocidal intent and the disproportionate and targeted deprivation of Ukrainians.[22] The record of Communist famines certainly shows that central directives could often be modified by local cadres, sometimes discreetly to ameliorate hunger, but also to intensify and target it. In the case of the Soviet famines of 1946–47, Filip Slaveski, Iurii Shapoval and Igor Caşu document how the most important apparatchiks in Ukraine and Moldova negotiated the burden of deprivation, acting simultaneously as 'implementers of central policies that were helping to make famine but, at the same time, the most effective advocates to alleviate the suffering caused by it, at least for some members of the affected population.'[23]

The Francoist regime in Spain also weaponized hunger and rationing for socio-political control.[24] This is a pattern that recurs into contemporary times. To give one example among many, the Nicolás Maduro regime in Venezuela has operated a system that translates scarcity of food and other essentials into a regime survival strategy. In the 2000s, the Bolivarian revolutionary government (then led by Hugo Chavez) used state resources to pay for welfare programmes that dramatically reduced poverty and hunger, after which political conflict against a counter-revolutionary coalition, including agricultural capitalists that still wielded great economic power, led to critical shortages of essential commodities, worsened by the combination of collapsing oil revenues and economic sanctions. The regime instrumentalized entitlement to rations and other benefits, using selective allocation of rations to consolidate its party base and punish opposition members. Meanwhile, it intensified illicit extractive and smuggling activities to enrich a new crony capitalist elite, utilizing the hunger crisis for a coercive restructuring of Venezuela's political economy.[25]

This volume highlights the issue of starvation diplomacy in a pathbreaking way. Contemporary humanitarian practitioners have devoted much attention to the principles and practices of negotiating access and protection in conflict zones—what has come to be called 'humanitarian diplomacy.'[26] Daniel Maul's chapter in this volume details an important early example of this, namely the role of the Quakers in Europe at the close of the First World War (WWI) and thereafter.[27] As its toll on the health and nutrition of 'innocent children' became apparent, American and British Quakers opposed the blockade of Germany and Austria and organized relief efforts, which in the immediate aftermath of the war played a major role both in feeding children and in promoting ideas of reconciliation—while navigating competing patriotisms and a spirit of internationalism. The initiative was championed and organized by Herbert Hoover, head of the American Relief Administration, who went on to mount another enormous relief effort in war-ravaged Russia.[28]

Relatively, scholars have neglected its counterpart, namely how those who wage wars manage mass starvation and its political fallout. The chapter by Ingrid de Zwarte and Miguel Ángel del Arco Blanco on British and American policymaking during WWII to enforce or relax the blockades of, respectively, Spain, Greece and the Netherlands is an exemplary case of filling this gap.[29] The British premise was that the humanitarian exceptions granted to the blockade during WWI, for German-occupied Belgium and northern France, were a strategic error that had assisted Germany's war effort, and therefore the principle that 'who brings food can win the war' should be more rigorously enforced this time around. Britain grudgingly allowed an exception for Greece on account of public pressure (this was the foundational cause for Oxfam) and political pressure from the United States. No exception was granted for the Netherlands, and airdrops largely served as a propaganda tool so that relief followed liberation. The case of Spain was more complicated insofar as the Allies' intent was to manage supplies in such a way that the Franco regime was kept on a leash that deterred it from joining the Axis.

Contemporary cases of starvation diplomacy in Syria, Yemen and the Gaza Strip highlight the historical relevance of WWII examples. The policy of 'kneel or starve' imposed on besieged enclaves in Syria by the regime of Bashar al-Asad was backed by Russia, which argued that the sovereign entitlement of the Syrian state trumped relief agencies' demands for cross-border access.[30] Russia was ready to use its UN Security Council veto to secure its interests. A comparable case, this time enforced by governments friendly to the United States—Saudi Arabia and the United Arab Emirates (UAE)—was the war of hunger in Yemen.[31] A notable difference between the two is that Saudi Arabia and the UAE sought to minimize the reputational damage by making ad hoc but highly publicized donations to the UN World Food Programme, while Russia did not do so.

Israel's 'diet' strategy for Gaza is a highly salient case of starvation diplomacy. In the 2000s, prior to Hamas's election victory, Dov Weisglass, advisor to Prime Minister Ohud Elmert, is reported to have said in a comment on the restrictions on supplies into Gaza: 'The idea is to put the Palestinians on a diet, but not to make them die of hunger.'[32] When Hamas took over the Gaza administration, this policy was formalized, its calculations contained in a document entitled 'Food Consumption in the Gaza Strip: Red Lines,' which determined a minimum diet of an average of 2,279 calories per person per day.[33] In the immediate aftermath of Hamas's attack on 7 October 2023 through Israel's border fence and its massacre of almost 1,200 Israelis, mostly civilians, and abduction of 250 hostages, Israel imposed a total blockade for nearly two months and a partial blockade for longer. Massive disruption, forced displacement and obstruction of humanitarian operations also made it extraordinarily difficult to gather humanitarian data. In April 2024, the IPC signalled that famine (under the IPC's precise definition) was imminent in northern Gaza.[34] The US Famine Early Warning System Network (FEWSNET) went further, claiming that the thresholds for determining famine had probably been breached.[35] This was accompanied by a public outcry in America and Europe and strong public and (reportedly) private statements by senior Americans.[36] Israel responded by loosening the siege and permitting larger amounts of relief supplies and commercial food into northern Gaza. The outcome, as documented by the IPC in June 2024, was that famine had been averted.[37] Meanwhile in southern Gaza, intensified military operations, further restrictions on humanitarian operations and evacuation orders worsened the already severe humanitarian disaster in other areas, at the same time as further obstructing humanitarian data gathering. Later in the year, when the US FEWSNET reported that the threshold for famine conditions had indeed been crossed in northern Gaza,[38] the Joe Biden administration suppressed the report.[39] This crude denial was followed the complete dismantling of FEWSNET by the incoming administration of President Donald Trump. Israel's 'diet' had been recalculated, not to avert starvation but to keep the data from Gaza just shy of the IPC's famine thresholds.

Humanitarian scripts

A third question is how humanitarian interests and scripts have shaped the representation of current and past famines, and relatedly, how those representations have shaped faminogenic policies and responses. Contributions to this volume help us unravel the social dimensions of humanitarianism and how it is always imbricated within relations of power, race and gender. The chapter by Mary Elisabeth Cox and Anne van Mourik on German representation of WWI hunger in film in the immediate post-war years vividly depicts this, at a time when no singular narrative had emerged.[40] One film satirizes the opulence of the philanthropic plutocrat 'Mr. Quaker' (a depiction of Herbert Hoover), foreshadowing an enduring mix of gratitude and resentment among recipients of charity.

The invention of humanitarianism was an exercise in creating a fiction that in war there is a space that is protected from the violent, escalatory logic of war-making and a post-war space in which human solidarity can flourish, overcoming bitter divisions. In essence, humanitarians are condemned to an enterprise akin to the unending task of Sisyphus, finding humanity amidst inhumanity and constructing a non-political representation of something intrinsically political.[41]

Famine memorialization is trapped in comparable, albeit less urgently painful, paradoxes. Musealizing mass starvation also entails constructing scripts, which are invariably framed by current circumstances and debates. Some of these issues are poignantly raised by Ó Gráda's chapter that places the recent memorialization of Ireland's Great Hunger in the context of contemporary Irish politics and its self-ascription as a leader in international humanitarianism.[42] Marguérite Corporaal's chapter in this book brings this into clear focus.[43] Drawing on examples from Finland, Ireland, the Netherlands, Scotland and Spain, she shows how contemporary political agendas have conscripted memories of past famines, while also providing an opportunity to surface forgotten famines and subaltern memories of recognized famines, including among diaspora communities for whom starvation may have been their parting experience. Corporaal addresses the challenges of representing famines in museums in a vivid manner, given the paucity of material artefacts specific to starvation and the difficulty of visually representing victims of hunger in a dignified manner, especially given that nineteenth and early twentieth-century philanthropists and journalists had few qualms about purveying barely human or spectral images of the starving. Rarely are the victims identified by name, or their stories told. These are themes of emerging scholarship in Europe and elsewhere in the world, keenly relevant to how we understand and respond to humanitarian emergencies today.[44]

Norbert Götz, Georgina Brewis and Steffen Werther usefully integrate diverse literatures on early and late twentieth-century relief efforts to develop a new timeline for the evolution of humanitarianism.[45] Their framing of 'expressive humanitarianism' for the period from approximately 1970 captures the new dynamics of race and power in two continents—Europe and North America—that confidently expected not to suffer hunger themselves. Necessarily, the institutions and discourses around famine in Europe shifted, and Götz et al.'s principal case study for this latter period is Ethiopia in 1984–85 when the Irish rock singer Bob Geldof recorded a song (Band-Aid's 'Do they know it's Christmas?') and organized a concert (Live-Aid) to raise funds. This chimes with Ó Gráda's suggestion that Ireland's national famine myth was forged from contemporary philanthropic enterprises, beginning with the prominent role of Irish missionaries in aiding Biafra in the late 1960s through the performative humanitarianism of Band-Aid/Live-Aid to the humanitarian diplomacy of President Mary Robinson in Somalia in 1992.

The vigorous confidence of Western humanitarians and their expectation that they could impose solutions went hand-in-glove with portrayals of the hungry as helpless 'others' awaiting salvation.[46] In turn, this contributed to a sense among Africans of alienation from the humanitarian international, with the consequences that too few scholars from the Global South are fully engaged in the field of humanitarian and famine studies and too many political leaders from those countries are ready to spurn external humanitarian action as an unwarranted intrusion into their sovereignty. Also, the often-degrading imagery used in the Western media and by international relief agencies raises the question of whether the affected communities' loss of agency over the portrayal of their experience contributed to the scarcity of local memorialization efforts.

The return of starvation to Europe during the Bosnian War (1992–95) unleashed some paradoxical dynamics. The imagery of starving camp inmates was unlike anything Europeans had seen since the 1940s, and the clamour for international military action was particularly loud. Unexpectedly, the Pentagon was prepared to intervene in Somalia on the argument that, in comparison to the former Yugoslavia, it would be a simple, safe and universally welcomed operation. President George H.W. Bush appeared to interpret the remark attributed to his predecessor that 'a starving child knows no politics' to mean that hungry Somalis would set aside political aspirations in order to be fed. The US Marines were soon disabused of this mistaken assumption, and the United States has never since dispatched troops on a primarily humanitarian intervention. When NATO intervened militarily in Bosnia and later in Kosovo, it did so with its own explicit political agenda, in support of some belligerents against others.

On the other hand, unfavourable comparisons were made between the relatively generous aid funds provided to Bosnia and the miserly amounts donated to Africa. This disparity recurred, sometimes with explicitly racist colouring, in the months following Russia's full-scale invasion of Ukraine in 2022. There was never any doubt that assistance to Ukraine was a political act. Some white journalists were candid that it was easier to feel compassion for people who looked like them.[47] But while Western outrage at Serbian and Bosnian-Serb starvation crimes in the 1990s readily translated into universal condemnation, comparable outrage at Russia's weaponization of food and starvation sieges was met with indifference or accusations of hypocrisy in many parts of the world. Suspicions of double standards appeared confirmed when the Joe

Biden Administration in Washington, DC, took on the role of arms supplier and apologist for Israel during its siege and onslaught on the Palestinians of Gaza.

Pasts and futures

The resurgence of scholarly interest in the history of famines has coincided with growing awareness of the legacies of slavery and colonialism—with starvation beginning to assume its rightful place in this catalogue of imperial horrors. The 'Rhodes must fall' movement awaits its counterpart for colonial-era starvation. With reference to the statue of Robert Clive, conquistador of Bengal who established a rule of plunder that created one of the subcontinent's most terrible famines in 1770 and whose statue stands between Britain's Treasury and its Foreign, Commonwealth and Development Office, I have proposed that 'Clive must fall.'[48] The lineage between the depredations of the East India Company, the attendant colonial tradition of a permissive approach to starvation crimes and British and American starvation blockades in the World Wars subsequently deserves more attention.[49]

The era of tolerating faminogenic practices appeared to have ended with the triumph of liberal norms in the early 2000s, capped with the unanimous adoption of UN Security Resolution 2417 on armed conflict and hunger in 2018. Resolution 2417 did not create a new law but enshrined an apparent consensus that war-induced hunger was a collective problem. Condemnation of starvation as a weapon of war appeared to unite Western nations, China and Russia with violations of this norm in Syria and Yemen regarded as outrages that should not be tolerated in the future. Götz et al.'s 'expressive humanitarianism' was becoming translated into international principles and law. However, exceptions and rules have since been inverted.

The wars in Ukraine and Gaza, coming in the immediate wake of massive starvation crimes committed with impunity in Ethiopia and Sudan, mark a reversion to custom. For the US, China and Russia, along with middle powers and increasingly European governments too, starvation diplomacy is ascendant over humanitarian norms while aid budgets are shrinking. Themes of starvation politics and diplomacy in this emergent era already rhyme with the histories in this volume, sadly making its scholarship likely to grow in relevance.

Notes

1 The 2024 version of the World Peace Foundation historic famine dataset has 80 'great famines' (defined as episodes of excess mortality of 100,000 or driven by hunger) from 1870 to 2022. Aggregate mortality in these episodes was approximately 144 million, with 93.4 million in Asia, 32.6 million in Europe, 15.3 million in Africa and 2.7 million in the Middle East.
2 Mike Davis, *Late Victorian Holocausts: El Niño Famines and the Making of the Third World*, Verso, 2002.
3 Norbert Götz, Georgina Brewis and Steffen Werther, 'Humanitarian Action: A Moral Economic Periodization of Famine Relief,' in this volume.
4 Filip Slaveski, Iurii Shapoval and Igor Caşu, 'Centre-Periphery Relations in the Soviet Post-War Famine of 1946–47,' in this volume.
5 Article 19, *Starving in Silence: A Report on Famine and Censorship*, London, 1990.
6 Stephen G. Wheatcroft and Filip Slaveski, 'Food Crises, Extreme Hunger and Famine in Russia and the USSR,' in this volume.
7 Amartya Sen, *Development as Freedom*, Oxford University Press, 1999.
8 Olivier Rubin, *Democracy and Famine*, London, Taylor & Francis, 2011.
9 Stanley Cohen, *States of Denial: Knowing about Atrocities and Suffering*, Cambridge, Polity Press, 2001.

10 Miguel Ángel del Arco Blanco, 'The Autarkic Policy: The Origin of the Spanish Famine, 1939–42, 1946,' in this volume.
11 Cormac Ó Gráda, 'Famine, Trauma and Memory: Commemorating the Great Irish Famine in the 1990s,' in this volume.
12 Janam Mukherjee, *Hungry Bengal: War, Famine and the End of Empire*, Oxford University Press, 2015.
13 Alex de Waal, 'See No Evil: How the United Nations Is Blind to the Famine in Tigray,' *Reinventing Peace*, World Peace Foundation, 24 September 2021, https://worldpeacefoundation.org/blog/see-no-evil-how-the-united-nations-is-blind-to-the-famine-in-tigray/
14 Naomi Fliss-Isakov et al., 'Nutritional Assessment of Food Aid Delivered to Gaza via Israel during the "Swords of Iron" War,' working paper, 2 June 2024, https://biochem-food-nutrition.agri.huji.ac.il/arontroen/publications/nutritional-assessment-of-food-aid-delivered-to-gaza
15 Francesco Checchi, Review of working paper by Fliss-Isakov et al. on food aid to Gaza, 27 May 2024, https://gisha.org/UserFiles/File/LegalDocuments/HCJPetition2024/Legal_Opinion_fchecchi_27052024.pdf
16 United Nations, 'Sudan on Sudan: Media Stakeout,' 28 June 2024, www.youtube.com/watch?v=FHUogxYnDQk
17 IPC, 'Famine Review Committee: Combined Review of: (i) The Famine Early Warning System Network FEWS NET-IPC Compatible Analysis for IDP Camps in El Fasher, North Darfur; and (ii) The IPC Sudan Technical Working Group Analysis of Zamzam Camp North Darfur, Sudan: Conclusions and Recommendations,' Rome, IPC, July 2024; Clingendael Institute, 'From Hunger to Death: An Estimate of Excess Mortality in Sudan, Based on Currently Available Information,' The Hague, May 2024.
18 Tatjana Tönsmeyer, 'War, Occupation and the Politics of Causing and Fighting Hunger in World War II,' in this volume.
19 Stephen Wheatcroft and Filip Slaveski, 'Food Crises, Extreme Hunger and Famine in Russia and the USSR,' in this volume.
20 Serguei Adamets, 'Famine in Nineteenth and Twentieth Century Russia: Mortality by Age, Cause and Gender,' in Tim Dyson and Cormac Ó Gráda (eds), *Famine Demography: Perspectives from the Past and Present*. Oxford University Press, 2002, p. 163.
21 Andrea Graziosi, *Stalinism, Collectivization and the Great Famine*, Cambridge, MA, Ukrainian Studies Fund, 2009. Raphael Lemkin famously described the famine as a paradigmatic case of genocide by starvation, see Raphael Lemkin, 'Soviet Genocide in Ukraine,' in Roman Serbyn, 'Lemkin on the Ukrainian Genocide,' *Journal of International Criminal Justice*, 7 (2009): 123–130.
22 Nicolas Werth, 'Food Shortages, Hunger and Famines in the USSR, 1928–33,' in Andrea Graziosi and Frank E. Sysyn (eds), *Communism and Hunger: The Ukrainian, Chinese, Kazakh and Soviet Famines in Comparative Perspective*, Toronto, Canadian Institute of Ukrainian Studies Press, 2016, pp. 10–24.
23 Filip Slaveski, Iurii Shapoval and Igor Caşu, 'Centre-Periphery Relations in the Soviet Post-War Famine of 1946–47,' in this volume.
24 Miguel Ángel del Arco Blanco, 'The Autarkic Policy: The Origin of the Spanish Famine, 1939–42, 1946,' in this volume.
25 Ragas, Jose, 'A Starving Revolution: ID Cards and Food Rationing in Bolivarian Venezuela,' *Surveillance & Society* 15.3/4 (2017): 590–595; Ana Felicien, Christina Schiavoni and Liccia Romero, 'The Politics of Food in Venezuela,' *Monthly Review*, 1 June 2018, https://monthlyreview.org/2018/06/01/the-politics-of-food-in-venezuela/#endnote-20-backlink; Eva van Roekel and Marjo de Theije, 'Hunger in the Land of Plenty: The Complex Humanitarian Crisis in Venezuela,' *Anthropology Today*, 36.2 (2020): 8–12; Katrina Burgess and Javier Corrales, 'Petro-states, Oil Shocks, and Regime Change: Venezuela and Ecuador, 2013–2023,' *Environment and Security* (2024), https://doi.org/10.1177/27538796241237287
26 Jan Egeland, 'Humanitarian Diplomacy,' in Andrew Cooper, Jorge Heine and Ramesh Thakur (eds), *The Oxford Handbook of Modern Diplomacy*, Oxford University Press, 2013. https://doi.org/10.1093/oxfordhb/9780199588862.013.0020; Elise Rousseau and Achille Pende, 'Humanitarian Diplomacy,' in T. Balzacq, F. Charillon and F. Ramel (eds), *Global Diplomacy*, Palgrave Macmillan, 2020, https://doi.org/10.1007/978-3-030-28786-3_18

27 Daniel Maul, 'Fight the Famine. American Quakers and Child Feeding in Germany, 1918–23,' in this volume.
28 Bertrand Patenaude, *The Big Show in Bololand: The American Relief Expedition to Soviet Russia in the Famine of 1921*. Stanford University Press, 2002.
29 Ingrid de Zwarte and Miguel Ángel del Arco Blanco, 'The Allied Blockade and British Policies of Food and Famine during World War II,' in this volume.
30 Jehan Bseiso, Michiel Hofman and Jonathan Whittal (eds), *Everybody's War: The Politics of Aid in the Syria Crisis*, Oxford, Oxford University Press, 2021.
31 Aditya Sarkar, '"Once We Control Them, We Will Feed Them": Mass Starvation in Yemen,' in B. Conley, A. de Waal, C. Murdoch and W. Jordash (eds), *Accountability for Mass Starvation: Testing the Limits of the Law,* Oxford, Oxford University Press, 2022.
32 Conal Urquart, 'Gaza on Brink of Implosion as Aid Cut-Off Starts to Bite,' *The Guardian*, 16 April 2006, www.theguardian.com/world/2006/apr/16/israel
33 Amira Hass, '2,279 Calories per Person: How Israel Made Sure Gaza Didn't Starve,' *Ha'aretz*, 17 October 2012, www.haaretz.com/2012-10-17/ty-article/.premium/israels-gaza-quota-2-279-calories-a-day/0000017f-e0f2-d7b2-a77f-e3f755550000; Gisha, 'Reader: "Food Consumption in the Gaza Strip - Red Lines",' www.gisha.org/UserFiles/File/publications/redlines/redlines-position-paper-eng.pdf
34 IPC, Famine Review Committee, 'Gaza Strip: March 2024, March 18, 2024,' www.ipcinfo.org/ipcinfo-website/alerts-archive/issue-97/en/
35 FEWS NET, 'Amid Uncertainty, It Is Possible Famine Is Ongoing in Northern Gaza,' Washington, DC, May 2024, https://fews.net/middle-east-and-asia/gaza/targeted-analysis/may-2024
36 Jennifer Hansler, 'USAID Administrator Says It Is "Credible" to Assess Famine Is Already Occurring in Parts of Gaza,' *CNN*, April 11, 2024, www.cnn.com/2024/04/11/politics/samantha-power-famine-gaza/index.html; Liam Stack, 'Parts of Gaza Are in Famine, World Food Program Chief Says,' *New York Times*, 4 May 2024, www.nytimes.com/2024/05/04/world/middleeast/cindy-mccain-gaza-famine.html
37 IPC, Famine Review Committee, 'Gaza Strip: Conclusions and Recommendations, June 2024,' www.ipcinfo.org/ipcinfo-website/countries-in-focus-archive/issue-105/en/
38 FEWS NET, 'A Famine (IPC Phase 5) scenario continues to unfold in North Gaza Governorate,' Washington DC, 23 December 2024. (No longer available online).
39 Alex de Waal, 'How to Measure Famine,' *London Review of Books*, 47.2, (2025) 13–16, www.lrb.co.uk/the-paper/v47/n02/alex-de-waal/how-to-measure-famine
40 Mary Elisabeth Cox and Anne van Mourik, '"I haven't Eaten So Well for So Long!": Representations of the Allied Blockade of Germany in German Textbooks and Film (1914–32),' in this volume.
41 Fiona Terry. *Condemned to Repeat: The Paradox of Humanitarian Action*. Cornell University Press, 2002; Hugo Slim. *Humanitarian Ethics: A Guide to the Morality of Aid in War and Disaster*. Oxford University Press, 2015.
42 Ó Gráda, Famine, Trauma and Memory, in this volume.
43 Marguérite Corporaal, 'Heritages of Hunger in Europe: Transnational Matter for the Present Day,' in this volume.
44 Marguérite Corporaal and Ingrid de Zwarte (eds), *Famines and the Making of Heritage*, Routledge, 2024; Camilla Orjuela, 'Remembering/Forgetting Hunger: Towards an Understanding of Famine Memorialisation,' *Third World Quarterly* 45.2 (2024): 259–276; Kavita Puri, 'Three Million: Episode 7, Road to the Past,' BBC Podcast, August 2024, www.bbc.co.uk/programmes/m0022clj
45 Norbert Götz, Georgina Brewis and Steffen Werther, 'Humanitarian Action: A Moral Economic Periodization of Famine Relief,' in this volume.
46 Alex de Waal, 'Humanitarianism Unbound? Current Dilemmas Facing Multi-Mandate Relief Operations in Political Emergencies,' London, Justice Africa Discussion Paper No. 5, November 1994; David Campbell, 'Imaging Famine,' *The Guardian*, 2005, www.david-campbell.org/photography/imaging-famine
47 Moustafa Bayoumi, 'They Are "Civilized" and "Look Like Us": The Racist Coverage of Ukraine,' *The Guardian*, 2 March 2022, www.theguardian.com/commentisfree/2022/mar/02/civilised-european-look-like-us-racist-coverage-ukraine

48 Alex de Waal, 'Clive Must Fall: Recapturing Anti-Colonialism's Famine Prevention Agenda,' *World Peace Foundation*, Reinventing Peace, 24 April 2024, https://worldpeacefoundation.org/blog/clive-must-fall-recapturing-anti-colonialisms-famine-prevention-agenda/

49 Cf. Nicholas Mulder and Boyd van Dijk, 'Why Did Starvation Not Become the Paradigmatic War Crime in International Law?' in Ingo Venzke and Kevin Jon Heller (eds), *Contingency in International Law: On the Possibility of Different Legal Histories*, Oxford, Oxford University Press, 2021.

References

Adamets, Serguei, 'Famine in Nineteenth and Twentieth Century Russia: Mortality by Age, Cause and Gender,' in Tim Dyson, & Cormac Ó Gráda (eds). *Famine Demography: Perspectives from the Past and Present*. Oxford University Press, 2002, pp. 158–180.

Article 19, *Starving in Silence: A Report on Famine and Censorship*, London, Article 19, 1990.

Bayoumi, Moustafa, 'They Are "Civilized" and "Look Like Us": The Racist Coverage of Ukraine,' *The Guardian*, 2 March 2022, www.theguardian.com/commentisfree/2022/mar/02/civilised-european-look-like-us-racist-coverage-ukraine

Bseiso, Jehan, Michiel Hofman and Jonathan Whittal (eds), *Everybody's War: The Politics of Aid in the Syria Crisis*, Oxford, Oxford University Press, 2021.

Burgess, Katrina and Javier Corrales, 'Petro-states, Oil Shocks, and Regime Change: Venezuela and Ecuador, 2013–2023,' *Environment and Security* (2024). https://doi.org/10.1177/27538796241237287

Campbell, David, 'Imaging Famine,' *The Guardian*, 2005, www.david-campbell.org/photography/imaging-famine.

Checchi, Francesco, 'Review of working paper by Fliss Isakov et al. on food aid to Gaza,' 27 May 2024, https://gisha.org/UserFiles/File/LegalDocuments/HCJPetition2024/Legal_Opinion_fchecchi_27052024.pdf

Clingendael Institute, 'From Hunger to Death: An Estimate of Excess Mortality in Sudan, Based on Currently Available Information,' The Hague, May 2024.

Cohen, Stanley, *States of Denial: Knowing about Atrocities and Suffering*, Cambridge, Polity Press, 2001.

Corporaal, Marguérite, 'Heritages of Hunger in Europe: Transnational Matter for the Present Day,' in this volume.

Corporaal, Marguérite and Ingrid de Zwarte (eds), *Famines and the Making of Heritage*, London, Routledge, 2024.

Cox, Mary Elisabeth and Anne van Mourik, ' "I Haven't Eaten So Well for So Long!": Representations of the Allied Blockade of Germany in German Textbooks and Film (1914–32),' in this volume.

Davis, Mike, *Late Victorian Holocausts: El Niño Famines and the Making of the Third World*, London, Verso, 2002.

De Waal, Alex, 'Humanitarianism Unbound? Current Dilemmas Facing Multi-Mandate Relief Operations in Political Emergencies,' London, Justice Africa Discussion Paper No. 5, November 1994.

De Waal, Alex, 'See No Evil: How the United Nations Is Blind to the Famine in Tigray,' *Reinventing Peace*, World Peace Foundation, 24 September 2021, https://worldpeacefoundation.org/blog/see-no-evil-how-the-united-nations-is-blind-to-the-famine-in-tigray/

De Waal, Alex, 'Clive Must Fall: Recapturing Anti-Colonialism's Famine Prevention Agenda,' *Reinventing Peace*, World Peace Foundation, 24 April 2024, https://worldpeacefoundation.org/blog/clive-must-fall-recapturing-anti-colonialisms-famine-prevention-agenda/

De Waal, Alex, 'How to Measure Famine,' *London Review of Books*, 47.2, (2025) 13–16, www.lrb.co.uk/the-paper/v47/n02/alex-de-waal/how-to-measure-famine

De Zwarte, Ingrid and Miguel Ángel del Arco Blanco, 'The Allied Blockade and British Policies of Food and Famine during World War II,' in this volume.

Del Arco Blanco, Miguel Ángel, 'The Autarkic Policy: The Origin of the Spanish Famine, 1939–42, 1946,' in this volume.

Egeland, Jan, 'Humanitarian Diplomacy,' in Andrew Cooper, Jorge Heine and Ramesh Thakur (eds), *The Oxford Handbook of Modern Diplomacy*, Oxford University Press, 2013, https://doi.org/10.1093/oxfordhb/9780199588862.013.0020

Felicien, Ana, Christina Schiavoni and Liccia Romero, 'The Politics of Food in Venezuela,' *Monthly Review*, 1 June 2018, https://monthlyreview.org/2018/06/01/the-politics-of-food-in-venezuela/#endnote-20-backlink
FEWS NET, 'Amid Uncertainty, It Is Possible Famine Is Ongoing in Northern Gaza,' Washington, DC, May 2024, https://fews.net/middle-east-and-asia/gaza/targeted-analysis/may-2024
Fliss-Isakov, Naomi, et al., 'Nutritional Assessment of Food Aid Delivered to Gaza via Israel during the "Swords of Iron" War,' working paper, 2 June 2024, https://biochem-food-nutrition.agri.huji.ac.il/arontroen/publications/nutritional-assessment-of-food-aid-delivered-to-gaza
Gisha, 'Reader: "Food Consumption in the Gaza Strip – Red Lines",' www.gisha.org/UserFiles/File/publications/redlines/redlines-position-paper-eng.pdf
Götz, Norbert, Georgina Brewis and Steffen Werther, 'Humanitarian Action: A Moral Economic Periodization of Famine Relief,' in this volume.
Graziosi, Andrea, *Stalinism, Collectivization and the Great Famine*, Cambridge, MA, Ukrainian Studies Fund, 2009.
Hansler, Jennifer, 'USAID Administrator Says It Is "Credible" to Assess Famine Is Already Occurring in Parts of Gaza,' *CNN*, 11 April 2024, www.cnn.com/2024/04/11/politics/samantha-power-famine-gaza/index.html
Hass, Amira, '2,279 Calories per Person: How Israel Made Sure Gaza Didn't Starve,' *Ha'aretz*, 17 October 2012, www.haaretz.com/2012-10-17/ty-article/.premium/israels-gaza-quota-2-279-calories-a-day/0000017f-e0f2-d7b2-a77f-e3f755550000
IPC, Famine Review Committee, 'Gaza Strip: March 2024, 18 March 2024.' www.ipcinfo.org/ipcinfo-website/alerts-archive/issue-97/en/
IPC, Famine Review Committee, 'Gaza Strip: Conclusions and Recommendations, June 2024,' www.ipcinfo.org/ipcinfo-website/countries-in-focus-archive/issue-105/en/
IPC, Famine Review Committee, 'Combined Review of: (i) The Famine Early Warning System Network FEWS NET- IPC Compatible Analysis for IDP Camps in El Fasher, North Darfur; and (ii)The IPC Sudan Technical Working Group Analysis of Zamzam Camp North Darfur, Sudan: Conclusions and Recommendations,' Rome, IPC, July 2024.
Lemkin, Raphael, 'Soviet Genocide in Ukraine,' in Roman Serbyn, 'Lemkin on the Ukrainian Genocide,' *Journal of International Criminal Justice* 7 (2009): 123–130.
Maul, Daniel, 'Fight the Famine: American Quakers and Child Feeding in Germany, 1918–23,' in this volume.
Mukherjee, Janam, *Hungry Bengal: War, Famine and the End of Empire*, Oxford, Oxford University Press, 2015.
Mulder, Nicholas and Boyd van Dijk, 'Why Did Starvation Not Become the Paradigmatic War Crime in International Law?' in Ingo Venzke and Kevin Jon Heller (eds), *Contingency in International Law: On the Possibility of Different Legal Histories*, Oxford, Oxford University Press, 2021.
Ó Gráda, Cormac, 'Famine, Trauma and Memory: Commemorating the Great Irish Famine in the 1990s,' in this volume.
Orjuela, Camilla, 'Remembering/Forgetting Hunger: Towards an Understanding of Famine Memorialisation,' *Third World Quarterly* 45.2 (2024): 259–276.
Patenaude, Bertrand M, *The Big Show in Bololand: The American Relief Expedition to Soviet Russia in the Famine of 1921*. Redwood City, CA, Stanford University Press, 2002.
Puri, Kavita, 'Three Million: Episode 7, Road to the Past,' BBC Podcast, August 2024, www.bbc.co.uk/programmes/m0022clj
Ragas, Jose, 'A Starving Revolution: ID Cards and Food Rationing in Bolivarian Venezuela,' *Surveillance & Society* 15.3/4 (2017): 590–595.
Rousseau, Elise and Achille Pende, 'Humanitarian Diplomacy,' in Balzacq, T., Charillon, F. and Ramel, F. (eds), *Global Diplomacy*, Palgrave Macmillan, 2020, https://doi.org/10.1007/978-3-030-28786-3_18
Rubin, Olivier, *Democracy and Famine*, London, Taylor & Francis, 2011.

Sarkar, Aditya, '"Once We Control Them, We Will Feed Them": Mass Starvation in Yemen,' in B. Conley, A. de Waal, C. Murdoch and W. Jordash (eds.), *Accountability for Mass Starvation: Testing the Limits of the Law*, Oxford, Oxford University Press, 2020.

Sen, Amartya, *Development as Freedom*, Oxford, Oxford University Press, 1999.

Slaveski, Filip, Iurii Shapoval and Igor Caşu, 'Centre-Periphery Relations in the Soviet Post-War Famine of 1946-47,' in this volume.

Slim, Hugo, *Humanitarian Ethics: A Guide to the Morality of Aid in War and Disaster*, Oxford, Oxford University Press, 2015.

Stack, Liam, 'Parts of Gaza Are in Famine, World Food Program Chief Says,' *New York Times*, 4 May 2024, www.nytimes.com/2024/05/04/world/middleeast/cindy-mccain-gaza-famine.html

Terry, Fiona, *Condemned to Repeat? The Paradox of Humanitarian Action*, Ithaca, NY, Cornell University Press, 2002.

Tönsmeyer, Tatjana, 'War, Occupation and the Politics of Causing and Fighting Hunger in World War II,' in this volume.

United Nations, 'Sudan on Sudan: Media Stakeout,' 28 June 2024. www.youtube.com/watch?v=FHUogxYnDQk

Urquart, Conal, 'Gaza on Brink of Implosion as Aid Cut-off Starts to Bite,' *The Guardian*, 16 April 2006, www.theguardian.com/world/2006/apr/16/israel

van Roekel, Eva and Marjo de Theije, 'Hunger in the Land of Plenty: The Complex Humanitarian Crisis in Venezuela,' *Anthropology Today*, 36.2 (2020): 8–12.

Werth, Nicolas, 'Food Shortages, Hunger and Famines in the USSR, 1928–33,' in Andrea Graziosi and Frank E. Sysyn (eds), *Communism and Hunger: The Ukrainian, Chinese, Kazakh and Soviet Famines in Comparative Perspective*, Toronto, Canadian Institute of Ukrainian Studies Press, 2016, pp. 10–24.

Wheatcroft, Stephen and Filip Slaveski, 'Food Crises, Extreme Hunger and Famine in Russia and the USSR,' in this volume.

World Peace Foundation, 'The History and Future of Famine,' 2024, https://worldpeacefoundation.org/project/history-future-of-famine/

Index

Note: Page numbers in *italic* indicate figures and in **bold** indicate tables.

For Product Safety Concerns and Information please contact our EU
representative GPSR@taylorandfrancis.com
Taylor & Francis Verlag GmbH, Kaufingerstraße 24, 80331 München, Germany

www.ingramcontent.com/pod-product-compliance
Ingram Content Group UK Ltd.
Pitfield, Milton Keynes, MK11 3LW, UK
UKHW050229200926
475702UK00020B/2938
9781032737638